How the World Cooks Chicken

How the World Cooks Chicken

H.J.Muessen

𝔰𝔇

STEIN AND DAY/*Publishers*/New York

First published in 1982
Copyright © 1981 by H. J. Muessen
All rights reserved
Designed by Louis A. Ditizio
Printed in the United States of America
STEIN AND DAY/ *Publishers*/Scarborough House
Briarcliff Manor, N.Y. 10510

Library of Congress Cataloging in Publication Data

Muessen, H. J.
  How the world cooks chicken.

  Includes bibliographies and index.
  1. Cookery (Chicken)   2.   Cookery, International.
I.   Title.
TX750.M84   641.6′65   80-51608
ISBN 0-8128-2740-6

To Carol, Henry, Lisa, Bill, Steve,
Hank, Linda, and Sarah

Contents

Acknowledgments

As with every book, and especially cookbooks, it is impossible to start at the beginning and go to the end without help; and I got plenty of that. I very gratefully acknowledge the advice and critique from my sisters Betty Lincoln and Joan Muessen, who both brought not only literary expertise to this manuscript, but their own experience from the kitchen, where they are both excellent cooks.

If Dianne Futerman, Mona Caparosa, Lynn Karson, and Ellen Peters hadn't helped me with the typing, the book probably wouldn't have been written. To those very good friends and business associates, Joe Mack, Steve Clow, and John Cross, my thanks for their continued interest, inspiration, and constructive criticism. I'd also like to thank my many friends who ate chicken at my house during the past five years (which was just about every time they came), for whether they knew it or not I made guinea pigs of them for the purposes of this book.

In researching these recipes, I contacted most of the United Nations representatives and many foreign Information Offices in New York City. There are too many to list, but they all have my thanks.

Fortunately, living in a suburb of New York City has made available to me a great many resources for material that most people would not have. First, the New York Public Library, and its branches, have hundreds of books, in and out of print, which provided not only recipes but background material on every country. Then *The New York Times* and New York *Post*, whose superb writers, Craig Claiborne, Pierre Franey, Mimi Sheraton, Julia Child, and others, I consulted constantly, and they have my deepest gratitude.

There are some authors also who have written books on individual cuisines that are so outstanding that I give them special mention in the appropriate chapter and recommend you consult them for the regional cookery they describe, which goes far beyond the chicken.

Finally, I acknowledge the trials I put my wife and children through. They were my "expert" panel and gave their enthusiastic advice and criticism ("Oh, no, not chicken again!") even when served chicken several times a week. They gave each dish a rating of from 1 (poor) to 5 (excellent), and on this basis the recipe was either included in the book or went back for more work. They were brutally frank and gave me no quarter, except my little one, Steve, who awarded each one a 7.

I hope you will award them 7's also.

Foreword

I once read that there are two basic kinds of cookbook, one that you read and one that you use. This seems a shame to me, for I've found that knowing a little about where a dish comes from, how it developed, or why and what its heritage is makes it a lot more interesting to serve. In this spirit, this book traces the birth and rise in popularity of chicken cookery throughout the world. It shows the regional influences that not only caused subtle changes in a cuisine but brought chicken to prominence, where a few years before it had never even been heard of. Thus the book is constructed as an information piece on the one hand, supported by authentic chicken and other fowl recipes, which describe the unique tastes of a country's cuisine.

In the vast majority of cookbooks a dish (chicken or otherwise) is labeled authentic merely by adding a name (in the language of the country it comes from) or an ingredient that is usually identified with the dish. *Cassoulet* is not a bean dish that's whipped up for dinner an hour before; done authentically, it takes a couple of days, and that doesn't include the time for preserving the goose wing in its own rendered fat. *Piripiri* isn't just ground chili peppers spread over chicken pieces for marinating and broiling; it's a marinade that—done correctly—takes 30 days to prepare. And then there are so many dishes (chicken or otherwise) that require something else to make them authentic—saffron in *Arroz con Pollo,* sambals in Southeast Asian cookery, dried shrimp and dende oil in the cooking of Brazil, or injera bread in Ethiopia's spectacular *Doro Wat.*

Authenticity is not the original method or recipe in every case. On the contrary, it is the time-honored taste or presentation that immediately associates the dish with its name—not just the chicken alone, but the total dish.

And that's what this book is all about.

My taste for food in general, and chicken in particular, was born in Denton on the Eastern Shore of Maryland, across the Chesapeake Bay from Baltimore. During the Depression years my parents took my sisters and me on frequent visits to see our grandparents, Ed and Lily Nichols. In those days there were no interstate highways, so the driving was slow, which made the trips seem interminable, and that made the anticipation of getting there almost unbearable.

But once there, it seems to me the ritual never changed—we hardly got in the door and through the hello's before we were sitting down to dinner, a meal that invariably featured a huge platter of Maryland Fried Chicken, lima beans served in their pot liquor, corn on the cob, cucumbers in vinegar, and every so often, the best fried crab cakes I've ever eaten.

Ed would start me out with three or four pieces of chicken, plus a mound of other food and, while Lily brought us up to date on the latest Denton gossip and goings on, I would silently plow my way through this gargantuan feast, saving one piece of chicken to the very last. And without fail, as soon as that last bone was picked clean, Ed would look over and say "Lily, that boy's got nothin' on his plate," then he'd spear two or three more pieces, and I'd start all over again.

Those were heroic repasts, to say the least, and they took much stamina and concentration to get through. (They also took much walking around afterwards to get over.) But one thing I remember with great pleasure was the side contest I always had with Lily on who could clean the neck bone the best. I don't recall ever beating Lily, but then she never beat Ed either, because he ate the chicken small bones and all, which to me was (and still is) utterly fascinating.

Our visits to Denton in those days usually lasted at least several days and often longer, so the chances were that we'd see chicken again before leaving. Now, however, Ed would put me to work. First he'd catch a chicken and, holding it by the legs, place it on the stump of a tree, and whack its head off. The first time I saw this should have been my last encounter with a chicken, for Ed released the bird to run headless around the yard, its heart still pumping out the blood. As I watched in stunned fascination, the dying bird suddenly turned and ran halfway up my leg, flapping its wings and clawing its feet, spewing blood all over my pants.

That should have ended any taste I had for chicken, but it didn't. Ed made me pick up the bird when it finally died, hold it by the feet in a tub of boiling water for several minutes, and then pluck out the feathers. This job was not only tedious but very hard on the fingers, for chicken feathers can hold a lot of hot water. Unless you're used to it, plucking three or four chickens at a time under these circumstances will parboil your hands.

Since that first time, I've seen many a chicken get its head lopped off and I've plucked many a feather. I never had the nerve or stomach for doing the act myself, though there is no doubt in my mind that a freshly killed chicken is superior to one that has been butchered and shipped to market from some mass production facility days and miles away.

Nowadays, of course, a freshly killed chicken is a rarity. You may find "recently" killed birds in some areas, and these are generally of good quality, but the vast amount of chicken meat comes to us neatly prepared and plastic-wrapped in the meat cooler section of our supermarket. I daresay that half the American population has never tasted freshly killed chicken, and that's a shame, for there is simply no comparison. Fresh chicken meat has a distinctive taste all by itself that adds great character to the dish being cooked. Supermarket birds are virtually tasteless by themselves and must rely almost entirely on a seasoning or a sauce to make the meat appetizing.

My legacy from Ed and Lily Nichols was a fondness for good, well-cooked food, with particular emphasis on chicken and other poultry. This was strongly reinforced while I was with the U.S. Navy during the early 1950s and came in contact with the cuisines of Hawaii, Korea, Japan, Hong Kong, Southeast Asia, and the Philippines right in their own backyards. At that time, with the exception of Korea, these countries had worked off many of the effects of World War II and their life styles were fairly normal. Fortunately neither Japan, Korea, nor the Philippines had become as Westernized as they were to become, so I had a chance to taste the offerings of the Orient pretty much the way they had been for centuries.

Once out of the Navy, I took up cooking as a hobby, beginning by trying to duplicate the flavors I had found in the Far East. At first, there was a great deal of experimentation, but as I got into it I began to try European, Middle Eastern, and even an African dish or two, sticking pretty much with the well-known chicken classics, but all the while compiling my own portfolio of recipes. After gathering a number of chicken dishes from around the world in a more or less haphazard manner, a certain pattern became apparent—a pattern that suggested there is a certain style or tradition that characterizes a cuisine and that the style seems to be present regardless of the food being eaten. For example, ask someone to describe "Indian cooking" and spices will probably be mentioned, or French and it will be wine and sauces. Italian cooking is garlic, onion, tomato, and pasta oriented, and Mexican is tortillas and chili peppers. It's the same throughout the world—certain condiments, ingredients, cooking techniques, utensils, even methods of presentation have come to identify a culinary style that moves across the cuisine of a region, a country, or an entire continent.

In gaining a familiarity with international chicken cooking, I got to know the chicken and other poultry very well, particularly how the chicken has been regarded as a food source through history and the role it plays now in the world's cuisines. Its ornithological name is *Gallus gallus,* and its earliest known ancester, the Red or Indian Jungle Fowl, roamed wild in India and Southeast Asia thousands of years before the birth of Christ. The Jungle Fowl was domesticated by the Chinese and became a staple in Oriental cuisines long ago, but it was centuries before it was introduced to European tastes and even longer before it came to America.

As a personality, the chicken leaves much to be desired: it is almost totally lacking in intelligence; it has little or no grace; it is completely unadaptable to training or useful work; it doesn't even fly, except briefly, and then only in extreme danger. The male is a ferocious fighter, an avid lover, and an automatic alarm clock, while the hen is prodigious in the art of laying eggs; but that's about the limit of their talents.

As a food source, however, the bird has many redeeming features. It provides not only meat, but eggs, for food; it is one of the most economical meats, and one of the easiest, in the world to produce; it has a protein value that ranks it nutritionally with other meats and fish; it is free from the taboos that involve beef, pork, and shellfish in some religions; it has a texture and flavor quality that lends itself to virtually every conceivable seasoning and method of preparation. These virtues have made the chicken one of the most commonly and frequently eaten meats on earth at the present time, a popularity that has come in comparatively recent years. In spite of all this, chicken is not considered the favored or traditional meat in any country, save perhaps China.

Fish is supreme in Scandinavia, Japan, Southeast Asia, and the Pacific Islands; beef and mutton are preferred in Great Britain and Australia; and lamb is favored in the Balkans, India, and the Middle East; beef is also the most popular meat in America, and in Argentina it's an institution; in Italy and Austria, veal is king; and pork, ham, and sausages are standard fare in East Europe. The French play no favorites—they have glorified fish, poultry, beef, pork, and lamb. It is only in China that chicken occupies a favored rank among meats, and even there it shares this distinction with pork.

Why is chicken meat seemingly held in such secondary regard? It isn't really. It's just that chicken has been chasing civilization since the dawn of history and has just now caught up. The meats associated so strongly with well-known national or regional cuisines are those that have been accepted or favored for centuries, and in some cases, thousands of years.

Since antiquity the hen has been bred essentially for the production of eggs. Centuries before the birth of Christ, both the Egyptians and the Chinese had developed highly efficient incubators, which could handle thousands of eggs at a time. The cock was bred for fighting and for its decorative feathers. In some ancient religions, the cock was thought to have magical powers, and in others was often the unhappy victim in sacrificial rites and divinations. Though the chicken was bred in ancient Persia, Greece, Egypt, and Rome, it vied with thrush, pigeon, peacock, wild gamebirds, and domesticated goose as a table meat and, among the aristocracy of these cultures, it was unanimously considered inferior. The fact that China did include chicken meat in its cuisine so long ago also explains why Chinese chicken cookery today is so far ahead of the rest of the world.

With the fall of Rome in A.D. 453, chicken breeding languished along with the rest of Europe's culture for the eight hundred years of the Dark Ages. The cuisines of the Middle East and the Orient continued expanding and gaining in sophistication, but nothing of gastronomic significance occurred in the West until the Renaissance dawned over Italy at the end of the thirteenth century. Even then the chicken wasn't known much beyond the Mediterranean. The Ottoman Turks introduced the bird to Eastern Europe five hundred years ago, and it only came to the Western Hemisphere a century later.

Since that time, however, chicken, goose, and turkey have become the preferred meats in many countries for important occasions. Goose is the Christmas or New Year's feast bird in Denmark, England, Austria, and Germany, while turkey is eaten in Brazil, Mexico, America, Canada, and the Ukraine at Christmas. (In America, of course, turkey is *the* bird at Thanksgiving.) Chicken, relatively scarce in Africa and Polynesia, is usually reserved for weddings and important guests. In a Dobreshe wedding in Romania, the newlyweds toast each other with a unique sour chicken soup. In Sri Lanka (Ceylon), a spicy chicken curry is prepared for special occasions, while in America, and throughout the Western world, Jews often serve a special chicken dish before, during, or after their many religious celebrations. Four hundred years ago, a French king campaigned for peasant support on the promise of a "chicken in every pot." This same slogan was attributed to an American presidential candidate earlier in this century, and during the Great Depression in America "chicken every Sunday" was something special to look forward to.

It is only since World War II that chicken cooking has really come into its own, and this recognition has been helped along by world food authorities and the medical profession. The population explosion, inflation, and the resulting shortages of fertilizer and grain have put beef, pork, lamb, veal, even fish out of the reach of hundreds of millions of people, and at the same time promoted the production of chicken. To produce one pound of meat, it takes two pounds of grain for chicken, four pounds for pork, and ten pounds for beef. Considering that grain is the staple food for most of the world's population, food authorities contend that even a small shift to chicken from beef or pork would alleviate a great deal of world hunger.

Health experts and nutritionists emphasize the value of chicken meat over beef and pork not only because the bird is a less expensive source of protein, but because it materially reduces the body's intake of fat and cholesterol.

The spotlight that has suddenly been turned on the bird as an economical and nutritious source of food has had a glorious effect on chicken cookery. Where it once was reserved for special occasions, it is now replacing century-old traditional dishes. Its popularity has increased all around the globe so rapidly in recent years, in fact, that the world's kitchens cook or prepare chicken in more ways than any other food—meat or otherwise.

For example: chicken is baked, braised, steamed, roasted, stewed, poached, grilled, or broiled (in the oven or over an open fire), smoked, as well as cooked in an underground pit or on a rotisserie. It is cooked in a casserole, in a pie, or in a soup. It is deep-fried, stir-fried, quick-fried, cooked by several methods in the same recipe, and even eaten raw. It is rolled, stuffed, filleted, pounded, flattened, cubed, cured, shredded, chopped, skewered, ground, and even encased in mud and cooked with the feathers still on. It can be served hot or cold or *en gelée,* or as a salad, a sandwich, a pudding, a custard, a loaf, in a crepe or an omelet. The world's kitchens turn out dishes in which a wide variety of nuts, fruits, spices, herbs, virtually all grains, as well as all other types of meat (lamb, pork, goat, beef, fish, shellfish, and game) are cooked in or with the fowl. Along with virtually every vegetable and vine type of food, there is frequent use of milk, honey, sugar, cream, cheese, yogurt, buttermilk, wine, beer, stock, sour mare's milk, sour cream, coconut milk, palm oil; and in Mexico, the classic fowl is cooked with chocolate. Almost every part of the chicken finds its way into some dish: besides the meat, the giblets are added to many gravies, and the livers make wonderful patés; chicken blood is added to sauces in some recipes; the feet and bones are essential to good, thick chicken soup, as any Jewish cook will tell you, and the fried skin (*grebenes*) and rendered fat are other mainstays of true Jewish cooking.

In one experimental kitchen in America recently, chicken feathers were actually ground up and successfully added to cookie dough for protein. In some parts of the world, the head and entrails are eaten, and in the Philippines, some natives find the unborn chick a delightful snack—eaten raw. And if that's not enough, the hen figures prominently in the aphrodisiac potions of Brazil's voodoo cultures.

In short, there's very little that can't be done with chicken.

Because it is so versatile in the pot and so commonly found in the kitchens of the world, it is probably the only meat (or food) that could serve to illustrate the comparative virtues of the world's cuisines. And that is the object of this book—to offer a compilation of chicken and other poultry recipes that will provide a comparison of the major cuisines around the globe as well as the nuances that invariably occur within a cuisine as a result of geographic, climatic, economic, or even ethnic conditions.

It took the cooks of the world over five thousand years to create the cuisines we enjoy today. In most cases, they were the result of a subtle cross-ruffing of life styles and cultures brought about gradually and peacefully through migration or trading. But in some cases the change was sudden and violent, as a result of invasion and occupation, where a radically different cuisine of one culture was suddenly thrust upon another. Twelve hundred years ago, for example, when the Middle Eastern Arabs overran North Africa, the change occurred overnight, but these same Arab Moslems introduced their cuisine to Southeast Asia beginning in A.D. 400, and over the centuries it was peacefully absorbed into the Indian/Chinese style of the area, where it is hardly discernible today.

It is only in the last half-century that many of the world's kitchens even rubbed shoulders with others. Now, however, as the technological wonders of the jet-television-satellite age shrink the globe, gastronomies are being thrown together on an almost hourly basis. If the past holds any clue, it is certain that the traditional cookery we enjoy today will be different tomorrow, but the odds are that the chicken will still be there to show off the new cuisines to their best advantage.

Chicken is the only vehicle that can make this claim, for it is the only food that is universally eaten—in every cuisine on earth. I acknowledge that fish is also universal to the world's cuisines like chicken, and is eaten far more frequently; but there are saltwater fish and freshwater fish, fish with red meat, white meat, and brown meat, shellfish, oily fish, and fish with dry flesh, and some water creatures that aren't fish at all. On the other hand, while there are many breeds of chicken, they all come from the same heritage, and with few exceptions they all offer the diner a selection of white meat and dark from the same bird.

With this as a prologue, I'm pleased to offer a selection of dishes showing the incredible variety of cooking and eating styles the people of the world enjoy. The great majority of these recipes are made of chicken, but I realized early on that there are poultry dishes other than chicken which are classic examples of a particular cuisine or so important to certain feasts or other occasions that they had to be included as well.

Perhaps the most difficult thing I encountered in putting this book together was finding certain ingredients. I happen to live in a suburb of New York City, and it occurred to me that if an ingredient was not available in this area it was highly unlikely that it would be available in other areas of the country. Surprisingly, there were few that I couldn't turn up with some diligent searching, but not all of them. So, in many cases, I have suggested substitutes. I want to emphasize that in every case a substitute will alter the dish in some way—in taste, in texture, even in appearance. It's unfortunate, but in some recipes it's the only way the dish can be done. In other cases the "exotic" ingredient can just as well be left out, and where this is possible I have so indicated.

Happily, major metropolitan areas all over the country abound in gourmet shops or department store sections that stock a wide variety of specialized spices, seasonings, or ethnic ingredients basic to certain cuisines. There are mail-order shops that specialize in foods and condiments of certain national cuisines. These are listed in the appropriate chapter.

Introduction

H. J. (Jim) Muessen has many qualities of the modern Renaissance person—a cook of the first order with one of the most sensitive palates I know, a gifted writer, a husband and father of the year and every year, and a successful businessman.

This is Jim's first book, and in it he shows clearly how acutely critical he is of what he eats. He has expressed his feelings about how the world cooks chicken in a highly personal manner.

How the World Cooks Chicken inspires at least two chickens in every pot—and what it promises is this: chicken, like bread, potatoes, and rice, can be eaten every day with interest, satisfaction, and relish. The chicken is truly omnipresent; it *is* the most popular food bird in the world, and it is cooked and served in hundreds of ways. Nowhere have I seen such an exhaustive, complete, mouth-watering set of recipes as there is in this book. Braised or broiled, poached or pan-fried, this cookbook clearly shows us in an exciting way how chicken lends itself to many compatible combinations in every part of the world.

Simon and Howe, in their *Dictionary of Gastronomy,** tell us that the earliest mention of the domestic fowl occurred in a passage by a Greek author, circa 570 B.C., about the same time that Aesop was admonishing the foolish milkmaid with, "Don't count your chickens before they are hatched." Well, Jim's chickens are all here in innumerable recipes ready for hatching and cooking.

*Andre L. Simon and Robin Howe, *Dictionary of Gastronomy* (New York: McGraw-Hill Book Company, 1970).

xxiii

If you love experimenting with good food, you'll achieve remarkable results with his recipes. If you'll read through them carefully, you'll find them quite easy to execute.

These are hearty, beautifully seasoned dishes that will rush you to the kitchen. Here is a wonderful cross-section of international chicken cookery, much of which has never been published in this country. It will be a fine and useful item on your cookbook shelf.

JOE FAMULARO

HOW
THE WORLD
COOKS
CHICKEN

✤ **Chapter 1** ✤

The Pacific

The Pacific Islands were originally settled by natives from Indonesia, who were among the earliest navigators of the high seas. In their wide-ranging proas, they explored the oceans from Madagascar to Japan, and their descendants are the rootstock of most Pacific Island cultures including the Philippines.

The islands that dot the Central and Western Pacific Ocean, stretching from Hawaii to New Zealand, are collectively called Polynesia. There is no political, religious, or economic unity among them, but similarities in customs, speech, religion, facial characteristics, and cooking methods strongly suggest some common ancestor. This is reinforced by massive temples and huge statues in the Egyptian and Indian tradition. These stone works are found all across the Pacific, and some speculate that these great sculptors might have reached Guatemala.

The gastronomies of Tahiti and Hawaii typify not only the style of cooking, but the techniques used throughout the Islands. Pork, fish, fruit, coconuts, and breadfruit dominate their cuisines, while beef (except in Hawaii) and chicken are rather scarce. Until the Westerners came, there was no such thing as a metal cooking utensil, so the Islanders adapted the broad ti leaf into a wrapper in which they cooked everything. The underground oven (*imu* or *hima'a*) became a community stove, and a common meal was prepared daily, by men only, for the entire tribe or group. Women were not allowed to eat until the men had finished; in fact, they weren't even allowed to watch. Happily, this tradition has gone by the boards today, and while the feast is still cooked by the men, the women now help in the preparation and in the eating.

The *imu* is also found in New Zealand and other Pacific Islands. Where it originated, no one knows, but the early Indonesian sailors probably helped it gain popularity across the ocean. A very similar underground oven called the *pib* has been used in Central America since antiquity, suggesting a legacy from ancient Polynesia. (Instead of ti leaves, however, the Central Americans tied up their food in banana leaves.)

After James Cook's visit in 1767, the French colonized Tahiti, and brought with them their newly emerging culinary skills. Though Tahitian cooking today remains very Oriental in style, the French presence is quite evident. Hawaii's cooking was strongly influenced by both Eastern and Western kitchens. The Chinese came to the sugar plantations as low-paid labor, and their cuisine is still basic to the Hawaiian style, with its bean sprouts, bamboo shoots, water chestnuts, and other traditional Chinese vegetables. The Portuguese seafarers introduced spices from the East and sausages from the West. The Japanese, who also came to work the fields, brought hibachi style cooking, and one of the world's great chicken hors d'oeuvre, *Rumaki.* The Spanish and Filipinos introduced the cooking of the Philippines, and the Americans, who were the last visitors to Hawaii, brought Yankee cooking from New England, many traces of which can still be found.

Besides *Rumaki,* Hawaii boasts two other world-famous dishes. Traditionally a pork feast, the luau more recently includes chicken, and is cooked in an underground oven over steam-heated rocks much like the *imu* or *hima'a.* The other, the classic Chicken and Pineapple, is probably served in every Polynesian restaurant in the world.

Filipino cuisine is actually a combination of native cooking (which originated in Indonesia and Malaya), American, Chinese, and Spanish. Fortunately, these culinary influences have remained rather distinct, as have the names of the dishes of each. Pork is the favored meat, despite the large Hindu and Moslem population, but chicken is also popular and both frequently find their way into the same pot. The national classic of the Philippines is *Adobo*—a Spanish dish with Filipino overtones that combines both pork and chicken (or uses either alone) in a faintly sour sauce. Another Filipino dish is *Rellenong Manok*—boned chicken stuffed with ground pork; of Chinese origin is *Pansit,* a pork, chicken, and noodle dish, with sausage sometimes added. The favorite snack of the Philippines is *Lumpia,* a chicken and pork roll fried in deep fat, which looks similar to the Spring, or Egg, Rolls of China and Indonesia.

The British came "down under" to Australia and New Zealand in the early nineteenth century, and many of the original Australian settlers were criminals and undesirables purged from Britain's jails.

They brought the English kitchen with them and it hasn't changed much since. Beef, mutton, and pork are the preferred meats, while poultry is a comparative luxury. Gamebirds, however, are fairly common and quail is a special favorite.

One of the more venturesome recipes directs that a quail be cleaned, but the feathers left on. A mud or clay pack is liberally applied until the bird is heavily covered (a half-inch thick). Then the package is buried in the embers of a hot wood fire and left for an hour or more, while the embers are fanned to keep them glowing. When the bird is done, the clay pack is pulled off and the feathers come with it. The meat is now ready to eat, very tender and with all the juices retained.

RECOMMENDED READING:

- Robin Howe, *Cooking for the Commonwealth* (London: André Deutsch, 1958)

HAWAII

RUMAKI—Chicken Livers with Water Chestnuts

This is a Japanese hors d'oeuvre, which they made famous in the Hawaiian Islands. It takes time to prepare, but cooks rather quickly, and can be completed at the table.

1 pound chicken livers	1 pound bacon, sliced
Pinch salt	1 cup water chestnuts
2 tablespoons soy sauce	Toothpicks
2 teaspoons freshly grated ginger	1 cup peanut or sesame oil

Cut the chicken livers in half. Combine the salt, soy sauce, and grated ginger in a bowl, stir well, then mix with the livers. Cut the bacon slices in thirds.

Now place one piece of chicken liver and one water chestnut on a piece of bacon, roll up tightly, and secure with a toothpick. Continue until all the chicken livers, water chestnuts, and bacon have been used. (This can be done ahead of time, and refrigerated until you are ready to cook the rumaki.)

To cook, heat oil in a skillet or chafing dish and deep-fry for 10 minutes or so, turning several times. This should make about 30-36 rumaki. Serve hot with a hot mustard (page 25) and/or *shoyu* sauce (page 52).

HAWAII

CHICKEN AND PINEAPPLE

Around the world this is the classic Hawaiian chicken dish, combining a Chinese style of chicken cookery with the Islands' best-known crop—pineapple.

1 3-pound cooked chicken, skinned, boned, and cut into 1-inch pieces	¼ cup (or more) peanut or sesame oil
2 teaspoons cornstarch	1 small clove garlic, minced
4 teaspoons water or stock	1 fresh pineapple, peeled, cored, and cut into 1-inch chunks
2 tablespoons soy sauce	2 tablespoons pineapple juice
	1 large piece ginger, chopped finely

Dissolve ½ the cornstarch in 2 teaspoons water or stock and add the soy sauce. Mix well. Add the chicken and turn several times to coat evenly, then let sit for 30 minutes, turning several times.

Bring the oil to high heat in a wok or large skillet and stir-fry the chicken pieces and garlic for 2 or 3 minutes. Reduce the heat and add ½ the pineapple chunks and 1 tablespoon of the juice. Cover and simmer for 5 minutes or so.

Dissolve the remaining cornstarch in water and mix in the remaining pineapple juice. Add to the wok with the ginger and cook for 2-3 more minutes, or until the sauce just begins to thicken. Remove from heat and serve hot, scattering the remaining pineapple chunks over all.

Serve with white rice. Serves 4.

POLYNESIA

Here are two examples of how chicken is cooked in a luau. One, from Tahiti, uses a sweet-sour sauce and the other, from Hawaii, combines chicken and fish. To be authentic both should be cooked in the *hima'a* or *imu,* the Polynesian underground pit, but this isn't recommended, because an imu is difficult to construct and use. An easier way is shown below. The chicken should be wrapped in banana or ti leaves (cellophane, cornhusks, parchment paper, or even foil will do) and then steamed over water.

TAHITIAN CHICKEN LUAU

1 3-pound chicken, cut into 12 or 16 pieces
Salt and pepper
4-6 tablespoons peanut or sesame oil
4 tablespoons wine vinegar

4 tablespoons lime juice
1 pound taro leaves or fresh spinach
½ cup light coconut cream (page 83)
12-16 ti or banana leaves (or other wrapper)

Rub the chicken pieces all over with a little salt and pepper. Bring the oil to moderate heat in a large skillet and slowly cook the chicken pieces on all sides for 10 minutes. Remove to drain when brown.

Mix together the vinegar and lime juice in a bowl and add the chicken, turning to coat each piece thoroughly. Place a piece of chicken on a taro or spinach leaf, brush on just a little of the vinegar-lime juice mixture, and add a small amount (1 teaspoon) of coconut milk. Fold the leaf carefully around the meat, then wrap the package in a ti leaf (or other wrapper). Be sure each package is securely tied.

Place a rack in a large kettle and fill with water to a point just below the rack. Bring the water to the boil, then reduce heat to a point where the water is just barely boiling and giving off good steam. Put the packages in carefully, one on top of the other, then cover and let steam for 1 hour. Be sure to check the water level every so often, and add some when it gets low.

Serve each guest an unopened package or two with rice, a salad, and fruit and, of course, the traditional Island accompaniment to all meals—poi. Serves 4. (Bottled poi is available in gourmet shops.)

HAWAII

HAWAIIAN LAU LAU—Chicken and Fish in Ti Leaves

Meat of 1 3-pound chicken, skinned, boned, and cut into large chunks
2 pounds fresh white fish, skinned, boned, and cut into large chunks
1 pound fresh taro leaves or whole-leafed spinach
Salt
2 tablespoons butter
12-16 ti or banana leaves (or other wrapper)

First rub salt on the chicken pieces and pour butter over the fish, coating thoroughly. Arrange one piece of fish and one piece of chicken on several taro or spinach leaves and fold into a package. Now place each package on a deveined ti leaf (or other wrapper) and fold and tie into a package.

Prepare a kettle as in the preceding recipe. Cover and bring to a boil, then reduce heat to moderate and steam for 2 hours. Serve the lau laus in their packages, for each guest to unfold and enjoy. Serves 6.

THE PHILIPPINES

LUMPIA—Chicken and Pork Rolls

This dish is very similar to the Chinese and Indonesian Spring

Rolls, but significantly different from the Egg Rolls of the Chinese-American kitchen.

Filling

1 3-pound chicken, cut up
Meat from 2 lean pork chops, cut into 1-inch cubes
2 cups water
1 stalk celery
2 onions, 1 quartered and 1 chopped finely
1 bay leaf
2 tablespoons salt

1 Chinese (or regular) cabbage
8 slices lean bacon
1 clove garlic, minced
1 cup bean sprouts
1 cup celery, diced
¼ cup dark soy sauce (or substitute 4 tablespoons soy sauce mixed with 2 tablespoons brown sugar)

Lumpia Wrappers

2 cups flour, sifted
2½ cups cold water

2 tablespoons (or more) vegetable oil

Place the chicken pieces and pork cubes in a Dutch oven or large kettle. Add the water, bring to the boil, then reduce heat to low. Skim off the scum that rises, then add the stalk of celery, quartered onion, bay leaf, and 1 tablespoon salt. Cover and cook for 45 minutes. When done, remove the meat and let cool, then remove the skin and bones from the chicken and dice the meat finely. Dice the pork also. Strain and reserve the pan liquid.

Clean the cabbage, quarter it and remove the cores, then cut the quarters into strips. In a separate skillet cook the bacon until it is crisp, then drain on a paper towel. Now sauté the second onion and garlic in a second skillet for 4 or 5 minutes over low heat. When done add the chicken and pork meat and cook slowly for another 5 minutes, turning constantly. Add the bean sprouts, celery, and cabbage a little at a time. Cook for 2 or 3 minutes, stirring constantly, then crumble the bacon into fine bits and add to the pan. Now add about ½ cup (or a little more) of the strained stock, the remaining salt, and the dark soy sauce. Continue turning the pot for 5 minutes, then empty the entire contents into a colander and let drain for 10 minutes. The filling is now ready.

Lumpia Wrappers

Combine 2 cups of flour in a bowl with 2½ cups of cold water and stir until all the lumps are gone. Now heat 2 tablespoons or more of vegetable oil (this will vary according to the size of the pan) in a hot skillet or griddle, and pour in a very thin layer of the mixture. If you keep the wrapper dough thin enough, it will take only 5-10 seconds to cook each wrapper. When browned, remove to a warm platter and dust with flour. Continue until all the lumpia wrapper mixture is used up, placing one done wrapper on top of the other.

To complete the lumpia, place 2 tablespoons of filling in the center of a wrapper in a cylindrical shape. Bring the ends up and over the filling, then roll the lumpia together and secure with toothpicks.

Now fill a deep fryer with about 3 inches of vegetable oil, and heat it to 375° F. Depending on the size of the pot, carefully place 2 or 3 of the rolls into the hot oil at a time. Turn them carefully to achieve a rich brown color all over, then remove to a large platter covered with paper towels to drain. It's best to keep the platter in the oven at a low setting so the lumpia won't get cold. This should make 18-24 rolls.

THE PHILIPPINES

CHICKEN AND PORK ADOBO

This is the national dish of the Philippines, having come there with the Spanish years ago. Originally made with pork, adobo is now made as often with chicken alone or with both at once. One of the best things about adobo is that it can be frozen or refrigerated and then reheated and served. This way it tastes even better.

2 tablespoons butter	⅓ cup soy sauce
2 tablespoons vegetable oil	⅓ cup cider vinegar
2 3-pound chickens, cut up	⅓ cup sherry
2 pounds lean pork meat, boned and cut into cubes	1 cup chicken broth
	3 cloves garlic, minced
½ cup water	½ teaspoon freshly ground
2 tablespoons cornstarch	pepper

Over moderate fire, heat the butter and oil in a large casserole or Dutch oven. Brown the chicken pieces, a few at a time, on all sides, then remove. Add the pork cubes to the same pan and brown slowly for 10 minutes, turning frequently.

Add the water, then cover the pot. Reduce the heat to low, simmer for 30 minutes, then remove the meat to a plate and keep warm.

Dissolve the cornstarch in the soy sauce in a small bowl, then add the cider vinegar, sherry, chicken broth, garlic, and pepper. Stir once or twice to blend, then pour the liquid into the pot. Cook for 1 minute over low heat to thicken a little, then remove from the fire. Return the chicken pieces and pork cubes to the pot and thoroughly coat each piece with the sauce.

(Note: At this point, you may let the adobo cool completely and put it away in the freezer or refrigerator for up to a week. When you are ready to cook it, just preheat the oven to 350° F and cook covered for 1 hour and 15 minutes.)

Preheat the oven to 350° F. Cover the pot and cook for 1 hour. Serve directly from the pot with rice. Serves 6-8.

THE PHILIPPINES

PANSIT—Chicken, Pork, and Sausage
After the Filipinos arrived, this dish also became very popular in Hawaii.

2 medium onions, 1 quartered and 1 sliced thinly
1 3-pound chicken, cut up
Salt and pepper
¼ cup peanut or sesame oil
1 large piece fresh ginger root, minced
Meat from 4 good-sized pork chops, cut into 1-inch cubes
10-12 large shrimp or prawns

2 medium Chinese or Spanish chorizo sausages cut into 1-inch pieces
¼ cup celery, cut into ½ inch pieces
¼ Chinese (or regular) cabbage, shredded
1 tablespoon paprika
1 pound Chinese (or thin Italian) noodles
1 quart water
3 tablespoons soy sauce
Fresh parsley for garnish

Quarter 1 onion and put it into a large kettle with the chicken pieces. Add salt and pepper and bring to the boil. Reduce heat to low and skim off the scum as it rises, then cover and cook for 35-40 minutes. Remove the chicken and let it cool. Strain and retain the stock. Heat the oil in a large skillet and sauté ½ the sliced onion and minced ginger root for 5 minutes, then add the pork cubes and brown slowly for 15 minutes. Remove the pork and set aside. When the chicken is cool enough to handle, remove the skin and bones and cut the meat into large (1-inch) chunks.

Cut the shrimp or prawns into 2 or 3 pieces each, depending on how large they are. Bring the oil in the skillet back to moderate heat and replace the pork cubes. Add the chicken chunks and prawns and the sausage pieces and cook for 2 minutes slowly, then add the remaining sliced onion, the sliced celery, the shredded cabbage, and the paprika. Now add 2 cups of the reserved stock. Cover and reduce heat to low and simmer for 30 minutes.

About 15 minutes before the meat and vegetables are done, bring a quart of water to boil in a large kettle (use the remaining stock, if any, also) and cook the noodles. When the meat mixture is nearly done, add 3 tablespoons soy sauce.

Arrange the noodles on a large serving platter and make a large well in the middle. Spoon the meat and vegetables into the well, and garnish with parsley. Serves 6-8.

Additions: Hard-boiled eggs, halved, and lemon wedges are ideal accompaniments to pansit.

THE PHILIPPINES

RELLENONG MANOK—Boned Stuffed Chicken

This is one of the national dishes of the Philippines, and its preparation takes a little doing. The carcass of the bird is removed, except the wing and the leg bones. The cavity is then filled with a pork stuffing and the bird sewn up and roasted. It is very similar to the Ashanti Chicken of Ghana, West Africa.

1 4-5-pound roasting chicken, boned	½ large green pepper, diced
Juice and grated rind of ½ lemon	2 tablespoons raisins
Salt and pepper	2 raw eggs
2 pounds pork, cut into strips	4 tablespoons butter, melted
1 pound ham, cut into strips	1 large onion, chopped coarsely
	4 hard cooked eggs, peeled

Boning a Chicken:

Boning a chicken is not difficult, but it does take care and patience. Start by laying the chicken on its breast and cutting the skin down the backbone. Gently cut the meat away from the neck bone, then work your way back to the tail, freeing the meat from the backbone on each side. Be careful not to pierce the skin or tear the meat. When you come to the joint where the wing meets the body, snip the cartilage with scissors and proceed, leaving the wing bones in. When you come to the thigh, find the joint that attaches to the carcass and snip the cartilage with scissors, then cut the meat away from the thighbone. The thigh meat should still be attached to the leg meat. Now gradually scrape the breast meat away from the bones. Lift out the skeleton and retain it for another time—it will find excellent use in making a stock or soup.

Preheat the oven to 350° F. Combine the lemon juice and rind with a little salt and pepper and rub it into the cavity of the bird. Pass the pork and ham strips through the fine blade of a grinder 2 or 3 times then, in a bowl, combine the meat with the pepper, raisins, raw eggs, 2 tablespoons melted butter, and chopped onions. Add a little salt and pepper, then mix the ingredients thoroughly with your fingers or a wooden spoon. Now pack the cavity about half full with the stuffing mixture and place the hard cooked eggs end to end down the center. Spoon in the remaining stuffing over the eggs, then gently bring the sides of the bird together and sew it up tightly.

Place the chicken, breast side up, on a rack in a roaster and shape it with your hands. Brush the skin all over with melted butter, then place the pan in the oven and roast it, uncovered, for 1½ hours or until done.

To serve, you may either place the whole chicken on a warm platter or remove the thread along the backbone and spread-eagle the bird, stuffing side down. In either case, slice the meat crosswise in 1-inch slices. Serves 6.

AUSTRALIA/NEW ZEALAND

CHICKEN AND ASPARAGUS IN FOIL

1 3-pound chicken, cut up	½ cup dry sherry
4 tablespoons butter or oil	6 slices smoked ham
12 large mushrooms, sliced	36 spears fresh asparagus
½ cup light cream	Salt and freshly ground pepper
	6 large squares of foil

Melt the butter in a large skillet and brown the chicken pieces slowly on all sides. Remove the chicken from the pan and cut the meat away from the bones in large pieces. Discard the skin and bones. Now cook the mushrooms in the butter until they are tender (about 5 minutes), then pour in the cream and sherry and a little salt and pepper and cook slowly for another 5 minutes. While the sauce simmers, preheat the oven to 350° F.

Arrange a slice of ham on each foil square and place on top a serving of chicken, 6 asparagus spears, 2 sliced mushrooms, a little salt and pepper, and 1 or 2 tablespoons of the sauce. Fold up each square securely, place in a baking dish, and bake for 20 minutes. Serve with rice, allowing each guest to open his package at the table. Serves 6.

❧ Chapter 2 ❧

The Orient

The collective cooking of China represents one of the two great culinary triumphs of the world. The other is the French. No other kitchens compare in innovation, discipline, or scope.

Though they stand on opposite sides of the globe as epitomes of Eastern and Western cooking, both owe their preeminence to a native genius for blending ingredients and seasonings and an almost fanatical attention to the details of preparation and presentation. If there is any superiority of one over the other, it might be in time only; the French kitchen "arrived" about four centuries ago, while the Chinese has been in existence for twenty or more.

The standards that made Chinese cooking into an art form were established by Confucius twenty-five hundred years ago. He applied the fundamentals of his philosophy of life not only to the preparation of food, but to the service, the etiquette, and the ritual of the table. He stressed the beauty of life and the harmonious existence of all things and, in this context, taught that food was not to be eaten just to sustain life, but that taste, flavor, aroma, color, and even texture, coming together in perfect harmony, were to be contemplated, discussed, and enjoyed as one would a painting, a piece of music, or a budding flower.

As European cuisines are classified as Spanish or French or Italian, according to remembered tastes or local ingredients, so are the regional Chinese cuisines distinguished for their own cooking styles, but they all follow the disciplines established by Confucius. There are essentially five, and they represent the major gastronomic regions of the country: Canton, Szechuan, Hunan, Fukien, and Shantung/ Peking. There are other lesser Chinese kitchens, but these are more ethnic or local in nature.

Cantonese ports were the first to be visited by Western civilizations, and it was from Canton that the greatest number of Chinese emigrated to America starting about a hundred and fifty years ago. So it is not surprising that the Cantonese style of Chinese cooking is the one with which the Western world is most familiar.

Canton's cooking is the most diverse and innovative in China and for good reasons: it is semi-tropical and it has the longest seacoast, which means that elaborate fish and shellfish dishes are common, as well as tropical fruits and coconuts. It is also the leading producer of rice and soy sauce. It is from Canton that America's favorite Chinese dishes, Egg *Fu-Yung,* Egg Rolls, and Chicken Chow Mein, originated.

Szechuan, a province in southwestern China, is famous for spicy dishes that utilize cayenne and the hot red chili pepper in a number of outstanding chicken and duck specialties.

Hunan, once the capital of China, is famous for its sauces. Located in China's central region, between Canton and Szechuan, Hunan borrows freely from both and blends them into a unique style which, though limited, is quite rich. Hunan cooking frequently uses wine and occasionally is very spicy but always is characterized by a certain elegance in presentation.

Fukien, a region that lies along the Formosan Straits, features fish, fruit, and paper-wrapped foods in its cuisine. It is probably the lightest and most delicate of all the classical cooking styles of China.

The fifth style of cooking was developed in Shantung, the great agricultural region in the north, where, between the Yellow and Yangtze Rivers, the first Chinese civilization appeared. The Shantung region is the largest producer of chicken and other poultry in China, so it is not surprising that there is a wider variety of chicken cookery here than in other Chinese kitchens. The Shantung style also features the stronger garden vegetables—garlic, scallions, and ginger—yet it retains a delicacy and refinement that does not show up in the neighboring Cantonese cuisine.

Shantung cooking is closely associated with the Peking style because of its proximity to Peking, which for centuries has been the seat of the country's government. The palaces of the emperors and mandarins were located in Peking, and in their kitchens was developed the haute cuisine of Chinese cooking—a style that became known as Peking or Mandarin cooking. But the delicacy of the Peking kitchen got its substance from the simpler Shantung cuisine as a result of the frequent trips of the Chinese lords and their retainers fleeing the Mongolian barbarians when they crossed the Great Wall of China and attacked the capital.

Cantonese and Shantung/Peking cuisines are easily the most comprehensive in China, and while there are many dishes in each, they share others, the preparation of which graphically illustrates the differences in style and technique. The Shantung/Peking kitchen, for example, also cooks an Egg *Fu-Yung,* but whereas the Cantonese use the whole egg and present a yellow dish, Shantung eliminates the yolk and offers a very light or white *Fu-Yung.* Similarly both cuisines include fried noodles, but the Cantonese will fry them to a golden brown in their woks, while the Shantung cook will soft-fry noodles for only a moment or so, leaving them white and pliable.

The Mongolians themselves added yet another cooking style called Chinese Moslem. Though less refined than those of the five regional cuisines, it has yielded some of China's greatest dishes. One of its features is cuisine of the campfire; for example, Barbecued Lamb, which is much the same as the Russian *Shashlik* or Middle Eastern *Shish Kabob,* and the Chinese or Chrysanthemum Hotpot. (The same device in Japan is called the Genghis Khan; in Korea, the *Sinsullo*; and in Singapore the Chinese Steamboat.) From the same kitchen, however, comes perhaps the most classic fowl dish in the Chinese repertoire—Peking Duck. It may also be the most complicated fowl dish to prepare that there is. Not only is the duck inflated, it is preserved or cured for a week by "wind drying" and then hung in the oven to be cooked.

The basic philosophy of the Chinese cook is to spend as little time at the stove and as much at the table as possible. The Chinese use one small stove—to cook rice, heat tea, and prepare six to ten dishes that will usually vary in cooking time. But over the past two millennia, remarkable innovations in technique and equipment permit them to work their culinary magic in such restricted circumstances.

One is the basket steamer, a device that is built in sections. One section sits on top of another, to permit four or more vegetables or meats to be steamed at the same time. The item that requires the most cooking goes in the bottom section and gets the most steam. The steamer also provides the Chinese cook with a way to heat a number of cooked dishes just before bringing them to the table.

Another is "crystal cooking," where the chicken is cooked in a tightly covered pot in rapidly boiling water for three to five minutes and then removed from the fire and allowed to sit covered for two hours. The chicken will be cooked to a turn without requiring any additional fire.

Because the cooking capacity of their range is so limited, the Chinese take elaborate pains to cut meats and vegetables to precise, bite-sized pieces well ahead of cooking time. Using a wok, a bowl-shaped metal pan with high sides that distributes heat over a wide area, a typical Chinese dish is cooked very quickly, and a number of dishes can be readied frequently in a matter of minutes.

Some Chinese dishes call for chicken that has been stripped from the bones and shredded so that it can be fried quickly. When the bone is left in, the chicken often will be chopped into sixteen or twenty pieces, again for quick cooking.

The Chinese give meats different priorities than do Western or Subcontinental cooks. Cattle are working animals, so beef is not a frequently eaten meat. Fish is a plentiful and popular dish, and the Chinese have any number of ways to cook it. Pork, though, is the mainstay of the Chinese diet all through the country. But if pork is the mainstay, fowl is the masterpiece. Chicken and duck are to the Chinese cuisine what veal is to the Italian, or sausage to the German. It is the meat reserved for festive, religious, or state occasions, and the Chinese have distinguished it in hundreds of ways. In keeping with the teachings of Confucius, they grow absolutely poetic when naming their chicken dishes, so that a diner may contemplate a mental image in anticipation of the gastronomic artistry that is to come.

Consider, for instance, sliced breast meat of chicken over asparagus. This simply cannot conjure up a taste as regal as "White Cut Chicken in Green Paradise;" nor does chicken marinated in sherry provoke by any means the same salivary stimulation of "Drunken Chicken;" and though on a less lyric note, "Ten-Ingredient Chicken" promises far more substance and character than simple Chicken Stew.

RECOMMENDED READING: Charmaine Solomon, *The Complete Asian Cookbook* (New York: McGraw-Hill Book Company, 1976); (A very new book) Lucille Liang, *Chinese Regional Cooking* (New York: Sterling Publishing Co., 1979); Robin Howe, *Cooking for the Commonwealth* (London: André Deutsch, 1958)

MAIL ORDER SOURCES FOR INGREDIENTS:

Mrs. DeWildt
RFD 1
Bangor, Pa. 18013

Liang's Oriental Gifts and Grocery, Inc.
8 Pleasantville Road
Pleasantville, N.Y. 10570

DIM-SUM—SMALL CHOW

The teahouse is a great tradition all over China, but the Chinese go there for more than tea. Some of the best known of China's dishes are served in teahouses as snacks—chow mein, congee, steamed buns, and dim-sum or "small chow," which are probably the closest thing China has to hors d'oeuvre. Here are several traditional dim-sum that feature chicken:

Chicken Wonton
Chicken Mixture

Breast meat of 1 small (2-2½-pound) chicken, cut into fine dice

2 tablespoons green pepper, chopped

1 scallion, chopped finely
1 teaspoon soy sauce
1 teaspoon sherry
1 tablespoon chicken stock
1 egg, well beaten
2 cups peanut oil

Wrappers
2 cups flour

1 teaspoon salt
Water

Combine the chicken meat in a large bowl with the pepper, chopped scallion, soy sauce, sherry, chicken stock, and egg. Turn with a wooden spoon for 1 minute, until the mixture is thoroughly blended. Let stand while you make the wrappers.

Sift the flour and salt together in a bowl, then add warm water to it, stirring until a smooth, pliable dough ball is formed. Dust a bread board with flour and knead the dough for 10 minutes with the heel of your hand, until it becomes slightly stiff. Now dust the board again and roll the dough out into a square as thinly as possible, then cut the dough into 3-3½-inch squares.

Place 1 teaspoon (or a little more) of the chicken mixture in the center of each square. Fold together two opposite corners, forming a triangle, then press the edges to form a seal. (The wontons may now be placed in the refrigerator for up to a week, until ready to be cooked.)

Heat the oil in a deep pan or wok and cook the wontons, a few at a time, for 2-3 minutes, until golden brown. Remove to drain and then keep warm until ready to serve. Serve with mustard and sweet and sour sauce. This should make 30-36 wontons.

Mustard Sauce

3 tablespoons dry mustard	1 teaspoon sesame oil
⅛ teaspoon salt	2 tablespoons soy sauce
2 tablespoons chicken broth	2 teaspoons vinegar

Mix together thoroughly and serve as a dip, or dribble the sauce over the wontons on a serving platter.

Sweet and Sour Sauce

1 tablespoon cornstarch	1 tablespoon sherry
3 tablespoons water	1 tablespoon vinegar
2 tablespoons soy sauce	1 tablespoon sugar
	1 tablespoon tomato sauce

Mix together the cornstarch and water until a smooth paste forms. Combine with the other ingredients until blended thoroughly, then heat over a low fire until the mixture begins to thicken. Serve as a dip.

Spring Rolls

The Cantonese brought this dim-sum dish with them to Hawaii and America, where it became known as egg rolls. Long before that, however, they introduced it to Indochina and the Philippines (*lumpia*). These are called "spring rolls" because the Chinese cooked them while celebrating the Chinese New Year. Spring came the next day, so everyone took a vacation and went home to his family.

Wrappers

3 cups flour	1½ cups (or more) cold water

Filling

2 cups plus 3 tablespoons peanut oil	2 cups bamboo shoots, cut into strips
1 scallion	2 cups bean sprouts
2 cups breast meat of chicken, cut into small dice	4 tablespoons soy sauce
1 cup fresh mushrooms (stems removed), chopped finely	4 tablespoons sherry
	Salt and pepper

Stir the water into the flour until a smooth ball of dough forms. Knead it with the heel of your hand for several minutes, then cover it and let stand for 10 minutes. Now roll it out into as thin a sheet as possible and cut the sheet into pieces 3x4 inches in size.

Bring the 3 tablespoons oil to fairly high heat in a wok or large skillet and stir-fry the scallion for a minute or so, then add the diced chicken. Stirring continually, fry the chicken for 4 minutes, then add the remaining ingredients. Lower the heat to medium and simmer for 3 minutes, stirring continually.

Place 1 heaping tablespoon of filling in the center of each dough rectangle, fold up the ends, then roll up lengthwise. Using a little water, seal the lapping edge. Bring 2 cups of oil to high heat and drop in 2 rolls at a time. Don't put in more at one time or they won't cook properly. Cook, turning gently, until the spring rolls are golden brown. Remove to drain. Serve hot (they may be reheated in the oven) with hot mustard and sweet and sour sauces (page 25). This recipe should make 30-36 spring rolls.

Fu-Yung

Fu-yung dishes are very popular in China, being enjoyed much as the French enjoy their omelets. The Cantonese brought it with them when they came to America, and "Egg Foo-Yung" with any number of meat and vegetable combinations is now a standard meal in Chinese-American restaurants. Here are two classic Chinese recipes made with chicken. In the first, from Peking, only the egg white is used; the second, from Canton, uses the whole egg.

Peking

White Fu-Yung

4 tablespoons chicken stock
6 egg whites
2 tablespoons white wine
1 teaspoon salt
2 teaspoons cornstarch

Breast meat of ½ chicken, chopped into fine dice
1 teaspoon white onion, minced (or prime white parts of one small scallion)
¼ cup peanut oil

Combine the stock, egg whites, white wine, salt, and cornstarch in a bowl and beat with a whisk. Add the minced chicken and onion and blend thoroughly.

Heat the oil in a wok or small iron skillet until rather hot. Gently spoon a little (1 spoonful) of the fu-yung mixture into the oil and cook until it is set. If necessary, turn the egg over for a few seconds, then remove to drain. Keep the egg pancakes covered on a warm plate until all have been cooked. Serve at once. Serves 4.

CANTON

Diced Chicken Fu-Yung

6 eggs	4 large mushrooms, chopped
Breast meat of ½ chicken,	Salt and pepper
chopped into fine dice	1 small onion, minced
3 tablespoons cornstarch	2 tablespoons white wine
	⅓ cup peanut oil.

Beat the eggs thoroughly with a whisk, then add the diced chicken, cornstarch, chopped mushrooms, a little salt and pepper, the minced onion, and the white wine. Stir together until the mixture is thoroughly blended.

Heat the oil in a large frying pan, then add a little of the mixture and cook until the fu-yung sets. (Use a spoon if you want small pancakes, or a ladle if you want them bigger.) When the pancake is fairly firm, turn it over gently and cook for another 10 seconds or so. Remove to drain and keep warm on a covered serving plate. Serve at once. Serves 4.

CANTON

CHICKEN CONGEE—Soft Rice with Chicken

Congee, in China, is not necessarily a main meal dish, although it is eaten frequently at breakfast. Congee is served as a snack in the many teahouses that appear all over the country. Congee is cooked in a great deal of water and comes out almost like a porridge, to which just about any combination of meat, fish, fowl, vegetable, egg, or nut can be added.

2 tablespoons soy sauce
2 pieces fresh ginger, minced
¼ cup sherry
2 scallions, chopped

Breast meat of whole chicken, skinned, boned, and cut into ½-inch cubes
½ cup chopped shrimp (or white fish, lobster, crab, etc.)
10 cups water or chicken stock
1 teaspoon salt
1 cup long-grained white rice

Make a marinade of the soy sauce, minced ginger, sherry, and scallions and stir in the chicken and shrimp, being sure to coat each piece. Let stand for 30 minutes.

Pour the water or stock, salt, and rice into a deep pot, and add the marinated chicken and shrimp (be sure to include the marinade). Stir together to blend thoroughly, then bring to the boil. Reduce heat to low, cover, and cook for 45 minutes. Serves 4.

PEKING

CHICKEN AND WALNUTS

1 cup walnuts
Water
1 tablespoon cornstarch
1, 3 cup sherry
1 teaspoon sugar
⅛ teaspoon salt
2 tablespoons soy sauce
Breast meat of 1 3-pound chicken, skinned, boned, and cut into ½-inch cubes

1/3 cup peanut or sesame oil
2 slices ginger root, chopped
1 clove garlic, minced
2 spring onions or scallions, sliced into ½-inch pieces
1 stalk celery, sliced into ½-inch pieces
5 water chestnuts, sliced
¼ cup chicken stock
½ cup bamboo shoots

Cover the walnuts with water and bring to the boil. After 3-4 minutes, remove from heat, drain, and let cool, then remove the skins.

Mix the cornstarch in 2 tablespoons water and stir until it dissolves. Add the sherry, sugar, salt, soy sauce, and chicken cubes and stir until the chicken pieces are completely coated. Set aside for 20 minutes.

Heat the oil in a wok or large skillet and fry the walnuts for several minutes, until they begin to change color. Remove immediately to drain.

Add the chopped ginger root and garlic to the pan and fry for 1 minute, then add the sliced onions, celery, and water chestnuts. Stir-fry for 3-4 minutes, turning constantly, then add the chicken and fry for another 3 minutes. Continue stirring.

Now add in any remaining marinade, the broth, bamboo shoots, and walnuts. Stir for 2-3 minutes or until the liquid begins to thicken. Serve hot with rice or noodles. Serves 4.

FUKIEN

CELLOPHANE-WRAPPED FRIED CHICKEN

The technique of cooking fish or fowl wrapped in paper is known and practiced throughout the world. Whether the Chinese developed it first is not known, but they have brought the art of cooking chicken in rice paper or cellophane to a high level.

Breast meat of 1 chicken, skinned and boned	2 tablespoons sugar
2-3 spring onions or scallions, sliced into 30 pieces	30 (4-inch square) pieces of cello- phane
2 tablespoons soy sauce	30 Chinese pea pods
30 thin slices ginger root	30 (inch-long) strips of smoked ham
2 tablespoons sherry	10 water chestnuts, sliced in thirds
	2 cups peanut oil

Slice the chicken thinly into 30 equal pieces. Mix together the onion slices, soy sauce, ginger root, sherry, and sugar. Then gently stir in the chicken. Stir a little to get each strip well coated, then let the bowl sit for 30 minutes.

Now place 1 strip of chicken in the center of a piece of cellophane. Arrange 1 onion slice, 1 pea pod, 1 strip of ham, 1 slice of ginger root, and 1 slice of water chestnut in the center with the chicken and pour over just a little (⅛ teaspoon) of the marinade.

Fold the bottom corner of the cellophane up over the chicken mixture, next fold the left corner over, and then the right. Now fold the top corner down and tuck it under the others securely.

Bring the oil to high heat in a deep-fryer, and slide the packets in very gently, just a few at a time. Deep-fry them for 5 minutes, turning gently once or twice. Don't put too many in at one time or the oil heat will drop, and the chicken won't cook through. As the packets are cooked place them on a paper-lined plate in a warming oven. Serve as hors d'oeuvre or as a meal, but serve them wrapped in the cellophane for the guests to open. Serves 6.

Peking/Shantung

PEKING DUCK

This is one of the most famous Oriental dishes of all, and one of the most time-consuming to prepare. In addition there is probably no cooking method more unique than the one employed here. Unfortunately you can't do this too well with a chicken, but because it's one of China's great recipes, I've included it.

First the bird is inflated. A tube (or straw) is inserted under the skin along the neck, and air is blown in to loosen the skin from the meat. Holding the neck firmly with one hand, the skin is worked with the other hand as the air is blown in, to help loosen it. It will take a while, but eventually the major part of the skin that covers the breast, thighs, and back will be loosened enough to permit the bird to be "inflated." Now the neck is tied up so air won't escape and the bird is "quick plunged" (held by the feet or with tongs) in a kettle of boiling water for a few seconds, then dried and hung up in a dry but open place for at least 6 hours but preferably overnight. In Peking the duck is rubbed with a sugar-water mixture and dried again before being hung in the oven and roasted. This can also be done on a rack in an open roaster with good results. Preheat the oven to 425° F and cook for 15 minutes. Then reduce the heat to 400° F and continue cooking for 45 minutes.

When the bird comes out the skin will be crackling done and the grease will be gone. With a sharp knife cut and peel off the skin carefully, then cut it into small pieces and keep warm. Cut the meat from the bones into smallish pieces and keep warm. Both will be served with pancake doilies when you are ready to eat.

Pancake Doilies

While the duck is cooking make the pancake doilies: Pour 2 cups of flour into a large bowl and gradually add 1 cup of boiling water. Stir into a smooth dough ball, then knead the dough for 10 minutes or so. Roll the dough into a long tube about 2 inches in diameter and cut the roll into ½-inch thick sections.

Now carefully roll the sections out to a diameter of 6 inches. Cook each doily in an ungreased skillet or griddle for 3 minutes on a side. When done keep them warm. Continue until all the pancake doilies are cooked. Now place them in a bowl and the bowl in a large kettle of water. The water should come about ⅔ of the way up the side of the bowl. Cover the kettle and bring to the boil. Steam the pancakes for 10 minutes (or use a basket steamer for the same length of time).

The crackling skin and pieces of meat are served on separate plates. Each guest helps himself to a piece of meat or skin (or both), wraps it in a doily, and eats it with his fingers. A variety of sauces and other dips should be available to enhance the flavor of the duck: bean paste, plum or apricot jam, soy sauce, vinegar, minced onion, and garlic are some popular accompaniments. The Chinese also serve stir-fried vegetables, cucumbers, and scallions.

TAIWAN

SHREDDED CHICKEN SOUP

Taiwan represents a microcosm of all of China's cooking, for when the Nationalist Chinese fled the mainland they took the best of each of the regional cuisines—and some of the cooks—with them.

1 3-pound chicken	1 cup fresh mushrooms, sliced
2 onions, peeled and quartered	¼ pound Chinese cellophane
2 quarts water	noodles
Salt	2 teaspoons soy sauce
1 pound small shrimp, cleaned,	2 tablespoons peanut oil
peeled, and cooked	4 scallions, cut into ½-inch pieces
	2 cloves garlic, minced

Place the chicken and onions in the water and sprinkle over a little salt. Bring the water to the boil, then reduce the heat to low, cover, and cook for 2 hours. Remove the chicken from the broth, and allow it to cool enough so you can handle it, then remove the skin and bones and discard and cut the meat into very thin strips. Return the chicken to the broth and increase the heat. Add the shrimp and mushrooms and boil for 5-6 minutes. Reduce the heat and add the noodles and soy sauce and simmer for 5-6 minutes more.

Meanwhile heat the oil in a small skillet and fry the scallions and garlic for 3-4 minutes, then remove with a slotted spoon and add to the soup. Serve hot in a large tureen. Serves 6.

SHANTUNG

MARINATED STEAMED-FRIED CHICKEN

Here's an excellent and delicious example of the multiphase cooking technique developed by the Chinese.

1 3-4-pound chicken	3 large slices ginger root, chopped
2 cups dry sherry	2 scallions, cut into ¼-inch slices
3 tablespoons soy sauce	3 tablespoons cornstarch
1 teaspoon sugar	6 tablespoons water
⅛ teaspoon each of cinnamon, star anise, fennel, clove powder, pepper	1 egg, beaten
	2 cups peanut oil
	Freshly ground pepper

First place the chicken in a large bowl and pour in the sherry. Let stand for 30 minutes or more. Pour off the sherry. Combine the soy sauce, sugar, and the five-spice powder (cinnamon, star anise, fennel, clove powder, and pepper) and rub the chicken with the mixture inside and out, covering completely. Return the bird to the bowl and add the ginger and scallions. Place the bowl in a large kettle with water (the water should come about ⅔ of the way up the bowl) and bring to the boil. Reduce the heat to medium, cover, and steam for 1½ hours. (Be sure to check the water occasionally so it doesn't go dry.) When done remove the chicken and let it cool, then cut it into serving pieces.

Dissolve the cornstarch in the water and gently beat in the egg, then coat the chicken pieces in this mixture. Bring the oil to high heat in a wok or large skillet and fry the chicken pieces, a few at a time, for 15-20 minutes. Remove to drain for a few moments, then place on a platter in a warm oven. When all the chicken is cooked, sprinkle pepper over and serve at once. Serves 4.

CANTON

LEMON CHICKEN

1 3-pound chicken, boned (skin stays on the meat)	2 tablespoons soy sauce
	2 eggs

2 tablespoons sherry

4 tablespoons cornstarch
2 cups peanut or sesame oil

Sauce

1 teaspoon salt
2 tablespoons sugar
Juice and grated rind of one
  lemon

1 cup chicken stock
1 scallion, cut into ¼-inch slices
Lemon wedges and parsley for
  garnish

Cut the chicken meat carefully into 1-inch cubes. Mix together the sherry and soy sauce and pour over the chicken pieces in a bowl. Toss several times to be sure each piece is evenly coated. Cover and let stand for 30 minutes.

Make a batter by mixing together the eggs and 3 tablespoons cornstarch (add just a little water if it's too thick). Bring the oil to high heat in a deep-fryer or wok, then dip each piece of chicken in the batter and drop into the oil for 2-3 minutes. Fry only 3 or 4 pieces at a time. When browned, remove to drain for a moment, then keep warm on a plate in the oven. When all the chicken pieces are browned, make the sauce:

Mix together the salt, sugar, 1 tablespoon cornstarch, the juice and grated rind of 1 lemon, and the chicken stock and stir for a few moments to dissolve the cornstarch. Heat a little oil in a wok or large skillet and quickly fry the scallion, stirring constantly. Gradually add the cornstarch mixture and stir until it becomes thoroughly blended and heated, then remove from the heat. Mound the chicken pieces on a warm platter and spoon the sauce over all. Garnish with lemon wedges and parsley and serve with rice or soft-fried noodles. Serves 4.

SZECHUAN

SPICY CHICKEN

This typifies Szechuan cooking at its best. Done authentically it's hot to the extreme, but this can be altered by reducing the chili pepper by half (or even less).

¼ cup fresh peanuts, shelled
5 tablespoons peanut oil
1 tablespoon vinegar
1 tablespoon dark soy sauce (or 2

parts soy sauce to 1 part brown
sugar)
1 or 2 tablespoons chili pepper,
chopped finely

2 pieces fresh ginger, chopped finely	Freshly ground pepper (black)
1 scallion, sliced thinly	1 pint water
2 cloves garlic, minced	Breast meat of 1 3-pound chicken, skinned and boned

Cover the peanuts with waxed paper and pound into a fine powder, then mix in 3 tablespoons peanut oil and stir until you have a smooth paste. Add the vinegar and dark soy sauce and stir until blended.

In a separate bowl, mix the chili pepper, ginger, scallion, garlic, and several grindings of pepper with 2 tablespoons peanut oil. Add this to the peanut mixture, and stir to blend completely.

Bring the water to the boil, and plunge the chicken meat in (with tongs) for 8 minutes. The chicken should be done. Remove to drain and cool, then shred the meat into thin strips, cutting across into 2-inch lengths. Place the chicken and sauce in the refrigerator for 1 hour, then mix together thoroughly before serving. Serves 2-4.

CANTON, SHANTUNG

CHAO (CHOW) MEIN—
Chicken and Pork with Fried Noodles

To Americans, *chao (chow) mein* means Chinese food. It's a noodle dish from the Canton and northern provinces that is made several ways and can include a variety of ingredients. In Shantung the noodles are first boiled and then soft-fried quickly in the oil left from cooking the meat and vegetables. The frying is really to heat them rather than cook them. In the Canton region, the noodles are fried for a longer period of time in oil, and pressed against the wok or pan so that they brown and become crisp.

2 quarts water	1 cup celery, chopped
Salt	½ cup pork meat, cubed
1 pound vermicelli, or very thin spaghetti	1 cup chicken meat, cut into thin 1-inch strips
4 fresh or dried mushrooms	2 tablespoons soy sauce
¼ cup peanut or sesame oil	1 1-inch piece fresh ginger, minced
2 cloves garlic, minced	
2 scallions, chopped	2 tablespoons sherry
1/3 cup bamboo shoots	1/3 cup water chestnuts
2 cups cabbage or spinach, shredded finely	

Bring 2 quarts of water to boil, add a little salt, then drop in the vermicelli slowly. Boil for 8-10 minutes, then drain in a colander under cold water to stop the cooking and prevent the noodles from sticking. Set aside.

Use fresh or dried mushrooms. If you use dried mushrooms, soak for 30 minutes, then slice them thinly and set aside. Bring 1 table-spoon oil in a wok or large frying pan to a rather high heat. Add the minced garlic, scallions, bamboo shoots, shredded cabbage or spin-ach, celery, and a little salt, and stir-fry for about 2 minutes. Now remove with a slotted spoon and set aside.

Now add 2 tablespoons oil to the wok and cook the pork for about 2 minutes, turning frequently. Then add the chicken and mushrooms, continuing to stir for 1 more minute. Add soy sauce, ginger, and 1 tablespoon sherry and stir-fry for 1 more minute. Then remove the meat from the wok with a slotted spoon and set aside.

Add the remaining oil and then the vermicelli. Stir-fry for a minute or so to heat them (or longer if you want them brown and crisp), then add back the vegetables and water chestnuts a little at a time, stirring all the while. When all ingredients are back in the pan, add the remaining sherry, stir 2 or 3 times, then turn out to a large warm serving platter. Serves 4-6.

Alternatives: Mix chopped, freshly scrambled eggs into the chow mein just before serving. Also bean sprouts or raw chopped cucumbers may be added for variation. Shrimp or beef may be used in place of pork.

CANTON

SHREDDED CHICKEN WITH BAMBOO SHOOTS

Breast meat of 1 whole chicken, skinned, boned, and cut into 1-inch strips	¼ cup peanut oil
	1 large slice ginger root, minced
	1 cup chicken stock
2 tablespoons cornstarch	2 tablespoons sherry
4 tablespoons water	1 tablespoon salt
White of 1 egg	1 cup bamboo shoots
	2 tablespoons sesame oil

Dissolve 1 tablespoon cornstarch in 2 tablespoons water. Beat the egg white with a whisk until frothy, then add to the cornstarch mixture. Stir once or twice, then add the chicken strips and turn for 1 minute with a wooden spoon or your fingers until each chicken piece is well coated.

Bring the peanut oil to high heat in a wok or large skillet and fry the ginger for 8-10 seconds. Remove from heat and pour off the oil. Now dissolve the remaining cornstarch in 2 tablespoons water.

Place the pan back on the heat and pour in the chicken stock, sherry, salt, and bamboo shoots. Cook briefly until the liquid starts to boil, then add the cornstarch mixture. Stir until the liquid begins to thicken, then add the shredded chicken and cook, stirring constantly, for up to 1 minute (depending on how thick you want the sauce).

Pour the mixture into a bowl and drizzle the sesame oil over. Serve with hot rice and a green vegetable. Serves 4.

Hunan

CHICKEN WITH BEAN SPROUTS

2 tablespoons cornstarch	1 cup peanut oil
6 tablespoons water	¼ cup pea pods, cut into strips
1 teaspoon salt	2 cups bean sprouts
White of 1 egg	4-5 oz. cooked ham, cut into thin
Breast meat of 1 whole chicken,	1-inch strips
skinned, boned, and cut into	2 tablespoons sherry
1-inch strips	1 tablespoon sugar

Dissolve 2 tablespoons cornstarch in 4 tablespoons water, then mix together in a bowl with ½ teaspoon salt and egg white. Mix in the chicken pieces and stir with a wooden spoon, or work with your fingers until each piece is well coated.

Bring the peanut oil to high heat in a wok or large skillet and fry the coated chicken pieces for 1 minute, stirring constantly. Remove to drain and then keep warm in the oven. Now stir-fry the pea pods and bean sprouts for 1 minute. Add back the chicken and ham and stir well. Add the sherry, ½ teaspoon salt, and the sugar. Dissolve 1 tablespoon cornstarch in 2 tablespoons water and add to the pot and stir until the liquid begins to thicken. Remove from heat and serve with rice. Serves 4.

PEKING/SHANTUNG

QUICK-FRIED CHICKEN IN SAUCE

This dish is popular all over China and, while other ingredients may be added, it is essentially a chicken chopped into 16 pieces and coated with a thin paste, then quick-fried twice in a wok or skillet.

To end up with 16 pieces, cut the leg and thigh sections and separate at the joint. Chop off the bottom bones of the legs, then cut the thighs in half. Cut off the wings (discard the tips) and cut in two at the joint. Now remove the breasts, split lengthwise, and chop across into thirds. That should add up to 16 pieces.

1 3-pound chicken	3 slices ginger root, sliced thinly
1 teaspoon sugar	1 tablespoon wine vinegar
1 scallion, sliced thinly	2 tablespoons sherry
3 tablespoons soy sauce	2 tablespoons water
½ teaspoon salt	2 tablespoons cornstarch
	2 cups peanut oil

Cut the chicken up as described above. Combine the sugar, scallion, soy sauce, salt, chopped ginger root, vinegar, and sherry in a large bowl. Mix together the water and cornstarch and add to the bowl, stirring to blend thoroughly. Now drop in the chicken pieces, turning them with a spoon to insure an even coating of each piece. Let stand for 2 hours.

Bring the oil to high heat in a wok or large skillet, and drop in a few chicken pieces at a time. Deep-fry for 3 minutes, turning several times, then remove to drain. When all are done, return the chicken to the hot oil and cook again for 5 minutes. (Most of this may be done ahead of time, if you wish. After the first frying, just cover the chicken pieces until you are ready to serve, then reheat the oil and complete the last step.)

Serve with rice, or soft-fried noodles. Serves 4-6.

SHANTUNG

DRUNKEN CHICKEN

Drunken Chicken is a great favorite in China and one of the country's best-known hors d'oeuvre. The recipe employs the Chinese method of quick or "crystal" boiling, where the bird is cooked in water or stock at a rolling boil for several minutes, then removed from the fire and let sit in the covered pot for 2 hours or so while the cooking completes itself. This is best done using a small, young bird to insure that the meat cooks through. After the chicken is crystal-boiled it is cut up, immersed in wine, and put in the refrigerator for up to a week. Use an authentic Chinese wine if available, but if you can't find one a good dry sherry is a satisfactory substitute.

1 2-2½-pound chicken	1 scallion, diced
2 tablespoons salt	1 clove garlic, minced
8-10 peppercorns	1 bottle Chinese wine, or sherry

Bring the water to a boil in a large kettle and add all the other ingredients except the wine. Place the chicken in the water and, after the water returns to the boil, cover and cook for 3-5 minutes. Remove the pot from the fire and let it sit covered for 2 hours or more.

Now remove the chicken from the pot and strip the meat from the carcass, discarding skin and bones, and cut it into 1-inch cubes. Put the chicken cubes into a large jar, pour in the wine or sherry, cover, and refrigerate for several days or a week.

Serves 6-8 as an hors d'oeuvre or 4 as an appetizer.

CANTON

TEN-INGREDIENT CHICKEN

There are a fairly large number of vegetables and other ingredients in this dish, so it's best to have them all prepared for cooking ahead of time.

2 tablespoons cornstarch	4 medium mushroom caps, quartered
4 tablespoons water	¼ cup bamboo shoots
2 tablespoons soy sauce	1-inch piece fresh ginger root, chopped
3 tablespoons peanut oil	2 cloves garlic, minced
¼ cup almonds, blanched and slivered	⅓ cup Chinese snow peas, or sliceed pea pods
Breast meat of 1 3-pound chicken, skinned, boned, and cut into ¼-inch dice	¼ cup water chestnuts, diced
	⅛ teaspoon pepper

3 spring onions or scallions, sliced
   into ½-inch pieces

½ cup smoked ham, cut into
   ¼-inch dice
½ cup chicken stock
2 tablespoons dry sherry

First dissolve the cornstarch in the water and soy sauce and set aside. Bring 2-3 tablespoons peanut oil to high heat in a wok or large skillet and fry the almond slivers for 1 minute, stirring constantly so they won't burn. Remove from the pan with a slotted spoon and set aside. Add the chicken meat to the pan and stir-fry for 2-3 minutes, then add the spring onions, mushrooms, bamboo shoots, ginger, garlic, snow peas (or pea pods), water chestnuts, and pepper and, stirring constantly, fry for 4-5 minutes.

Now add the diced ham and the cornstarch mixture and stir into the pan. Reduce the heat to low, then add the stock and stir-fry for 4 or 5 minutes or until the sauce becomes slightly thickened. Stir in the sherry just before serving. This goes best with cooked white rice. Serves 4.

Alternative: Substitute ½ cup cooked, coarsely chopped shrimp for the ham.

SZECHUAN

SWEET COOKED CHICKEN

In this recipe the chicken is "wind dried" or cured in the open air before quick-frying in a wok.

Meat from a 3-pound chicken,
   shredded into small, thin strips
1 tablespoon sugar
1 tablespoon soy sauce
Small pinch ground chili pepper

1 tablespoon wine vinegar
⅔ tablespoon bean paste
⅔ tablespoon *hoisin* sauce*
2 teaspoons cornstarch
4 teaspoons water
3 tablespoons peanut oil

Spread the shredded chicken on a large flat cookie sheet and let stand in an airy place for 2 or 3 hours.

When the chicken is ready to cook, mix together the sugar, soy sauce, chili pepper, vinegar, bean paste, and hoisin sauce. Blend the cornstarch and water until smooth and add to the sauce.

*Hoisin sauce is a brownish-red sauce available in most specialty food stores.

Bring the peanut oil to high heat in a wok or large skillet and quick-fry half the shredded chicken for 2 minutes or so, turning frequently so each piece cooks evenly. Remove with a slotted spoon and keep warm, then cook the remaining chicken and when done remove to the warming plate.

Reduce the heat to low and add the sauce mixture to the wok and heat for a few moments, then add back the chicken pieces. Stirring constantly, heat for a minute or so until the sauce starts to thicken. Serve immediately with rice. Serves 4.

SZECHUAN

SHREDDED CHICKEN IN WINE SAUCE

Not all Szechuan cooking is hot and spicy. This is a quick and easy, though classic, chicken dish served in a wine sauce that might just as well have come from neighboring Hunan. The Chinese have a variety of their own wines, which they frequently use in cooking, but in the event you cannot find authentic Chinese wine, dry sherry is a satisfactory substitute.

Breast meat of 2 3-pound chickens, skinned, boned, and shredded into thin strips
½ teaspoon salt
2 egg whites

2 tablespoons sherry
4 tablespoons cornstarch
1 cup Chinese pea pods, sliced into ⅛-inch strips
2 cups bean sprouts

Sauce
3 teaspoons cornstarch
6 teaspoons water
2-3 scallions, sliced into ½-inch pieces
2 pieces fresh ginger root, chopped

6 tablespoons Chinese wine or dry sherry
⅛ teaspoon salt
¼ teaspoon sugar
¼ cup chicken stock
4-6 tablespoons peanut oil

Combine the shredded chicken in a bowl with the salt, egg whites, and sherry and blend thoroughly. Add the cornstarch and stir to dissolve.

Now make the sauce: First dissolve the cornstarch in water, then combine with all the other sauce ingredients.

Bring the oil to high heat in a wok or large skillet and stir-fry the chicken shreds for 15-20 seconds. Remove to drain. Pour off all but 1 tablespoon oil and add the sliced pea pods and bean sprouts. Stir-fry for 8-10 seconds, then add back the chicken. Stir the pan, constantly turning and tossing the ingredients, for another 8-10 seconds. Now pour in the sauce, reduce heat to low, and stir the pan until the sauce starts to thicken. Serve with rice. Serves 2-3.

PEKING/SHANTUNG

VELVET CHICKEN
The white appearance in this recipe is reminiscent of the fu-yung style; however, instead of individual pancakes, the entire egg-chicken mixture is brought to the table when done and apportioned there.

4 tablespoons cornstarch	2 cups peanut oil
1 teaspoon salt	4 tablespoons water
½ cup chicken stock	½ cup snow peas or ¼ cup sliced
2 tablespoons sherry	pea pods
1 teaspoon sugar	4 mushrooms, sliced thinly
Breast meat of 1 3-pound chick-	½ cup smoked ham, diced
en, skinned, boned, and cut	coarsely
into fine dice	¼ cup bamboo shoots, sliced
5 egg whites	thinly

Combine 2 tablespoons cornstarch, salt, stock, sherry, and sugar. Stir to blend thoroughly, then add the diced chicken and mix well. Beat the egg whites with a whisk until stiff, and gently fold into the mixture. Bring the oil up to medium heat and slowly pour in the egg-chicken mixture, stirring so that the egg begins to set in a smooth consistency. This should take no more than 20-30 seconds. Remove with spoon or spatula to drain.

Dissolve the remaining cornstarch in 4 tablespoons water. Pour off all but 1 tablespoon of oil and stir-fry the snow peas (or pea pods), mushrooms, diced ham, and chopped bamboo shoots for 2-3 minutes. Then quickly return the chicken-egg mixture. Stir rather rapidly for a few moments. Now add the dissolved cornstarch and stir until it just starts to thicken, then remove from the heat. Serve on a warm platter immediately. Serves 4.

Hong Kong/Kowloon

SUGAR-SMOKED DUCK (or Chicken)

The Chinese use hickory, walnut, or other woods in smoking their meats just as we do, but another method, which gives an entirely different taste, is sugar smoking. This is best done in an outdoor covered barbecue, but it can be done in your oven, although one should have the exhaust fan on throughout.

This also represents China's unique multiphase cooking technique.

1 4-pound duck (or 3-pound chicken)	1 onion, quartered
	Salt
1 quart water	10 peppercorns
	½ cup brown sugar

Marinade

6 tablespoons peanut oil	1 clove garlic, minced
¼ teaspoon anise seed powder	6 tablespoons soy sauce
	3 tablespoons sherry

Place the bird in the water in a large kettle and bring to the boil. Reduce heat, skim off the scum, then add the onion, salt, and peppercorns. Cover, and cook slowly (duck 1½ hours, chicken 1 hour). Now cut the bird into individual servings or into 16 pieces if you wish. (See page 37.)

Mix together the marinade ingredients and stir to blend thoroughly. Pour the marinade over the chicken pieces in a large bowl, turning to coat each piece. Let stand, covered, for 1 hour.

When the meat is ready, preheat the oven to 375° F. Line the bottom of a large, ovenproof pot with foil and place a small rack inside. Add ½ the sugar. Place the meat on the rack and cover the kettle with foil, then place a lid on tightly, forming a seal. Put the kettle in the oven for 10 minutes, and allow the sugar to burn and thus smoke.

Now remove the kettle and reline the pan if necessary, and add the remaining sugar. Reline the top of the kettle, and return to the oven to smoke for another 10 minutes. The meat should turn a rich mahogany color, and the sugar-smoke taste will have permeated the meat. Brush lightly with a little peanut oil and serve. Serves 4-6.

CANTON

WHITE CUT CHICKEN

This is a classic Chinese delicacy which, like Peking Duck, is first "air dried" or cured. However, instead of being roasted, the bird is crystal boiled and then cut into small pieces and served. White Cut Chicken is usually served with ham, but when accompanied by a green vegetable, it picks up rather descriptive names such as Jade Tree Chicken or White Cut Chicken in Green Paradise. Call it what you will, it is one of China's masterpieces.

1 small 2-2½-pound chicken	1 large bunch of broccoli
1 quart water	Salt
3-4 ounces cooked ham	1 tablespoon cornstarch

If you wish to make this as authentically as possible, wash and dry the chicken and rub all over, inside and out, with salt and pepper. Hang the bird in an open, airy place for 24 hours. (This step may be omitted.)

Bring one quart of water to the boil, put in the chicken, cover, and let boil for 3-5 minutes. Turn off the heat and let the pot stand for 2 hours, covered, while the chicken cooks.

When the chicken has cooled, remove from the pot and reserve the stock. Cut away the leg pieces and separate at the joints. Cut off the wings and separate these at the joints also, discarding the tips. Now cut away the breasts and remove the meat, leaving the skin intact. Slice the breast meat in thin slices about 2 inches long.

Arrange the chicken legs and wing pieces on a serving platter in a circle. Slice the ham into thin slices approximately the size of the breast slices, then lay the ham and chicken in the center of the platter in alternating slices. Cover the platter and place in a warming oven.

Cut the broccoli flowerets off, and peel the stems. Cook in 2 cups of reserved chicken stock until done and then arrange these alongside the leg and wing pieces on the platter.

Now make a sauce by bringing 1 cup of stock to the boil. Add a large pinch of salt. Add the cornstarch and stir to dissolve and mix thoroughly. When the liquid begins to thicken, remove from the heat and spoon some over the meat. Serve the remaining sauce at the table. Serves 4.

PART II

Korea and Japan

China's imprint on the cultures of Korea and Japan is unmistakable. For centuries Korea existed as a sort of small territorial adjunct to China, paying her tribute, but left fairly much alone to manage her own affairs. The Koreans even spoke and wrote Chinese until the fifteenth century, when they adopted their own alphabet and language, and their cooking and eating techniques still are carbon copies of the Chinese.

Similarly, virtually every aspect of Japan's culture has been patterned after, or borrowed from, China. Early in the sixth century, Buddhism came to Japan from China. The monks were well steeped in Chinese civilization, and introduced not only the Buddhist philosophy but Chinese art, music, literature, architecture, even the methods of public administration that the Chinese emperors and mandarins had developed over centuries to govern their vast country. For the next thousand years this cultural dependence was reinforced by a steady intercourse between Japanese monks, merchants, and government officials and their Chinese counterparts. The Japanese *hibachi* was developed from the Chinese charcoal stove; their chopsticks came from China; and the shallow, metal bowl (wok) for quick-cooking over a charcoal fire was also a Chinese innovation.

The cuisines of Korea and Japan were born in the Shantung kitchens of China, but there the similarity ends, for neither goes so far in scope nor includes the flair and innovation of the Chinese.

Fish and rice are the predominant features of the Korean and Japanese meal for rich and poor alike. Both have extensive seacoasts and fishing is a major industry, and since both countries are ruggedly

45

mountainous most of the tillable land area is given over to the production of rice. This leaves little room for beef, pork, or lamb, although—paradoxically—for centuries the national meat dishes of both countries have been made with beef. In Korea it is *bul goki,* which is thin, marinated beef slices grilled over charcoal, and in Japan it's the classic *suki-yaki,* sliced beef and vegetables fried in oil on a hibachi. Fowl cookery is gaining in popularity in both Japan and Korea, and both offer several chicken dishes, which illustrate not only the characteristics of each nation's cooking but the preparation of their meals as well.

Suki-yaki, originally a beef and vegetable dish, is now frequently made with chicken or pork. As in Chinese cuisine, the meats and vegetables are cut to exact size, then neatly arranged on a platter for the guest to admire as much before it is cooked as after.

There are two unique characteristics of Korean cooking: sesame seeds and *kim-chi.* No other cuisine on earth uses the sesame seed to such a degree as does Korea's. The seeds are used whole or ground to a powder for cooking, and the oil is used for frying.

The main Korean meal usually includes a soup, and in two outstanding chicken soups, the flavorful essence is extracted from the sesame seed and returned to the broth. Kim-chi is a pickled cabbage which, because it is served so frequently, is made in large quantities. The Koreans pack the prepared cabbage into huge jars, then seal them and store them in the ground for a week or a month depending on how cold the weather is, and let the kim-chi ferment. It's an anxious moment when the jars are opened, for depending upon the original preparation and the correctness of the fermentation, the kim-chi will either be a lip-smacking triumph or a long-term disaster.

RECOMMENDED READING: Charmaine Solomon, *The Complete Asian Cookbook* (New York: McGraw Hill, 1976); Judy Hyun, *The Korea Cookbook* (Chicago: Follette Publishing Co., 1970)

MAIL ORDER SOURCES FOR INGREDIENTS:

Liang's Oriental Gifts and Grocery, Inc.   Mrs. DeWildt
8 Pleasantville Road   RFD 1
Pleasantville, N.Y. 10570   Bangor, Pa. 18013

KOREA

DAK TWIKIM—Deep-Fried Chicken

Breast meat of 1 3-pound chicken, skinned and boned
1 egg
4 tablespoons water

⅓ cup cornstarch
Pinch salt
2 cloves garlic, minced
2 scallions, minced
1 cup peanut or sesame oil

Slice the breast meat into thin, narrow 2-inch strips. Beat together the egg and water, then the cornstarch, salt, minced garlic, and scallions and blend thoroughly. Now coat the chicken strips in this mixture.

Bring the oil to high heat in a deep-fryer and drop in the coated chicken strips a few at a time. Fry for 1 minute, then remove to drain. When all the strips have been fried once, return them to the egg-cornstarch mixture and coat them again. Now fry the chicken pieces a second time, again only a few at a time. When they float, they're done. Drain again and serve with rice and kim-chi (page 55). Serves 4.

JAPAN

OYAKO DONBURI—Chicken with Eggs

This translates into "parent and child" or "mother and child," because the dish contains both chicken and eggs. This recipe also illustrates the Japanese method of cooking rice. The rice water is brought to the boil, then the heat is reduced to low. With a cover on, the rice cooks for 15 minutes, then is set aside to steam for 15-20 minutes. The important thing is to leave the lid on so the steam doesn't escape.

1 cup of rice in 2 cups of water
Breast meat of 1 3-pound boiled chicken, skinned, boned, and sliced thinly
1 cup dashi (or substitute, page 48)
⅓ cup soy sauce

⅓ cup mirin (sweet rice wine), sake, or sherry
2 scallions, cut into ¼-inch slices
6-8 mushrooms, sliced thinly
4 eggs
1 thin slice each of green and red pepper, chopped
Parsley for garnish

Cook the rice as described above. Refrigerate the chicken slices for 15 minutes. Combine the dashi, soy sauce, and wine in a saucepan, and place over low heat. Add the chicken slices, sliced scallions, and mushrooms and simmer for 5 minutes.

By now your rice should be done. Divide it into 4 individual bowls. Beat the eggs together until frothy, then pour over the chicken and cover. Turn the heat down to very low and cook for 3 minutes or until the eggs set. When done, spoon the chicken and egg mixture equally over the rice. Garnish with chopped peppers and parsley. Serves 4.

JAPAN

CHAWAN-MUSHI—Chicken Custard or Soup

Chawan-mushi is one of the few Japanese dishes eaten with a spoon, and this is because some of the liquid is served with the cooked vegetables and meat. *Dashi* is a stock made from kelp and dried, shaved bonita and is found in countless Japanese soups, stews, and sauces. It's usually available in dried form in specialty food stores. If you don't find it, an adequate substitute is chicken stock, to which is added (per quart of stock) ¼ cup soy sauce and 2 tablespoons sake or dry sherry.

Breast meat of 2 chickens, skinned and boned	6 cups dashi (or substitute)
6 large shrimp, shells removed and deveined	4 eggs, well beaten
½ cup sake or dry sherry	1 teaspoon salt
½ cup soy sauce	6 large fresh mushrooms, chopped finely
	½ cup fresh spinach, chopped finely

Put the chicken meat through the fine blade of a meat grinder (or use a blender) or chop it into fine dice. Now do the same with the shrimp. Combine the sake (or sherry) and soy sauce and divide equally into 2 bowls. Marinate the chicken and shrimp separately.

Bring the dashi (or substitute) to medium heat, and slowly pour in the beaten eggs. Add the salt and stir several times to blend thoroughly. Remove from heat and set aside. Now pour off any marinade liquid from the chicken and shrimp and divide each equally into 6 custard cups or small, deep bowls. Divide the mushrooms and spinach equally into the bowls. Now fill each cup slowly with the egg broth mixture.

Preheat the oven to 350° F. Place the cups in a large, deep baking pan and fill with water, until the water level comes about halfway up the sides of the cups. Place the pan in the oven and bake for 35 minutes or until the custard sets. Serves 6.

JAPAN

YAKITORI—Grilled Marinated Chicken

This is outstanding as an appetizer or as a main dish, although the quantity of ingredients for a full meal would have to be increased by 2 or 3 times for several people.

Breast meat of 1 whole chicken, skinned and boned

¼ pound chicken livers, cut in half

10-12 scallions, cut into 1-inch lengths

¼ pound chicken gizzards, cut in half (optional)

1 pound large fresh mushrooms, cut in half

1 clove garlic, minced

⅓ cup soy sauce

1 piece ginger root, minced

⅓ cup sake, mirin, or dry sherry

1 tablespoon sugar

Cut the breast meat into strips, 1 inch long and ½ inch wide. On a bamboo skewer alternately thread 1 strip of chicken, then 1 piece of scallion, ½ chicken liver (or gizzard, or both), ½ mushroom, another strip of chicken.

Combine the garlic, soy sauce, ginger root, sake (or wine), and sugar in a large flat baking dish, and mix together well. Place the bamboo skewers in the sauce, turning to coat each one well. Set aside for 15-20 minutes, turning the skewers every 5 minutes or so. Prepare a charcoal fire and, when the coals have burned down to a white ash, grill the Yakitori for several minutes. Turn the skewers and brush the meat and vegetables with marinade sauce frequently to insure even cooking without burning. (This can also be done the same way in an inside broiler.) Serves 4-6 as an appetizer or 2 as a main dish with rice.

JAPAN

CHICKEN IN ORANGE-SOY SAUCE

1 cup chicken stock
1 3-pound chicken, cut up into 16 pieces (page 37)
1 teaspoon salt
3 radishes, sliced thinly
6-8 mushrooms, sliced thinly

1 small head Chinese (or regular) cabbage, chopped coarsely
Juice and grated rind of 4 oranges
1 cup soy sauce
6 tablespoons sake or dry sherry
1 tablespoon sugar
3 scallions, chopped finely

Bring the stock to the boil, add the chicken pieces and salt, cover, and reduce heat to moderate. Simmer the chicken for 30 minutes. Now add the sliced radishes, mushrooms, and cabbage, cover, and cook an additional 15 minutes. Mix the rind and juice of the orange in a bowl, then stir in the soy sauce, wine, and sugar. Blend well, then divide the sauce equally into serving cups to be used as dips. Divide the chopped scallions equally, to be used as a dip.

Turn the chicken pieces and vegetables into a chafing dish and keep hot at the table. The guests should serve themselves, using the dips to flavor the dinner. Serves 4-6.

JAPAN

YOSENABE—Chicken and Shellfish

Yosenabe translates into something like "leftover," and virtually any meat or fish is frequently included.

2 quarts dashi (or substitute, page 48)
Breast meat of 1 chicken, skinned, boned, and cut into strips
12 shrimps, shelled and deveined
12 chunks crabmeat or lobster
12 oysters or clams (optional)
½ pound spinach, cut into strips
2 carrots, sliced thinly lengthwise

3 scallions, cut diagonally into 1-inch pieces
½ pound Chinese cabbage, shredded
¼ cup bamboo shoots
6-8 large mushrooms, sliced thinly
1 pound Udon noodles or vermicelli (see note)

Heat the dashi in an electric skillet. Arrange the meat, shellfish, and vegetables attractively on a serving platter and bring all to the table.

First cook the meat and shellfish for 3-5 minutes (only enough for a small serving to each guest) and serve it. While this is being eaten cook half the vegetables and serve them, then the remaining meat and fish, and finally the remaining vegetables. Serve with several dips, such as minced peppers, vinegar, sake, soy sauce, horseradish, beaten egg, shoyu sauce (page 52), or lemon juice mixed with soy sauce. Serves 4.

Note: Udon noodles are available in Oriental and some specialty food stores.

JAPAN

CHICKEN SUKI-YAKI

Suki-yaki is best known in Japan as a beef dish, but chicken is becoming more and more popular. This recipe, typical of the Japanese style, requires that all ingredients be prepared in advance and then brought to the table in an attractive arrangement and cooked. Though the Japanese traditionally use a hibachi, an electric frying pan is ideal for cooking suki-yaki.

The Japanese use shirataki noodles for suki-yaki dishes. This is a standard Japanese noodle made in long thin strips like vermicelli (a good substitute) from the starchy substance of a plant called Devil's Tongue. Shirataki is available in specialty stores in wet or dry form.

1 3-pound chicken, cut up, skinned, and boned	8 large mushrooms, sliced thinly
1 pound piece of bean curd	1 cup celery, sliced diagonally into 1-inch pieces
6-8 scallions, sliced diagonally into 1-inch lengths	1 pound shirataki noodles
2 onions, sliced thinly	¼ cup peanut or sesame oil
1 cup bamboo shoots, sliced into thin strips	½ cup soy sauce
	6 tablespoons sake or dry sherry
	2 tablespoons sugar

Cut the chicken meat into the thinnest possible slices. Broil the bean curd lightly and cut into ½-inch squares. Arrange all ingredients neatly in rows on a platter and bring to the table. Cook the shirataki noodles until tender, then bring to the table in a separate dish.

Heat the oil and fry the chicken slices on both sides for 1 minute, then push to one side of the pan. Pour in the soy sauce, sake (or sherry), and sugar, then add the vegetables. Keep the heat fairly low. Stir the vegetables for about 3 minutes in the pan. The guests should serve themselves with noodles, then the meat and vegetables. If the number of guests is larger than 4, increase the quantities accordingly, and cook only ½ the food at a time. Serves 4.

JAPAN

MIZUTAKI—Simmered Chicken with Shoyu Sauce

Mizutaki is a well-known dish of ancient origin that shows off the Japanese style at its best. Shoyu sauce is made with barley and soy beans and is to Japanese cooking what plain salt is to American. It finds its way into practically all meat, fish, and vegetable dishes as well as being used as a dip for hors d'oeuvres and appetizers.

4 cups (or more) dashi (page 48) or chicken stock
1 3-pound chicken, cut up, skinned, and boned
1 medium onion, quartered
1 slice ginger root, chopped coarsely
Salt and pepper
8-10 large mushrooms, sliced
2 cups shredded cabbage
8-10 scallions, cut diagonally into 1-inch sections
1 cup bamboo shoots
¼ pound bean curd, cut into ½-inch squares
1 cup shoyu sauce (see below)
3-4 large radishes, grated
lemon wedges
1-2 red chili peppers, chopped very finely

Bring the dashi or stock to a boil. Reduce heat and then drop in the chicken pieces, onion, ginger root, and a little salt and pepper and cook for about 15 minutes.

Arrange the mushrooms, cabbage, scallions, bamboo shoots, and bean curd squares on a platter for the dinner guests to help themselves. The vegetables should be dropped into the boiling dashi or stock and cooked quickly at the table.

Serve each guest ⅓ cup of shoyu sauce for dip and a dish of grated radish, with lemon wedges, and finely chopped red peppers for garnish.

Shoyu Sauce

Shoyu is available in specialty stores in bottles, but you may make a suitable substitute in the following way:

1 cup soy sauce
1 tablespoon cornstarch

6 tablespoons brown sugar
⅔ cup water
2 teaspoons minced scallion

Combine all ingredients and bring to the boil. Remove from heat, stir several times, and let sit for a few minutes if you want the sauce hot, or for 1 hour to serve cold.

KOREA

TAK KUI—Broiled Chicken
Korean cooking, like Chinese and Japanese, is done mostly on a charcoal fire, so "broiling" actually is a form of frying. The Koreans use just a small amount of oil to keep the meat from sticking.

1 3-pound chicken, skinned and
  boned
¼ cup soy sauce
2 tablespoons sesame mash (see
  page 56)

1 scallion, chopped finely
1 small clove garlic
1 tablespoon sugar
2 tablespoons sesame oil
½ cup water

Cut the chicken meat into bite-sized pieces. Combine the remaining ingredients (except the oil and water) in a large bowl and mix well. Now add the chicken and mix well again. Let this stand for 30 minutes. Heat 2 tablespoons oil in a skillet and brown the chicken slices slowly on both sides. When all the pieces are cooked, return them to the skillet, add ½ cup of water, and cover. Cook the chicken for 20-30 minutes over low heat until done. Serve with rice and kim-chi (page 55). Serves 4.

KOREA

DAK-JIM — Chicken with Vegetables
1 3-pound chicken, skinned and
  boned
2 scallions, sliced thinly
1 carrot, sliced thinly lengthwise
2 large mushrooms, sliced thinly
1 tablespoon sesame seed

Salt and pepper
1 tablespoon sugar
2 tablespoons soy sauce
1 quart water
1 egg prepared for decoration
  (see page 56)

¼ cup sliced bamboo shoots   3 tablespoons chopped walnuts
⅓ cup water chestnuts   (optional)

Remove the meat from the bones and place in a stewpot or Dutch oven. Add the sliced scallions, carrot, mushrooms, sesame seed, bamboo shoots, water chestnuts, a little salt and pepper, sugar, and soy sauce. Add 1 quart of water (more or less—you want just enough to cover the meat and vegetables). Bring the liquid to the boil, then reduce heat and simmer slowly for an hour or so or until the meat is tender. Turn into a bowl and serve with egg decoration and chopped walnuts. Serves 4.

KOREA

CHO-KAY TANG—Chicken Sesame Soup

1 2½-pound chicken   1 tablespoon sesame oil
1 quart water plus 1 cup   4 large mushrooms, sliced thinly
2 scallions (green parts also)   2 eggs cooked for decoration
¼ teaspoon grated ginger root   (page 56)
Salt and pepper   2 pears or apples, peeled, cored
2 cups sesame seed   3 tablespoons chopped pignolia
3 cucumbers, sliced thinly   (pine) nuts

Cover the chicken with 1 quart of boiling water. Add the scallions, ginger root, and a little salt and pepper, and simmer, covered, until tender. When done, let the chicken cool a little, then cut it up and remove and discard the skin and bones. Cut the chicken meat into long, thin strips. Let the broth cool completely, then skim and blot away all fat.

While the chicken cooks, pour the sesame seeds into a blender, add 1 cup of water, and blend at a medium high speed for a minute or so, then strain the liquid into the cold chicken broth. Cut the cucumbers into long, thin, flat slices, then sprinkle with a little salt and set aside for 5 minutes. Pour off any water that forms. Now heat the oil in the skillet and cook the cucumbers slowly for 1 minute. Remove to drain and reserve. Slice the mushrooms in long, thin slices and cook gently for 1 minute in the oil. Remove to drain and reserve.

Prepare the two eggs for decoration and set aside. Now slice the pears or apples in long, thin slices, and mix well with the cucumbers, mushrooms, and egg strips. Add this mixture along with the chicken strips to the cold broth and serve in soup plates. Sprinkle a little of the chopped pignolia nuts on each plate of soup. Serves 4.

KOREA

DAK POK KUM—Sesame Chicken
(Wild gamebirds, particularly pheasant, are also excellent cooked this way.)

1 3-pound chicken, skinned and boned	3 tablespoons sesame mash (see page 56)
1 quart water	Salt and pepper
½ cup soy sauce	1 teaspoon sesame oil
2 scallions, chopped coarsely (green tops also)	2 tablespoons sugar
	4 large mushrooms
1 large clove garlic, chopped	2 cups reserved broth

Cut the meat into large bite-sized chunks. Bring the quart of water to the boil, then reduce heat to low and cook the chicken for about 30 minutes, until it is partly done. Pour off 2 cups of broth and reserve the rest for another use.

To the chicken, add the remaining ingredients and 2 cups of broth. Mix well and continue cooking over a low fire for another 30 minutes. Serve with rice. Serves 4.

ACCESSORIES TO KOREAN COOKERY

Kim-chi, egg decoration, and sesame mash are three ingredients used in, on, or with almost all Korean dishes. Preparing each is relatively simple, and including them will make your Korean meal a little more authentic.

KIM-CHI
Although kim-chi should be packed in a container and left to sit for several days or longer, this is not practical for the occasional

Korean meal. Here's one that can be made and enjoyed the same day. While it's not the real thing, the flavor is similar and it serves its purpose very well. Kim-chi is available, bottled, in many specialty food stores.

1 Chinese cabbage cut into strips 2 inches by 2 inches 1 tablespoon vinegar	1 tablespoon dark soy sauce (substitute 2 parts soy sauce to 1 part brown sugar) 1 teaspoon cayenne pepper

Blend all ingredients and toss together with the cabbage. Place in a covered container and let sit until ready to serve.

EGG DECORATION

Egg strips are used to garnish most Korean meat dishes and are particularly attractive served over rice. One egg is usually enough for a meal for 4-6 people, but add another if you serve more.

Beat one egg with 2 tablespoons of water and a pinch of salt. Pour a little of the mixture into a large heated, oiled skillet. Work the pan back and forth until the egg covers the bottom very thinly. Let the egg sit over low heat until it is done. Remove and keep warm. Repeat until all the egg mixture is used up. Slice the omelets into ½-inch wide strips and lay over the rice or meat. If you separate the yolks and whites, and cook each the same way, you have egg garnish in two colors.

KAE—Sesame Mash

Roast sesame seeds in a skillet over a low fire. *USE NO OIL.* When golden brown, remove from heat and cool, then mash the amount you need to a coarse powder. The roasted seeds or powder will keep for several months.

❧ Chapter 3 ❧

Asia

PART I

Southeast Asia—Indonesia, Malaysia

The southern corner of Asia and the islands adjacent to it were developed culturally in three different phases. The ancient civilizations of China provided Southeast Asia with its earliest culture, and gastronomically this legacy is still apparent in every country. The wok is used throughout the area, as are stir-frying, the charcoal stove, grilled skewered meat, bean curd, and the Chinese cellophane noodle, *laksa*.

Although they dominated the mainland region for over a thousand years, the influence of the Chinese was gradually eroded by the immigration of Buddhists and Hindus from India, beginning in the fifth century. Over the next thousand years the social and cultural fabric of Southeast Asia slowly became that of her neighbor to the west: art and architecture, music, language, even the tradition of the god-king, which flowered in the Khmer kingdom, centered in Angkor Thom in Cambodia, eight hundred years ago.

When the Moslems overran India, they too continued eastward, blending their religious and social customs with those already existing. But the Moslems were not just after converts, they were interested in spices. Even though the Roman Empire had fallen only three hundred years before, and the Western world was suffering through the miseries of the Dark Ages, the demand for spices among Europe's nobility, and their ability to pay exorbitant prices, was undiminished. For seven hundred years (until Vasco da Gama discovered the sea route to India), the Moslems controlled what was probably the most lucrative international trade that ever existed until modern times.

Britain, France, Portugal, and the Netherlands vied for control of Southern Asia from the sixteenth to the twentieth centuries, but despite the fact that they held absolute control over the entire region, nothing of gastronomic significance was introduced by the Europeans. The French style is still evident in Vietnam, but in restaurants, not in home cooking. The same is true of the British in Singapore and Burma, but again British food is found only in public eating places and was never assimilated into the native cuisines.

The British, however, were indirectly responsible for creating a unique cuisine in Malaysia in the nineteenth century. They imported Chinese men by the thousands into Singapore to work the sugar plantations. Since China forbade the emigration of women, these men intermarried with women of Malayan and Indian extraction. Their descendants, the Straits Chinese, developed *nonya* (the Straits word for "housewife") cooking, which combines the gentle style of the traditional Chinese kitchen with the chili-oriented, volcanic Malaysian cuisine to produce something as distinctive as it is delicious.

With the exception of Singapore, which is overwhelmingly Chinese, Indonesia and Malaysia remain essentially Moslem and Hindu, and the taboos that govern eating in India are present here too, though their observance is not nearly so strict. Therefore, pork, beef, and lamb are seldom eaten except among the more affluent.

Common to all countries is a fish sauce of rather vile odor (but surprisingly good taste) to the uninitiated, which is added to everything, including chicken dishes, essentially for the same seasoning purposes that we use salt. It is *Nam Pla* in Thailand, *Nguoc Nam* in Cambodia, *Trassi* in Indonesia, and *Nuac Mam* in Vietnam. You may have trouble finding these in any but a metropolitan area, but an acceptable substitute can be made by mixing equal parts of soy sauce and anchovy paste.

Over the centuries, rice has played such a fundamental role in the day-to-day existence of the Southeast Asians that it has acquired a mystical quality and reverence which follows the natives from the cradle to the grave and perhaps beyond. In Thailand, Buddhist monks beg for rice rather than money, and natives give it hoping to gain a better life the next time around. In Java, the first thing a newborn baby sees is a rice cone placed there by his parents to insure future emotional self-reliance.

The dependence of the Indonesians and Malaysians on rice has produced a number of dishes of international distinction, and some of the best-known include chicken. One is *nasi goreng,* fried rice, in which quick-fried cubes of meat are added to cooked rice, and the whole is quick-fried again. Quite taken with this dish, the Dutch brought it back, and its popularity in the Netherlands today is greater than most traditional Dutch dishes.

Another gastronomic triumph of Indonesia is the *Rijsttafel,* or "rice table," and though it's a Dutch word, the meal and the cooking are purely Indonesian. The rijsttafel originated several centuries ago when the rich Dutch colonists, perhaps weary of the monotony of plantation life, vied with one another to see who could offer the finest feast. Originally it was simply a large platter of rice accompanied by a variety of other foods, but it soon developed into an eating orgy rivaling those of ancient Rome. One planter outdid another; massive platters of rice were followed by endless lines of servants carrying different dishes of meat, poultry, fish, vegetables, fruits, sweets, sambals, and tea and beer. It was originally intended to offer enough variety that no matter how choosy a guest might be, sooner or later something would come along that he liked. That day is past and the excesses are gone, but the rijsttafel idea is still a part of Indonesia, and the Netherlands as well, and it is a superb feast.

Spices of every variety are grown throughout Southern Asia, but their popularity varies from one country to another. Burmese and Thai cooks tend to use a greater assortment in their chicken dishes than do other cuisines, but a Burmese chicken curry will generally be rather mild while a similar dish cooked in Thailand will be hot. Indonesians and Malaysians use red, white, and black pepper copiously in their cooking and add chili peppers to produce the most fiery cuisine in the world. But nearby in Cambodia, Laos, and Vietnam, the mild spices such as *laos,* lemon grass, and ginger find favor, perhaps reflecting the nature of the people.

Coconuts are also used extensively in Asian cooking and, because of the lack of a dairy industry in Southern Asia, coconut milk is used instead of butter. It is not only the basic cooking liquid, but serves as the base for fish and fowl sauces and marinades, and as an ingredient in almost everything—stews, soups, puddings, curries, and in coffee. In other recipes, the coconut meat is shredded and either heated in water to produce milk or cream, or added to innumerable dishes as a flavoring agent.

The Portuguese are said to have brought the capsicum or "chili" pepper from the New World to the East Indies, where it was enthusiastically adopted and cultivated. As a consequence East Indian food is hot to the extent that the average Westerner cannot tolerate it. On top of that, the meal generally includes a variety of side dishes called *sambals,* which are there to blend or to sharpen the taste of the food, and these can be extremely hot also. Several of the most typical sambals for chicken and vegetable dishes are included among the recipes, and you should choose two or three to accompany your meal, but the chili content of each has been lowered to "reduce the heat" to tolerable levels. The purist may add back up to twice as much ground or chopped chili peppers and be pretty close to the real thing.

The Southern Asian kitchen offers perhaps the widest ranging culinary experience in the world. Its spectrum of tastes moves from the almost apologetic gentleness of Cambodia to the chili-oriented violence of Indonesia, pausing for a moment of truce in the *nonya* cuisine of Malaysia. Threading its way through this maze of tastes is the chicken, whose ancestor originated in the local jungles. It's small wonder that chicken cookery in Southern Asia has reached a level equal to any other in the world—*Soto Ajam, Bahmi Goreng, Mi-Krob, Rijsttafel,* and *Nasi Goreng* to name just a few examples.

But there is one dish that has achieved international acclaim not only for its outstanding taste, but also because of its preparation. It is *Saté*, and both Indonesia and Malaysia claim it as their national dish. The chicken version is *Saté Ajam,* but there is also great demand for beef, fish, pork, goat, caribou, and turtle saté.

Saté Ajam consists of strips of chicken, marinated in a dark, sweet soy sauce mixture, and grilled quickly over charcoal. It is served with a peanut and chili sauce that blends spectacularly with the marinade to make a chicken dish of unusual distinction. Saté Ajam is served at home or in restaurants throughout both countries as a snack or a full meal, but it is the saté vendor who gives the dish its international appeal. He carries a large yoke across his shoulders from each end of which is suspended a basket-like receptacle, one of which holds his meats, sauces, and marinades, and the other a charcoal brazier. This colorful character appears after sundown and wanders the streets far into the night, rattling porcelain clappers or tinkling a small bell to attract his customers. Once a sale is made he puts the yoke down, cooks the saté to order, and serves it on the spot.

Should you ever have occasion to enjoy saté under these conditions, the sound of a rattling clapper or a tinkling bell will provoke a Pavlovian response for a culinary experience of unforgettable delight.

RECOMMENDED READING: Robin Howe, *Cooking for the Commonwealth* (London: André Deutsch, 1958); Charmaine Solomon, *The Complete Asian Cookbook* (New York: McGraw-Hill, 1976); Yohanni Johns, *Dishes from Indonesia* (London: Chilton Book Co., 1971)

MAIL ORDER SOURCE FOR INGREDIENTS:

Mrs. DeWildt
RFD 1
Bangor, Pa., 18013

INDONESIA

BAHMI GORENG—Chicken with Fried Noodles

2 raw whole chicken breasts, skinned, boned, and cut into thin narrow strips

4-6 tablespoons ketjap manis (page 81)

1 pound Chinese noodles (laksa) (page 80)

2 eggs, cooked, for decoration (page 82)

1 cup peanut or coconut oil

6 onions, finely chopped

2 cloves garlic, minced

1 inch-long piece green ginger, chopped

1 teaspoon ground cardamom seeds

½ Chinese cabbage or 3 cups shredded green cabbage

½ pound fresh or 1 8-ounce can bean sprouts

½ cup bamboo shoots

2 scallions, chopped (both white and green parts)

6 large prawns, shelled, deveined, chopped, and cooked

Lemon wedges and fried onion flakes for garnish

Marinate the chicken strips in the ketjap manis for about 2 hours, making sure the meat is completely covered with the sauce. Prepare the noodles by cooking in hot water for 15 minutes. Remove to drain and let sit for 30 minutes. Prepare the eggs for decoration and set aside.

Heat some oil in the same pan, or a wok, and sauté the onions, garlic, ginger, and ground cardamom seeds. Remove with a slotted spoon and keep warm. Add a bit more oil and turn the heat up to moderate. Stir-fry the chicken strips for about 5 minutes, then remove and keep warm. Stir-fry the shredded cabbage, the bean sprouts, the bamboo shoots, and chopped scallions for 3-4 minutes, then add the chopped cooked prawns and stir-fry for another 5 minutes. Reduce the heat to low and return the chicken and the onion and garlic mixture to the pan and cook for another 5 minutes. Add the noodles, toss well, and cook slowly for 5 more minutes.

Turn the bahmi out into a platter and arrange the omelet strips around and over it. Garnish with lemon wedges and sprinkle with fried onion flakes. Serves 4-6.

MALAYSIA/INDONESIA

AJAM SIMUR—Chicken in Soy Sauce

1 3-pound chicken, cut up	1 teaspoon nutmeg
4-6 tablespoons butter	½ teaspoon clove powder
2 cloves garlic, minced	1-2 cups water
2 scallions, sliced thinly	¼ cup soy sauce
Salt and freshly ground pepper	¼ pound laksa (cellophane noodles) (page 80)

Heat the butter in a large skillet and sauté the garlic and scallions gently for about 5 minutes. Now sprinkle in the pepper and salt and add the chicken pieces and cook slowly for 10-15 minutes. Add the nutmeg, clove powder, water, soy sauce and cover and cook for 1 hour over low heat. Add the noodles, check the water, adding more if necessary, then cook covered an additional 15 minutes. Serve with a green vegetable and a salad. Serves 4.

INDONESIA

GINGER CHICKEN WITH MUSHROOMS

1 3-pound chicken, skinned and boned	1 large onion, chopped
	½ cup water
2 tablespoons peanut or coconut oil	Salt and pepper
	6-8 mushrooms, sliced
1 clove garlic, minced	3 slices green ginger
	1 teaspoon cornstarch

Cut the chicken meat into small cubes. Heat the cooking oil in a large skillet or wok and sauté the garlic and onion slowly for about 5 minutes. Add the chicken meat and continue cooking until the meat is browned slightly, then add the ½ cup water and the salt and pepper. Cover and cook over low heat for about 10 minutes, then add the mushrooms and ginger. Re-cover and cook a final 15 minutes.

Remove the chicken and mushrooms from the pan and keep warm. Thicken the pan juices with a little cornstarch and serve in a sauceboat. Serve the chicken and mushrooms with rice or noodles and a vegetable. Serves 4.

Malaysia/Indonesia

SATE AJAM—Grilled Chicken with Peanut Sauce

Made by the colorful vendor who carries his kitchen on his shoulders, saté ajam is first marinated, then grilled over charcoal, and then served with one of the most unusual sauces you'll ever taste. Finally, cold cucumber slices are served to top it all off.

This can be served with equal success as an appetizer or a main dish at dinner. The number of chickens you use will be determined by the size of your guest list and how you plan to serve it. The following recipe will make enough appetizers for 6-8 people.

Breast meat of 1 chicken, skinned
 and boned
2 cloves garlic, minced

1 cup soy sauce
6 tablespoons molasses
3 tablespoons brown sugar
2 tablespoons water

Peanut Sauce
1 tablespoon peanut oil
2 scallions, chopped
5 macadamia nuts, crushed
¼ cup crunchy style peanut butter, or ¼ cup raw peanuts fried
 lightly in oil

2 tablespoons brown sugar
2 teaspoons ground chili peppers
½ cup coconut milk (page 82)
2 tablespoons marinade sauce
 (see below)
Lemon wedges
Sliced cucumbers

Slice the chicken meat into long flat slices about ¾ inch thick. Now cut the meat crosswise into ¾-inch strips and thread 4 or 5 strips onto each bamboo skewer. Mix the garlic, soy sauce, molasses, and brown sugar with the water in a saucepan and heat gently, stirring until the sugar melts. Pour this mixture into a long shallow dish and marinate the chicken for 2 hours.

In an electric blender combine the oil, scallions, macadamia nuts, peanuts (or peanut butter), sugar, and chili. Grind at a fairly high speed until a paste is formed, then cook gently in a skillet for a minute or so. Add the coconut milk and the marinade and cook slowly for another 1-2 minutes or until the sauce begins to thicken. Grill the skewered chicken over charcoal and serve on a plate with peanut sauce, a lemon wedge, and several slices of cold cucumber.

INDONESIA

GULAI AJAM—Indonesian Chicken Curry

Gulai (gulè) is the Indonesian version of the Indian curry, and is popular throughout the country. The dish varies in the spices used according to where you happen to be in Indonesia, and it can be cooked as a beef, mutton, egg, fish, or vegetable dish, as well as chicken.

1 3-pound chicken, cut up	5 dried chilies, ground to a powder, or 1 teaspoon sambal oelek (page 80)
2 cloves garlic, minced	
1-inch piece green ginger	
½ teaspoon turmeric	4 macadamia nuts, crushed
⅛ teaspoon each cumin, coriander, fennel seeds	¼ teaspoon laos
	1 tablespoon coconut or peanut oil
2 small yellow onions, chopped finely	
	1 teaspoon lemon grass powder
	Juice and grated rind of 1 lemon
	2 cups coconut milk (page 82)
	2 tablespoons grated coconut
	Salt and freshly ground pepper

With a mortar and pestle, or in an electric blender, make a paste of the garlic, ginger, turmeric, cumin, coriander, fennel, chopped onions, ground chili (or sambal oelek), macadamia nuts, and laos and stir into a large skillet with the oil. Blend the paste over low heat for a few minutes, then add the lemon grass, the lemon juice, and grated rind and stir into the mixture. (If it appears to be too dry, add 1 or 2 tablespoons of coconut milk.) Increase the heat to medium, then add the remaining coconut milk, grated coconut, the chicken, and a little salt and pepper, and cook for 2 minutes. Spoon the sauce over the chicken pieces and turn the heat to low. Simmer for 40 minutes, or until the chicken is tender. Do not let the pan boil or the coconut milk with curdle. It is also important to stir the pan frequently. When done serve with rice. Serves 4.

Alternative: Gulai Itik is virtually the same recipe, using duck instead of chicken. Green chilies, which are readily available, are better here than red, and the coconut milk should be replaced with 1 cup of water.

INDONESIA

OPOR AJAM—Chicken in Mild Sauce

This is outstanding with plain white rice, but even better with *nasi langi* (yellow rice).

1 3-pound chicken, cut up
4 macadamia nuts
1-inch piece green ginger
2 medium yellow onions, chopped
2 cloves garlic, minced
½ teaspoon cumin
2 tablespoons coriander

1 piece lemon grass, or ¼ teaspoon lemon grass powder
Salt and freshly ground pepper
2 tablespoons coconut or peanut oil
⅛ teaspoon mace
⅛ teaspoon laos
2 cups coconut milk (page 82)
2 tablespoons tamarind or lemon juice

Grind the nuts, onions, and garlic in 1 tablespoon oil in a mortar or electric blender, until they blend into a smooth paste. Now in a wok or skillet, combine the paste with the mace, laos, cumin, coriander, and lemon grass and stir-fry in the remaining oil for 1 minute. Add the chicken pieces and season with salt and pepper. Stir all together well, then cover and cook over moderate heat for 10 minutes. Add the coconut milk and slowly bring to the boil, stirring constantly. Now reduce the heat to simmer and re-cover the pan. Cook slowly for 30 minutes or until tender. About 5 minutes before chicken is done, add the tamarind or lemon juice. Serve with white rice or *nasi langi*. Serves 4.

Nasi Langi—Yellow Rice

In the top pan of a double boiler combine 1 cup of white rice, 1 cup of fresh chicken stock, 1 cup of coconut milk, 4 tablespoons freshly grated coconut meat, a little salt, and 2 tablespoons turmeric. Bring the water to the boil and cook the rice for 20 minutes or until all the liquid is absorbed. Serve in a bowl with chopped green and red peppers as a garnish.

INDONESIA/MALAYSIA

NASI GORENG DJAWA—Javanese Fried Rice

One of the most classic examples of Far Eastern cooking, nasi goreng was brought back to the Netherlands by the Dutch, and it became a national favorite there as well.

Seasoning

1 onion, chopped finely
2 garlic cloves, minced
Salt and black pepper
1 teaspoon trasi (page 80)
2 teaspoons ground red pepper
½ teaspoon turmeric
2 tablespoons peanut or vegetable oil
2 cups cooked, shredded white meat of chicken

3 cups raw shrimp, shelled, deveined, and chopped coarsely
1 tablespoon ketjap manis (page 81)
¼ cup green pepper, chopped coarsely
½ cup celery, chopped coarsely
4 cups cooked, long grain white rice
2 eggs, cooked, for decoration (page 82)

Place all seasoning ingredients in a mortar or electric blender and pound or mix to a smooth paste. Bring the oil to a fairly high heat in a wok and cook the paste for 2 minutes stirring all the while (add just a little more oil if the mixture starts to dry).

Now add the chicken, shrimp, and ketjap manis. Stir-fry the ingredients for 4-5 minutes, then add the green pepper and celery. Continue stirring for 1 minute, then add the rice a little at a time, tossing and stirring until each kernel is covered with oil and the mixture is thoroughly blended.

When done turn the nasi goreng out onto a platter or bowl and garnish with omelet cut into thin strips. Serve with vegetables and krupuk (page 80). Serves 4.

Indonesia/Malaysia

SOTO AJAM—Chicken Soup (Stew)

A soto comes in many variations throughout these countries. It is not a soup in the traditional sense, nor is it a stew, but something in between. It is not served as a part of a meal as much as a between-meal snack, or a light repast after the theater or a party. Sotos are best known as chicken dishes, but they can also be made with beef.

1 3-pound chicken	10 peppercorns
4 scallions	1 tablespoon coriander seeds,
3 macadamia nuts, crushed	ground
1 tablespoon laos	1 stalk lemon grass
1 teaspoon turmeric	1 cup coconut milk (page 82)
1 clove garlic	1 cup Chinese noodles (laksa)
1 ¼-inch piece green ginger	page 80)
2 quarts water	½ pound bean sprouts
Salt	2-3 hard cooked eggs
	½ cup chopped celery leaves

Chop 2 scallions finely and combine with the nuts, laos, turmeric, garlic, and ginger in a mortar or blender and grind to a paste. Bring the water to the boil, put in the chicken and 1 tablespoon salt, then cook for 10 minutes or so, skimming the scum off as it rises. Now add the paste and peppercorns, coriander and lemon grass. Reduce heat to low and simmer the soto for 30-40 minutes until done. Remove the chicken from the pot and cut away the meat, discarding skin and bones. Cut the meat into strips and place in a large tureen or bowl.

Slice the remaining 2 scallions into 1-inch pieces and add with the coconut milk, lemon grass, noodles, and bean sprouts to the broth. Simmer for 10 minutes or so until done. Slice the eggs in half and place them in the tureen with the chicken. Now pour the broth into the tureen and sprinkle chopped celery leaves over the top. Serves 4.

THAILAND

MI-KROB—Thai Fried Noodles

This dish typifies Thai cooking at its best. Either Chinese vermicelli or Thai rice noodles are suitable. They are fried until crispy brown, then served with a variety of meats and side dishes. Mi-krob is flavored with *nam pla,* a traditional Thai fish sauce that is readily available in Oriental food stores. A reasonable substitute, however, is regular soy sauce seasoned to taste with anchovy paste.

1 pound Chinese vermicelli or Thai rice noodles
Boiling water to cover
6 tablespoons oil
3 cloves garlic, minced
2 large scallions, chopped finely
½ pound pork (meat from 2 chops), cubed
1 whole chicken, skinned, boned, and cubed

12 shrimps, shelled, deveined, and chopped
½ cup canned or fresh crabmeat (optional)
¼ pound yellow bean cake, sliced thinly
1 teaspoon sugar
4 tablespoons nam pla, or substitute (above)
Juice of ¼ lemon or lime
4 eggs
1 cup bean sprouts

Drop the noodles or vermicelli into the boiling water and scald for a few moments, then drain and spread out for 15-20 minutes on a towel to dry. Now heat 4 tablespoons oil in a large skillet and fry the noodles until crispy brown. Remove, to drain and reduce heat to low. Remove most of the oil from the pan and sauté the garlic and scallions, then add the pork and chicken cubes. Cook for 8 minutes, then add the shrimp. Cook an additional 5 minutes, then add the crabmeat if desired, and the bean cake slices. Stirring constantly, add in the sugar, nam pla, and juice. Cook for 2 or 3 minutes. Add a little more of the cooking oil if the mixture begins to get dry.

Break the eggs in a bowl and whip together, then stir into the mixture. Cook until the eggs have set, then crumble the noodles over the top. In a separate pan, heat 2 tablespoons of oil and fry the bean sprouts lightly for 2 minutes, then serve as a garnish sprinkled over the mi-krob. Serves 4-6.

Additions: Other garnishes which should accompany the mi-krob are chopped red chilies, chopped chives, grated orange rind, and chopped coriander leaves.

Straits Chinese

CHICKEN WITH PLUM SAUCE

The Straits Chinese brought their fondness for fruit with them from China and include it in many dishes. Here's one that is typical of the Chinese combination of plums and chicken in a sweet and sour sauce.

Salt and pepper
1 3-pound chicken, cut up
4 tablespoons vegetable oil or
    butter
6 tart plums, peeled, pitted, and
    chopped finely
2 tablespoons cornstarch

1 or 2 large pieces fresh ginger
    root, chopped finely
2 tablespoons soy sauce
2 tablespoons sherry
1 clove garlic, minced
2 tablespoons cider vinegar
1 cup chicken broth
6 macadamia nuts, crushed

Rub salt and pepper all over the chicken pieces. In a large Dutch oven, heat the butter or oil and brown the chicken slowly and lightly. Remove the chicken and set aside to keep warm.

Combine the chopped plums and cornstarch in the Dutch oven off the heat, and stir until smooth. Add the remaining ingredients and stir until thoroughly blended, then add the chicken pieces back to the pot, spooning the sauce over. Preheat the oven to 350° F. Cover the Dutch oven, place it in the oven, and cook for 45 minutes. Serve directly from the pot with salad and rice. Serves 4.

Vietnam

CHICKEN AND BAMBOO SHOOTS

1 3-pound chicken, cut up
3 quarts water
1 1-pound can bamboo shoots

2 tablespoons *nuoc mam* sauce,
    or substitute (page 60)
3 scallions, sliced thinly

Place the chicken pieces in a large kettle with 3 quarts of water. Add the bamboo shoots to the pot along with the remaining ingredients. Cook slowly for 1½ hours, uncovered. Serve with rice. Serves 4.

THAILAND

KAENG PHET—Thai Chicken Curry

A typical Thai meal consists of a number of dishes, one of which is a curry, served with a large bowl of rice. The Thai curries, like others, have their roots in India, but the Thai version uses plenty of red chilies and is therefore much hotter. This one is an authentic Thai recipe, although it should be adapted to reduce some of the heat.

1 3-pound chicken	1 cup fresh sweet basil leaves
	3 cups coconut milk (page 82)

Curry Mixture

5 chilies (or less)	2 tablespoons nam pla, or substi-
1 teaspoon peppercorns	tute (page 60)
1 teaspoon coriander seeds	1 teaspoon lemon grass powder
2 teaspoons cumin seeds	½ teaspoon powdered laos
1 tablespoons salt	Grated rind of ¼ lemon or lime
	4 cloves garlic, minced
	1 onion, finely chopped

First make the curry mixture: Combine the chilies, peppercorns, coriander, cumin seeds, and salt in a blender and grind to a powder. Add the nam pla (or substitute), lemon grass, laos, lemon (or lime) rind, garlic, and onions and grind to a paste. Add a little coconut milk if it gets too dry.

Strip the chicken meat, discarding bones and skin, and cut into cubes. Bring 1 cup coconut milk to the boil in a wok and add the chicken cubes. Simmer for 15 minutes, stirring every 2 or 3 minutes, then add the curry mixture and cook for another 10 minutes. The coconut milk by now will be almost gone. Add the remaining coconut milk and the fresh basil and cook for another 5 minutes. Serve with rice, a soup, and mixed vegetables. Serves 4.

Burma

CHICKEN COCONUT SOUP

1 3-pound chicken, cut up
3¼ cups peanut or vegetable oil
2 onions, chopped finely
2 tomatoes, peeled, seeded, and
  chopped

Salt and pepper
2 cups water
2 cups coconut milk (page
  82)
Lemon or lime slices

Seasoning

1 teaspoon grated ginger
1 clove garlic, minced
1 small stick cinnamon, crushed

Seeds from 2 cardamoms,
  crushed
1 teaspoon turmeric
1 teaspoon coriander
½ teaspoon cumin

Sauté the chopped onions in the vegetable or peanut oil gently for about 5 minutes, then add the seasoning. Cook slowly for 3 or 4 minutes, then put in the chicken pieces, the tomatoes, and a little salt and pepper. Pour in the remaining water, cover, and simmer for 1 hour. Now add the coconut milk and cook slowly uncovered for another 10 minutes. Serve with lemon or lime slices. Serves 4.

Thailand

KAENG RON—Chicken Soup with Shrimp, Pork, and Cucumbers

¼ cup each:
  raw chicken meat, shredded
  raw chopped pork
  raw shrimp, chopped coarsely
    or sliced
2 tablespoons butter or vegetable
  oil
1 clove garlic, minced
1 onion, chopped finely
1 teaspoon ground coriander
  seeds

¼ teaspoon freshly ground
  pepper
2 teaspoons light soy sauce
2 quarts chicken stock
1 medium cucumber, thinly sliced
8 large mushrooms, chopped
2 eggs beaten with 2 tablespoons
  water
Coriander or parsley leaves for
  garnish

First prepare the meat: Heat the oil in a wok or large frying pan and cook the garlic, onion, coriander, and pepper gently for about 5 minutes. Now stir in the soy sauce and mix well. Add the chicken and pork and increase the heat to high. Stir-fry until the meat is brown, about 5 minutes. Then add the stock, cucumber slices, shrimp, and mushrooms. Cover and simmer for 30 minutes. When the dish is done, whip the eggs together with 1 or 2 tablespoons water and add to the pot a little at a time, stirring constantly. Let simmer for about 5 minutes.

Serve in a large tureen garnished with fresh coriander or parsley leaves. Serves 4.

VIETNAM/CAMBODIA

GINGER CHICKEN

2 cloves garlic, minced	Gizzard, heart, and liver,
4 tablespoons butter or oil	chopped finely
Meat from 1 pork chop, cubed	4 large mushrooms, sliced thinly
1 3-pound chicken, cut into 16	2 slices green ginger, chopped
pieces (page 37)	finely, or 1 teaspoon powdered
1 teaspoon sugar	ginger
1 teaspoon vinegar	1 tablespoon flour
1 tablespoon nguoc nam sauce	1 cup chicken stock
(see below)	Chopped chives for garnish

In a large skillet or wok sauté the garlic in butter until it turns golden. Add the pork and cook for 5 minutes, turning frequently. Add the chicken, sugar, vinegar, and nguoc nam sauce, stir for 5 minutes over moderate heat, then add the chicken giblets. Continue stirring for another 5 minutes. Now add the mushrooms and ginger and continue stirring for 5 more minutes. Mix the flour and stock together and stir into the pot. Cook 5 minutes more, then serve garnished with chopped chives. Serves 4.

Nguoc Nam (Nuoc Mam) Sauce

Nguoc nam in Cambodia is the same as the Vietnamese *nuoc mam,* and both are used much as salt is used in America. An agreeable substitute, should you not be able to find either in Chinese or specialty food stores, is a mixture of equal parts of soy sauce and anchovy or shrimp paste.

VIETNAM

LEMON GRASS CHICKEN

1 3-pound chicken, cut up
2 tablespoons lemon grass
  powder
4 scallions, sliced thinly
Salt and pepper

Peanut or vegetable oil
1 red chili pepper, chopped finely
1 tablespoon nuoc mam sauce
  (see Ginger Chicken, page 75)
2 tablespoons chopped roasted
  peanuts (or peanut butter)

Combine the powdered lemon grass, scallions, and salt and pepper with 2 tablespoons oil, then brush it over each of the chicken pieces. Let stand for 30 minutes.

Heat 2 tablespoons oil in a large skillet and add the chili pepper and chicken pieces. Keep the heat fairly low and let the chicken brown slowly for 30 minutes or so, turning once or twice. Add the peanuts and nuoc mam sauce.

Continue cooking slowly for another 10-15 minutes or until the chicken is tender. Turn several times to avoid burning. Serve with rice or Chinese noodles. Serves 4.

BURMA

KAUKSE HIN—Burmese Chicken Curry

The Burmese enjoy curries as much as the Indians, but theirs are generally milder. Kaukse hin is served with noodles rather than rice, but it is accompanied by similar side dishes and relishes to those of its Indian cousins. Though it is not a hot curry, one of the side dishes is usually ground chilies, which you can add as you wish to achieve the desired heat.

1 3-pound chicken, cut up
Liver, heart, and gizzard,
  chopped finely
4 cloves garlic, minced
3 onions, chopped coarsely
1 teaspoon turmeric

½ teaspoon cumin
1 tablespoon coriander
Salt
Freshly ground pepper
2 cups coconut milk (page 82)
½ cup peas
Juice of 1 lemon

Place the chicken, chopped giblets, garlic, and onions in a kettle. Mix the turmeric, cumin, coriander, salt, and pepper together, then add 1 cup coconut milk. Stir to blend thoroughly, then pour over the chicken, making sure each piece is well coated. Simmer the chicken uncovered for 1½ hours. About 20 minutes before done, add ½ cup peas and the remaining coconut milk.

When the meat is done, sprinkle it with lemon juice and serve with Chinese noodles or vermicelli. Serves 4.

MALAYSIA (STRAITS CHINESE)

SINGGANG AJAM—Spread-eagled Chicken

This dish is similar to others enjoyed in China, the Caucasus, and the Balkans. As all of these areas came into contact at one time or another with the Mongols and Tartars of Central Asia, or peoples fleeing from them, it's an interesting speculation that these dishes all may have a common origin.

1 3-pound chicken	1 teaspoon fresh green ginger, ground
⅔ cup vegetable or peanut oil	¼ teaspoon lemon grass powder
2 cloves garlic, minced	⅓ teaspoon turmeric
2 small onions, chopped	½ teaspoon salt
5 red chilies (or less), minced	4 cups coconut milk (page 82)
1 tablespoon ground coriander	6-8 candlenuts or macadamia nuts, crushed

Remove the backbone from the chicken and pound it until the breast and rib bones separate from the meat. Remove the breastbone and the cartilage and flatten the chicken with a mallet. Heat the oil in a large skillet and sauté the garlic and onions slowly for about 5 minutes, then add the ground chilies, coriander, green ginger, lemon grass, turmeric, and salt and cook slowly for about 2-3 minutes.

Place the flattened chicken in a flat dish and spoon the sauce over it, coating it well. Let sit for 2 hours. When ready to broil the chicken, pour the coconut milk and crushed nuts into a pan and heat very slowly. Stir continuously or the milk will curdle. After 10 minutes, place the chicken in the coconut milk sauce and cook for 15 minutes very slowly. Spoon the sauce and the marinade over the chicken and turn several times. Now start a charcoal fire, then grill the chicken, turning frequently to allow it to broil evenly. Brush the chicken with the sauce as it cooks. Serve on a platter with a salad and plain rice. Serves 4.

INDONESIA

AJAM PANGGANG BUMBU RUDJAK—
Broiled Spiced Chicken

This dish is marinated, then partially cooked on the stove and finished over a charcoal fire. The slow cooking lets the spices penetrate better.

1 3-pound chicken, split down the breastbone	½ teaspoon powdered lemon grass
3 red chilies	1 cup coconut milk (page 82)
2 teaspoon laos powder	1 tablespoon ketjap manis (page 81)
2 cloves garlic	Juice of 1 lemon
1 onion, chopped finely	½ cup water
1 teaspoon trasi (page 80)	

Run a skewer through the lower part of the bird and stick the legs under it, so the chicken lies spread-eagled and flat. With a sharp knife, lightly score the meat in several places. Grind the chilies, laos, garlic, onion, and trasi in a mortar or an electric blender to a paste, then coat the chicken with it on all sides, and let stand for 1 hour.

While the chicken marinates, prepare a charcoal fire in a hibachi or small barbecue. Combine the lemon grass, coconut milk, ketjap manis, lemon juice, and water in a large skillet and bring to the boil. Put in the chicken, reduce the heat to low, and simmer for 20 minutes, spooning the sauce over it from time to time. Now remove the chicken to the barbecue and cook for another 20 minutes, basting with the pan sauce. (You may also put the chicken under the broiler for about 10-12 minutes, turning and basting just once.) Serve with rice and vegetables. Serves 4.

INDONESIA

AJAM BUMBU BASENEK—Spicy Chicken

Bumbu Basenek identifies a certain spice mixture which, like *rudjak,* is so popular in various parts of Indonesia that it is prepared in quantity and used frequently.

1 3-pound chicken, cut up	1 onion, chopped
Salt and freshly ground black pepper	1 cup coconut milk (page 82)
3-4 tablespoons peanut or vegetable oil	2 tablespoons ketjap manis (page 81)
	Juice of 1 lemon

Bumbu Basenek

1 onion, chopped finely	2 garlic cloves, minced
½ teaspoon trasi (page 80)	2 teaspoons ground laos
5 macamia nuts, crushed	2 tablespoons peanut or vegetable oil
½ teaspoon ground cumin	
1 teaspoon sambal oelek (page 80), or 1 teaspoon red pepper	1-inch piece of green ginger, sliced thinly

Sprinkle the chicken pieces with salt and pepper and let sit for 30 minutes. Crush the ingredients for bumbu basenek in a mortar or grind together in an electric blender. In a wok, sauté the paste in half the oil for 2 minutes, then remove from the heat and set aside. In a separate skillet or wok heat the remaining oil and brown the onion slowly. Now add the chicken and brown on all sides for about 10 minutes, then add the spice paste and the coconut milk, stirring constantly. Cook for 3 minutes, and add the ketjap manis.

Continue stirring for 1 minute, then add the lemon juice. Reduce heat to low and cover the pan. Simmer for 30 minutes, then serve with rice. Serves 4.

ACCESSORIES TO THE SOUTHERN ASIAN MEAL

It isn't enough to cook a chicken meal with just rice to savor fully the taste of Southern Asian cooking. Likewise, it isn't really fair to the Indonesian or Malaysian style to leave out some of the special accessories that are unique to their cuisines.

Almost all of the recipes on the preceding pages call for one or more of these special ingredients, or for vegetable dishes, sambals, or sauces to accompany them. Although the several examples listed here don't even scratch the surface of what's usually served, these will help round out your meal and perhaps make it a little more authentic and enjoyable.

Trasi

This is a shrimp concentrate that comes in cakes. It is used in almost everything, and has no substitute. If you can't find it, add a little salt.

Krupuk

This is a cracker made with shrimp and sago or tapioca. It is purchased already processed and ready for deep-fat frying. Krupuk is served with virtually all meals and is readily available in specialty or gourmet stores. In hot oil it needs only about a second or two to cook fully.

Laksa

Cellophane noodles—available in specialty stores. As a side dish, serve laksa that have been dipped for an instant into boiling oil in a wok or frying pan. They'll puff up, so take them out almost immediately. Drain and sprinkle with a little salt before serving.

Sambals

These are the fiery hot side dishes that make the Indonesian cuisine a thing apart. Many sambals take the name of the particular dish in which they are used exclusively (*sambal nasi goreng*—the sambal used with fried rice), but others are more general and found in a variety of dishes. There are no "right" or "wrong" sambals for most Indonesian dishes—use the one that suits your taste, or all of them.

Sambal Oelek—This is simply red chilies chopped into fine dice or crushed into a paste with water and a little salt. It is violently hot and should be used with care. Though not as popular in Southern Asia, green chilies will give excellent results with nowhere near the heat.

Sambal Goreng

2 tablespoons finely chopped
 onions
1 tablespoon laos
Juice of ¼ lemon
Salt

2 cloves garlic, minced
1 tablespoon sambal oelek (page
 80)
Peanut or vegetable oil
1 tomato, peeled and chopped
4 tablespoons coconut milk

Grind the onions, laos, lemon juice, salt, garlic, and sambal oelek to a paste in a mortar or electric blender, then sauté in a little oil, stirring constantly. After a minute or so, add the chopped tomato and continue stirring over low heat for 5 minutes. Remove from the fire and let sit for a minute or so, then blend in the coconut milk. (For where to get laos, see page 63 for mail order source.)

Sambal Badjak

This can be very hot, and while excellent with chicken and meat, it is not good with vegetables.

6 candlenuts or macadamia nuts,
 crushed
1 tablespoon brown sugar
4 cloves garlic, minced
2 onions, finely chopped

2 teaspoons sambal oelek (page
 80)
1 teaspoon trasi (page 80)
Salt
1 tablespoon lemon juice
Peanut or vegetable oil
4-6 tablespoons coconut cream
 (page 82)

Grind the nuts, sugar, garlic, onions, sambal oelek, trasi, and lemon juice into a paste in a mortar or electric blender, then sauté in a little oil for a minute or so, stirring constantly. Add the coconut cream and continue stirring for several more minutes. The mixture should begin to get dry. Remove from heat and let cool.

Ketjap Manis

This is a sweet soy sauce made simply by combining 2 parts of soy sauce with 3 parts of brown sugar or dark corn syrup. Although the ingredients are different, the American "ketchup" or "catsup" originated from this sauce.

Egg Decoration

Egg decoration is not exclusive to Southern Asia. In Korea, for example, there is scarcely a meat and rice or noodle dish that doesn't have thin strips of omelet arranged around and across it to make it both attractive and tasty. Cook an omelet as you normally would and cut it into long, thin strips. Then add it to any dish you like just before serving. (Also see page 56 for the Korean method of making egg decoration.)

Rudjak

This is a spicy sauce, somewhat on the sweet side, which finds frequent use in Indonesian cooking. It is served over cooked or raw vegetables and is splendid with chicken.

1 red chili, chopped, or 2 tablespoons sambal oelek (page 80)
½ teaspoon trasi (page 80)

4 tablespoons ketjap manis
  (page 81)
Juice of 1 lemon
Peanut or vegetable oil
½ cup thick coconut milk
  (below)

Combine the chili, trasi, ketjap manis, and lemon juice in a mortar or electric blender and grind to a paste. Sauté in the oil for a minute or two, stirring constantly. Remove from heat and let cool and then stir in the coconut cream.

Coconut Milk and Cream

There are several ways to make coconut milk. The easiest is to buy a can of it in a gourmet or specialty shop, but the canned product doesn't have the fresh pure taste of newly made milk.

Another way is to use grated unsweetened coconut, which is sometimes available in supermarkets, but again the freshness is usually gone.

The real way is to make it from scratch, and in America even that can present problems. Depending on how long the nuts have been sitting in some warehouse, coconuts sometimes become rancid in their shells. You can't tell how fresh any given nut is until you open it, but if you want the real thing it's worth the risk.

To open the coconut, punch out the three eyes at one end and drain the liquid. Lay the coconut on its side on a hard surface and whack it with a hammer about one-third of the way down from the eyeholes. Coconuts are tough, so it will take several good whacks, but if you revolve the nut each time you hit it, it will eventually crack. Once it does, it is easy to break it into pieces.

Now cut the white meat away from the shell in as large chunks as you can. There is a brown skin between the meat and the shell, and that should be peeled or scraped off and discarded. Now grate the coconut meat coarsely in a blender, and pour in very hot (not boiling) water. For each cup of coarsely grated coconut meat you should add 1 cup of hot water, which in turn will make about 1 cup of coconut milk.

Let the coconut meat and water sit for 10-15 minutes, then turn the blender up to the purée setting and blend for 1 minute. Stop it and scrape down the sides with a rubber spatula, then purée it again for 1 more minute. By now you will have a smooth paste.

Now line a large fine sieve with a double thickness of dampened cheesecloth and set it over a bowl. Scrape the entire contents of the blender into the sieve and, with a wooden spoon, press down as hard as you can to extract the milk. When you have gotten as much milk out as you can with the spoon, bring the ends of the cheesecloth together, enclosing the pulp, and squeeze hard on the ball. This should extract whatever milk is left in the pulp; you may then discard the pulp ball.

What you have now is thick coconut milk, and this is used in more recipes than either thin milk or cream. However, recipes frequently call for one or the other, and to obtain them merely let the bowl sit for an hour or so for the cream to rise to the top. Gently ladle or spoon the coconut cream off—what's left is thin coconut milk.

Tightly covered, coconut milk or cream will keep in the refrigerator for several days or in the freezer for several months.

PART II:

The Asian Subcontinent

The Subcontinent, or "underbelly," of Asia stretches from Bangladesh in the east through India, Sri Lanka (Ceylon), Pakistan, and Afghanistan to Iran in the west. Except for Iran, the cooking of this vast region is generally categorized as Indian, and it is considered by many to be as sophisticated and elegant as any other in the world. One reason for this is the spectacular use of spices characteristic of all Subcontinental cooking, and another may be the culinary influences of the Byzantine and Persian kitchens introduced by the Moslem and Mogul conquerors.

The eating habits and cookery of India and surrounding nations are probably more affected by religious, social, and economic restrictions than any other in the world. Over four thousand years ago the Buddhist and Brahmin sects laid down the precepts of Buddhism and Hinduism, including the do's and don'ts of cooking and eating. The Moslems came in the ninth century and added Islam's taboos. On top of these, the population, which is second only to that of China in size, is among the poorest in the world, so for millions upon millions the standard of living is barely above the starvation level.

The strictest religious sects forbid the eating of anything that ever had animal life in it at all. Some believers even wear masks over their faces to avoid accidentally inhaling a stray insect. The Buddhists proclaimed the cow to be sacred, so beef is rarely on the menu, and the Moslems forbade pork in any form, so this meat is not frequently found on the table. It's small wonder that this area is home to the largest number of vegetarians in the world.

Where and when meat is eaten, it is usually chicken, lamb, fish, kid,

85

or goat. The Jungle Fowl, ancestor of today's domestic chicken, originated in India and Indochina; thus these cultures have had a centuries-long head start in chicken cookery over the Western world, and they have made the most of it.

The style and the taste of the cooking of India changes drastically as one moves from north to south. Delhi is the capital of India today, as it was in the days when the Moguls ruled. Baber led his Aryan forces through Persia and the Khyber Pass into India in the sixteenth century and overthrew the Moslems. He was enraptured with the Persian civilization and borrowed freely from its cuisine: pilafs (or *pulaos*), *kababs*, yogurt, sweet desserts, and the *tandoor* oven were just some of the items he brought with him. Despite the coming and going of the British and French in ensuing centuries, the north of India has retained much of this early Persian influence. The cuisine of northern India is well seasoned, to be sure, but the hot spices are not used to nearly the degree as in the cooking of the south.

Wheat is widely grown in the north (in fact it was actually cultivated before rice), and some of India's best known foods are bread products—*nan, partha,* and *chappatis. Nan* is a yeast dough made with yogurt and sugar, which the Indian cook shapes into a moist, oblong loaf, and then slaps against the top or other inside wall of the tandoor oven to bake at the same time the *Tandoori* chicken is grilled over a hot charcoal fire at the bottom. Served with *dhal,* which accompanies about everything in India, tandoori chicken is one of India's most famous, and most delightful, dishes.

In southern India and Sri Lanka (Ceylon) the cuisine takes on a decidedly different character. There are more people, more poor, more vegetarians, and more of the hot spices are used in cooking. Rice is the staple, in fact the only, food for most. A great many more fish and shellfish appear in southern Indian meals, and coconut milk is a common ingredient. Though hotter and spicier and less cosmopolitan than the Mogul kitchen of the north, some of the classic dishes of India come from her southern kitchens: the *Biryanis* (rice dishes with meat), the *Kormas* (rich ragouts that usually contain yogurt), and the *Vindaloos* (frequently seasoned with vinegar to give them a tart taste) are just three that are outstanding when made with chicken.

Spice seasoning, the most obvious characteristic of Indian cooking, was originally found to help preserve meat in a continually hot climate. Pepper was one of the first spices used for this purpose, for it also masked the taste of decaying meat. The recipes used by the women of India go back centuries in time. These dishes are seasoned with spice combinations that are ground daily, for there's no such thing as premixed curry powder in India as there is in the West. In fact, the Indians don't even refer to their spice mixtures or dishes as curries—this is a term (from the Tamil word *Kari*) which the British used to describe all spice mixtures.

An Indian cook will, however, prepare an especially favored combination of spices in fairly large quantity to produce a *massala,* which she will use again and again. One of India's most famous chicken dishes is *Murgh Massalam* which, though it differs from cook to cook, is roasted or simmered in a favorite combination of spices.

In addition to the spice tradition there are other unique elements in Indian cooking. One is *ghee,* or clarified butter, where butter is melted and the butter fat strained out. Cooking with ghee substantially reduces the possibility of the fat burning and creating an unwanted and unfavorable taste in the food. But ghee is actually used only on occasion. The Indian dairy industry is relatively small, so butter is both scarce and expensive. Vegetable or other oils are the common cooking media, while ghee is reserved for special dishes or occasions.

Another tradition involves chicken: the Indian usually removes the chicken skin before cooking, considering it to be unclean and, therefore, unfit for consumption. In all likelihood, this tradition has its roots in antiquity. The skin and fat of chicken will spoil very quickly, giving off an unpleasant odor. The meat, even unrefrigerated, will keep longer, and any off-odors were easily masked with pepper or other spices.

Finally, there is chutney. Americans, and others, are apt to consider chutney as one mixture that comes in a bottle and is readily available in every grocery store. There is no such thing in authentic Indian cooking, and most likely little or no bottled chutney is available in India.

Chutneys are side dishes and perhaps six or eight are served with any given meal. They have their counterparts in Indonesian, Chinese, and Middle Eastern cooking and, though all vary widely in form and number, their purpose is the same. They are there to enhance a taste, to blend various elements of the meal, or to put out the fire if the seasoning is especially hot. In a multi-course meal, the chutneys will change with the entrée.

Two pages of chutney recipes have been added from which you should choose several to accompany your Indian meal (107-8). Look closely and you'll notice that some of the popular Indian chutneys—bananas, peanuts, cucumbers, tomatoes, and raisins, among others—are nothing more than foods you've been eating and enjoying all your life.

RECOMMENDED READING: Madhur Jaffrey, *An Invitation to Indian Cooking* (New York: Alfred Knopf, 1973); Robin Howe, *Cooking From the Commonwealth* (London: André Deutsch, 1958); Charmaine Solomon, *The Complete Asian Cookbook* (New York: McGraw-Hill, 1976)

MAIL ORDER SOURCE FOR INGREDIENTS:

Mrs. DeWildt
RFD 1
Bangor, Pa., 18013

INDIA

CHICKEN VINDALOO

This curry comes from the coastal regions of southern India and was highly popular in the old Portuguese enclave of Goa. Vindaloos show the use of vinegar and mustard oil in a preparation which is rather rare in other parts of India.

Seasonings

1 teaspoon cumin
2 teaspoons turmeric
1 red chili pepper, ground
1-inch piece ginger, ground
1 tablespoon coriander
½ teaspoon each salt and pepper
6 cloves
½ cup wine vinegar (or a little more)

1 3-pound chicken, cut up, skinned, boned, and the meat cut into 1-inch cubes
3-4 tablespoons mustard oil (or ghee, page 108)
1 large onion, sliced thinly
3 cloves garlic, minced
4 hard cooked eggs

In a mortar or blender combine all the seasonings and grind together until thoroughly pulverized and blended. Add the vinegar and stir into a smooth, rather thick paste. Add the chicken cubes and turn all together to coat the meat completely on all sides. Cover and refrigerate for 12-24 hours. (This will make the curry hotter. If a mild curry is desired, do not marinate but go right to the cooking step described below.)

Heat the mustard oil (or ghee) in a large skillet with a cover. Sauté gently the sliced onions and minced garlic, then add the chicken and spice mixture. You may want to add a little more vinegar along with the ½ cup hot water—this is a matter of taste. Cover and simmer for 1 hour. About 10 minutes before serving, add the hard-cooked eggs and spoon some sauce over each. Re-cover and finish cooking. Serve the vindaloo with rice and the eggs sliced in half. Serves 4.

India

CHICKEN KORMA

1 3-pound chicken, cut up, skinned, boned, and cut into 1-inch cubes
4 hard cooked eggs, halved
1 large onion, chopped finely

1 large clove garlic, minced
3-4 tablespoons ghee (page 108)
1 tomato, peeled and chopped
2 cups yogurt
Salt
Chutney

Curry Mixture

1 teaspoon grated fresh ginger, or ½ teaspoon powdered ginger
1 teaspoon turmeric
1 teaspoon freshly ground black pepper

1 teaspoon coriander
1 teaspoon cumin
1 teaspoon mustard powder
1 teaspoon poppy seed
4 cloves, crushed
¼ teaspoon cinnamon

Mix together the chicken meat, the egg halves, the onions and garlic, and the curry mixture in a bowl, and marinate for 1 hour. Heat the ghee and cook the meat gently for 5 or 6 minutes in a large skillet, turning constantly with a wooden spoon. Now add the tomato and yogurt, cover, and cook for 30 minutes over low heat. When nearly done, sprinkle over a little salt. Serve with plain boiled rice and chutney. Serves 4.

India

MOGLAI CHICKEN

This dish has its origins in the great Mogul courts of three to four hundred years ago. The Persian influence shows up in the use of yogurt, which the Moguls brought with them when they conquered India.

2 onions, chopped finely
1 teaspoon fresh ginger, ground
4 cloves garlic
Water
½ cup ghee (page 108)
1 3-pound chicken, cut up and skinned

1 tablespoon *garam masala* (page 108)
½ teaspoon ground turmeric
¼ teaspoon red pepper (or ground chili powder)
2 cups yogurt
1 tablespoon saffron
½ cup coconut milk (page 82)

Put the onions, ginger, garlic, and ¼ cup of water in a blender and grind to a smooth paste. Cook over a slow fire for 10-12 minutes, stirring frequently so it doesn't burn. Melt about half of the ghee in a large skillet. Add the onion paste, then the chicken pieces a few at a time. (You may need more ghee.) Turn the chicken frequently to coat on all sides and to brown evenly. Don't let the fire get too hot. Remove and keep warm.

Mix the garam masala, turmeric, and red pepper and add to the pan and cook for 5-6 minutes very slowly. Add the rest of the ghee, then return the chicken to the pan and spoon the sauce over each piece. Cook for 3 minutes, then add the yogurt. Stir well for a minute, then cover and cook over low fire for 30 minutes.

While the chicken cooks, grind the saffron and soak it in a little warm coconut milk. When the chicken is ready, pour this over and cook another 5 minutes, uncovered. Serve with rice, vegetables, and chutney. Serves 4.

INDIA/PAKISTAN

MURGH TIKKA—Skewered Chicken

This is typical of northern Indian cooking—sharp and peppery but not as hot as they like it in the south. Murgh tikka is usually cooked in India's unique oven—the tandoor.

1 3-pound chicken, cut up and skinned	1 tablespoon *garam masala* (page 108)
½ teaspoon coriander	2 tablespoons lemon juice
½ teaspoon cumin	1 cup yogurt
1 onion, chopped finely	Salt and pepper
1 teaspoon paprika	1 clove garlic, minced
	1 teaspoon freshly grated ginger

Cut the meat from the bones in as large pieces as possible, then cut it into 2-inch cubes. Combine the remaining ingredients in a bowl and mix thoroughly. Add the chicken cubes and mix well with a wooden spoon to coat each piece all over. Set aside, covered, for 2 hours or longer.

Thread the cubes on skewers and cook in the broiler or over a charcoal fire for about 10 minutes, turning once. Brush the meat once or twice with the spiced yogurt sauce. Serve with rice and vegetables and nan bread (page 102). Serves 4.

INDIA

CHICKEN CHAAT—Spicy Chicken Appetizer

Breast meat of 1 chicken, skin removed
3 cups fresh chicken stock
2 green chilies, chopped
½ cup fresh coriander leaves, chopped
½ cup fresh mint leaves
2 large onions, chopped
Large pinch red or cayenne pepper
1 clove garlic, chopped finely
¼ teaspoon powdered coriander seed

1 piece fresh ginger, grated (1 teaspoon)
4 medium tomatoes, 2 skinned and chopped finely
Salt and freshly ground pepper
¼ cup fresh lemon juice
3 tablespoons yogurt
2 tablespoons grenadine syrup (optional)
½ cucumber, peeled and diced finely
Garnishes: orange sections, banana slices, and fresh coriander leaves
Lettuce leaves

Place the chicken and broth in a pan and bring to a boil. Reduce heat, cover, and simmer for 15 minutes, then let stand for 1 hour.

In a blender, combine the chilies, coriander leaves, mint, half the onions, red pepper, garlic, powdered coriander, ginger, 2 chopped tomatoes, salt and pepper, lemon juice, yogurt, and the grenadine syrup, and blend at a medium setting for 15-20 seconds.

When the chicken is cool, remove it from the pan and shred the meat, discarding the bones. (The stock may be retained for another use.) Place the shredded meat in a large bowl. Cut the 2 remaining tomatoes into small dice and add to the bowl, then mix in the remaining chopped onion and the cucumber. Now pour in the sauce from the blender and mix in the bowl thoroughly, then refrigerate for 1 hour.

To serve, place a large fresh lettuce leaf on a plate and spoon a portion of the chaat into the center. Garnish with orange sections, banana slices, and coriander leaves. Serves 4-6.

PAKISTAN

MURGHI PULAO—Chicken with Rice

Rice dishes are the backbone of Subcontinental cooking, and there seems to be no end to their number and variety. Usually chicken, lamb, vegetable, or a fish accompaniment is cooked separately and the rice is fried for a few minutes in ghee, then added to the liquid to complete the cooking. When done the rice and meat are combined and then left to sit while the grains separate.

This recipe includes a small piece of mutton or lamb to provide a richer broth.

1 pound lamb or mutton, cut into small pieces	1 cup white rice
	1 teaspoon grated ginger
3 quarts water	4-6 cloves
1 3-pound chicken, skin removed	Seeds from 6 cardamom pods
1 teaspoon salt	¼ teaspoon mace
6 onions	1 teaspoon ground coriander (or less)
½ cup ghee (page 108)	1 teaspoon freshly ground pepper
	4-6 hard cooked eggs

Place the lamb or mutton pieces, water, chicken, salt, and 2 onions (quartered) into a large kettle and bring to the boil. Skim off the scum as it rises. Reduce the heat to moderate and cook, uncovered, for about 45 minutes, or until the chicken is done. Remove the bird and set aside. Cook the broth down a bit, then strain it into a bowl, pressing all the flavor from the lamb cubes. Reserve 2 cups for the rice and save the rest for another use.

Slice the remaining onions thinly and cut the chicken into pieces. Heat the ghee in a skillet and fry the onion slices to a golden brown, then remove with a slotted spoon. Now fry the chicken pieces on all sides until lightly brown. Set these aside with the onions and keep hot. Now fry the rice in the skillet for 3 minutes. Be sure to stir constantly so that all of the kernels are well coated with ghee.

Grind the ginger, cloves, and cardamom seeds together in a mortar or electric blender and add to the rice, stirring to blend thoroughly. Now add the reserved broth, the mace, coriander, a little salt, and several grindings of fresh pepper. Cook the rice, covered, for 20 minutes or so, then add the chicken pieces. Re-cover and set aside for about 20 minutes.

Turn the rice out onto a serving platter and surround with the chicken pieces and hard cooked eggs. Garnish with sliced, fried onions. Serves 4.

INDIA

MURGH MASSALAM I—Roast Stuffed Chicken

1 4-pound roasting chicken, skin   Salt and pepper
  removed

Stuffing

2 hard cooked eggs, chopped   2 tablespoons raisins
1 medium onion, chopped   2 tablespoons almonds, blanched,
1 teaspoon grated ginger   peeled, and chopped
                                    Juice of 1 lemon

Spicy Sauce

2 tablespoons grated coconut   2 tablespoons garam masala
  (unsweetened)   (page 108)
2 cloves garlic, crushed   ½ tablespoon turmeric
1 small onion, minced   ⅓ cup ghee (page 108)
                                    2 cups plain yogurt

Rub the chicken inside and out with a little salt and pepper. Combine all the ingredients for the stuffing in a bowl and mix well, then stuff the bird and skewer or truss the cavities closed.

Combine the sauce ingredients and mix well. Heat the ghee in a small skillet and gently cook the sauce for 3 minutes or so, then stir in the yogurt and simmer very slowly for 1-2 minutes, then remove from the fire.

Preheat the oven to 325° F. Place the chicken in a casserole and spoon the sauce over it, being sure to coat the bird thoroughly. Now cover the casserole tightly and roast in the oven for 1½ hours, or more if necessary, basting with the sauce every 20 minutes or so. Serves 4-6.

MURGH MASSALAM II—Marinated Chicken

1 3-pound chicken, cut up and   4 hard cooked eggs
  skin removed

Marinade

4 cloves garlic, chopped
1 tablespoon grated ginger
1 teaspoon salt

1 tablespoon garam masala
  (page 108)
¼ teaspoon cayenne
½ teaspoon turmeric
⅓ cup yogurt

Spicy Sauce

⅔ cup ghee (page 108)
2 large onions, chopped finely
6 almonds, blanched, peeled, and
  crushed
1 tablespoon ground coriander
1 teaspoon ground cumin
⅛ teaspoon ground cardamom
  seeds

¼ teaspoon each of ground
  cloves, cinnamon, nutmeg,
  mace, and cayenne pepper
⅛ teaspoon salt
⅛ teaspoon freshly ground
  pepper
Juice of 1 lemon
5-6 tablespoons water

Prick the chicken pieces all over with a sharp fork and place in a large bowl. Combine all the marinade ingredients and mix well, then spoon over the chicken, coating it thoroughly. Let sit for 2 or more hours.

Heat half the ghee in a large skillet and cook the chopped onions over low heat for 5 minutes. Remove the onions to a blender, but save the cooking oil. In a separate dry skillet, brown the almonds gently and add to the blender. Then, in the same skillet, toast the coriander and cumin very slowly (don't allow them to burn). When done add to the blender, along with the remaining spices, lemon juice, and water. Now blend at medium speed for 15-20 seconds.

Add the remaining ghee to the reserved cooking oil and bring up to moderate heat. Brown the chicken pieces on all sides for about 8-10 minutes, removing each piece as it's done. When all pieces are browned, cover them thoroughly with the spicy sauce and return them to the skillet. Reduce the heat to low, add a little water, cover, then cook for 30 minutes. Turn the pieces once, adding a little more water if the sauce begins to thicken. Peel the hard cooked eggs and add them to the skillet about 10 minutes before the meal is ready.

Serve the chicken on a warm platter with the eggs. Pour any remaining sauce over all and serve with rice, tomato wedges, and several chutneys. Serves 4.

Sri Lanka (Ceylon)

CHICKEN AND POTATOES IN COCONUT MILK

1 3-pound chicken, cut up and skinned
1 medium onion, chopped
3 tablespoons ghee, coconut oil, or peanut oil
¼ teaspoon cayenne pepper
Large pinch turmeric
1 large clove garlic, minced
1 teaspoon green ginger, crushed
⅛ teaspoon freshly ground black pepper
2 large potatoes, peeled and diced
1½ cups thin coconut milk (page 82)
¼ cup lime juice

Heat the oil in a large skillet and slowly sauté the onions until golden, then add the cayenne pepper, turmeric, garlic, ginger, and black pepper. Cook over low heat for 4 minutes. Turn the heat up a little, add the chicken pieces, and fry for about 10 minutes, turning frequently to brown on all sides. Now add the diced potatoes and the coconut milk. Turn the heat back to low, cover, and simmer for 1 hour or until tender. Turn out onto a platter and sprinkle with lime juice. Serve with rice. Serves 4.

India

CURRIED DUCK (or Chicken)

1 4-5 pound duck, cut up and skinned
4 tablespoons peanut or coconut oil
1 medium onion, chopped
1 1-inch piece green ginger, crushed, or 1 teaspoon green ginger powder
2 cloves garlic, chopped finely
½ teaspoon cumin
1 red chili pepper, chopped finely, or 1 teaspoon red pepper
2 tablespoons coriander
1 cup water
1 teaspoon salt
1 cup thin coconut milk (page 82)
Juice of 1 lemon

Heat the oil and sauté the chopped onions lightly, then brown the duck pieces for about 5 minutes. Remove the duck and keep warm. Add the ginger, garlic, cumin, chopped chili pepper or red pepper, and coriander to the pan and cook slowly for 3 minutes.

Now add the water and salt and stir well to blend, then add back the duck pieces. Cover and cook gently for 1 hour or until the meat is tender. Add the coconut milk and cook slowly another 15 minutes uncovered, then stir in the lemon juice. Remove from heat and serve immediately with rice. Serves 4.

INDIA

MARINATED FRIED CHICKEN

1 3-pound chicken, cut up and skinned	¼ teaspoon freshly ground black pepper
1 teaspoon turmeric	2 cloves garlic, minced
1 red chili pepper, chopped finely	Salt
Juice and grated rind of 1 lemon	4 tablespoons ghee (page 108),
1 teaspoon cumin	coconut oil, or peanut oil

With a sharp fork, prick the chicken pieces all over. Now mix together the turmeric, minced chili pepper, lemon juice and rind, cumin, pepper, garlic, and salt, and rub this mixture thoroughly into the chicken pieces. Cover the chicken and let sit for 1 hour.

Heat the oil or ghee in a large skillet and slowly fry the chicken for 30 minutes or until done. Serves 4.

BANGLADESH

BENGALESE CHICKEN CURRY

1 3-pound chicken, cut up and skinned	1 chili pepper, chopped finely
Paprika	¼ teaspoon each of cumin and dried mustard
Salt	Large pinch each of turmeric, ground cardamom, and ground cinnamon
4 tablespoons peanut or coconut oil	
2 onions, chopped coarsely	1 cup chopped tomatoes
1 clove garlic, crushed	1 teaspoon coriander powder
	½ cup water

Sprinkle the chicken pieces with a little paprika and salt, then, in a large skillet, brown them slowly in the oil for 10 minutes. Remove from the pan and keep warm. In the same oil cook the onions and garlic until golden, then add the chili pepper, cumin, mustard, turmeric, cardamom, and cinnamon and cook slowly for about 5 minutes. Now add the chopped tomatoes, coriander, and water and simmer for 15 minutes.

Empty the skillet into a bowl, then replace the chicken pieces in the skillet. Sprinkle again with a little salt, then pour the curry sauce over the chicken, coating each piece thoroughly. Cover the pan and simmer over low fire for 1 hour. Serve with rice. Serves 4.

INDIA

BAKED CHICKEN WITH TOMATO-YOGURT SAUCE

1 3-pound chicken, cut up and
  skin removed
½ cup fresh grated coconut meat
1 clove garlic
1 chili pepper (or less), chopped
  finely
1 1-inch piece green ginger, or 1
  teaspoon ginger powder

1 cup plain yogurt
1 teaspoon salt
1 large onion, sliced thinly
Juice and grated rind of 1 lemon
1 cup tomatoes, chopped
⅛ teaspoon saffron
⅓ cup slivered almonds
Parsley for garnish

In a mortar or electric blender, grind the coconut, garlic, chili pepper, and ginger to a powder. Combine the yogurt, salt, sliced onions, lemon juice and rind, chopped tomatoes, and saffron and stir well to blend, then mix thoroughly with the powdered seasoning. Prick the chicken pieces all over with a sharp fork, then place them in a large shallow baking dish and spoon over the seasoning mixture. Sprinkle liberally with slivered almonds, then seal with foil, cover tightly, and set aside for 1 hour.

Preheat the oven to 375° F. Place the sealed baking dish in the oven and bake for 1¼ hours. When done garnish with parsley and serve with rice. Serves 4.

AFGHANISTAN

KABAB I MORGH—Grilled Chicken

This can also be cooked on a rotisserie, in which case the oil and garlic mixture is used for basting.

1 3-pound chicken, cut up
6 tablespoons peanut or vegetable oil
Salt and pepper
2 cloves garlic, minced

1 onion, chopped finely
1 tomato, peeled and chopped finely
Parsley for garnish
4-6 hard cooked eggs
Nan bread (page 102)

Heat the oil in a saucepan and sauté the garlic until golden. Rub the chicken with salt and pepper and brush liberally with the oil and garlic mixture. Place under the broiler for about 10 minutes on each side. Mix the chopped tomato with the onion and let sit for a while at room temperature, then spread over the chicken pieces, when serving, along with parsley sprigs for garnish. Surround with hard cooked eggs and serve with nan bread. Serves 4.

Note: Once out of the oven the nan will rapidly become fairly firm. Cut off a piece 4 or 5 inches square and serve each with a piece or two of chicken and an egg on top.

INDIA

BLACK PEPPER CURRY

1 3-pound chicken, cut up and skinned
2 teaspoons black pepper
½ teaspoon salt
½ teaspoon turmeric
1 teaspoon cumin
2 teaspoons coriander

6 tablespoons vegetable or peanut oil
1 large onion, chopped coarsely
1 tablespoon green pepper, minced
½ cup water
1 cup thick coconut milk (page 82)

Combine the black pepper, salt, turmeric, cumin, and coriander and rub the mixture into the chicken pieces.

Heat the oil in a large skillet and cook the onions slowly until golden. Add the minced pepper and the chicken pieces and fry for 10 minutes, turning once. Now add the water, cover, and simmer for 30 minutes. When the chicken is nearly done, add the coconut milk and cook slowly for 10 more minutes. Serve with rice and a green vegetable. Serves 4.

Mauritius

CHICKEN BABAJEE

This is adapted from a book of some years ago, in which the birds used were pigeons, not chicken. But pigeons in this country are rare, and so is their cousin, the dove, so this recipe calls for chicken.

Mauritius is an island situated in the Indian Ocean between India and Africa. There are no "Indian" ingredients in babajee, which may mean that this dish came to Mauritius with the Europeans.

1 3-pound chicken, cut up	1 tablespoon fresh parsley,
Salt and pepper	chopped
5 tablespoons butter or oil	1 egg
2 onions, chopped coarsely	1 tablespoon water
1 cup fresh chicken stock	4 slices white bread, toasted
1 teaspoon thyme	Parsley for garnish

Rub the chicken pieces with salt and pepper and then brown them in 5 tablespoons butter or oil. Add the chopped onion, chicken stock, thyme, and chopped parsley and cook over medium heat for 5 minutes. Now reduce the heat to low, cover, and cook for 30 minutes.

When done, remove the chicken pieces and keep warm. To the pan, add the egg beaten with 1 tablespoon of water and stir into the sauce for about 5 minutes. The sauce should just begin to thicken a little (if it doesn't, increase the heat slightly but continue stirring). Remove from the heat and keep warm.

Arrange the chicken pieces on the slices of toast on a warm platter and spoon on a little of the sauce, passing the rest in a sauceboat. Garnish with parsley sprigs and serve. Serves 4.

Sri Lanka (Ceylon)

ALBASSARA—Chicken Pancakes

This is a Moslem dish that must be served piping hot or it loses its flavor and character.

1 3-pound chicken, cut up	½ teaspoon freshly grated ginger
4-6 tablespoons ghee (page 108)	Salt and freshly ground pepper
2 onions, chopped finely	1 cup (or less) chicken stock

Pancakes

5 eggs	Salt and pepper
2 cups milk	3 tablespoons flour
	1 tablespoon butter

Heat the ghee in a large skillet and sauté the onions gently for about 5 minutes, then brown the chicken pieces on all sides. Now sprinkle with salt, pepper, and ginger and add the stock. Simmer over low heat for about 30 minutes, until the chicken is done.

Remove the chicken pieces from the pan and cut away the meat, discarding skin and bones. Shred the chicken meat into small strips and return to the sauce in the pan to keep hot.

Make a batter by mixing together thoroughly the first 4 pancake ingredients. Melt 1 tablespoon of butter in a large skillet and drop in a small amount of batter. The pancakes should be very thin and light, very much like crepes, and about 3 inches or so in diameter. Do not let them get too brown. Make as many pancakes as the batter allows. Serve either by spreading 5 or 6 pancakes on a plate and spooning the chicken mixture over, or rolling a pancake up with some chicken inside. Serve as hot as possible. Serves 4-6.

INDIA/PAKISTAN

TANDOORI CHICKEN

This dish originated in the Punjab, part of which lies in northern India and part in Pakistan. The chicken is marinated in a spicy mixture for 24 hours and then is roasted or barbecued in a unique cylindrical oven called a *tandoor*. Though the dish is mostly Indian, the oven was brought by Baber and the Moguls from Persia in the sixteenth century.

The tandoor is a primitive device 4 or 5 feet high, constructed of straw and mud and sunk partially in the ground. A fire is banked in the bottom and when just right chicken, lamb, or fish on long skewers are plunged in to broil. As a tandoor is not commonplace anywhere except in India, this recipe has been adapted to the standard charcoal fire.

3 3-pound chickens, halved, skinned, and backs removed	2 lemons or limes, quartered

Marinade

2 onions, coarsely chopped
6 cloves garlic, peeled and
    chopped
1 teaspoon grated ginger
Juice of 1 lemon
1 cup yogurt

2 tablespoons garam masala
    (page 108)
1 teaspoon turmeric
$\frac{1}{3}$ cup ghee (page 108)
$\frac{1}{4}$ teaspoon mace
Salt

First combine the marinade ingredients and mix well. Lightly slash the meat of each chicken half in 5 or 6 places, then place the pieces in the marinade in a shallow dish and coat each thoroughly. Cover and let stand for 6-8 hours.

Prepare a charcoal fire and when hot cook the chicken pieces for 5-6 minutes on each side very close to the fire, then raise the chicken and let finish cooking slowly for 15 or 20 minutes, turning several times and basting with the marinade.

This can also be either broiled or roasted in a very hot oven. Serve with rice and nan bread and lemon or lime wedges. Serves 6.

Nan Bread

Nan is just one of a number of excellent Indian breads, and it is cooked simultaneously in the tandoor with the chicken. The cook slaps the moist, oblong-shaped dough against the top or side of the oven and lets it bake as the chicken barbecues.

1 package dry yeast
1$\frac{1}{4}$ cups warm water
2 teaspoons salt
1 tablespoon sugar

4 tablespoons yogurt
1 egg, beaten
3 cups flour
$\frac{1}{3}$ cup ghee (page 108)

Dissolve the yeast in 3 tablespoons warm water. Combine salt, 4 tablespoons ghee, yogurt, sugar, and the remaining water, stir well, then add the egg and yeast. Add the flour and work together to form a dough ball. Cover and set aside in a warm draft-free area for 1 hour. Knead the dough ball for 10-15 minutes, then divide it into 6 evenly sized balls.

Preheat the oven to 450° F, then form each ball into an oval shape about $\frac{1}{4}$ inch thick. Brush the tops with the remaining ghee, place them on a baking sheet, and bake for 10-12 minutes until brown. Serve hot, one to each person, with the tandoori chicken.

INDIA/SRI LANKA (CEYLON)

SOUTH INDIAN CURRY

1 3-pound chicken, cut up and
  skinned
¼ cup ghee
1 large onion, chopped
¼ teaspoon mustard seeds (or ⅛
  teaspoon mustard powder)
1 tablespoon coriander
¼ teaspoon freshly ground
  pepper
¼ teaspoon ground red chilies

1 teaspoon turmeric
¼ teaspoon aniseed
2 cloves, crushed
1-inch stick cinnamon, crushed
Seeds from 2 cardamom pods,
  crushed
1-inch piece ginger, crushed
Salt
2 cups coconut milk (page 82)

Heat half the ghee in a large skillet and sauté the onion slowly for several minutes until golden. Add the mustard seeds (or powder) and cook for another 5 minutes. Now add the remaining ghee and the curry mixture. Cook slowly for 2 minutes, then add the chicken pieces and cook slowly for 7-10 minutes, until they color a bit. Now sprinkle over a little salt and the coconut milk, uncover, and cook for 30-40 minutes, until done. Serve with rice or potatoes and vegetables. Serves 4.

Note: Subcontinental cooks prepare potatoes in the same way as Western cooks except for baking them. If boiled, potatoes are usually served sliced or mashed. Most of the time they are peeled and cubed and fried in a spice mixture. Try adding potatoes cut in half-inch cubes directly to this curry about 20-25 minutes before it is done.

INDIA

SPICY CHICKEN WITH TOMATOES

1 3-pound chicken, cut up,
  skinned, boned, and cut into
  1-inch cubes
¼ cup ghee (page 108)
2 medium onions, chopped
  coarsely
2 cloves garlic, minced
1 teaspoon ginger
1 teaspoon cumin

1 tablespoon coriander
6 cloves, crushed
½ teaspoon turmeric
1 teaspoon freshly ground black
  pepper
¼ teaspoon cayenne pepper
3 tomatoes, peeled and chopped
1 cup yogurt
Salt
Water

Heat the ghee in a large skillet with a cover or a Dutch oven. Sauté the onions and the garlic until golden, then add the spices and cook very slowly for about 3 minutes. Now add the chicken pieces and cook for 10 minutes over low heat, turning constantly to coat each piece. Add the tomatoes and let cook for 4-5 minutes, stirring continuously, then pour in the yogurt, a little salt, and about ½ cup water. Cover and simmer over low heat for 45 minutes. Serve with rice. Serves 4.

INDIA/PAKISTAN

MURGHI BIRYANI—Chicken and Rice

This is one of the most famous of the rice dishes of India and Pakistan. It is a Mogul dish resembling a pilaf, and can be cooked with either chicken or lamb. The rice is first partially cooked, then added to the spiced, marinated meat in another pan. This combines and distributes the flavors in a way which couldn't be done by just stirring the rice and meat together.

1 3-pound chicken, cut up, skinned, and boned	1 onion, chopped
12 threads saffron	Salt
2 cups plain yogurt	6 cloves, ground
2 teaspoons grated ginger	¼ teaspoon cardamom seeds, ground
2 teaspoons turmeric	1 cup white rice
1 clove garlic	2 cups water
¼ teaspoon ground cinnamon	2 tablespoons almonds, blanched and crushed
1 teaspoon ground coriander	2 tablespoons raisins
1 teaspoon ground cumin	2 hard cooked eggs, quartered
¼ teaspoon ground mace	Parsley for garnish
⅓ cup ghee (page 108)	

Grind the saffron in a mortar and soak in 2 tablespoons of yogurt for 2 hours. Cut the chicken meat into 1-inch squares. Now grind the ginger, turmeric, and garlic together in the blender with the cinnamon, coriander, cumin, and mace. Mix with 1 cup of yogurt. Pour this mixture over the chicken pieces in a bowl, coating each piece thoroughly, and let sit for 2 hours.

Heat 3 tablespoons of ghee in a large skillet and brown the chicken pieces for 20 minutes, until completely cooked, turning frequently. In a second skillet, heat the remaining ghee and sauté the onion until brown, then remove and keep warm. Now put the saffron, salt, cloves, cardamom seeds, and rice into the same pan. Stir continuously to coat each rice kernel for a minute or so, then pour in 2 cups of boiling water. Cook over medium to high heat for 8-10 minutes, or until the rice is half cooked.

In a casserole, spoon in half the rice, then add a layer of onions, almonds, chicken pieces, and raisins. Add the remaining rice, then pour over the remaining yogurt. Place the pot on a very low fire, cover, and cook until the yogurt has been absorbed (about 10 minutes). Serve from the casserole or turn the rice out into a warm serving platter. Garnish with quartered ha-d cooked eggs and parsley. Serves 4-6.

INDIA/SRI LANKA (CEYLON)

MULLIGATAWNY SOUP—Pepper Water

This is one of the world's great soups, and while its origin is in South India and Ceylon, it was conceived by the British. The word has been Anglicized from the Tamil words which sound like *molega* and *tonee* or "pepper water." There are many recipes for mulligatawny soup varying from an extremely hot version, used to moisten rice dishes, to this one, which is really British and contains either chicken or cubed lamb.

1 3-pound chicken, cut up and skinned	2 tablespoons oil
3 quarts water	1 lime, quartered
6 onions, sliced	Small piece ginger
2 cloves garlic	Small piece cinnamon
1 medium onion, chopped	4 large tomatoes, peeled and chopped
1 cup thick coconut milk (page 82)	2 bay leaves
	Pinch coriander
	Salt

Seasoning

5-10 dried chili peppers	1 teaspoon turmeric
1 tablespoon coriander seeds	1 teaspoon grated ginger
½ tablespoon cumin seed	
8 peppercorns	

Place the chicken pieces and water in a large soup pot. Bring to the boil and skim off the scum as it rises. Reduce the heat to low and add the onions, cloves, ginger, cinnamon, tomatoes, bay leaves, coriander, and salt, then cover and cook for 1 hour. Now remove the chicken and strain the stock, then skim off the fat and return the stock to the pot. Bone the chicken and cut the meat into bite-sized pieces and set aside.

Now make the seasoning: You may vary the number of dried chilies to suit your taste (or leave them out altogether), because this is where the heat comes from. In a blender grind the chili peppers, coriander, cumin, peppercorns, turmeric, and ginger together until a paste is formed. Mix it with the coconut milk and stir this mixture into the soup. Sauté the chopped onion gently in oil until golden, then add to the soup. Return the chicken pieces to the pot and continue to cook for another 5 minutes, stirring once or twice. Serve the soup in a tureen or in individual bowls. Cooked rice with slices of lime are usually served with the soup. Serves 6-8.

ACCESSORIES TO SUBCONTINENTAL COOKING

Chutney

Chutneys are side dishes somewhat like pickles, and while some are there merely to put out the fire, all are superb additions to a curry or other meal. Chutney is a matter of pride to the Indian housewife, who would never serve bottled chutney any more than she would use prepared curry powder. She mixes these side dishes daily to go with her curries, pilafs, and other foods.

Mint Chutney

This may be the most universally enjoyed chutney of all.

1 or 2 small green chili peppers	½ small clove garlic
1 teaspoon chopped ginger	Juice of 1 or 2 limes (to taste)
1 scallion (white part only)	4-6 fresh mint leaves, chopped

Pound the ingredients together in a mortar, first removing the mint leaves from the stems. Add the lime juice and stir to desired consistency and taste.

Bananas

Slice bananas crosswise on the diagonal and serve cold.

Cucumber Chutney

Chop fresh, peeled cucumbers and serve in a little salt and vinegar.

Tomato Chutney

Peel several tomatoes and chop them finely. Add a little minced onion and a drop or two of lemon or lime juice.

Peanuts

Fresh-roasted nuts are a common and delicious side dish. Serve them whole or crushed.

Green Peppers

Coarsely chop a small green bell pepper, and serve in a small amount of vinegar and salt.

Coconut Chutney

Combine unsweetened, or freshly grated, coconut with chopped mint leaves, a pinch of cayenne pepper, cumin and salt, and a few drops of lemon.

Date Chutney

Pit and chop the dates. Season them with a little turmeric, coriander, salt and pepper, and lemon juice.

Raisin Chutney

Raisins alone are an outstanding side dish, but they can be flavored with a little ground ginger, sugar, cayenne, pepper, vinegar, and powdered mustard.

Onion Chutney

This is also very popular. Slice the onions paper-thin and mix with a little minced green pepper, lime juice, and salt.

Lemon and Lime

Though not actually a chutney, lemon and lime wedges or slices are almost always present on the dinner table to add that extra touch to the flavor of the food.

Ghee

Ghee is made simply by melting butter and straining it through cheesecloth. This removes the solids, which prevents the butter from burning and turning brown when used in cooking.

Garam Masala

Though the Indian cook uses a wide variety of spices, and will grind them daily according to her need, she frequently will combine a specially favored blend of spices and make up a fairly large supply for future use. Called a *garam masala,* this blend probably comes in as many versions as there are cooks in India, and can be very hot, very mild, or very fragrant. Here's one version which will make a half cup or so. (Kept tightly closed, garam masala will keep for several months.)

3 tablespoons coriander seeds
3 tablespoons cumin seeds
½ tablespoon whole black pep-
    percorns

1 teaspoon cardamom seeds
1 3-inch stick cinnamon
4-6 whole cloves

Combine all in an electric blender and grind at high speed for 20-30 seconds.

🌿 Chapter 4 🌿

The Middle East

Writings of the Pharaonic ages show the presence of chicken as well as other fowl in their cuisines. It is known that Egypt developed an incubator so efficient it could handle thousands of eggs at a time. The eggs were probably meant for eating, as chicken meat was not held in the same regard as pigeon, thrush, or other exotic birds, which the peasants snared with nets stretched between long bamboo poles. But both the chicken and the egg played prominent roles in Egypt's religion and superstitions, and cockfighting was the favorite sport. It is not unlikely that many a loser found his way into the soup pot. Pigeons were the food of royalty, held in high respect, and were actually bred for the table. This practice has survived, and today Egypt is one of the few countries in the world that produces domestic pigeons for eating.

The Egyptian cuisine today is quite similar to that of her Arab neighbors to the east, but there are two peasant dishes—*Melokhia* and *Ful Medames*—that were probably enjoyed by the peasants of the Pharaonic dynasties just as they are now. Melokhia, a soup considered the national dish of Egypt, is the wedding of a long-boiled chicken in its broth with the spinach-like herb melokhia. It is not likely to appeal to the taste of the average Westerner, but to the Egyptian it is manna. Ful medames is a bean dish usually served with hard boiled eggs, and it too continues, three millennia later, as a standard daily meal for the peasants. With the virtual disappearance of the ancient Egyptian cuisine, there remain today three distinct cooking styles in the Middle East—Persian, Turkish, and Arabic. One might add Armenian cooking also, for though Armenia is now a part of the U.S.S.R. its roots are Middle Eastern, and the influence of its gastronomy on the others of the region is very noticeable.

The standout cuisine in the Middle East belongs to Persia, and it is more responsible for the character of Middle Eastern cookery than any other. Persian food is richly spiced, but not nearly as hot as that of the other Middle Eastern countries, and one reason for this is that Persians use yogurt (*mast*) frequently, both as an ingredient and as a side dish to help keep the heat down. It is also used as a base for flavoring numerous sauces that are poured over virtually everything—meat, vegetable, salad, or rice.

Two of the outstanding features of Persian cooking are their rice preparations and the *Koreshe*. The Persians cook rice with the same reverence as do the Indonesians, and they do it in two ways: *Chelo* and *Polo*. Chelo is steamed rice, cooked alone, which acts as the base or center over which the koreshe or other foods are served. In preparing chelo the rice is cooked and drained. Butter is then melted in a pot and the rice is spooned back in the form of a cone. The pot is covered with towels to absorb the steam, then the rice is cooked again for 30 minutes or more. When done, the rice cone will have a golden crust at the bottom while the rest will be pure white.

Polo (which becomes *Pollo, Pilau, Pulao, Pilaf,* or *Pilaff* as one goes east or west) is a dish in which rice and other ingredients such as meat, vegetables, nuts, spices, and herbs are cooked together, all at once. Two polo dishes containing chicken have gained an international reputation. *Morg Polo,* chicken and rice (this became *Murgh Pulao* when the Moguls took it to Afghanistan), is a favorite on such festive occasions as weddings, feast days, and particularly the Persian New Year. The other is *Shirini Polo,* a dish served exclusively to royalty. *Shirini* means "sweet," and the sweetness in this dish comes from candied orange peels and carrots. A koreshe is a sauce in Persia, but Westerners would liken it more to a stew. A wide variety of ingredients can go into a koreshe, and they are invariably served over chelo. Koreshe dishes also illustrate the Persians' uninhibited use of fruit, for pomegranates, apples, peaches, prunes, cherries, quinces, and apricots are all featured each in its own koreshe. Persia's classic koreshe is *Fasenjam,* which was originally a wild duckling sauced with a walnut and pomegranate mixture. It is still their supreme masterpiece, but today chicken frequently replaces the duck.

Turkish cooking is very different from that of Iran, though it too has its roots in one of the Middle East's ancient civilizations—the Byzantine Empire. The cuisine is substantial and varied and has distinct Eastern overtones where the country borders Armenia, but it lacks the flair and imagination of the Persian kitchen. In western Turkey, lamb is the staple meat, as it is throughout the Middle East, but when the Turks celebrate, the occasion usually features a fowl. Whether it is chicken, turkey, goose, duck, or gamebird, it is most frequently cooked in one of two ways—stuffed (*dolmasi*) with rich mixtures of nuts, bulgur (or burghul), couscous, or fruits and then roasted; or cut up and cooked as a *yahni,* which is a stew richly flavored with spices, vegetables, nuts, or fruit. In eastern Turkey one finds a strong Armenian influence featuring traditional kababs and pilafs of wide variety and perhaps the world's most versatile dish, *Circassian Chicken.* Here the meat is shredded and served with pilaf, over which a well-seasoned walnut sauce is spooned. It can be the main entrée, an hors d'oeuvre, a sandwich filling, or a salad.

Chicken is a very popular meat in Turkey, and so is turkey, and it provides one of the area's interesting culinary footnotes. Turkey (the bird) is featured in Turkey (the country) on New Year's Eve. The Turks call it *hindi* and serve it with chestnuts (*Kesteneli Hindi*) or filled with a pine-nut stuffing (*Hindi Dolmasi*). But the turkey is native to Central America and was brought back by the Spanish and Jesuit priests to Europe only four centuries ago. The name hindi allegedly was given by the Turks, who thought the bird came from the Far East, which is what the New World was thought to be at first.

The last true Middle Eastern cooking style belongs to the Arabs, and it is simpler and less sophisticated than the others. The desert Arabs live on lamb or goat (and an occasional camel), rice, and yogurt (*laban*). Chicken and beef are scarce because of the climate and lack of pasturage, and pork is rarely found except in the most cosmopolitan restaurants, since both Jewish and Moslem dietary laws forbid it. Though chicken is rare in the desert, there is one unique dish, *Foudja Djedad* (diced chicken-stuffed apples), which has become something of a national favorite in Saudi Arabia.

The Arab cuisine improves immensely as one moves away from the desert to the metropolitan centers of Lebanon, Syria, Jordan, Iraq, and Israel. Lamb is still the favored meat, but the simplicity of Arab cooking is well illustrated by a number of chicken dishes in which a single seasoning or two will flavor the dish rather than a blend— cinnamon chicken pilaf, garlic chicken, sesame chicken, to name just a few.

The Israeli cuisine is not particularly distinct from the Arab. One thing that does stand out, however, is that Israeli cooking is not that of the Central European Jews, even though immigrants from these countries do make up the majority of Israel's current inhabitants.

Because of the climate the heavy gastronomy of Europe finds no place in the Middle East.

The desert Arabs' cooking may not have the sophistication of the Persians and Turks, but they do have one dish that's in a class by itself. It's the largest single dish in the world, and it includes chicken. According to the *Guinness Book of Records,* the Bedouins will occasionally roast a whole camel for a wedding feast. "Cooked eggs are stuffed in fish, the fish stuffed in cooked chickens, the chickens stuffed into a roasted sheep carcass and the sheep stuffed into a whole camel."

RECOMMENDED READING: Rachel Hogrogian, *The Armenian Cookbook* (New York: Atheneum, 1971); Claudia Roden, *A Book of Middle Eastern Cookery* (New York: Knopf, 1972); Sonia Uvezian, *The Cuisine of Armenia* (New York: Harper & Row, 1974)

MAIL ORDER SOURCE FOR INGREDIENTS:

Mrs. DeWildt
RFD 1
Bangor, Pa., 18013

TURKEY

CIRCASSIAN CHICKEN

1 3-pound chicken	1 celery stalk, sliced lengthwise
2 quarts water	Salt
1 carrot, scraped and cut length-	½ teaspoon paprika
wise into 4 pieces	1 tablespoon chopped parsley
	Black olives, pitted and sliced

Place the chicken in a large pot with the carrot, celery, and a little salt and add 2 quarts of water. Bring to the boil, skim, then cover and cook over moderate heat for about 40 minutes or until the chicken is tender. Remove the chicken and let cool but retain the broth. When cooled, debone the chicken and discard the skin, then shred the meat into small pieces and set aside and keep warm. Strain the stock—this should produce enough for the walnut sauce and the pilaf.

Make the walnut sauce (see below) and mix the shredded chicken with about 1 cup of the sauce. Then make a plain pilaf (see recipe below). Mound the pilaf in the center of a serving platter and spoon the chicken mixture over. Now spoon the walnut sauce over the chicken, sprinkle with paprika, and garnish with chopped parsley and sliced black olives. Serves 4-6.

Note: This recipe calls for serving the chicken and sauce (below) warm. Both can be served cold, however, in a salad or sandwich, without the pilaf.

Walnut Sauce

1½ cups stock from chicken	1 clove garlic, chopped
2 cups shelled walnuts	1 medium onion, chopped
3 slices bread, crust removed	Salt and pepper

Soak the bread in a small amount of chicken stock so it is moist. Put into a blender with half the walnuts, half the onions and garlic, and about ¾ cup of chicken stock. Cover and blend at medium speed for about 10 seconds. Add another slice of bread, half the remaining walnuts, onions, garlic, and half the remaining chicken stock and blend another 10 seconds. Now add all the remaining ingredients and blend until the entire mixture has reached the consistency of a smooth paste. Adjust the consistency to your liking by the amount of stock you add.

Pilaf

1½ cups long grain rice   2½ cups chicken stock
6 tablespoons butter   Salt and freshly ground pepper

Soak the rice in hot water for about 15 minutes, then drain. Melt 2 tablespoons butter in a saucepan, add the chicken stock and salt and pepper, and bring to a boil. Add the rice, stir a moment, then cover and reduce heat to low. Simmer for about 20 minutes until the pan liquid is absorbed. Remove from the heat, add the remaining butter, and replace cover with a napkin or towel. Let stand for 20 minutes before serving.

TURKEY

TUVUKLU BULGUR—Chicken with Bulgur

1 3-pound chicken, cut up   Seeds from 2 cardamom pods,
4 tablespoons butter   ground
Salt and freshly ground pepper   ½ teaspoon ground coriander
2 medium onions, chopped   1 teaspoon whole cumin seed,
1 large (or 2 small) garlic cloves,   ground
   chopped   Grated rind and juice of ½ lemon
1 cup bulgur   2 cups fresh chicken stock

Preheat oven to 350° F.

Melt the butter in a skillet and brown the chicken on all sides, sprinkling on a little salt and pepper as it cooks. Remove the chicken, then sauté the onions and garlic gently until golden. Add the bulgur and stir thoroughly until the pan liquid is absorbed and the onions and bulgur are mixed.

Place the chicken pieces in a medium to large casserole and sprinkle with a little more salt and pepper. Add the cardamom, coriander, and cumin and the rind and juice of lemon. Pour in the chicken stock and then spoon the bulgur on top of the chicken. Cover and bake for 1 hour. Serve directly from the casserole. Serves 4-6.

Bulgur Pilaf

An excellent variation of this is a bulgur pilaf. Cook the chicken, onions, and garlic as above, then remove the chicken pieces and keep warm. Pour the cup of bulgur into the pan and mix with onions and garlic. Pour in 1½ cups of chicken stock and salt and freshly ground pepper. Bring the pot to the boil, then reduce the heat to low and cook slowly for 30 minutes. Mound the pilaf on a platter and place the chicken pieces around it and serve.

Other variations include the addition of small amounts of cubed tomatoes, or cheese, or 1 tablespoon of pine (pignolia) nuts, walnuts, or almonds.

TURKEY

TUVUKLU GUVEC—Chicken and Vegetable Casserole

1 3-pound chicken, cut up	2 onions, chopped coarsely
6-8 tablespoons butter	1 pound peas
Salt and pepper	1 pound string beans
1 medium eggplant	6 medium potatoes, peeled and
1 medium squash	quartered
2 green peppers, cut into strips	½ cup water

Preheat the oven to 350° F.

In a skillet, sauté the chicken pieces in 4 tablespoons of butter until golden. Place the chicken in a large casserole and add salt and pepper.

Peel and slice the eggplant and squash and sauté in the skillet, adding more butter if necessary, for about 2-3 minutes. Add to the casserole. Sauté the peppers very lightly and add with the onions to the casserole. Add the peas, beans, potatoes, and tomatoes to the pot and sprinkle with a little salt and pepper. Now pour in ½ cup water, cover, and bake in the oven for 1 hour. Serves 4-6.

TURKEY

KOFTIT FERAKH—Chicken Balls

This is a delightful appetizer but can be enlarged to make a main dish as well.

2 cooked chicken breasts	1 small onion, chopped finely
2 slices white bread, crusts re-moved	⅛ teaspoon turmeric
	¼ teaspoon sage
½ cup milk	¼ teaspoon rosemary
1 egg	Juice of ½ lemon
Salt and pepper	Flour
	Oil for frying

Remove the chicken meat from the bones and discard the skin. Soak the bread in the milk and squeeze almost dry, then put the meat and bread through the fine blade of a grinder. Place the meat and bread mixture in a bowl, add the salt and pepper, egg, then the onion, turmeric, sage, rosemary, and lemon juice and combine thoroughly. Roll the mixture into small balls for appetizers or large for a main dish (this recipe should be doubled for a main dish for 4 persons). Roll the balls in flour and fry in deep oil, then serve immediately. Makes 12-16.

TURKEY

HINDI DOLMASI—Stuffed Turkey (or Chicken)
This is also a favorite of the Turkish community on Cyprus.

1 cup long or medium grain rice	⅔ cup butter
3 cups fresh chicken stock	¼ cup pignolia (pine) nuts
1 8-10-pound turkey with heart, liver, and gizzard	Salt and freshly ground pepper
	¼ cup black currants
	2 onions, chopped finely

Cover the rice in a bowl with very hot water. Add 1 tablespoon salt, then let soak for 15 minutes.

Preheat the oven to 350°F. Place the turkey in a roasting pan, breast side up, and smear it liberally with butter. Add 1 cup of stock, cover, and roast for ¾ hour. Dice the giblets and sauté in a little butter until they lose their pink color—about 5 minutes. Stir constantly or they'll burn. Set aside.

Melt 4 tablespoons butter in a saucepan and sauté the pignolia nuts and rice over low to moderate heat for 10 minutes, again stirring continuously. Now add the salt and pepper, currants, and 1 cup of boiling stock. Stir, cover, and cook for 15 minutes over moderate heat, then add the sautéed giblets and the onions. Mix well and remove from the heat.

When the turkey has been roasted for 1 hour, remove and stuff the cavity with the rice-onion-giblet mixture. Reserve any that is left over. Sew or skewer the cavity closed and return the bird to the roasting pan. Roast for 1¼ hours, covered, basting frequently. Add more stock if it evaporates. Remove cover and roast another 15 minutes so that the turkey is a nice golden brown.

The leftover rice may be used to supplement the stuffing at the table. Add ½ cup of boiling stock to the rice in a saucepan. Cover and cook until the liquid is absorbed. Remove from heat and place a towel over the pan, then re-cover and let sit for 30 minutes or so. Serves 6-8.

TURKEY

TAVUK YAHNI—Chicken Stew
This is a close cousin, and possibly the forerunner, of the Greek *kota yahni.*

1 3-pound chicken, cut up	1 tablespoon flour
4 tablespoons butter	4 medium tomatoes, peeled and
12 small white onions	chopped
Salt and pepper	¾ cup water
½ teaspoon paprika	4 tablespoons red wine

Heat the butter in a medium-sized casserole or Dutch oven, then brown the chicken pieces on all sides. Remove the outer skins of the onions, and place them over and between the chicken pieces. Add salt and pepper to taste and sprinkle with paprika and flour. Now spoon in the chopped tomatoes and pour in the water. Cover and cook over medium heat for 30 minutes. Uncover, add the wine, and cook for another 2-3 minutes, then serve right from the casserole. Serves 4.

TURKEY

TAVUKLU BOEREK—Chicken-Filled Pastries
This can be made in several different ways. A boerek can be a main dish, a luncheon side dish, or an unusual new picnic dish. The pastry dough is *yafka,* the Turkish version of the better known *phyllo* (or *fila*) of Greece. (It's also known as *brik* or *malsouka* in Tunisia.)
Boerek is a pastry, and its filling can be virtually anything that pleases you: a nut-honey mixture, tuna fish, cheese and mushrooms, or creamed cheese; in fact it's excellent with the walnut sauce in Circassian Chicken. Here's one version using chopped chicken with onions and tomatoes.

1 3-pound chicken, cut up
8 ounces butter or oil
4 onions, chopped finely
2 cups fresh chicken stock

2 tomatoes, peeled and chopped
Pinch rosemary
Salt and pepper
1 teaspoon parsley flakes
12 phyllo or yafka sheets

Heat the oil in a skillet and brown the chicken pieces until golden, then set aside. Now add the chopped onions to the pan and sauté gently until tender. Add broth, tomato, rosemary, and a little salt and pepper and return the chicken pieces. Cover and cook on a low flame for about 40 minutes. Set aside to cool.

Skin the chicken pieces and remove the bones. Cut the meat into small 1-inch squares and return to the pan. Add parsley and stir well.

Preheat the oven to 350° F. Lay one sheet of phyllo pastry on a bread board, brush with butter, then lay another sheet on top. Put one-sixth of the chicken mixture in the center and fold the phyllo pastry sheets across from each side. Brush again, then fold the ends to make a square package. Repeat this step with the remaining mixture and sheets. Now place the boerek on a greased pastry sheet and bake for 30 minutes in the oven until a golden brown. Serves 6.

TURKEY/ARMENIA

PILIC DOLMASI (POROV HAV)—Stuffed Roast Chicken

1 cup long or medium grain rice
Salt
½ pound lean lamb or veal, minced
Oil or butter

¼ cup pignolia (pine) nuts
¼ cup raisins or currants
1½ cups fresh chicken stock
2 onions, chopped finely
1 4-pound roasting chicken
Parsley for garnish

Cover the rice in a bowl with very hot water. Add 1 tablespoon salt and let soak for 15 minutes. Sauté the lamb or veal lightly in 2 tablespoons butter or oil for 5 minutes, stirring constantly. Remove from heat and set aside.

Melt about ¼ cup butter or oil in a saucepan. Drain the rice and add to the pan with the pignolia nuts and sauté gently for 8-10 minutes, then add the raisins and a cup of stock. Bring to the boil quickly, stirring, then reduce the heat to moderate, cover, and cook for about 10 minutes. Now add the lamb and onions and continue cooking for 5 more minutes, stirring frequently. Brush the chicken liberally with melted butter, then fill the cavity with the rice and meat stuffing. Reserve any leftover rice mixture to supplement the main course. Roast the chicken uncovered at moderately low heat (325-350° F) until golden and tender. This should take about 20-30 minutes per pound. Baste frequently.

If you wish to supplement the rice for the main course, add about ½ cup of stock to the remaining rice mixture and cook over low heat for 10 minutes or until the liquid is absorbed. Remove from the heat and cover the pan with a towel. Then replace the cover and let the rice sit for 30 minutes or so, keeping warm.

Place the chicken on a serving platter, garnish it with parsley, and serve the remaining rice in a separate bowl. Serves 4-6.

IRAN

EGGAH—Chicken and Egg Pancake

No Middle Eastern cookery book would be complete without an eggah recipe. An *Eggah* is an Arabian omelet, though it's more like a piece of bread or toast when it's finished. It is speculated that the Moors brought the original eggah back with them from Spain centuries ago.

Here's one eggah recipe (there are many), which uses chicken or turkey and which can be served either as a first or a main course.

2 chicken breasts, cooked and cut into small cubes	6 eggs
	1 clove garlic, minced
1 medium onion, chopped finely	1 teaspoon cumin powder
Butter or oil for frying	1 teaspoon parsley flakes
	Salt and pepper

In a large skillet sauté the chopped onion in oil gently until golden. Beat the eggs in a bowl and add garlic, cumin, parsley, and a little salt and pepper. Mix well, then stir in the onion and the chicken cubes.

Return the mixture to the skillet with a little more butter or oil. Cook over very low heat for about 30 minutes or until well set. Now turn the eggah and brown the other side, or put it under the broiler to finish the top until browned. Turn onto a heated platter and serve at once. Serves 4-6.

IRAN

MORG POLO—Chicken with Rice

Morg polo is the favorite dish in Iran on festive occasions such as weddings or holidays, and particularly on the Persian New Year.

1 3-pound chicken	¼ teaspoon cinnamon
2/3 cup butter or oil for frying	Salt and pepper
1 large onion, chopped finely	½ cup dried apricots, chopped
½ teaspoon sage	2½ cups rice
½ teaspoon thyme	⅔ cup seedless raisins or currants

Heat 2 tablespoons butter or oil in a large skillet and sauté the onions, then remove from the pan and set aside. Combine the sage, thyme, salt, pepper, and cinnamon and sprinkle over the chicken. Add 4 tablespoons butter to the pan and brown the chicken slowly on all sides for 10 minutes, then remove and set aside. While the chicken cooks, wash and soak the raisins or currants in cold water for 5 minutes. Melt 1½ tablespoons butter or oil in the same skillet and sauté the raisins (or currants) and apricots on a low fire for 3 minutes, then set aside. Cook the rice as in the chelo recipe (page 124) but after putting ½ the boiled rice in the pot over butter, add the sautéed chicken, onions, raisins, and apricots over the rice. Add the rest of the rice and pour over the remaining butter. Cover and cook over low fire for one hour. Serves 4-6.

IRAN

KORESHE HOLU—Chicken with Peach Sauce

1 3-pound chicken, cut up	1 onion, chopped
Salt and pepper	3 tablespoons lemon juice
¼ teaspoon paprika	4 large firm peaches, sliced as for a pie
8 tablespoons butter	2 tablespoons lime juice
2 cups water	½ cup sugar

Sprinkle the chicken pieces with salt, pepper, and paprika and brown lightly in 4 tablespoons butter. Add 1 cup of water, cover, and simmer for about 30 minutes. Now melt 2 tablespoons butter in a skillet and sauté the chopped onions gently for 2-3 minutes. Remove and add 1 tablespoon of lemon juice. In a third skillet, melt 2 tablespoons butter and sauté the sliced peaches over low heat for 2-3 minutes.

Now add the onions to the chicken and spoon over the peaches. Mix the remaining lemon and lime juice together and pour over the chicken. Add 1 cup of water, cover, and simmer for 20 minutes. Serve over chelo (see below). Serves 4.

Note: This recipe can be altered to include oranges, plums, apricots, or sour cherries.

Chelo

In Iran, there is a very special way of cooking a chelo. If you use Iranian rice or any other long grain rice, cover it with water and soak it for an hour or two with 1½ tablespoons salt for every pound of rice. Then pour off the soak water and slowly add the rice to boiling water (3 cups of water per cup of rice). Boil for 10-15 minutes, stirring every few minutes. Now rinse the rice in a strainer with lukewarm water, then add 4 tablespoons of melted butter to the pot in which the rice was originally cooked. Return the rice on top of the butter, spooning it in carefully to form a cone. Add 2 tablespoons water at the same time. Melt 4 more tablespoons butter and pour over the rice. Now put two layers of paper toweling over the pot, cover, and cook for 10-15 minutes on medium heat. The toweling will absorb the excess moisture and permit the rice to steam without getting soggy. Lower the heat and cook for 35-40 minutes.

The rice will form a golden crust at the bottom while the rest remains white. If desired, add more melted butter before serving. You should be able to serve 4 people comfortably with each cup of rice.

IRAN

KORESHE MAST va KARI—
Curried Chicken with Yogurt Sauce

1 3-pound chicken, cut up	1 teaspoon ground pepper
3 cups water	1 stalk celery
2 teaspoons salt	1 carrot

Yogurt Sauce

4 cups yogurt
2 eggs
1 onion, chopped finely
½ teaspoon allspice

¼ teaspoon each of ground coriander, cumin, clove, black pepper, and cardamom seed
1 tablespoon flour
1 tablespoon butter

Place the chicken in a Dutch oven with the water and 1 teaspoon each of salt and pepper and the celery and carrot. Cover, bring to the boil, then reduce heat and simmer for 1 hour, skimming off the scum as it rises. Remove the chicken and let cool, then remove the skin and bones and cut the meat into strips about ¼ inch wide.

Put the yogurt into a double boiler with the eggs, the chopped onion, the remaining salt, the allspice, and the curry spices. Beat thoroughly, then add flour and the butter, a little at a time, stirring constantly. Now put the double boiler over low heat and stir continuously for 10 minutes, until the sauce thickens. Be sure not to cover or overheat the mixture or it will curdle. Now add the chicken strips to the sauce and cook for another 5 minutes. Serve over chelo (page 124). Serves 4-6.

IRAN

KORESHE FESENJAM—Duck (or Chicken) with Pomegranate and Nut Sauce

1 4-pound duck, or 3-pound
  chicken, cut up
8 tablespoons butter or oil
2 teaspoons salt
½ teaspoon turmeric
½ teaspoon freshly ground
  pepper

1 large onion, chopped finely
2 cups walnuts, crushed
4 cups water
½ teaspoon cinnamon
¼ cup lemon juice
¼ cup pomegranate syrup
2 teaspoons tomato sauce
1-2 tablespoons sugar (to taste)

Sauté the duck or chicken pieces in 6 tablespoons butter or oil with salt, turmeric, and pepper until golden brown on all sides (about 10 minutes). Put aside. Add 2 tablespoons butter to the skillet and sauté the chopped onion gently, then add the walnuts and heat over medium fire for 5 minutes, stirring constantly. Be careful not to burn the walnuts. Now add water, cinnamon, lemon juice, and pomegranate syrup and the tomato sauce. Cover and simmer for about 30 minutes. Add sugar (to taste) to the sauce if it is too sour. Return the duck or chicken to the skillet, cover, and let simmer for 30 minutes. Serve with chelo (page 124). Serves 4-6.

IRAN

SHRINI POLO—Chicken with Sweet Rice

8 tablespoons butter
Peels of 2 oranges, cut into strips lengthwise
3 carrots, peeled and cut into 1-inch long strips about ¼-inch wide
1 cup almonds
1 cup sugar

1 teaspoon saffron, ground and dissolved in 1 teaspoon warm water
¼ cup pistachios, chopped
¼ cup olive oil
1 3-pound chicken, cut up
Salt
3 cups water
2 large onions, quartered
4 tablespoons butter, melted
½ pound long grain white rice
Parsley for garnish

Prepare the rice for chelo (page 124).

Blanch the orange peels by putting them into a pan of boiling water for 1 minute. Take from the fire, pour off the hot water, and immerse in cold. Set aside. Repeat with the almonds, discard the skins, and set aside.

Melt 8 tablespoons butter in a large skillet, then add the carrots and cook over moderate heat for 15 minutes. Do not brown. Now add the orange peel, almonds, sugar, and saffron and stir for a few moments to be sure the sugar dissolves, then cover and simmer for 20 minutes. This will candy the carrots and the orange. Add the pistachio nuts and continue simmering for 5 minutes, then remove the pan from the heat and set aside.

Heat the oil in a Dutch oven and brown the chicken pieces thoroughly, a few pieces at a time. When done, remove the chicken and pour off the remaining oil, then return the chicken to the pan, and sprinkle with salt. Now add 3 cups of water and the onions, cover, and simmer for 30 minutes.

While the chicken cooks, bring 3 cups of water to the boil and add the rice. Boil actively for about 5 minutes, then drain through a sieve. In the same pot melt the remaining 4 tablespoons butter, then spoon in ½ the rice. Add ½ the carrot and orange mixture on top of the rice, then add the remainder of the rice, then the remainder of the candied carrots and orange peel. Cover and simmer for 30 minutes.

When both the chicken and rice are done, mound the rice in the center of a serving platter, and arrange the chicken pieces around it. Garnish with parsley. Serves 4-6.

EGYPT

MELOKHIA

This is the national peasant soup of Egypt and is eaten once or twice a day. *Melokhia* is a green leafy herb that looks much like spinach, but is earthier in taste and much stronger. Melokhia is cooked in water with other vegetables, or with chicken or other meat, or is eaten fresh during the summer. It is also dried and stored for other seasons. I have found the dried form in some specialty or gourmet stores in America.

Before cooking the dried melokhia, however, it must be crushed between your fingers or in a blender, then soaked in a little hot water, the amount depending on how much you are preparing. The idea is to get the crushed leaves to swell to about double in size, so add only enough for the leaves to absorb.

Make the stock by covering a chicken with water and boiling it for 2 hours or more until the meat is just falling off the bones. Slice a carrot and a stalk of celery and add with some salt and pepper. You want to end up with about 8 cups of stock (which is about 2 quarts), so you may have to adjust the water as you go along. Remove the bird and bone it, saving the meat. Strain the stock and bring to the boil, then add the soaked and strained melokhia leaves.

Boil over low heat for 30 minutes. Chop up 4 cloves of garlic and sauté for 5 minutes with salt. Add ⅛ teaspoon red pepper and cook for 1 minute more. Add this to the melokhia about 10 minutes before it is ready, stir once or twice, then cover and finish cooking. This preparation can be eaten as a soup or with rice and chicken meat from which the stock was made.

Egypt

CHICKEN WITH HOMMOS (Chickpeas)

1 3-pound chicken, cut up	4 medium tomatoes, peeled and
6 tablespoons butter	chopped
1 clove garlic, sliced	2 tablespoons tomato paste
12 small white onions, peeled and	1 10-ounce can chickpeas
washed	Salt and pepper
	Paprika
	1 cup fresh chicken stock

Melt 3 tablespoons butter in a large skillet and sauté the garlic and onions (whole) for about 5 minutes, stirring continuously. Remove onions and brown the chicken pieces in the same butter, adding a little more if necessary. Remove the chicken from the pan when golden and keep warm.

Melt 3 tablespoons butter in a saucepan and add the chopped tomatoes, tomato paste, and stock. Cover and cook over low heat for 30 minutes. When done, drain and wash the chickpeas under hot water, and add to the pot. Now add the onions, cover, and cook for an additional 10 minutes. Pour the vegetable mixture over the chicken in the frying pan. Add salt, pepper, and paprika and the stock to keep the dish moist. Cover and cook for about 20 minutes over moderate heat. Serves 4.

Egypt

CHICKEN LIVER PILAF

1 onion, chopped	½ pound chicken livers
2 tablespoons butter	1 cup long grain rice
½ green pepper, seeded and diced	2 cups fresh chicken stock
10 medium to large mushrooms,	Salt and pepper
sliced	1 tablespoon almonds, blanched,
	peeled, and crushed

Preheat the oven to 400° F. Sauté the onion and green pepper gently in 1 tablespoon butter for 5 minutes, then add the sliced mushrooms and cook for another 5 minutes. Remove all with a slotted spoon and set aside. Now sauté the chicken livers for 3 minutes or so, until the pink color is lost. Remove from the heat and slice. Heat the remaining butter in a saucepan and pour in the rice. Stir constantly for a minute so that every grain is covered with butter.

Now mix together thoroughly in a casserole the onions, peppers, mushrooms, chicken livers, and the rice. Pour in 2 cups of chicken stock, season with salt and pepper and stir in the crushed almonds. Bake for 20 minutes in a hot oven (400° F), then serve with roast chicken or other meats. Serves 4.

Note: This pilaf makes an excellent stuffing for chicken. Increase the recipe slightly if you want extra for a stuffing. Also try the pilaf with the *hamud* (page 130).

EGYPT

HAMAM MAHSHI—Braised Stuffed Pigeons (or Spring Chickens)

This is an Egyptian classic. Pigeons are a great delicacy in Egypt, where they are bred for the table, and Egypt is one of the few countries where this is still done. In America squab or young gamebirds, or a small, fresh spring chicken will do very well. This dish should be made with *fireek,* which is a coarsely crushed whole-wheat grain similar to Turkish bulgur. Depending on the number of pigeons, you will need about ½ cup of stuffing each. This recipe is for 4 pigeons or doves about 1 pound each, or for two small spring chickens.

4 pigeons or doves, or 2 small spring chickens	2 cups fireek (or substitute an equal amount of bulgur or cracked wheat)
¼ pound butter for frying	
1 medium onion, chopped finely	Salt and pepper
2 cups chicken stock	4 cups fresh chicken stock
Hearts, gizzards, and livers, chopped finely	Parsley flakes

Preheat the oven to 350° F. In about 4 tablespoons of butter sauté the chopped onions for 5 minutes, then add the chopped giblets and sauté another 5 minutes. Add the fireek (or bulgur) and salt and stir for 2 or 3 minutes, making sure to cover each wheat grain with butter. Now season each bird inside and out with salt and pepper, then stuff each with the fireek mixture. Retain the remaining fireek. Skewer or truss both neck and breast cavities of each bird and smear liberally with the remaining butter. Place the birds, breast side up, in a large casserole and pour in 2 cups of stock. Bring to the boil on top of the stove, then put into the oven, cover, and cook for about one hour, basting frequently.

When the birds are half cooked, bring the remaining stock to the boil and add the leftover fireek, stirring constantly. Reduce heat and simmer until the birds are ready. All the liquid should be absorbed by the fireek.

Serve the pigeons on a platter sprinkled with parsley flakes, and the fireek in a separate bowl. Serves 4.

EGYPT

HAMUD—Chicken Soup with Lemon
This is actually more than a simple chicken soup. Hamud may be served twice in the same meal—as a soup at the beginning and again as a sauce for rice or meat in a later course.

1 chicken carcass and giblets	2 cloves garlic
2 quarts water	1 tablespoon salt
2 stalks celery, sliced	⅛ teaspoon pepper
2 carrots, sliced	Juice of 1-2 lemons
2 shallots, sliced	5-6 tablespoons cooked rice

Put the chicken bones and giblets in a large saucepan with the celery, carrots, shallots, garlic, salt and pepper, and 2 quarts of water. Bring to the boil, then add the juice of one lemon. Reduce heat to low and simmer for 1 hour, skimming off the scum as it rises. Now remove the chicken carcass, let it cool, then pick off all the meat and return it to the soup. Add more lemon juice to give it the level you desire. Some cooked rice may be added just as it is served, and this will add to the body and character of the hamud.

ARAB

BARBECUED GARLIC CHICKEN
(with Lemon, and with Mint)
Garlic grows profusely in the Middle East and is very popular in all cookery of the area. Here are two Arab standards, the first of which modifies the garlic taste with lemon and the second with mint.

With Lemon

1 3-pound chicken, cut up	Salt and pepper
5 cloves garlic	Juice of 2 lemons
	Oil or butter

Crush the garlic and mix well with salt and pepper and 1 tablespoon lemon juice. Rub a little of this mixture on each piece of chicken. Prepare a marinade of ½ cup oil and the remaining lemon juice and pour over the chicken. Let marinate for 1 hour.

Over a hot charcoal fire, or under the broiler, cook the chicken on both sides until done. Baste with remaining garlic and lemon marinade. Serve with rice. Serves 4.

With Mint

8 tablespoons butter	¼ teaspoon freshly ground
6 cloves garlic	pepper
1 teaspoon salt	1 3-pound chicken, cut up
	½ cup flour
	½ cup fresh mint

In a large skillet, melt 2 tablespoons butter and brown the garlic slowly. Combine salt and pepper and the flour and dredge each piece of chicken thoroughly. Remove the browned garlic pieces from the skillet and melt the remaining butter. Add the chicken and fry until browned (30 minutes) over moderate to low heat. After the chicken pieces are done, add the mint, cover, and let sit for several minutes to absorb the flavor. Serve with rice. Serves 4.

SAUDI ARABIA

FOUDJA DJEDAD—Baked Chicken-Stuffed Apples

Breasts from 1 3-pound chicken,	¼ teaspoon clove powder
skin removed	Pinch ginger
Water	Pinch cinnamon
Salt and pepper	6 large cooking apples
3 tablespoons butter	Brown sugar
	½ cup breadcrumbs

Preheat the oven to 350° F. Cover the chicken with lightly salted

water and boil for 1 hour. Cut the meat from the bones and dice into
½-inch cubes. Mix with a little salt and pepper and then add 2
tablespoons soft butter, the clove powder, ginger, and cinnamon.
Core the apples but don't cut all the way through. Stuff the apples
with the mixture, spread over a little brown sugar, and top with
breadcrumbs. Place in a baking dish, cover, and bake for 30 minutes.
Reduce heat about 5 degrees every 6 or 7 minutes to be sure the apples
don't burst. After 30 minutes, remove the cover and bake for another
5 minutes to brown crumbs. Serves 6.

ARAB

CHICKEN WITH DATES

1 3-pound chicken, cut up
2 tablespoons butter or oil
Salt and pepper
Juice of 1 orange
1 cup chicken stock
1½ tablespoons cornstarch

Pinch each of cumin powder, coriander powder, clove powder, black pepper, nutmeg, and cinnamon
1 medium onion, chopped finely
Juice of 1 lemon
1 cup dates, pitted and chopped
½ green pepper, sliced
Orange slices

Preheat the oven to 350° F. In a casserole or Dutch oven, heat the
butter or oil, season the chicken with salt and pepper, then brown on
all sides until golden. When done remove the pieces to a plate and
pour off the excess oil.

While the chicken browns, combine the orange juice in a bowl with
the stock, cornstarch, cumin, coriander, clove, pepper, nutmeg, and
cinnamon, and the chopped onion and lemon juice. Pour into the
casserole and, over high heat, stir until the sauce thickens.

Now replace the chicken, spooning the sauce over each piece so all
are thoroughly covered. Put a cover on the casserole and place it in the
oven. Bake for 45 minutes. When done, place the chopped dates and
green pepper slices over the top of the chicken pieces along with
several orange slices as garnish. Serve directly from the casserole.
Serves 4.

ARAB

CINNAMON CHICKEN PILAF

2 3-pound chickens, cut up	2 teaspoons cinnamon
6 tablespoons oil or butter	2 cups long grain rice
Water	2 teaspoons blanched almonds,
Salt and freshly ground pepper	peeled and slivered
½ teaspoon allspice	2 teaspoons pignolia (pine) nuts

Heat the oil or butter and brown the chicken, a few pieces at a time, until golden. Put all the pieces in a Dutch oven and add water to cover (about 4 cups), salt and pepper, allspice, and cinnamon. Bring the pot to the boil quickly, then reduce the heat and simmer for 1 hour. Remove the chicken and strip the meat from the wings, legs, and thighs and cut into small cubes. Keep the remaining pieces warm.

Adjust the pot liquid to 4 cups by adding more water. Return the diced chicken, add the rice to the pot, cover, and place on simmer. While the rice cooks, sauté the blanched almonds and pignolia nuts very lightly in oil and stir into the pot. After 20 minutes or so, the water should be absorbed by the rice. If not, let the pot sit covered for a few more minutes off the fire.

Now mound the rice on a large platter, arrange the chicken breasts around it, and serve. Serves 4-6.

ARAB

SESAME CHICKEN

4 tablespoons butter or oil	1 cup flour
1 cup sesame seeds	1 egg
1 teaspoon paprika	¼ cup fresh chicken stock
Salt	1 3-pound chicken, quartered

Preheat the oven to 350° F. Heat the butter or oil in a large skillet. Combine the sesame seeds, paprika, a little salt, and the flour. Beat the egg and mix it with the stock, then dredge each chicken quarter first in the flour mixture, then in the egg, and then in the flour mixture again, and place in the skillet. Fry 2 or 3 pieces at a time until all are brown. Place the browned quarters in a baking dish and bake for 30 minutes. Serves 4.

ARAB

CHICKEN AND RICE CASSEROLE

1 3-pound chicken, cut up	½ cup heavy cream
8 tablespoons butter	½ cup milk
1 cup rice	1 cup fresh chicken stock
Salt and freshly ground pepper	½ teaspoon cinnamon

Preheat the oven to 375° F. Melt 4 tablespoons butter in a 2-3 quart casserole and brown the chicken pieces on all sides. Remove the chicken and keep warm. Now melt 2 more tablespoons butter in the casserole and pour in the rice. Remove from the heat and stir the rice so that each kernel is thoroughly coated with butter. Arrange the chicken pieces over the rice. Now bring the cream, milk, and stock to high heat (don't boil) in a saucepan, and pour it over the chicken in the casserole. Sprinkle salt and a few grindings of fresh pepper over the chicken and then sprinkle on the cinnamon. Cover and bake for 30 minutes. When done remove the casserole from the oven and let it rest, covered, for 15 or 20 minutes and then serve. Serves 4.

ARAB

CHICKEN WITH VERMICELLI

1 3-pound chicken	1 cardamom pod (cracked)
Salt and freshly ground pepper	4 quarts water, plus 1 cup
Juice and grated rind of ½ lemon	1 pound vermicelli
1 tablespoon olive oil	2 tablespoons butter
	1 teaspoon cinnamon

Season the chicken with salt and fresh pepper, inside and out. Rub the lemon juice and rind all over the chicken, then place it in a large casserole with the olive oil, cardamom pod, and 1 cup of water. Cover and cook the chicken for 1 hour, turning it occasionally and checking the water so it doesn't go dry.

When done, remove the meat from the chicken, discarding skin and bones, and cut it into small chunks. Reserve the pan liquid.

While the chicken cooks, bring 4 quarts of water to the boil and cook the vermicelli for about 5 minutes. Remove the chicken from the casserole, add the butter and pan liquid, and place half the partially cooked vermicelli in the bottom. Arrange the chicken over the vermicelli and sprinkle each piece with a little cinnamon, then spread the rest of the vermicelli over the chicken. Cook uncovered for 5 or so minutes, then serve with green vegetables. Serves 4.

❧ Chapter 5 ❧

Russia

Occupying the largest land area of any single country in the world, Russia borders China, the Subcontinent, the Middle East, and Europe, and the development of her gastronomy has been strongly influenced by all of her neighbors. During the prehistoric era, the land was home to Slavic nomads in the West and Asian Mongols in the East. The Slavs were people of the soil and are credited with developing the first agriculture in Russia. On the other hand, the Asians practiced no agriculture at all, but were savage warriors who lived in tents, moved constantly, and prided themselves on their fast horses and fearlessness in battle.

The gastronomy of the Slavs was coarse and heavy, dependent upon grain, soup, and root vegetables, and accented with the traditional ingredients of the Asians—sour cream (*smetna*), fermented mare's milk (*kumiss*), tea, sauerkraut, and horse meat, which was either raw and ground, or grilled on a sword. The amalgamation of these cooking styles became the early Russian cuisine, and this is what the Slavs and Tartars brought to eastern Europe during the Dark Ages.

The Tartars from Central Asia ruled Russia from the thirteenth to the fifteenth century, and their occupation merely reinforced the Asian influences that by then had become a featured part of the Russian cuisine. The Tartars were forced out in the fifteenth century by Ivan the Great and his son, Ivan the Terrible, who was crowned czar in 1547. During their rule, Russia became a feudal monarchy which was harshly oppressive to the peasants. A vast gap existed between the nobility, who lavished fortunes on their leisure, and the peasant, who barely scratched his subsistence from the soil. Despite their love of luxury, however, the banquet tables of the nobility were something less than elegant. Although vast quantities were consumed at each meal, the food was unseasoned and otherwise cooked with little imagination. No manners were expected or displayed, and no refined table service. Food was passed in bowls or on platters from person to person, in a manner still known as "Russian Service."

The style of the Russian court changed dramatically in 1762, when a German princess became Catherine the Great, Empress of Russia. Appalled by the lackluster food, vulgar service, and gross table manners of her court, Catherine trained her servants in the art of "French Service," where the food is placed on a plate and served individually to a guest. She hired master chefs from France and a platoon of culinary artists steeped in every phase of haute cuisine. Her lead was quickly followed by the Russian nobility, and in a short time French chefs were commanding a station and authority approaching that of the nobility itself.

French cooking and French chefs remained a part of Czarist Russia until the Revolution, with the exception of one brief period when Napoleon invaded the country. For a while then, everything French was frowned upon, but the Russians' newly acquired taste for *haute cuisine* led to an early forgiveness. During this century and a half some of the classic Russian dishes we know today were invented by Frenchmen for Russians. The great chicken salad—*Salade Olivier*—was created by a French chef for Czar Nicholas II, and Beef Stroganoff by another for the Count of that name. Perhaps the best-known Russian dish of all—Chicken Kiev—was inspired by the French school, at least the version that uses paté de foie gras instead of sweet butter.

While the French were transforming the nobles' cuisine, the peasant farmwife was developing her own traditional dishes. Buckwheat was the staple food of Old Russia, so she tried it with everything. Buckwheat groats (*kasha*) were eaten daily with cream and butter, or used as a stuffing for chicken. When ground into flour, kasha became the dough for a *Pirog,* a large pastry filled with meat or chicken and vegetables, or the cover for a *Pashtet,* a meat or vegetable pie.

Not all of Russia eats in the same manner as the Slavs of Great Russia and the Ukraine. The Baltic nations Lithuania, Estonia, and Latvia enjoy a cuisine very similar to that of their Scandinavian neighbors. This means fish is plentiful and chicken cookery scarce, although Latvia presents one interesting dish, a chicken pudding. On the other side of the nation lie the enormous and largely uninhabited areas of Central Russia and Siberia. This is an Asian land and offers little of interest in fowl cookery.

The Caucasus, however, presents an entirely different cuisine. This small and mountainous corner of Russia has a Middle Eastern heritage, and has borrowed a great deal from its Turkish neighbors. The Caucasian *Plov* (or *Palov*) is the Turkish *Pilaf,* a rice dish most often made with lamb, but more frequently now with chicken. Caucasians also make a chicken soup with lemon quite similar to the Turkish *Baud Lamon* or the Greek *Avgolemono.* On New Year's Day, the Armenians serve chicken in pomegranate sauce, a dish that appears to have originated in Persia and traveled to Turkey. But the Georgians have a unique chicken dish that is all their own—*Tabaka.* Here, the back is cut away and the wings tucked under the body. The bird is then placed on a grill with a heavy weight on it. In this condition, the chicken is grilled very quickly, and when finished retains its flattened shape. This method of cooking chicken and other birds was brought to the Balkans by the Bulgars a thousand years ago, but it has its origin in the campfires of ancient Tartary.

RECOMMENDED READING: Rachel Hagropian, *The Armenian Cookbook* (New York: Atheneum, 1971); Sonia Uvezian, *The Cuisine of Armenia* (New York: Harper & Row, 1974)

LATVIA

Huhner (Chicken) Pudding

1 3-pound chicken, skinned and
  boned
3-4 slices stale white bread
1 medium onion, minced
3 eggs, separated and beaten

3 tablespoons sour cream
½ cup fresh chicken stock
Salt and white pepper
2 tablespoons butter
Breadcrumbs for topping

Soak the bread in water, then squeeze almost dry. Put the chicken meat and the bread through the coarse blade of a meat grinder 2 or 3 times into a bowl. Add the minced onion, the beaten egg yolks, sour cream, stock, salt, and white pepper (or black pepper if white is not available). Thoroughly blend the mixture with a wooden spoon, then fold in the egg whites.

Preheat the oven to 350° F. Grease a small baking dish with part of the butter, then pour in the chicken mixture. Top with pats of butter and breadcrumbs and bake for 30 minutes. Serve hot with a sour cream or mushroom gravy along with boiled potatoes and a green salad. Serves 4.

ARMENIA

AJEM PILAF—Baked Chicken Pilaf

3 cups chicken stock
Salt and pepper
2½ cups rice

¼ teaspoon allspice
1 3-pound chicken, cut up
3 tablespoons butter

Preheat the oven to 325° F.

Bring the chicken stock to the boil in a saucepan, add salt and pepper, then the rice and the allspice. Reduce the heat to low, cover, and simmer for 10 minutes. Brown the chicken pieces for 15 minutes on both sides.

Now arrange the chicken pieces in a casserole and sprinkle with salt and pepper, then pour in the rice and stock. Dot with butter, cover, and place in the oven for half hour or until the chicken is tender. Serves 4-6.

Alternatives: Add a pinch or two of cinnamon to the rice for a sweeter version. Or add 2 chopped, peeled tomatoes to the pot about 10 minutes before serving (but omit the cinnamon).

UKRAINE

SALADE OLIVIER—Chicken Salad

A French chef in the service of Czar Nicholas II concocted Salade Olivier, which when first introduced to the Czar was pronounced a triumph and became an immediate sensation. It may be one of the best-known chicken salads in the world, and is the ancestor of one of the most popular luncheon dishes in America today.

1 3-pound chicken, cooked and the meat cubed	½ cup sour cream
	Salt and pepper
4 boiled potatoes, peeled and sliced	1 head lettuce, washed and shredded
4 hard cooked eggs, sliced	2 tablespoons capers
2 dill pickles, thinly sliced	½ cup small black or green olives
¾ cup mayonnaise	3 tomatoes, cut in quarters

Mix the chicken, potatoes, eggs, pickles, mayonnaise, and sour cream. Add the salt and pepper to taste, then serve on shredded lettuce garnished with capers, olives, and tomatoes. Serves 6.

UKRAINE

CHICKEN KIEV

This may be one of the most famous chicken dishes in the world. Originally a rather bland dish, a variety of herb combinations has made it quite the opposite. Here's one basic recipe plus several variations:

3 large, whole chicken breasts, wings attached	2 eggs, beaten
	Salt and freshly ground pepper
8 tablespoons unsalted butter	1 cup dry breadcrumbs
Flour for dredging	Vegetable oil for frying

Remove the wing tips and the second bone, leaving only the leglike bone. Split the chicken breasts and remove the breast bones. Lay a piece of waxed paper over each chicken breast and pound gently until flattened, taking care not to break off the wing bone. Prepare the butter by dividing it into 5 portions and rolling each portion into a cylindrical shape about the size of your little finger. Roll each butter cylinder in flour and put in freezer for 30-45 minutes.

When you are ready to cook the chicken, place one finger of butter on each piece of chicken. Wrap the chicken fillets around the butter, tucking in the ends to be sure the butter can't escape (use a toothpick to secure each cutlet, but remove them when serving). Dredge the cutlet in flour, being sure to cover thoroughly. Pat the cutlets into an oblong shape, then dip them into the beaten eggs, again being sure the entire cutlet is covered. Now roll in breadcrumbs and refrigerate for one hour before deep-frying. Heat the oil in a deep-fat fryer to 360° F, then fry each cutlet until golden brown—about 20 minutes. As each cutlet is done remove and keep warm. Serve at once. Serves 6.

Variations: All the variations have to do with the butter mixture. Some rather dramatic effects can be achieved. Here are a few:

Pâté de foie gras—Combine 4 tablespoons butter with 4 tablespoons pâté de foie gras, in place of 8 tablespoons of butter, and complete the recipe as above.

Mushrooms—Chop 4 tablespoons mushrooms finely and add to the butter. Add also a pinch of cayenne pepper.

Herb seasoning—Cream the butter by mashing it with a spoon and mixing in 1 teaspoon fresh lemon juice, 1 teaspoon tarragon, ½ teaspoon salt, several grindings of fresh pepper, and 1 clove of garlic, crushed. (Try also with ½ teaspoon rosemary instead of the tarragon.)

Chive or parsley butter—Chop up finely about 4 tablespoons of fresh chives and mix with the butter. Similar and just as good is chopped fresh parsley mixed with butter.

MOLDAVIA

CHICKEN AND POTATO SOUP WITH SMETNA
(Sour Cream)

Some Central Asian natives still use sour mare's milk (*kumiss*) to cook their fowl, as did their Tartar ancestors. But in the more populated areas of Russia sour cream or yogurt has taken its place.

1 3-pound chicken, quartered	1 onion, chopped
1 teaspoon salt	1 stalk celery, sliced
2 quarts water	1 tablespoon vinegar
Chicken giblets, trimmed of fat and muscle	1 pound potatoes, peeled and diced
2 tablespoons butter or oil	2 tablespoons smetna (sour cream)
1 carrot, sliced	Dash cayenne pepper
1 parsnip, sliced	Chopped dill for garnish

In a saucepan, place the chicken quarters and giblets and cover with 8 cups of water (2 quarts). Add salt and bring to the boil. Heat the butter or oil in a skillet and sauté the carrot, parsnip, onion, and celery and add with the vinegar to the chicken. Cover and simmer over low heat for 2 hours.

Remove the chicken and keep it warm. Strain the stock and set aside for 10 minutes to cool, then skim the fat off. Now add the diced potatoes and cook, covered, over moderate heat until done, about 15-20 minutes, then add the smetna and cayenne pepper and stir well.

Place one quarter of chicken in a soup plate and spoon the chicken potato broth over it, being sure to include the potatoes. Sprinkle with dill and serve hot. Serves 4.

OLD RUSSIA

CHICKEN IN SMETNA (Sour Cream Sauce)

1 3-pound chicken, quartered	Salt and pepper
2 tablespoons flour	4 tablespoons butter or oil
	Parsley sprigs for garnish

Smetna Sauce

½ cup smetna (sour cream)	1 tablespoon flour
2 tablespoons butter	½ cup fresh chicken stock
	Salt

Cover each chicken piece with flour, then sprinkle it with salt and pepper. Heat the butter or oil in a large skillet, then fry the chicken, turning frequently, for 30 minutes over moderate heat, until nearly done. Meanwhile prepare the smetna sauce.

Keeping the heat low, melt 2 tablespoons butter in a saucepan and blend in the flour, then gradually stir in the stock. Add the smetna and a little salt and mix thoroughly. Now drain the fat from the chicken and pour in the smetna sauce. Do not allow the sauce to get too hot. Simmer for about 8 minutes and then remove from the heat. Serve the chicken on a platter with some sauce poured over, and the rest in a sauceboat. Garnish with parsley. Serves 4.

OLD RUSSIA

CHICKEN WITH KIZIL (Cherry) Sauce

1 3-pound chicken	1 carrot, sliced
Salt and pepper	1 stalk celery, sliced

Kizil Sauce

8 ounces bing cherries (see note)	2 teaspoons butter
1 cup stock	1 teaspoon sugar
1/3 cup seedless raisins	1 cup water
	4 teaspoons flour

Place the chicken, carrot, and celery in a saucepan and cover with water. Add 1 teaspoon salt and a little pepper, then simmer over low heat for 2 hours or until tender. Remove the chicken and keep warm, then strain the stock and reserve 2 cups.

Cook the cherries in a little water over low heat for about 15 minutes, until they are soft, then strain the juice and set aside. Rub the cherries through a fine sieve, return to the juice and add the raisins, sugar, salt, and stock. Blend the butter with the flour, dilute with a little of the liquid, and add to the cherry sauce. Stir well, then bring to the boil over high heat. Reduce heat to low and simmer for 10 minutes, stirring frequently.

Cut the chicken pieces into serving pieces, arrange on a platter, and pour the kizil sauce over all. Serves 4.

Note: Cherries grown in Old Russia, Armenia, and the Middle East are on the sweet side. This dish is also made with a slightly acidic (tart) cherry, which I think has more flavor. Our bing cherry is excellent in the dish, but don't use canned ones.

THE CAUCASUS

TCHAKHOHBILI—Caucasian Chicken Stew

1 3-pound chicken, cut up	1 tablespoon vinegar
4 tablespoons butter or oil	1 bay leaf
2 onions, chopped coarsely	2 tablespoons tomato paste
1 teaspoon salt	1/4 cup chicken stock
1/2 teaspoon freshly ground	2 tomatoes, quartered
pepper	1 lemon, sliced
1/4 cup vodka	Parsley sprigs or dill for garnish

Heat the butter or oil in a Dutch oven, and brown the chicken pieces until golden. Remove the chicken pieces to a platter, then sauté the onions until soft and tender. Return the chicken to the pot, add salt and pepper, vodka, vinegar, bay leaf, tomato paste, and the stock, then cover and simmer for 45 minutes. Remove the cover, add the tomato quarters, then cook an additional 10 minutes.

Place the chicken on a platter and garnish with lemon slices and chopped parsley or dill. Serves 4.

UKRAINE

SALADE BAGRATION

The creation of a French chef, this salad is named after the great Russian general, Prince Peter Bagration, who defeated Napoleon at Eylan.

1 cup celery, sliced crosswise	1½ cups mayonnaise
1 cup cooked artichoke hearts	3 tablespoons chili sauce
½ cup vinaigrette dressing	4 hard cooked eggs
2 cups cooked breast of chicken, cubed	¾ cup minced ham
	½ cup minced parsley
2 cups cooked elbow macaroni	¾ cup minced black olives or truffles

Marinate the celery and artichoke hearts in vinaigrette dressing for 30 minutes. Mix in the cubed chicken and macaroni, then mix in the mayonnaise and chili sauce and combine thoroughly. Put this mixture into a serving bowl and smooth the top. Separate the yolks and whites of the hard boiled eggs, and chop each separately. Sprinkle each over the smoothed chicken mixture. Then sprinkle over this the minced ham, parsley, and black olives (or truffles). Toss at the table. Serves 6.

AZERBAIJAN

CHICKEN PLOV (PILAF)

Azerbaijan is the republic next door to the Caucasian republics of Georgia and Armenia. This area is very much like its Middle Eastern neighbors in way of life, religion, language, and particularly in cuisine. A *Plov* is the areas version of the Turkish *Pilaf.* It is a rice dish, altered in any number of ways and tastes by the addition of nuts, meats, vegetables, seasonings or, in this case, fruits. Do not be limited in your choice of fruits; virtually anything will do.

1 pound assorted dried fruits	2 medium onions, chopped
1 3-pound chicken, cut up	coarsely
4 tablespoons butter or oil	1 cup rice
	2 cups water, or chicken stock
	Salt and pepper

Soak the fruit in hot water for 1 hour. Preheat the oven to 350° F.

Cook the rice in water or stock in a double boiler over high heat for 15 minutes. Melt the butter in a large skillet and brown the chicken pieces on all sides for about 10 minutes. Remove and keep warm. Sauté the onions in the same skillet until golden, adding more butter or oil if necessary.

Now cover the bottom of a medium-sized Dutch oven or casserole with the sautéed onions and arrange the chicken pieces on top. Add salt and pepper to taste. Spoon about half of the partially cooked rice over the chicken, then add some of the fruit, then the rest of the rice, and finally the remaining fruit. Cover and cook in the oven for 45 minutes. Serves 4.

OLD RUSSIA

COTLETKI POJARSKI—Chicken Cutlets

The origin of this dish seems to be a popular carriage stop on the road between Moscow and St. Petersburg in the early nineteenth century. Pojarski, or his successors, allegedly used gamebirds, but there are other versions that use chicken or veal or a combination of both.

1½ pounds raw white meat of
  chicken (about 3-4 breasts)
4 slices white bread, crumbled
½ cup milk

1 egg white
½ cup heavy cream
8 tablespoons butter
Salt and pepper
½ teaspoon nutmeg
¾ cup dry breadcrumbs

Put the chicken meat through the fine blade of the meat grinder. Soak the crumbled bread in milk for 10 minutes, then squeeze out excess milk. Mix thoroughly the chicken, bread, egg white, cream, 3 tablespoons butter, salt and pepper (about 1 teaspoon salt and ½ teaspoon pepper), and nutmeg. Divide the mixture into 6 cutlets or cakes and roll in breadcrumbs. Heat the remaining butter in a skillet and sauté the cutlets over moderate to low heat until golden brown on all sides, about 20 minutes. Serves 6.

Note: An excellent hot hors d'oeuvre can be made from the same mixture. Just make the balls very small, like large marbles, then roll in the breadcrumbs and sauté the same way, though not so long.

THE CAUCASUS

GRILLED CHICKEN WITH TKEMALY SAUCE
The wild plums of Georgia give their name to this sauce. The chicken can be grilled in an oven, but the wood or charcoal smoke from an outdoor fire gives it an added flavor. This recipe is also outstanding with squab or Rock Cornish game hen. You won't find Georgian plums in this country, but fresh domestic plums make a very adequate substitute.

2 2-3-pound chickens, quartered
4 tablespoons butter
Salt and freshly ground pepper
4-6 ripe plums
2 cloves garlic, crushed

1 cup smetna (sour cream)
1 cup water
Dash cayenne pepper
Pinch basil
Pinch chopped dill

Rub the chicken quarters all over with salt and freshly ground pepper. If the meat is to be grilled indoors, put it in the broiler for 10-12 minutes on a side. If cooked outdoors, arrange on skewers or a spit, coat with melted butter, and grill, turning frequently. Baste liberally with butter every 5 minutes or so.

Stew the plums in water until they are soft. Remove the stones and rub the plums through a sieve, then mix in the smetna and simmer over low heat, stirring constantly. (Don't let the pan get too hot or the sour cream will separate.) After 5 minutes add a little salt, the cayenne, crushed garlic, basil, and dill. Adjust the consistency with a little plum juice to achieve the thickness of heavy cream. Serve the chicken with a spoonful (or more) of tkemaly sauce poured over. Serves 8.

CHICKEN PIE

The Russians frequently eat chicken or meat pies, and they cook them in several different ways. Two that are world-famous are the *Pirog* from Old Russia and the *Pashtet* from the Ukraine. Both combine chicken, hard cooked eggs, and rice covered with a pastry crust. The difference is that in the pirog, the cooked chicken meat is cut into very small (diced) pieces and mixed with the rice, eggs, and other ingredients, while the pashtet is made with slices of chicken.

OLD RUSSIA

CHICKEN PIROG

1 3-pound chicken	1 parsnip, sliced
1 carrot, sliced	Salt and pepper
1 stalk celery, sliced	1 cup rice
1 onion, chopped	4 hard cooked eggs, chopped
	2 tablespoons butter, melted

Pie Pastry

1 pound flour	½ cup cold water
14 ounces butter	Juice of ½ lemon
½ teaspoon salt	1 egg, beaten

Place the chicken in a saucepan with the carrot, celery, onion, parsnip, and a little salt and pepper. Cover and cook for 2 hours. Remove the chicken and strain the stock, reserving 2 cups. Cook the rice for about 20 minutes in the stock in the double boiler, adding a little more salt and pepper.

Remove and discard the skin and bones from the chicken, then cut the meat into very small pieces. When the rice is done, combine it with the chicken, chopped eggs, and melted butter and mix well. Cover and set aside and make the pie pastry.

Pie Pastry

Cut up the butter into small pieces and drop into a mixing bowl. Sift the flour and salt over the butter and work it all together with a knife or spatula. Make a hole in the center and pour in ½ cup of very cold water and the juice of ½ a lemon. Knead for about 10 minutes, then refrigerate for 1 hour. Roll the dough out, fold over in thirds and refrigerate again for 30 minutes. Repeat three more times. Now roll the dough out to about ¼-inch thickness.

Preheat the oven to 425° F. Cut the dough in half and lay 1 sheet in a baking dish, trimming the edges. Spoon in the chicken mixture and cover with the other pastry sheet. Trim and press together the edges with a fork to seal. With the tip of a knife or fork, prick the pastry for steam vents and brush the top with a beaten egg. Bake the pie for 10 minutes, then reduce the heat to 375° F and cook for 25 more minutes. Serve directly from the baking dish. Serves 4.

UKRAINE

PASHTET

2 cups rice	3 hard cooked eggs, sliced in
4½ cups chicken stock	eighths
8 tablespoons butter	1 3-pound chicken, roasted,
2 tablespoons chopped dill, or	boned, and sliced
½ tablespoon dill powder	Salt and pepper
3 onions, chopped coarsely	Pie pastry (above)

Cook the rice in a double boiler in 4 cups of stock for 20 minutes or until done, then mix in 3 tablespoons of butter and the dill. Cover and let stand for 10 minutes.

Preheat the oven to 425° F. Heat 2 tablespoons butter in a skillet and then sauté the chopped onion until golden. Grease a 6- x 9-inch baking dish and lay a little rice on the bottom; cover with some of the onions, then a layer of hard cooked egg slices, then the chicken.

Cover the chicken with the remaining onions, then the remaining egg slices and the remaining rice. Season each layer with just a little salt and pepper, add ½ cup of the stock, and dot with the remaining butter. Make a pie pastry, only cut the recipe in half, as only a top sheet is needed. Cover the pie, trim and seal the edges with a knife, prick, and brush the top with melted butter, then bake the pie in a 425° F oven for 10 minutes. Now reduce to 375° F and bake for an additional 20 minutes. Let the pie stand when done for 5 minutes, then serve hot right from the baking dish. Serves 4.

CHICKEN FILLETS

In addition to Chicken Kiev, the Russians have developed other very interesting dishes made from the filleted chicken breast. Some of the best come from Old Russia, Byelorussia (which borders Poland), and the Ukraine.

OLD RUSSIA

ROLLED CHICKEN BREASTS

Whole breast of 1 3-pound chicken	Breadcrumbs
	Salt and pepper
2 hard cooked eggs	6-8 tablespoons butter

Remove the breastbone and ribs and slice the raw breasts into thin, wide fillets. (One full breast should make 4 fillets.) Cut the hard cooked eggs in half, and place each half on a fillet. Sprinkle with breadcrumbs and a little salt and pepper and roll up carefully. Secure each roll with toothpicks, then dust again with breadcrumbs. Now fry in butter over medium heat until golden brown, about 15-20 minutes. Serves 4.

BYELORUSSIA

REBRA KURITSKY—Chicken Breast Fillets

3 full chicken breasts, with wings, split	3 tablespoons smetna (sour cream)
Salt and pepper	2 eggs
½ cup butter	1½-2 cups fine dry breadcrumbs

½ pound chicken livers
2 medium onions

½ cup water
2 tablespoons flour mixed with 2 tablespoons water
Parsley sprigs for garnish

Make a 3-inch slit in each breast just above the rib bones. Sprinkle with salt and pepper.

Heat 1½ tablespoons butter in a small skillet and sauté the liver and onion gently for 10-15 minutes. Chop the liver into small pieces, then mash it together in a small bowl with the onions until thoroughly blended into a paste. Add a little salt and pepper and sour cream, mixing again until a fairly firm consistency is achieved.

Now place equal portions of the stuffing in the slit in each fillet. Be sure each cavity is full, then secure the slit with toothpicks. Beat the eggs slightly in a shallow dish, and put the breadcrumbs in another. Dip the fillets into the egg, turning to cover completely, then roll them in the breadcrumbs, covering each thoroughly. Repeat this step with each fillet.

Over moderate heat melt ½ cup butter in a large skillet and fry each fillet until golden brown, about 5 minutes on each side. Add ½ cup water, cover, and reduce heat to low. Simmer gently for 30 minutes, adding a little more water if necessary. Remove the chicken fillets to a warm platter and deglaze the pan with the flour and water mixture. Stir constantly for 3 minutes, then pass the sauce in a sauceboat. Garnish the chicken with parsley sprigs and serve. Serves 6.

UKRAINE

SCHNICEL—Fried Chicken Fillets

3 large whole chicken breasts
½ cup flour
1 egg, whipped

Salt
1½ cups small cubes white or French bread
1 cup butter or oil

Preheat the oven to 325° F. Split the breasts and remove the skin and bones. Split each breast just enough so it will lie flat. Now coat each fillet with flour dipped in egg and sprinkle with a little salt. Press both sides of the fillets into the small bread cubes, being sure to cover thoroughly. (Press the bread in with your fingers if you have to.)

Heat the butter or oil over medium high heat and brown the fillets quickly. Remove the fillets to a baking sheet and bake in a slow oven (325° F) for 15 minutes. Serves 4-6.

🌿 Chapter 6 🌿

Africa

Perhaps the last place that comes to mind when one thinks of classic gastronomy is Africa. Since World War II, however, the world has become increasingly aware of the emergence of New African nations, and while we have been witness to agonizing episodes of political unrest and social turmoil, we have simultaneously been made more aware of the cultural traditions of the African people and particularly the singular, sometimes spectacular, culinary art that they have achieved.

Africa has three major geographic features—the vast and arid Sahara Desert in the north, the dense jungles in the central lowlands, and the grassy veldts and savannahs of the south. In broadest gastronomic terms Africa also presents three faces to the world, and these coincide with the continent's geography and history. In the Sahara north the people are overwhelmingly Arab, and so is the cooking, although one finds many reminders of the British and French kitchens left behind from the colonial period.

In the south there is an amalgam of European and Asian cooking, which developed as the colonies developed and as Asian slaves, exiles, and servants were imported by British and Dutch merchants. Only in the lowlands will one find a cuisine that could be described as native African.

One won't find much chicken cooking in the desert, where mutton or goat is eaten if any meat is eaten at all. But on the coast of the Maghreb (the Arab name for Morocco, Tunisia, and Algeria) there are a number of interesting dishes that feature chicken, fish, beef, and lamb. Two in particular stand out, and both might be called national favorites of the African Arab—the *Tagine* (pronounced ta-hee-na) and *Couscous*. A tagine is a stew, which takes its name from the special pot in which it's cooked. A rich, spicy mixture of vegetables and meat, it has endless variations and frequently includes more than one type of meat.

Couscous also has its own special pot—the *couscousière*. Couscous is a semolina-type grain, which is painstakingly rolled by hand into fine pellets and then steamed until done. It found its way to western Africa, and crossed the Atlantic to Brazil with slaves impounded by the Portuguese for their New World colony, and today it has become one of the national dishes of the Bahian or Afro-Brazilian culture.

On the northeast coast of Africa lies Ethiopia, a mountainous country that was first black, then Christian, then settled by Moslems six hundred years ago. This is ancient Nubia, the home of the Nubian chicken (guinea fowl) of Roman days, and it is also the land where coffee originated. The one dish that stands out as an international classic is *Doro Wat,* which, in its true form, is shredded chicken doused with a *berbere* (red pepper) sauce that is hot to the extreme. It is served with *injera* bread, which is a yeast bread fried or baked in pancakes two feet in diameter. The wat and the bread are presented on wicker tables specially designed for the meal. One eats it with one's fingers, breaking off a piece of bread and scooping up a little of the wat from the center of the communal table. Doro Wat is a popular dish with the middle and upper class families of Ethiopia, but injera bread is such a staple among the natives that the women bake it several times a week to assure an everyday supply.

The central part of the continent lays claim to no such spectacular dish as Doro Wat, but it does have its surprises. It offers perhaps the only authentic "African" cuisine the continent can claim. It's the land of *Jollof* rice, *Mealies* (green corn), *n-ghumbo* (okra), *jindungo* (chili peppers), and groundnuts (peanuts)—colorful names but really not much different from the everyday food we eat in this country.

Until recently, the African diet was virtually void of animal protein, except along the coast where fish was available. Protein-rich okra and groundnuts were daily staples and were frequently added to chicken soups, stews, and stuffings. Two unique chicken dishes of Central Africa include peanuts. One, from the Ashanti region of Ghana, calls for the removal of the backbone, breastbone, and ribs of a fresh roasting chicken while keeping the flesh intact. The cavity is then filled with a mixture of sausage and groundnuts, after which the reconstructed bird is sewn up or skewered closed and roasted. Another, which is finding a following in Europe, is *Groundnut Chop,* a rich chicken and vegetable stew that includes groundnuts and chili peppers.

One technique we owe the Africans is tenderizing chicken with buttermilk. Until recently, chicken was rather scarce in Central

Africa, so for the most part the bird was reserved for special occasions. Even so, the average chicken was tough, scraggly, and underweight. Long ago the African cook learned to tenderize the meat by steaming a cleaned and dressed bird over buttermilk and then simmering it slowly in the remaining liquid. This technique is very popular in the Southern United States, and probably has its origins with the slaves.

The eastern nations of Central Africa are populated essentially by native blacks. But one finds more of a European and Asian influence in the local gastronomy, particularly as one moves down the coast. A favorite dish in Uganda is a simple chicken stew made with plantains (a close cousin to the banana), while in neighboring Kenya, Tanzania, and Malawi, spicy chicken curries are preferred. In Mozambique, a former Portuguese colony, the natives took to the chili pepper and make Chicken *Piripiri,* one of Africa's most delightful surprises. *Piripiri,* or *jindungo,* is a seasoning made of dried, pounded red chilies, which takes thirty days to make properly. The chili pepper, of course, is native to South and Central America, and the Portuguese brought it to their colonies in East Africa four hundred years ago.

Once the sea route to India was opened in 1498 and the Arab blockade of the spice trade broken, Southern Africa became a hub of activity. As trade with the East increased, however, there was a radical improvement in South Africa's cooking, and it wasn't the Europeans who were responsible for it; it was the Asians. Traders came from India and Southeast Asia, and many of them stayed. Others came as exiles or servants, and some were brought in as slaves—which seems almost paradoxical, for Africa has been looted of its people since antiquity. In the seventeenth century the Dutch transported thousands of Malaysian slaves from their colonies in the East Indies to their colonies in South Africa. Combining their culinary skills with the produce and spices the Dutch had in great abundance, the new residents created the "Cape Malay" style, which became, and still is, one of the most sophisticated in Africa. Chicken is the featured meat of the Cape Malay kitchen with chili peppers. The names of the dishes remain Dutch—*Hoender en Aardappel, Hoender Pastei, Gesmoorde Hoender*—but there the similarity ends.

Though chicken cookery in Africa is a sometime thing and varies in popularity from one region to another, it provides some of the best examples of the widely diverse styles that the continent as a whole has to offer. Try them all and be surprised—"Darkest Africa" has some of the brightest and most innovative chicken dishes you will ever taste.

RECOMMENDED READING: Hilda Gerber, *Traditional Cookery of the Cape Malays* (1957); Mrs. H. M. Slade, *Mrs. Slade's South African Cookery Book* (1957); Sandy Lesberg, *The Art of African Cooking* (New York: Dell, 1971); Dinah Ameley Ayensu, *The Art of West African Cooking* (New York: Doubleday); Robin Howe, *Cooking for the Commonwealth* (London: André Deutsch, 1958)

SOURCE FOR INGREDIENTS:

Mrs. DeWildt
RFD 1
Bangor, Pa. 18013

PART I:

North Africa

COUSCOUS

Couscous is the national dish of the Maghreb (Algeria, Tunisia, and Morocco). It is found today in all North African countries from the Atlantic to the Suez, and is also served in many West African nations. Couscous is a standard in Brazilian cooking also, having come to South America with slaves imported by the Portuguese.

Couscous is not only the basic vehicle for a meat or vegetable stew, but it is prepared as a stuffing and a dessert as well. The less well-to-do eat couscous plain two or three times a day, but those better off are limited only by time, imagination, and the ingredients at hand.

Perhaps the most interesting thing about couscous is the way it is cooked. A special pot called a *couscousière,* which is similar to our double boiler, is used. The upper pot is earthenware and has small holes in the base like a sieve to allow steam to escape from below. The bottom vessel is made of metal.

The meat and vegetables are cooked in the lower pot. The couscous is soaked, then put into the top pot and steamed. Then the couscous is mounded in the center of a platter or large serving dish and the vegetables and pieces of meat are arranged around it. Some of the broth is poured over the meat and vegetables, and the rest is served in a sauceboat. Here's the basic couscous recipe using chicken:

1 pound couscous	1½ quarts beef broth or water
3 cups boiling water	2 cups garbanzos
½ cup oil or butter	2 large tomatoes, peeled and
2 3-pound chickens, cut up	chopped

159

3 large onions, chopped
1 teaspoon each salt and black
  pepper
⅛ teaspoon cayenne pepper
½ teaspoon turmeric
1 teaspoon saffron

2 zucchini or yellow squash,
  sliced
3 carrots, sliced lengthwise in
  quarters
1 handful raisins
Parsley sprigs for garnish

In a large bowl, pour 1 cup of boiling salted water over the couscous. Let stand for 8-10 minutes; repeat twice. The couscous should double in size.

While the couscous is soaking, heat the butter or oil and brown the chicken a few pieces at a time, transferring them to the bottom pot of a couscousière. (This recipe can be made beautifully in two separate pots also—see below.) Add butter or oil if needed, then sauté the onions until tender and add to the meat. Pour ½ cup of the broth into the frying pan, stir well, and pour into the pot. Now add the salt, pepper, cayenne, turmeric, and saffron. Pour in the broth and bring to a simmer.

Now, if you are using a couscousière, place the top pot with the soaked couscous grains onto the bottom pot with the stew in it. (Make sure the top pot doesn't touch the stew or broth). The steam will be forced through the small sievelike holes and will cook the couscous. Simmer and steam both stew and couscous for one hour. Remove the top pot and stir the couscous with a fork to separate the grains. Add the carrots, zucchini, tomatoes, garbanzos, and a little salt and pepper to the lower pot, return the top pot with the couscous, and simmer for 45 minutes. Now add the raisins to the lower pot, stir the couscous again, and simmer for about 15 minutes. Toss the couscous with a little butter, and then mound it in the center of a large platter or serving dish. Arrange the meat and vegetables around the couscous and pour over the broth. Garnish with parsley sprigs. Serves 6-8.

In all likelihood you won't own or have access to a couscousière, but this dish can be made just as well by cooking the stew as above in a covered stewpot or casserole. To cook the couscous, use a saucepan that will accommodate a colander. Partly fill the pan with water, then line the lip of the pan loosely with foil to create a seal. Now line the colander with one thickness of cheesecloth, and pour in the couscous, after soaking it in boiling water as described above. Make sure the water in the saucepan does not touch the bottom of the colander.

Bring the water to the boil and then turn down the heat to maintain a very gentle boil. Insert the colander, making sure that no steam escapes around the edges, and steam for 2 hours. Serve in the same manner as described above.

Note: Couscous is not always eaten with meat and vegetables as a stew. In the Maghreb it is used frequently as a stuffing, while in Egypt the couscous is cooked as usual, but a little confectioner's sugar and one teaspoon of chopped nuts (peanuts, almonds, walnuts, or pistachios) are added, and it's eaten as dessert. A much expanded version of this "sweet" version is a North African recipe that combines not only sugar and chopped nuts, but dates, almonds, raisins, grated orange rind and juice, curaçao, and currants, all of which are folded into the couscous just before serving.

MOROCCO

ROAST CHICKEN WITH ALMOND STUFFING

1 3-pound chicken	1 tablespoon basil
1 cup breadcrumbs	Freshly ground black pepper
½ cup fresh almonds, crushed	Salt
1 egg, whipped	¼ cup olive oil
	¼ cup honey

Crush the fresh almonds with a mallet and combine with the breadcrumbs, whipped egg, basil, and black pepper. Mix well with your fingers. Rub the chicken cavity with salt and a little more black pepper, then fill with the stuffing.

Mix the olive oil and honey. Gently score the breast, legs, and thighs of the chicken with a knife, then brush the chicken all over with half the oil and honey mixture. Place the chicken in a roaster, cover, and cook in a moderate oven (350° F) for 45-50 minutes, depending on the size of the bird, brushing frequently with the remaining oil-honey mixture and pan juices. Uncover and roast the last 15 minutes so that the chicken becomes a golden brown, continuing the basting all the time. Serves 4.

TUNISIA/MOROCCO

DJAJMAHSHI—Roast Chicken with Lamb and Pine Nut Stuffing

Lamb is more popular in North Africa than chicken—but here's a preparation that uses both. Next time you have a leg of lamb, cut off ½ pound before you cook it and keep it for this dish.

1 4-pound roasting chicken	15 peppercorns, crushed
Honey for basting	2 tablespoons butter
½ pound lamb, ground	½ teaspoon powdered cinnamon
1 onion, diced	¼ teaspoon nutmeg
¼ cup pine nuts (pignolia)	1 clove, crushed
Salt	½ cup cooked rice

First prepare the stuffing: Brown the ground lamb in a dry skillet and add the diced onion, pine nuts, salt and peppercorns, butter, cinnamon, and nutmeg and clove and cook for 3 minutes longer. In a large mixing bowl, combine the cooked rice with the stuffing and mix together thoroughly. Rub the cavity of the chicken with salt and pepper and stuff with the warm mixture.

Preheat the oven to 350° F. Roast the chicken for 1 hour, covered, basting with honey or butter every 10-15 minutes. Remove the cover for the last 15 minutes to brown the breast and legs. Serves 4-6.

MOROCCO

LEMON CHICKEN WITH OLIVES

1 chicken, cut up	½ cup chicken stock
1 medium onion, chopped	½ cup green olives, pitted and
Olive oil	sliced
1 lemon	½ cup black olives, pitted and
	sliced

Sauté the onion in oil until tender in a large skillet. Cut ¼-inch thick slices from ½ the lemon and juice the remaining half. Grate the rind of the remaining half lemon and set aside. Slide ½ slice lemon under the skin of each chicken piece, then place one or two ½ slices of lemon on top of each piece. Add the lemon juice and rind to the sautéed onion and heat a few minutes.

Now place the chicken in the skillet, add the stock, cover with a tight lid, and cook over medium heat for about ½ hour. Drain the black olives, slice them, and add to the pan, then cover and cook for another ½ hour.

When done, serve the chicken on a platter of white rice, garnished with green olives and parsley. Serves 4.

MOROCCO

CHICKEN GDRA—Chicken with Chickpeas

In the Maghreb, a very popular dish is the *Tagine* (ta-hee-na). Actually the pot is the tagine, but because it is prepared so frequently, the dish has acquired that name also. This is a traditional tagine recipe from Morocco, in which one onion is cooked with the meat or chicken as a flavoring agent, while the remaining onions are added toward the end, as an accompaniment to the stew.

1 3-pound chicken, cut up
3 tablespoons butter
⅛ teaspoon ground saffron (optional)
Salt and ground black pepper
1 teaspoon cinnamon
3 medium onions, chopped coarsely

1½ cups chickpeas, soaked overnight, or 1 16-ounce can of chickpeas
Pinch ground coriander
1 tsp. parsley flakes
½ cup almonds, blanched and peeled
Juice and grated rind of ½ lemon

In a large stewpot or Dutch oven, melt the butter, stir in the salt, saffron, and a few grindings of black pepper, the cinnamon, and 2 onions and cook for several minutes until golden, then add the chicken and chickpeas. Cover with water and simmer for 1½ hours or until the chicken is tender. Add water as necessary. During the last hour add the remaining onions, the coriander, the parsley, and the almonds and cook until the onions are soft and the sauce is reduced.

This should be served over rice, which is cooked using some of the sauce from the tagine. When done, arrange the rice on a platter with the chicken around it, and pour some of the sauce over the meat.

Sprinkle the lemon juice and the grated rind over all and serve the remaining sauce in a sauceboat. Serves 4.

Note: With most stews, there are infinite combinations of ingredients, and a tagine is no exception. To the basic stewed chicken (or other meat) can be added almonds, hard-boiled eggs, or assorted fruits, and the stew is always eaten with rice or couscous or with just plain Arabian bread.

ETHIOPIA

DORO WAT—Chicken with Berberé Sauce and Injera Bread

Doro wat is the national dish of Ethiopia. It is a stew cooked with many spices and served with *injera,* a fermented bread made of teff. Injera is eaten several times a day in Ethiopia, so a small amount of fermented batter is usually reserved from each fresh batch to serve as a leavening agent for the next batch.

The wat is spooned onto the injera, which is then folded and eaten with the fingers. A gracious hostess will offer "just one more bite" to her guests as a sign of goodwill or friendship at the conclusion of the meal.

1 3-pound chicken, cut up	2 teaspoons ginger
Salt	1 teaspoon nutmeg
2 cups water	1 teaspoon paprika
½ cup lemon juice	¼ teaspoon cardamom powder
2½ cups onions, chopped finely	Pinch salt
2 garlic cloves	½ cup dry white wine
6 tablespoons oil or butter	6-8 hard cooked eggs
Berberé sauce (see below)	Ground black pepper

Wash the chicken pieces and pat dry. Rub each piece with salt and place in a large bowl. Prepare a marinade of 1½ cups cold water, lemon juice, and ½ cup chopped onions, and pour over the chicken. Make sure each piece is completely coated with the marinade. Let stand for 1 hour at room temperature, turning the chicken at least 3 or 4 times.

Now make the berberé sauce and set aside. Heat the butter or oil in a large Dutch oven or stewpot, and sauté the remaining chopped onions over moderate heat. Add berberé sauce, garlic, ginger, nutmeg, paprika, cardamom, and a pinch of salt and cook over low heat for about 3 minutes, stirring constantly. Increase the heat to high, add wine and water, and bring rapidly to the boil. Reduce heat to medium and cook for 5 minutes. The pan liquid should then be somewhat thickened. Now reduce heat to simmer.

Remove the chicken from the marinade and pat dry. Add the chicken to the Dutch oven, making sure each piece is completely coated with the sauce. Cover and simmer for 30 minutes. Now add the eggs and stir into the sauce. Simmer for 15 more minutes or until the chicken is done. While the doro wat cooks, make the injera bread (recipe follows).

Transfer the entire stew to a serving dish or platter. Grind fresh black pepper over and garnish with the hard cooked eggs. Serve with injera bread and white rice. A good dry white wine is an excellent accompaniment. Serves 4-6.

Berberé (Red Pepper) Sauce

This will make enough for one doro wat recipe.

1 teaspoon onions, chopped finely
1 large garlic clove, chopped finely

⅛ teaspoon each of ground ginger, ground coriander, ground cardamom, cinnamon, nutmeg, fenugreek, and paprika
1 teaspoon ground red pepper
Salt and freshly ground pepper
1 tablespoon red wine
¼ cup warm water

In a small saucepan, mix the ginger, cardamom, coriander, cinnamon, nutmeg, and fenugreek and roast over low heat for 1-2 minutes. Stir constantly and don't burn. Let cool for 10 minutes, then mix in the onions, garlic, a pinch of salt, and the wine and blend them into a paste.

In a separate saucepan, combine the paprika and red and black pepper and roast for 1-2 minutes over low heat, stirring continuously. *Do not burn.* Add the water and the spice paste in the saucepan and simmer for about 10 minutes. Use this in the above recipe as indicated.

Injera (Fermented Teff Bread)

Injera is the fermented dough of *teff* (or millet), but barley or cornmeal or wheat can be used. One authentic recipe for making injera is shown below. Because of the time involved and the difficulty you will encounter finding teff in this country, a substitute recipe, which is fairly similar, follows.

2 pounds teff (or other grain)   1 cup leavening (or leftover batter
3 quarts water   from a previous teff dough or a
                                            sourdough starter)

The grain should be finely ground. In a large bowl, mix slowly with cold water, being sure to keep from lumping. Make a fairly thick mixture. Add the leavening, mix well, cover with a lid, and leave overnight. If no leavening dough is available, let the teff mixture sit for 2 or 3 days covered. It will ferment in this time. Pour off carefully any water that may accumulate on top of the dough.

Take 1 cup of the new mixture and thin it in water in a saucepan. Stirring constantly, cook this well until it becomes rather thick. Cool and return it to the original bowl with the other teff mixture. Thin the entire mixture with a little cold water, then cover and let the dough rise. The batter is now ready (reserve one cup of the batter if you expect to make more in the future).

To cook injera bread, grease and heat a griddle or iron skillet over moderate heat and pour the batter on, making sure it spreads evenly. Cook for 1 minute, then cover. Injera will rise as it cooks and can be removed easily. Do not cook too long and do not brown.

Alternate Recipe
5 tablespoons sifted flour   ½ teaspoon baking soda
3 cups buckwheat pancake mix   5 cups water

In a large mixing bowl, combine all the ingredients, stirring continuously to make a smooth batter. Be sure all lumps are gone. Heat a greased griddle, then pour in the injera batter to cover, making sure it's even all around. Cook over moderate heat for a minute or so, until the bread is barely moist, with airholes on top. Do not brown the bottom. Remove to a plate and keep warm. Repeat until all the batter is used.

PART II:

West Africa

TOGO

GUMBO—Chicken Okra Soup

This version of gumbo has been popular in many African states for several centuries. *Gumbo* is a Bantu word, which is defined by Webster as "a soup thickened with okra pods and usually containing vegetables with meat or seafood," and that's exactly what it is in both Africa and America.

2 quarts water	¼ teaspoon grated ginger
1 3-pound chicken, cut up	1 clove garlic
2 cups onions, chopped	2 tomatoes, peeled and chopped
Salt and pepper	2 red peppers, seeded and sliced
	2 cups okra, chopped

In a large saucepan, place the chicken pieces, 1¼ cups of chopped onions, salt and pepper, ginger, and the garlic clove. Add two quarts of water, cover, then simmer for 1 hour. Remove cover, then add the tomatoes and peppers and bring to the boil for 5 minutes. Reduce heat, add the remaining onions and chopped okra, and cook for another 10 minutes. Serve in soup plates, spooning the soup over a piece of chicken. Serves 4-6.

LIBERIA

PERLEAU—Chicken with Ham and Cabbage

1 3-pound chicken, cut up	1 large onion, chopped
Salt and pepper	2 medium tomatoes, chopped
4 tablespoons butter or oil	1 cup cabbage, chopped
1 cup cooked ham, cubed	1 cup rice
1½ quarts water	Parsley for garnish

Rub the chicken pieces with salt and pepper. In a skillet, heat the butter or oil and fry the chicken lightly on all sides. Remove the chicken to a 5 or 6 quart Dutch oven, then sauté the ham cubes in the skillet. Add the ham to the Dutch oven also. Add water, the chopped onion, chopped tomatoes, and the cabbage, then cover and simmer for 40 minutes.

After about 20 minutes take 2 cups of broth from the chicken and add it to the pot with the rice. Re-cover the chicken and continue cooking for another 20 minutes.

Bring the broth to the boil, then reduce the heat and cook the rice for 20-25 minutes. Mound the rice on a serving platter and arrange the chicken around it. Garnish with parsley and serve. Serves 4.

GHANA

GROUNDNUT CHOP—Chicken Stew with Peanuts

Ghana lays claim to this recipe, but it is popular throughout Middle Africa and is even finding a following in Europe. It can be made with almost any kind of meat, and along the coast fish, shrimp, or crabs are often added. Like the other great African stews, *Thiou* and *Mafe,* there is no end to the combinations and they are all good.

2 3-pound chickens, cut up	1 cup coconut milk (page 82)
1 large onion, sliced	4 cups peanuts, shelled and
1 teaspoon salt	blanched (or substitute ½ cup
4 cups water	peanut butter)
3 large tomatoes, quartered	2 cups chicken stock
3 chili peppers, washed and	3-4 cups hot cooked rice
seeded	6 hard cooked eggs, shelled

If you use peanuts, grind or pound them to a powder, add hot water, and stir until a paste forms. Simmer for an hour, then mix in 1 cup of coconut milk.

If peanut butter is used, put the chicken, salt, and onions into a stewpot with 3½ cups of water, bring to the boil, then simmer covered for 1 hour. In a saucepan combine the tomatoes, peppers, and ½ cup of water. Bring to the boil, then simmer, covered, 8-10 minutes. Now force this mixture through a sieve. Mix the peanut butter, tomato mixture, and stock and add it to the meat. Simmer until the chicken is tender, about 10 minutes.

Mound the rice on a serving platter, and arrange the meat and hard cooked eggs around it. When serving, put a helping of rice in a soup plate, place an egg in the center with a piece or two of meat, and cover with the stew. Serves 6-8.

Groundnut chop is a real feast, to which may be added a number of garnishes. Here are just a few: Whole or crushed roast peanuts, chopped onions, banana cubes, fried lightly, or fresh, freshly grated coconut, okra, squash slices, lemon or lime slices, diced green peppers, diced red peppers.

SENEGAL

YASSA—Spicy Marinated Chicken

This is a dish that can be marinated for 10 minutes or for 24 hours. If you wish to choose the short marinade, score the pieces first very lightly with a knife or prick them gently all over. Yassa should be broiled, either indoors or out, or pan-fried.

1 3-pound chicken, cut up

Marinade

3 large onions, chopped   Salt and pepper
2 small cloves garlic, crushed   Juice of 4 lemons
½ teaspoon red pepper   1 tablespoon peanut or vegetable
¼ teaspoon ginger   oil
                                       1 cup water

Mix together all marinade ingredients including the lemon rinds in a large bowl. Stir well, then add the chicken pieces and allow to marinate for several hours (up to one day). Be sure each piece is either immersed in marinade or turned occasionally to be evenly coated.

When ready to cook the chicken, remove it and pat dry with a towel but reserve the marinade.

Pan-Fried

Heat 3 teaspoons of peanut or vegetable oil in a large skillet and brown the chicken, a few pieces at a time, turning frequently. As they brown, remove to a plate.

Now return the chicken to the skillet, and add 2 teaspoons of the liquid marinade and ½ cup of water. Bring to the boil, then simmer, partly covered, for 30 minutes. Serve with rice and vegetables. Serves 4..

Broiled or Barbecued

Grill over a charcoal fire (4 inches from the heat) for 10 minutes on a side or broil in an oven. Return the chicken plus ½ cup water and the solid marinade to the skillet. Cover and simmer for 20-30 minutes. Serve with rice.

NIGERIA

Jollof Rice

Jollof is a stewlike dish named for the Wolloff tribe of Senegal, West Africa. *Jollof* means "one pot," and permits virtually any combination of meat, fish, poultry, or vegetable. It is usually reserved for high occasions such as weddings or when special guests arrive.

4 tablespoons peanut oil
1 pound lean stewing beef, cut into small cubes
1 3-pound chicken, cut up
1 pound lean pork, cut into large cubes
2 large onions, chopped coarsely
2 large tomatoes, peeled and chopped
Salt and pepper
3 green peppers, seeded and chopped
2 cloves garlic, sliced

1 cup chicken stock
2 cloves
½ teaspoon nutmeg
⅛ teaspoon parsley flakes
Pinch thyme
1 bay leaf
3 cups water
2 2-ounce cans tomato paste
1 chili pepper, chopped finely
1½ cups white rice
1 small cabbage
2 zucchini or yellow squash, cut crosswise into ¼-inch slices

Rub the chicken pieces with salt and pepper. Heat the oil in a large stewpot, brown the chicken pieces thoroughly for 10 minutes, and set aside. Add the beef and pork and brown on all sides, then add one chopped onion, tomatoes, peppers, and garlic, cover, and cook for 15 minutes. Pour in the chicken stock, reduce heat, and simmer for 10 minutes more. The pan liquid should be substantially reduced and thickened. Return the chicken and add the cloves, nutmeg, parsley, thyme, and bay leaf. Simmer an additional 15 minutes, covered.

When done, remove the chicken, beef, and pork and keep warm. Pour a little sauce over to keep moist. Add 3 cups of water to the pan along with the tomato paste, and chopped chili, and the remaining chopped onion. Bring to the boil, add the rice, then reduce heat to moderate, cover, and cook for 30 minutes. Remove from the heat but leave covered for 10 minutes so that the rice can absorb all the pan juices.

Wash and cut the cabbage into 6 pieces and cook in salted water for 15 minutes. Cook the squash in a separate saucepan for 15 minutes. Drain and season each vegetable with salt and pepper.

Shape the rice into a mound on a serving platter and sprinkle with nutmeg. Arrange the chicken, beef, pork, and vegetables around and serve immediately. Serves 6-8.

IVORY COAST

CHICKEN A LA N'GATIERO—Chicken in Peanut Sauce
This recipe is very similar to *Mafe* from Niger, though it calls for more peanuts or peanut butter. Groundnuts (peanuts) are rich in protein and are thus a staple in the diets of many African nations.

1 3-4-pound chicken, cut up	1 teaspoon tomato paste
2 tablespoons peanut oil	7 cups water
2 shallots, cut up	8 ounces peanut butter
1 medium onion, chopped	½ teaspoon red pepper
2 large tomatoes, diced	1 bay leaf
	½ teaspoon salt

Heat the peanut oil in a Dutch oven or deep saucepan and brown the chicken pieces on all sides. Add the shallots, onion, tomato, and tomato paste and cook for 1-2 minutes. Add water, bring to the boil, then cover and cook over low heat for 10 minutes. Meanwhile make a creamy paste of the peanut butter by stirring in a little water. Add this to the pot, with red pepper, bay leaf, and salt. Reduce heat and simmer for 30 minutes. Serves 4.

Gambia

CHICKEN THIOU—Chicken Vegetable Stew

A typical West African stew, this uses many of the vegetables common to the area. It can be cooked with chicken or beef (or both) with equally good results.

1 3-pound chicken, cut up	2 medium sweet potatoes, sliced
¼ cup oil or melted butter	2 pimentos (or sweet red peppers)
2 large onions, chopped	2 carrots, sliced
1 tablespoon tomato paste	2 turnips, chopped
¼ medium cabbage, shredded	1 bay leaf
4 medium tomatoes, peeled and chopped	Salt and pepper
	4 cups water

Heat the oil in a Dutch oven and sauté the onions lightly, then remove with a slotted spoon and set aside. Brown the chicken pieces on all sides in the remaining oil, then add the tomato paste and stir in a little water. Add the vegetables to the pot along with the bay leaf and a little salt and pepper. Return the onions, add the remaining water, and bring to the boil. Now reduce the heat to low and simmer covered for an hour. Serves 4-6.

Note: A variation of this includes the addition of peanut butter. Mix ¼ cup of crushed peanuts or peanut butter with a little water to make a smooth paste. Add to the pot after the chicken and vegetables have cooked for 30 minutes. Serve with rice.

Ghana

ASHANTI CHICKEN—Chicken with Peanut Butter and Sausage Stuffing

In Ghana this recipe calls for the complete boning of the chicken from the backbone to the breastbone, taking care not to break the flesh. The stuffing is then added and the deboned chicken is reconstructed and sewn or skewered together. This takes a bit of talent and practice, and may be unnecessary; a whole chicken, properly stuffed, provides the same outstanding taste as the original, without all the work.

1 4-pound roasting chicken	1 large tomato, diced
½ pound bulk sausage	⅛ teaspoon black pepper
2 medium onions, chopped	1 tablespoon butter or oil
1 tablespoon groundnut paste (peanut butter)	⅛ teaspoon salt

Mix the sausage, onion, groundnut paste (or peanut butter), tomato, salt, and pepper in a bowl. Heat the oil in a skillet and cook the mixture for 5 minutes. Lard the chicken well, and then fill the cavity with the mixture. Now close the cavity with a skewer or truss and place the chicken in a roasting pan. Cook in a moderate oven, covered, for 1 hour and 15 minutes, basting frequently. Remove the cover and roast 15 minutes longer so the breast is cooked to a golden brown. Serves 4-6.

Note: If you wish to debone the chicken, see page 14 for directions.

NIGERIA

PALM OIL CHOP—Chicken Stew with Palava and Foofoo

A "chop" is a stew of sorts, or a soup if the pan liquid is not reduced too much, and it has a great many variations. The chop is made of a *palava* sauce and is served with *foofoo*. The sauce is the broth or stew and *foofoo* is a moist meal or paste prepared from the fermented root of the cassava plant. One Nigerian recipe (which may be where the dish originated) calls for such native herbs as *egusie* seeds, *bologie* leaves, both of which are probably impossible to find in this country, so this is an adaptation. Palm oil, incidentally, can be found in most specialty stores that feature Near Eastern or Latin American foods. If you can't find it, use olive or peanut oil.

1 3-pound chicken, cut up	½ cup palm oil
2 cups spinach, chopped	1 large onion, sliced
1 pound pork, cut into cubes	2 tomatoes, chopped
1 pound beef, cut into cubes	2 cups okra, chopped

2 shallots, chopped   Pinch cayenne pepper
2 quarts water   Salt

Boil the spinach in 1 cup of water for 10 minutes, strain, and set aside. Put the pork, beef, and chicken pieces and shallots into a pot with salt, cover with water, and simmer for 15 minutes. Do not cover.

Heat the palm oil in a large Dutch oven and sauté the sliced onion and chopped tomatoes gently for about 5 minutes. Now add the meat, chicken, okra, spinach, and cayenne pepper. Sprinkle over a little salt and simmer gently for one hour or until the meat is tender. Serves 6-8.

Foofoo

Foofoo is an African staple (also *fu-fu* or *fou fou*) that shows up in the cooking of many African nations. One method of preparing foofoo is to pound the fermented root of the cassava plant and strain it through a fine sieve. The meal is then left to stand in water for an hour. It is then strained again and cooked with a little lime juice. When the mixture is firm, it is molded onto a dish, to be served with the stew. (Cassava is found in some specialty shops in the North and rather commonly in the South.)

A poor substitute (and not recommended unless you can't find the real thing) uses instant mashed potatoes, which are easily obtained in America. Mix 1 cup of potato starch with 1 cup of instant mashed potatoes in 3 cups of water, then cook for about 5 minutes, stirring constantly to avoid lumping. When the mixture becomes very thick, remove to a large bowl, then shape into balls, and serve with the stew and palava sauce.

PART III:

Central Africa

ZAIRE (CONGO)

CHICKEN WITH GREEN PEPPERS

1 3-pound chicken	6 green peppers, sliced in rings
Salt and pepper	and seeded
½ cup butter	⅓ cup peanut butter
2 tablespoons chopped parsley	1 cup roasted peanuts (unsalted)

Preheat the oven to 350° F. Rub the chicken all over with salt and pepper, then smear a little butter over the breast, legs, and wings. Mix the chopped parsley with the remaining butter and pack it into the cavity. Put the bird into a roaster and then into the oven for 1 hour. Baste every 15 minutes or so. After 20 minutes, add the pepper slices, and cover these with butter drippings.

When the chicken is done, spread a thin layer of peanut butter over the breasts, legs, and wings and then scatter the roasted peanuts on top, making sure they stick. Return the pan to the oven and roast another 10 minutes. Serve the chicken on a platter with the pepper slices scattered over and around, with a bowl of white rice. Serves 4.

ZAIRE

ROAST CHICKEN WITH GROUNDNUT STUFFING

1 4-pound roasting chicken

Stuffing

¾ cup breadcrumbs	¼ cup butter
2 cups groundnuts (peanuts), crushed	2 onions, chopped coarsely
	2 eggs
	Salt and pepper

Mix the stuffing ingredients together and stuff the bird. Sew or skewer the cavity, then roast and serve the bird as you normally would. Serves 4-6.

A guinea fowl is frequently cooked this way in Africa; just increase the stuffing ingredients slightly.

ZAIRE

CHICKEN MOUAMBA—Chicken in Palm Oil Sauce

1 3-pound chicken, cut up	Salt and freshly ground pepper
	½ cup palm oil

Palm Oil Sauce

¼ cup palm oil	3 tablespoons peanut butter
1 onion, chopped finely	1 6-ounce can tomato paste
	1 cup fresh chicken stock

Sprinkle each chicken piece with salt and pepper. Heat ½ cup palm oil in a heavy skillet and brown the chicken on all sides. Now remove the skin and bones and cut the meat into small cubes. Set aside.

While the chicken is cooking, prepare the sauce: Heat the remaining ¼ cup of palm oil in a saucepan. Add the onion, peanut butter, tomato paste, stock, and a little salt and pepper. Bring the mixture to the boil, then add the diced chicken. Reduce to low heat and cook until the sauce thickens. Serve over rice. Serves 4.

PART IV:

East Africa

MOZAMBIQUE

GALINHA CAFEAL—Broiled Marinated Chicken with Coconut Sauce

2 3-pound chickens, cut up	1 teaspoon salt
1 cup strained lemon juice	2 tablespoons butter or oil
½ teaspoon red pepper	1½ cups coconut milk (page 82)

Place the chicken in a large, deep bowl. Combine the garlic, the lemon juice, red pepper, and salt and pour over the chicken. Turn the pieces several times to be sure each is completely covered with the marinade. Marinate at room temperature for 2 to 4 hours or in the refrigerator for 4 to 6 hours. Turn from time to time.

Next make the coconut milk. Preheat the oven to broil. (This dish, incidentally, is excellent cooked over an outside charcoal fire.)

Arrange the chicken pieces, meat side down, on the rack of the broiling pan. Prepare an oil and coconut mixture and brush each chicken piece, then broil about 4-5 inches from the heat for 8 minutes. Now baste the pieces with the oil-coconut mixture, broil again for 8 minutes, then turn and repeat the process on the other side.

Remove the chicken pieces to a heated platter and keep warm. Pour the pan juices into a small skillet, and add the remaining oil and coconut mixture. Stirring constantly, cook over low heat for several minutes until the sauce is thoroughly heated. (If you barbecue the chicken, you won't need a gravy, so just pour any unused basting juice

177

over the chicken and serve it.) Do not boil the coconut sauce. Now pour the sauce into a sauceboat and serve with the chicken. Serves 6-8.

MOZAMBIQUE

CHICKEN PIRIPIRI

This is really a barbecue recipe, which may take a short time to cook, but a long time (if you do it the right way) to prepare.

Piripiri is a seasoning made of dried, pounded red chilies in olive oil. It is actually called piripiri in Portugal, but in Portuguese Africa it also goes by the name of *jindungo*. It can be substituted for very easily with tabasco sauce, but it is so easy to make (provided you want to wait that long) that the real thing should be tried.

You need a glass bottle with a very tight stopper. Fill the bottle with one part dried, chopped red chilies and two parts olive oil. Let sit for 30 days, tightly closed.

1 3-pound chicken, cut up	¼ cup lemon juice
1 cup piripiri	Lemon peels
2 cloves garlic, chopped	½ teaspoon salt

Make a marinade of the piripiri, garlic, lemon juice and peels, and salt. Put in a large bowl and add the chicken pieces, turning occasionally to get complete coverage. Marinate for 2-4 hours.

Broil the chicken over a good charcoal fire. Brush occasionally with the marinade, and cook for about 30 minutes, or until done. (This can also be cooked in the oven broiler at high heat. Baste as above.) Serve with rice and vegetables, or with green mealies (see page 179) and tomatoes. Serves 4.

MALAWI

CURRIED CHICKEN STEW WITH MEALIES

2 small frying chickens, cut up	1 tablespoon ground coriander
2 medium onions, chopped	1 tablespoon ground cumin
Oil for frying	⅛ teaspoon black pepper
Salt and pepper	¼ teaspoon ground cardamom
2 large tomatoes, chopped	¼ teaspoon ginger
	⅛ teaspoon clove powder

Heat the oil in a stewpot, and sauté the onions until golden but not brown. Now add the chicken and a little salt and brown well on all sides. Add the chopped tomatoes and the spices and cover. Reduce the heat and cook for 1 hour. Add a little water if necessary. Serve with mealies baked with tomatoes and rice. Serves 6-8.

Mealies Baked with Tomatoes

Mealies, in Africa, are corn on the cob. They are eaten either green (which is how this recipe was originally written) or ripened.

3 cups mealies (from about 4 medium cobs), or one 8-ounce can of corn, or 3 cups frozen, defrosted corn)	1 onion, chopped finely 3 tomatoes 2 eggs, separated Salt and pepper 2 tablespoons breadcrumbs

First cook the corn until it is done. Then cut the kernels away from the cob into a large mixing bowl. Mix in the chopped onion, chopped tomatoes, and the salt and pepper. Beat the egg yolks and add them to the pot. Now beat the egg whites until stiff and fold into the mixture. Layer the breadcrumbs on top. Dot the entire mixture with butter. Bake in a 325° F oven for 15 or 20 minutes, until well cooked.

KENYA

SAFFRON CHICKEN WITH RAISINS

2 3-pound chickens, cut up	½ teaspoon cinnamon
8 tablespoons butter	½ teaspoon cardamom
2 medium onions, chopped	½ teaspoon saffron
2 cups white rice	½ cup raisins
½ teaspoon ground cloves	5 cups chicken stock
¼ teaspoon paprika	Salt and ground pepper

In a casserole heat the oil or butter and sauté the onions lightly. Add the rice and brown, pour in 4 cups of stock, a little salt and pepper, and simmer for 30 minutes. (The pan liquid should be nearly gone.) While the rice is cooking, mix together the ground cloves, paprika, cinnamon, and cardamom in a small bowl. Now rub the spice mixture into each piece of chicken thoroughly.

Sprinkle the remaining spice mixture plus half the saffron and raisins over the rice. Now place the chicken pieces on top of the rice, add the remaining cup of stock, and sprinkle the rest of the saffron and raisins over. Bake in a moderate oven (350° F) for 30 minutes. Serves 6-8.

UGANDA

CHICKEN STEW WITH PLANTAINS

Plantains are a close cousin to the banana. They look the same but are not sweet like the banana and must be cooked. They are used extensively as a vegetable in African cookery and when cooked in the green, or unripe, state and then mashed, resemble the potato in both look and taste. Plantains were known in the Middle East in Alexander's time and today are common throughout Central America and the Caribbean Islands.

In the following recipe, use regular potatoes or yams if you cannot find plantains.

2 pounds plantains
Salt and pepper
1 3-pound chicken, cut up

4 tablespoons palm or peanut oil
2 onions, chopped
2 tomatoes, chopped
2 cups water

Heat the oil in a Dutch oven and brown the chicken on all sides. Add the onions, tomatoes, and water, then salt and pepper to taste, cover, and simmer 1 hour.

Peel the plantains and place on a rack in a pot above the level of a little water. Add salt and pepper and bring the water to the boil. Now reduce the heat and cover, and steam the plantains for 40 minutes. Remove and mash, and keep warm in indirect heat until ready to serve.

Place the plantains in the center of a platter and arrange the chicken pieces around. Pour sauce over all. Serves 4-6.

PART V:

South Africa

CAPE MALAY

GESMOORDE HOENDER—Chicken and Green Chilies

The combination of chicken and green chilies in a white wine sauce may appear a little unusual, but the taste is outstanding.

1 chicken, cut up	2 onions, sliced
2 green chilies, diced	½ cup white wine
2 tablespoons butter	Salt and pepper
	Pinch nutmeg

Heat the butter in a skillet and brown the chicken all over. Remove the pieces and keep warm. Fry the onions gently, return the chicken, and add the wine, salt and pepper, nutmeg, and diced chilies. Cover tightly and simmer 1 hour. Serve with cooked rice and a green salad. Serves 4.

CAPE MALAY

HOENDER EN AARDAPPEL—Chicken and Potatoes in White Wine Sauce

1 3-pound chicken, cut up	Salt and pepper
2 tablespoons butter	½ cup white wine
Gizzard, heart, and liver, chopped	1 tablespoon parsley flakes
	Parsley for garnish
1 pound potatoes, peeled and diced	4 tablespoons cornstarch

Rub the chicken with salt and pepper and let sit for 5 minutes. Sauté the chicken pieces in butter and set aside and keep warm. In the same skillet add the chopped giblets and sauté for a minute or so, until they just lose their pink color. Don't overcook. Remove the browned giblets and put with the chicken pieces. Now sauté the potatoes lightly, being careful not to brown. Add a little water, if necessary.

In a casserole large enough to hold the chicken and potatoes comfortably, place the chicken and giblets and add the potatoes on top. Salt a little and add a few grindings of fresh pepper. Add ¼ cup of white wine, cover, and cook in a moderate oven (350° F) for about 40 minutes. Remove the chicken to a warm platter. Spoon the potatoes into a mound in the center of the platter and arrange the chicken pieces around it. Sprinkle all lightly with parsley flakes and garnish with sprigs of parsley. Serve with white wine sauce. Serves 4.

White Wine Sauce

From the casserole, take about ¾ cup of pan fluid and let cool. Mix in 4 tablespoons cornstarch. Stir well, smoothing out all lumps. Now stir this mixture back into the pan liquid. Add ¼ cup of white wine and bring to the boil, then reduce heat and cook, stirring constantly, for about 5 minutes, or until the sauce thickens to desired consistency. Pass in a sauceboat.

CAPE MALAY

HOENDER PASTEI—Chicken Pie

2 onions, chopped	1 tablespoon sago (tapioca)
3 teaspoons allspice	4 tablespoons butter
⅛ teaspoon mace	Salt
6 peppercorns	2 egg yolks
1 3-pound chicken, cut up	Juice of 1 lemon
2 tablespoons vermicelli	3 slices ham
	Pastry

Combine in a cloth bag one chopped onion, the allspice, mace, and peppercorns. Tie the bag and drop it into a saucepan. Add the chicken pieces, the other chopped onion, and the stock. Bring to the boil, then reduce the heat and simmer for about 30 minutes. Now add the vermicelli and sago (tapioca) and butter and a little salt. Cook for another 15 minutes, until the chicken is tender. Stir frequently to be sure the sago and vermicelli don't stick and burn.

Remove the bag and discard. Whip one egg yolk with the lemon juice and stir into the broth. Remove all skin from the chicken pieces, bone each piece, and cut the meat into chunks about 1 inch square. Chop the ham slices coarsely.

Line a baking dish with pastry (see below) and put in the chicken and ham and pour over the sauce. Now cover with a pastry top, and brush with egg yolk. Place in a hot oven (400°F) and cook until golden brown. Serves 4.

Pastry

2 cups sifted flour	⅔ cup shortening
1 teaspoon salt	5-6 tablespoons ice water

Sift the flour and salt into a bowl, then add the shortening. Blend until the mixture looks coarse or mealy. Slowly add ice water, stirring with a fork. Shape a ball out of the pastry, then roll it out into ⅛-inch thickness on a floured pastry board.

CAPE MALAY

GEBRAAIDE HOENDER—Spiced Roast Chicken

1 3-pound chicken, cut up	1 clove garlic, crushed
Salt	⅛ teaspoon each of:
1 cup water	turmeric
1 pound potatoes, diced	fenugreek
Oil	cumin
1 onion, chopped finely	fennel
Pinch ginger	allspice

Rub each piece of chicken with salt and place the pieces in a skillet with 1 cup of water. Cover and simmer gently.

After 15 minutes, add the potatoes, a little oil if necessary, and the onion. Add also the spices and the ginger and garlic. Now simmer for an additional 30 minutes. Serve with rice or vegetables. Serves 4.

❧ Chapter 7 ❧

Eastern Europe

East Europe is a territorial corridor of ten nations running from the Baltic Sea to the Aegean. Over the centuries these countries played host to, among others, the Greeks, the Romans, the Huns, the Avars, the Slavs, the Bulgars, the Magyars, the Khazars, the Mongols, Charlemagne's armies, the Venetians, the Crusaders, the Ottoman Turks, and even the Russians and Americans in the twentieth century. Most brought their culinary traditions with them, and so many have endured that East Europe today presents perhaps the most dramatic examples of Eastern and Western cooking combined in the same pot. Despite this sharing of a turbulent history, the cooking of the northern countries in the corridor is radically different from that of the Balkans.

The Northern Countries

The northern countries were home to semisavage hunters and warriors, and their early gastronomy reflected it: thick stews and soups, served with dumplings (which in time became *galuska* in Hungary, *spaetzle* in Germany, and *knedlichy* in Czechoslovakia), roast pork and sausages, stuffed goose, wild game, noodles, black bread, red and green cabbage, and beer.

Eastern influences on this hearty diet came at first with Attila and the Huns in the fifth century and were reinforced by invaders over the next seven hundred years. All brought the cooking of Central Asia with them—grilled and raw chopped meat, sour cream, yogurt, pickles, and most particularly sauerkraut, which the Asians themselves had borrowed from the Chinese. Although obviously more sophisticated now in preparation and presentation, the general cuisine of the northern countries today is probably more like that of antiquity than of any other in Europe.

The two best examples of ancient cooking are the *Bogracsos* of Hungary and the *Bigos* of Poland, both of which were born over a thousand years ago, and both of which remain the national dishes of their countries. The original *Bogracsos* was a communal meal of the Magyars and was cooked outdoors in a large metal pot (*bogracs*) over a wood fire. The men of the tribe would forage for food, and what they brought back went into the pot regardless of whether it was wild or domestic meat, fowl, vegetable, root, or herb.

It has come down to modern times as a superb stew, which can be

187

varied endlessly, and in Hungary today chicken is very frequently the meat of choice.

While the bogracsos was a peasant meal, the bigos was strictly for the aristocracy. Polish nobility, with an entourage frequently numbering in the hundreds, would take to the forests at regular intervals to indulge in their favorite pastime, hunting. The day's bag was heated in huge kettles that never stopped cooking. Today's catch was tossed into the pot on top of what remained from yesterday's and the whole thing cooked again, so that the meat extracts and vegetable juices were continually reduced to a rich essence of extraordinary taste. In this same tradition, the bigos of today is cooked the day before it is to be served, and then cooked again.

Fowl cookery is enormously popular in all five northern countries, but not so much chicken as duck, goose, or wild gamebirds. The birds are more often roasted than not and either stuffed or served with potatoes, noodles, sauerkraut, or dumplings.

But chicken wasn't even known in East Europe until five hundred years ago, when it was introduced by the Ottoman Turks. Perhaps the Turks made their most noteworthy contribution when they introduced the sweet red pepper called *paprika,* and the plump tender chicken. The Hungarians lost little time in combining the two into one of the world's classics—*Csirke Paprikas,* or chicken paprika. From this early beginning both the chicken and paprika went on to greater glories all over Europe. Austria, for instance, adopted the spice and the bird and created *Paprikahuhn,* only they cooked it in sweet cream instead of sour.

The Austrian cuisine is more diverse and sophisticated than the others of East Europe. Vienna was the seat of the powerful Hapsburg dynasty, and the kitchens were commanded by some of the finest Italian and French chefs on the continent. These artists not only brought the greatness of their own cooking to Austria, they improved on the native cookery they found.

East Europe was also home to the largest concentration of European Jews. Pork was alien to their religion, and beef too expensive, so poultry became their staple. Not being wealthy, the Jews found a use for everything—the feet were used to add body to soup, the fat for frying, the giblets for gravies, and the neck (skin and meat) for *Helzel,* ground or chopped chicken or goose meat sewn into the neck skin and either boiled or roasted with the bird.

Jewish cooking is now found in most Western cuisines. Coinciden-
tally, it was during the great Jewish migration to America in the last
century that the domestic poultry industry in this country began to
flourish.

Austria

SACHER HUHN—Chicken with Sausage and Sweetbreads

An Austrian dish with Italian overtones, this was originally made with small wild gamebirds, but is outstanding with Rock Cornish game hen or small young chicken.

1 pound Italian sweet sausage	Salt and freshly ground pepper
Liver from the chicken, chopped finely	¼ cup port wine
2 lamb sweetbreads, chopped	1 4-pound roasting chicken
	Parsley sprigs for garnish

Preheat the oven to 350°F. Mix the sausage, chopped livers, and chopped sweetbreads together, then sprinkle over a little salt and freshly ground pepper. Cook in a skillet over a low flame for 10 minutes, stirring frequently, until the mixture has browned slightly. When nearly done, add the port wine and stir for a moment, then remove from the heat. Stuff the chicken with the mixture, and pour over the remaining pan liquid. Truss or skewer the cavities and roast, covered, for 1 hour. Baste every 10-15 minutes. Remove cover and brown the breast and legs for 15 minutes, then serve garnished with parsley sprigs. Serves 6.

Austria

PERL HUHN—Roast Guinea Fowl

Because the guinea fowl has naturally dry meat, it is usually larded, and this is done with a larding needle. Bacon fat strips are threaded through the eye of the needle, then inserted and pulled through the skin, where they are left to keep the meat moist while cooking.

6-8 long, thin strips bacon fat	½ calve's brain
1 6-8-pound guinea fowl, or 2 3½-4-pound roasting chickens	½ cup white wine
1 large onion	2 mushrooms, sliced
12 cloves	1 cup heavy cream
Salt and pepper	1 egg yolk
Butter	¼ cup chicken stock
	Fried toast

Preheat the oven to 375° F. Using a larding needle, insert the bacon fat under the bird's breast and thigh skin (omit this step if chicken is used).

Stick the cloves into the onion and place that inside the bird. Now sprinkle and rub salt and pepper all over the bird and roast it for 1 hour in 6 tablespoons of butter. Baste every 10-12 minutes.

Clean the calve's brain of all skin and blood, and soak, in well-salted water for 20 minutes. Cut the brain into small pieces and sauté gently for 5 minutes in 2 tablespoons butter. Pour in the wine, add the mushrooms and the stock, and simmer for 20 minutes. Then beat together the cream and egg yolk and add to the brains. Let simmer for 5-6 minutes, until it starts to thicken, and then pour into a sauceboat. Fry 6-8 pieces of de-crusted white bread and arrange these on a large serving platter around the guinea fowl. Spoon equal portions of the brains in their sauce onto each piece of toast and serve one with each portion of fowl. Serves 6-8.

AUSTRIA

PAPRIKAHUHN—Chicken Paprika

Austria and Hungary have shared a great deal of history and in the process have traded many culinary secrets. One was chicken paprika. Austria was quick to find and adopt this classic recipe from Hungary, but she cooked it with sweet cream instead of sour, or with a mixture of some of each.

1 3-pound chicken, cut up	1 medium tomato, peeled and
6 tablespoons butter	chopped
1 onion, chopped	Salt and pepper
1 carrot, chopped	1 cup chicken stock
1 stalk celery, chopped	1 cup sweet cream
2 tablespoons paprika	1 tablespoon grated cheese
3 tablespoons flour	Parsley sprigs or watercress for
	garnish

Melt 4 tablespoons butter in a large, deep skillet or Dutch oven, and brown the chicken pieces on each side. Remove and set aside. Add the remaining butter and the chopped onion, carrot, and celery and cook over low heat for 10 minutes, stirring 2 or 3 tines. Add 2 tablespoons paprika and, stirring continuously, cook for another 2-3 minutes. Remove the pan from the heat and stir in the flour, tomato, and salt and pepper, then add the stock and return to the fire. Raise the heat and stir the mixture until it comes to the boil, then reduce it to low and simmer for 15 minutes.

Now return the chicken pieces to the pan, spoon over the sauce, and cover and cook slowly for 40 minutes. When done, arrange the chicken pieces on a serving platter. Add the sweet cream to the sauce with 1 tablespoon of grated cheese. Stir to blend thoroughly, then spoon the mixture over the chicken pieces. Garnish with parsley sprigs or watercress, and serve with spaetzle. Serves 4.

Spaetzle

3 quarts water, plus 1 cup	1 egg
4 teaspoons salt	Melted butter
2½ cups sifted flour	½ tablespoon paprika

Bring 3 quarts of water to the boil and add 3 teaspoons salt. Beat together 1 egg and 1 teaspoon of salt in 1 cup of water, then slowly blend in the sifted flour until a smooth dough is formed. Drop the dough into the boiling water in ½-teaspoon amounts—they should be about 1 inch thick when they rise to the surface. Cook for 10 minutes, then remove and keep warm. Repeat this process until all the dough is used.

Drizzle melted butter generously over the spaetzle and then sprinkle on the paprika for color.

AUSTRIA

ESTRAGON HUHN—Tarragon Chicken

One of the great fowl dishes of France has its Austrian counterpart. Here's one version with a spectacular white wine gravy:

1 cup chicken broth	1 stalk celery, sliced across very
Salt and pepper	thinly
1 teaspoon tarragon	1 leek, sliced
2 bay leaves	3 tablespoons flour
1 3-pound chicken, cut up	¾ cup light cream

2 carrots, sliced across	1 egg yolk
¼ cup mushrooms, washed and sliced	¾ cup dry white wine

Bring the chicken broth to the boil in a Dutch oven, then add ½ tablespoon salt, pepper, tarragon, and bay leaves. Add the chicken pieces, reduce the heat to low, cover, and simmer for 30 minutes. Now add the carrots, sliced mushrooms, celery, and leek to the pot and cook covered for 30 minutes. Remove the meat and vegetables to a platter and keep warm. Strain the pan liquid and reserve 1 cup of the fluid.

White Wine Gravy

In a bowl, mix together the flour, cream, and egg yolk and stir until smooth. Now add the cup of pan fluid and wine to the Dutch oven and bring the heat up to medium. Pour the cream mixture in a little at a time, stirring continuously, and cook over low heat until smooth and slightly thickened. Remove from the heat and spoon the gravy over the chicken. Serves 4.

AUSTRIA

HUHNER MIT GRUNER—Chicken with Green Gravy

2 tablespoons butter	Salt and freshly ground pepper
1 stalk celery	1 3-pound chicken, cut up
1 medium onion, chopped finely	1 cup chicken stock
	1 8-ounce can mushroom soup

Green Gravy

4 tablespoons finely chopped chives	3 tablespoons butter
	2 tablespoons flour
4 tablespoons finely chopped parsley	1 cup chicken stock
	1 cup light cream

In a deep pan, slice the celery thinly and sauté gently with the chopped onion in butter until golden and soft. Add salt and pepper to the chicken pieces and a little to the sauté vegetables, then place the chicken pieces in the pan and pour in the stock and mushroom soup.

Simmer gently for 1 hour, then remove to a serving platter and serve with green gravy.

To make the green gravy, chop the chives and parsley, then mash the pulp to extract some of the juice. Over low heat, melt the butter and stir in 2 tablespoons flour until smooth, then add the stock and cream a little at a time, stirring constantly. When the gravy is thickened, stir in the parsley and chives and their juice. When completely blended the gravy should be a bright green. Serve with the chicken in a gravy boat. Serves 4.

CZECHOSLOVAKIA

ROAST GOOSE (OR CHICKEN) WITH SAUERKRAUT AND KNEDLIKY

Roast goose is a favorite in Czechoslovakia and is frequently accompanied by *knedliky,* a dumpling made in a variety of different ways, which takes the place of bread or potatoes.

Note: If you cook a 4-5 pound chicken, reduce all other ingredients by half.

1 8-10 pound goose, or 4-5 pound chicken	4 pounds fresh sauerkraut
6 tablespoons butter or oil	1 teaspoon caraway seeds
2 onions, chopped finely	3 tablespoons flour
1 cup water	2 tablespoons sugar
	Salt and freshly ground pepper

Preheat the oven to 350° F. Wash the goose inside and out with cold water. Sprinkle with salt and a few grindings of pepper all over the outside and rub it into the bird. Rub more salt into the cavity. Place the goose into a roaster and add 1 cup of water. Cover and roast for 2-2½ hours, basting frequently. (Note: If you use chicken, roast for 1 hour and 15 minutes.) When there is about 1 hour of cooking time left for the bird begin preparing the sauerkraut.

Brown the onion in butter or oil in a medium saucepan. Add water, the sauerkraut, and the caraway seeds and simmer over low heat for 45 minutes, stirring well every 5 minutes or so. Add the flour and sugar and a little salt and freshly ground pepper, and mix thoroughly. Simmer for 5 minutes.

Serve the goose or chicken on a warm platter and the sauerkraut in a separate bowl. Serve with knedliky. Serves 6-8 for goose, 4-6 for chicken.

Bramborovymi Knedliky—Potato Dumplings

4 cups cooked mashed potatoes	1 cup flour
2½ tablespoons salt	1 egg
½ cup farina	½ cup melted butter

Make a dough by combining the potatoes, ½ teaspoon salt, farina, flour, and a beaten egg. Knead for 10-15 minutes, then make the dumplings. These can be any size or shape you choose, but round or oval dumplings, each using from ¼ to ½ cup of dough, are preferable. Bring 2 quarts of water to the boil in a large saucepan and add 2 tablespoons salt. Add the dumplings one or two at a time until they are all in the water, then simmer for 15 minutes. Remove to a serving dish and pour on the melted butter, then serve with the goose and sauerkraut.

GERMANY

HUHN IN SPECKSAUCE—Chicken in Bacon Sauce

1 3-pound chicken, cut up	1 shallot, chopped finely
4 tablespoons butter	2 cups chicken stock
4-5 strips fat bacon, diced	Salt and freshly ground black
Livers of the chicken, diced	pepper
Juice and grated rind of 1 lemon	Parsley for garnish

Melt the butter in a large deep skillet with a cover, and brown the chicken pieces on all sides. Add the diced bacon and livers, then add the lemon juice and grated rind, the shallot, the broth, and the salt and fresh pepper. Bring to the boil, then cover and reduce heat to low. Simmer for 30-40 minutes, until done. Remove to a warm platter and arrange the parsley over and around the chicken. Serve the gravy in a sauceboat. Serves 4.

GERMANY

HUHN MIT LEBERKNODEL—
Chicken with Liver Dumplings

1 3-pound chicken, cut up	¼ teaspoon rosemary
2 slices bacon	⅛ teaspoon thyme
3 onions, chopped coarsely	⅛ teaspoon sage
3 carrots, quartered lengthwise	1 bay leaf
3 stalks celery, sliced across	2 cups water
2 cups chicken stock	4 tablespoons flour
Salt and freshly ground pepper	Parsley sprigs for garnish

Liver Dumplings

Liver from the chicken	1 tablespoon chopped parsley
2 eggs, separated	Salt
1 teaspoon butter, creamed	1 teaspoon fine breadcrumbs

Brown the bacon until crisp in a large Dutch oven or casserole. Remove and set aside. Sauté the chicken pieces, a few at a time, in the bacon fat, until brown on all sides, then add the onions, carrots, celery, stock, salt and pepper, rosemary, thyme, sage, and bay leaf. Crumble the bacon into small bits and sprinkle them into the pot, then add 2 cups of water. Bring the pot to boiling, then reduce the heat to low, cover, and simmer gently for 1 hour. When the chicken and vegetables are done, remove them to a platter and keep warm.

Strain the broth, return it to the pan, and bring it to the boil. Combine all the liver dumpling ingredients and blend thoroughly in a bowl. Moisten a teaspoon in the boiling broth and then drop in spoonfuls of the liver mixture. When they are done they will rise to the top. Remove and keep warm.

When the dumplings have finished cooking, blend the flour and ½ cup of the broth together until smooth, then pour back into the gently boiling broth. Stir constantly until the liquid begins to thicken, then remove from the heat and serve in a sauceboat. Serve the chicken, vegetables, and dumplings on a platter, garnished with parsley sprigs. Serves 4.

GERMANY

HELZEL—Stuffed Goose (or Chicken) Neck

In this country, helzel is commonly associated with the Jewish kitchen, but in Eastern Europe, particularly Germany, it is enjoyed by Jew and gentile alike. Helzel can be made in many different ways, but the two most popular are either a ground meat mixture of beef, veal, and goose meat or simply a mixture of grain. It is probably the closest thing to a poultry sausage there is.

Necks of one goose or 4-6 chickens	1 teaspoon flour
½ cup ground veal	½ cup chicken stock
½ cup ground chuck	1 teaspoon lemon juice
1 clove garlic, crushed	Salt and pepper
4 slices white bread (1 cup), shredded into very small pieces	2 eggs
2 medium onions, chopped finely	1 cup water
2 tablespoons butter	1 bay leaf
	1 carrot, peeled and sliced
	6 peppercorns

Gently pull the skin off the neck, taking care to avoid breaking or tearing the skin. Pick off all the flesh that's on the neck bone and chop or grind it finely. Now mix together the goose, veal, and ground chuck in a bowl. Add the garlic, the shredded bread, and chopped onion, and mix together thoroughly.

Melt 1 tablespoon butter and stir in the flour until it browns slightly. Add the stock and stir until smooth. Now add the meat mixture, lemon juice, and a little salt and pepper. Simmer for 20-30 minutes, until the meat is done. Cool, then beat and stir in the eggs.

Sew up one end of the goose neck and fill it with the mixture. Sew up the other end and any vents or tears in the skin. Melt the remaining butter and brown the necks on all sides. Then put them in a pan with the water, bay leaf, carrot, and peppercorns and cook for 30 minutes. Serves 2-4.

GERMANY

SAUERES HUNCHEN—Sour Chicken

1 3-pound chicken, cut up
1 quart water
1 cup vinegar
¼ teaspoon grated nutmeg

1 medium onion, chopped
    coarsely
½ bay leaf
3 whole cloves
1 cup sour cream

Place the chicken pieces in a large pan or Dutch oven and add water, vinegar, nutmeg, and onion. Add 1 bay leaf and 3 cloves in a small cheesecloth bag. Cover and cook over low heat for 1½ hours. When done remove the chicken pieces and the cheesecloth bag. Stir in the sour cream and simmer for an additional 10 minutes until the pan liquid is reduced somewhat, then pass in a sauceboat. Serves 4.

AUSTRIA

WIENER BACKHUHN—Viennese Fried Chicken

1 3-pound frying chicken, cut up
Juice of 1 lemon
Salt and pepper
Flour

2 eggs, beaten with 3 tablespoons
    water
Breadcrumbs
⅔ cup melted butter
Lemon slices and parsley springs
    for garnish

Remove the skin from all chicken pieces except the wings. Flatten the breast pieces, removing bones as necessary so they will fry evenly. Sprinkle the chicken with lemon juice and let stand at room temperature for 1 hour. Sprinkle with salt and pepper and dredge lightly with flour, by putting 3 or 4 pieces in a bag with flour and shaking.

Now dip each piece into beaten egg, then dredge with breadcrumbs. Melt the butter in a deep skillet, add the chicken, and fry slowly over moderate heat, turning once so that both sides become golden brown. When brown, lower heat, and fry for another 8 to 10 minutes on each side.

Arrange the fried chicken pieces in a single layer in an open baking pan. Pour the melted butter from the skillet over each piece and bake in a preheated 325° F oven for 10 minutes or until the breading is dry and crisp. Garnish with lemon slices and parsley sprigs. Serves 4.

HUNGARY

CSIRKE PORKOLT—Chicken Stew with Dumplings

One of the trademarks of Hungarian cooking is the accompanying noodles, dumplings, or potatoes. This is hearty fare, and is served with virtually every meal, whether soup, stew, or just bread alone is offered. These dumplings are very similar to the famous Hungarian galuska (page 203).

2 tablespoons butter	2 teaspoons paprika
2 onions, chopped	Chicken giblets, chopped
1 clove garlic, sliced	coarsely
1 3-pound chicken, cut up	2 tablespoons tomato paste
Salt	4 cups chicken stock
	2 tablespoons parsley flakes

In a large casserole, melt the butter and gently sauté the chopped onions and garlic. When soft and golden, add the chicken pieces and sprinkle with a little salt and paprika. Add the chopped giblets, tomato paste, and the chicken stock. Reduce heat, cover, and simmer over low heat for 1½ hours.

While the chicken cooks, prepare the dumplings:

1 cup flour	1 egg
⅛ teaspoon salt	Water

Sift the flour and salt into a bowl. Make a well and break the egg into it. Stir the egg into the flour thoroughly then, adding several teaspoons of water at a time, continue stirring until a firm dough forms. Be sure all the flour has been stirred in. Now roll the dough out on a board to about ½-inch thickness. Cut into ½-inch strips, then cut the strips into ½-inch pieces. Drop the pieces into the pot one at a time to prevent sticking.

When the chicken is done, remove the pieces to a platter and sprinkle with parsley. Strain the liquid and serve separately as a gravy or sauce and the dumplings in a bowl. Serves 4-6.

HUNGARY

BOGRACSOS CSIRKE—Casserole Chicken

2 3-pound chickens, cut up
Salt
3 tablespoons butter
1 red onion, chopped finely
1 tablespoon paprika
¼ pound mushrooms, sliced

½ cup tomatoes, peeled
1½ cups chicken stock
2 pounds small, new potatoes, peeled
1 cup sour cream
Parsley sprigs for garnish

Preheat the oven to 350° F. Sprinkle the chicken with salt. Melt the butter in a casserole, and add the paprika and chopped onion and the chicken pieces. Brown on all sides, add the mushrooms, tomatoes, and chicken stock, then cover and put in the oven for 1 hour.

While the chicken cooks, parboil the potatoes, then add them to the stew about ½ hour before it's done. Stir one cup of sour cream into the gravy just before serving. Sprinkle with parsley, then serve in the casserole pot. Serves 4.

AUSTRIA

HUHNERPALATSCHINKEN—Chicken Pancakes

Pancake Batter

1 cup milk

3 ounces flour
2 eggs

Mix together the pancake batter ingredients, blend well, and let stand for 1 hour.

3½ tablespoons butter
Juice and grated rind of ½ lemon
1 whole chicken breast, cooked and diced
½ cup mushrooms, sliced
1 teaspoon chives, chopped finely

Salt and pepper
Pinch nutmeg
½ tablespoon flour
2 tablespoons light cream
3 tablespoons grated Romano or Parmesan cheese, or 1½ tablespoons of each, mixed

In a skillet with a cover, melt 2 tablespoons butter and stir in the juice and grated rind of the lemon. Set the heat very low and stir in the diced chicken, mushrooms, chives, salt and pepper and nutmeg. Cover and cook for 10 minutes. Mash the flour together with ½ tablespoon of butter to make a smooth cream, then add to the chicken mixture. Add the cream and stir all together thoroughly, then cover and cook for another 5 minutes. Remove from the heat and keep warm.

Preheat the oven to 400° F. While the chicken mixture finishes cooking, make the pancakes. Melt the remaining butter and pour a little in a skillet or small omelet pan. Pour in the batter and brown, then toss or turn over and brown the other side. Use all the batter to make 4 or 6 pancakes, then put 3 tablespoons of the chicken mixture equally on each pancake, fold over, and place in a baking dish. Pour the remaining chicken mixture over the pancakes, sprinkle the cheese over all, and brown in the oven for a few minutes. Serves 4-6.

HUNGARY

MAZSOLA CSIRKE—Chicken with Raisin Sauce
This recipe is traditional for weddings in eastern Hungary.

2 quarts water plus ½ cup	½ cup raisins
1 3-4-pound chicken	½ cup sugar
2 teaspoons salt	1 cup white wine
1 lemon	2 teaspoons flour
½ cup vinegar	3 teaspoons butter

Bring 2 quarts of water to the boil in a saucepan and add the salt. Place the chicken in the pan, reduce heat to low, and cook slowly for 2 hours. Remove the chicken when done to a platter. Reserve one cup of broth.

Slice the lemon as thinly as possible, then put into a small pan with the vinegar and ½ cup water and cook slowly for 20-30 minutes. Drain, reserving the slices. Combine the raisins, sugar, and wine in the saucepan and cook gently until the raisins are full and plump.

Arrange the lemon slices all over the bird. Now blend the flour and butter together over low heat, add the cup of chicken broth, and stir into a smooth, somewhat thick paste. Add the raisins in wine and continue stirring. Serve the sauce in a sauceboat. Serves 4.

HUNGARY

CSIRKE PAPRIKAS—Chicken Paprika

The Ottoman Turks are as much responsible for this dish as the Hungarian, for the Turks introduced both the chicken and paprika to East Europe five hundred years ago.

2 2½-3-pound chickens, cut up	½ teaspoon paprika
Salt	2 teaspoons vinegar
6 tablespoons butter or oil	1 cup chicken stock
3 medium onions, chopped	⅓ cup sour cream
coarsely	Parsley sprigs for garnish

Rub the chicken pieces in salt and soak in cold water for 15 minutes. Heat 3 tablespoons of butter or oil in a large deep skillet. Drain the chicken pieces, but do not dry. Add to the skillet, a few pieces at a time, and fry lightly. They should be golden but not brown.

As the chicken fries, melt 3 tablespoons of butter or oil in the bottom of a Dutch oven or stewpot. Add the onions and sauté gently but do not brown, then stir in the paprika and vinegar. Now add the chicken pieces and the stock. Cover and stew for about 1 hour over low heat.

Remove the chicken from the pot and keep warm on a serving platter. Blend the sour cream into the liquid in the pot and pour some of the sauce over the chicken and the rest into a gravy boat. Sprinkle the chicken lightly with paprika for color and garnish with parsley. Serve with potatoes or galuska. Serves 6-8.

Note: Csirke Paprikas can be varied in several interesting ways:

1. Use tomato paste (⅓ cup) to make the gravy, instead of sour cream.

2. Use the same recipe, but instead of frying the chicken pieces lightly, put them directly into the Dutch oven or stewpot and stew over low heat for about 1½ hours. For color, combine ½ teaspoon paprika with melted butter and a little water and pour over the chicken.

3. Potatoes, carrots, and onions may be added to the stew after about ½ hour.

Galuska

3 tablespoons butter or oil	1 cup flour
1 cup water	2 eggs

Heat the butter or oil, add the water, then stir the flour in slowly to make a smooth paste. Beat the eggs lightly and stir into the paste.

In a deep saucepan, bring salted water to the boil. Using a teaspoon, drop small bite-sized pieces of dough into the water and let them boil, a few pieces at a time, for about 10 minutes. Remove the dumplings from the water with a slotted spoon and then hold them under cold running water. Pour melted butter over the dumplings and sprinkle with salt before serving.

HUNGARY

CSASZAR JERCE—Chicken in Cream and White Wine Sauce

1 3-pound chicken, cut up	1 cup heavy cream plus 2 table-
Salt	spoons
½ pound butter	1 cup dry white wine plus 2 table-
	spoons

Sprinkle the chicken pieces with salt a few pieces at a time and brown on all sides in butter in a large Dutch oven. Add 1 cup each of wine and cream to the pot, cover, and cook slowly for 45 minutes. When tender remove the chicken from the pot and keep warm. Add 2 tablespoons each of cream and wine to the pot juices and heat quickly on top of the stove. After the gravy thickens a bit, serve in a sauceboat along with rice or potatoes. Serves 4.

Note: This can be just as easily braised in a moderate oven (325-350° F) for the same length of time with the gravy made in the same way.

HUNGARY

CHICKEN WITH NOODLE STUFFING

This stuffing can be used with chicken, duckling, goose, or even turkey. The recipe makes about 3-4 cups of noodle stuffing, which is ample for any bird up to about 6 pounds. Adjust accordingly for larger or smaller birds.

1 4-pound roasting chicken
½ pound egg noodles
2 quarts water
3 tablespoons butter
1 small onion, chopped finely
Liver, gizzard, and heart, cleaned
    and diced

¼ pound paté de foie gras (or
    liverwurst), diced
2 tablespoons chopped fresh
    parsley
½ tablespoon paprika
¼ teaspoon sage
Salt and pepper

Add 1 tablespoon salt to 2 quarts of water and cook the noodles until tender. Drain and keep hot. Sauté the onions gently in butter until golden, then add the diced giblets and paté and cook slowly for 5 minutes. Now combine the onions, liver, and paté with the noodles. Pour in the cooking butter also. Add the parsley, paprika, sage, and a little salt and pepper. Toss well with forks to mix all ingredients evenly, then stuff the bird and roast it as you usually would. Serves 4-6.

CZECHOSLOVAKIA

ROAST CHICKEN WITH CARAWAY
This is similar to the great Scandinavian roast chicken, which has a butter and fresh parsley stuffing. The difference is there is less of the butter here, but the Czechs add caraway seeds for a totally different taste.

1 3-pound chicken
Salt and pepper
10-12 sprigs fresh parsley,
    chopped

8 tablespoons butter
2 tablespoons caraway seeds
4 slices bacon
6 potatoes, peeled

Preheat the oven to 350° F. Rub the chicken with salt and pepper inside and out. Mash the chopped parsley, caraway seeds, and 4 tablespoons butter together and stuff the body cavity. Place the bacon strips in the neck cavity under the skin. Place the chicken and potatoes in a roaster with the remaining butter, cover, and roast until tender, about 1 hour, basting frequently. Take the lid off for the last 15 minutes to brown the breast and legs. Serves 4.

POLAND

CHICKEN WITH ANCHOVY STUFFING

1 3-pound chicken	4 slices white bread, shredded and
2 strips bacon	crusts removed
1 small onion, chopped	¼ cup milk
Meat from 1 or 2 lean veal chops,	4 anchovies, washed
cubed	¼ cup butter
	2 eggs, separated
	Salt and freshly ground pepper
	Juice and grated rind of ¼ lemon

Preheat the oven to 350° F. Fry the bacon until crisp, then remove and sauté the chopped onion gently until golden. Add the veal meat and cook for 5-6 minutes, stirring frequently, then remove the onion and veal from the pan to cool.

Put the shredded bread in a bowl and pour in the milk a little at a time, turning the bread constantly to moisten all the pieces. Add the veal and onions to the bread and mix thoroughly. Now mash the anchovies with the butter and mix with the egg yolks. Stir this into the bowl and season with salt and pepper and the lemon rind and juice. Finally beat and fold in the egg whites. Stuff the bird and sew up the cavities, then roast, covered, for 1 hour. Remove the lid and brown· the breast and legs for an additional 15 minutes. Serves 4-6.

POLAND

BIGOS—Hunter's Stew

Originally, bigos was made for royal hunting parties in large outdoor cauldrons, with today's catch added to the remains of yesterday's. The result was a very rich and ever-changing stew. In this same tradition, bigos is now often made a day or two before it is to be served, and reheated.

2 cups boiling water	1 3-pound chicken, cut up
4-6 very large, fresh mushrooms	1 pound lean beef, cubed
6 tablespoons butter	½ pound lean pork, cubed
4 medium onions, chopped	1 cup chicken stock
1 cooking apple, peeled, cored,	1 cup Madeira wine
and chopped	½ pound kielbasa, sliced across in
	½-inch pieces

1 pound sauerkraut
½ pound cabbage, cored and
   shredded
6 medium tomatoes, quartered

Pinch each of clove, nutmeg, and
   cinnamon
Salt and pepper

Soak the mushrooms in boiling water for an hour or two, then slice very thinly. Reserve the water. Preheat the oven to 350°F.

In a heavy, 6-quart Dutch oven, sauté the chopped onions and apple in 2 tablespoons butter over low heat for about 5 minutes, then remove from the heat and stir in the tomatoes, sauerkraut, sliced mushrooms, and cabbage.

Melt 2 tablespoons butter in a large skillet and brown the chicken, beef, and pork cubes separately, adding butter as needed and turning frequently. When browned, transfer the pieces to the Dutch oven. Deglaze the pan by pouring in the stock and the Madeira and stirring for a minute or so to loosen all the meat particles, then pour this into the Dutch oven. Add also the soaking water from the mushrooms.

Now add the kielbasa slices, the spices, and the salt and pepper, then cover the Dutch oven and bake for 2 hours (remove the cover for the final 30 minutes). Serve directly from the pot. This is excellent with a good, dark beer. Serves 6-8.

Note: Goose or duck pieces are just as good as chicken. Also wild game such as rabbit, venison, boar, pheasant, or quail add a special flavor, which gets better and better each time it is reheated.

GERMANY

DUCKLING (OR CHICKEN) IN BEER

1 4-6-pound duckling or roasting
   chicken
Giblets of the duck, with mem-
   branes removed
6 ounces (½ bottle) dark or bock
   beer, or ale
4 tablespoons honey
½ teaspoon thyme

⅛ teaspoon clove powder or
   crushed clove
Pinch nutmeg
2 cups white bread, shredded
   finely, or breadcrumbs
2 egg yolks
6 tablespoons butter
1 orange, sliced
Parsley for garnish

Chop the giblets very finely and add them to a saucepan with ½ cup dark beer or ale, 2 tablespoons honey, thyme, cloves, and a pinch of nutmeg. Simmer gently for 15 minutes. Remove from the heat and cool, then mix in the shredded bread or breadcrumbs and the 2 egg yolks. Now stuff the bird.

Preheat the oven to 350°F. Melt 6 tablespoons of butter in a roasting pan and add ½ cup of the dark beer or ale and the remaining honey. Stir well and put the duck into the pan. Spoon some of the sauce over the bird, then cover and roast for 2 hours, basting every 15-20 minutes. Place the bird on a warm platter and pour the sauce on. Arrange orange slices on and around the duckling or chicken and add parsley sprigs for garnish. Serves 4-6.

POLAND

VOLHYNIAN CHICKEN—Parsley-Stuffed Roast Chicken

From southeastern Poland, which is now part of the U.S.S.R., this may be served either hot or cold.

1 4-pound roasting chicken	1 cup white bread, shredded
Salt and freshly ground pepper	coarsely (crusts removed)
Liver of the chicken, deveined	¼ cup milk
and chopped finely	6 tablespoons butter
2 cups fresh parsley, chopped	2 eggs
coarsely	Juice of ½ lemon

Preheat the oven to 375°F. Wash the chicken in cold water and pat dry, then rub it with salt and pepper inside and out.

Combine the chopped liver, parsley, shredded bread, and milk in a bowl and, with your fingers, work the mixture until blended thoroughly.

Now separate the eggs. In a separate bowl cream the egg yolks and 4 tablespoons butter together, then add to the liver and parsley mixture. Beat the egg whites until stiff and fold into the mixture, then stuff the bird and truss the cavity closed.

Place the chicken in a roasting pan. Melt 2 tablespoons butter, add the lemon juice, and pour or brush over the chicken so that it is completely covered, then turn the chicken onto its side. Cover and roast for 15 minutes, then turn the chicken onto its other side. Baste the bird, return the cover, and roast for another 15 minutes.

Now remove the cover, baste again, turn the chicken onto its back, and roast for 30 minutes or until done, uncovered. Serves 4-6.

The Balkans

The southern tier of East Europe is made up of the Balkan nations—Romania, Yugoslavia, Bulgaria, Greece, Albania (and European Turkey). Originally of Celtic and Dacian ancestry, the Balkan natives only partially accepted the Moslem religion when occupied by the Ottoman Turks in the fourteenth century, but they adopted the Moslem cuisine almost totally. One finds traces of the ancient Slavic gastronomy in Bulgaria and Romania; however, the cookery of all five countries has such a strong Middle Eastern flavor that many of the dishes even retain the Turkish names. The Turks introduced *meze*—the hors d'oeuvre of a hundred varieties—and they brought *yafka,* the paper-thin pastry dough that became *phyllo* in Greece and *strudel* in Germany. The great chicken pie of the Greeks, *kotopitta,* is a direct descendant of the Moorish *bstilla,* which was born in Spain and the Maghreb. Both use yafka or phyllo sheets on the bottom as well as the top so that the pie when served is completely surrounded by crust.

Turkey's *Tavuk Yahni* is very similar to the Greek *Kota Yahni,* and both are outstanding chicken stews. The Bulgarians offer chicken *Kesteni,* chicken cooked in a sweet chestnut sauce, which is patterned directly after the Turkish *Hindi Kesteneli* (although the Turks prefer turkey). The world classic *Ajem Pilaf* (chicken and rice) of Armenia found its way to Greece, where it is equally enjoyed as *Kotopoulo Atzem Pilafi,* only with a few onions added.

Avgolemeno is copied, or finds its roots (who can be sure) in the

Turkish *Baud Lemon*; but whatever the origin both are superb soups or sauces made of chicken stock with egg and lemon.

Though Turkey occupied Yugoslavia for years, Dalmatia on the Adriatic Coast was long a vassal of Venice, so fish and olive oil cookery predominate there. The northwestern states of Croatia and Slovenia show the influence of their Austro-Hungarian neighbors in such dishes as schnitzels and dumplings, pork and sauerkraut, black bread, beer, and chicken paprika, though the Yugoslavs make theirs into a stew with dumplings.

All Balkan countries have one or more versions of chicken simmered in sour cream, and one of the best, from Romania, contains small whole mushrooms, which are simmered in the sour cream sauce until done, thereby retaining the firmness they usually lose when sautéed.

Sour soups are another legacy of the Slavic tradition, and these too are found in most of the Balkan nations. In southern Romania a chicken and vegetable soup, *Reikachen mit Huhn,* includes rice and raisins as well as sour cream, and is traditionally served at weddings. Another chicken and vegetable soup is *Kisela Corba,* and it is equally popular made with sour cream, vinegar, sauerkraut juice, or lemon juice and sweet cream.

Early in the eighteenth century, tomatoes found their way into the Balkans from the New World, and were adopted enthusiastically. The Greeks and Bulgarians, in particular, added tomatoes to a great many stews; in fact both enjoy chicken and tomato stew regularly.

Despite all the outside influence, however, Balkan cooking has developed characteristics of its own. Though lamb is the principal meat of the Balkans, a great deal of fish, beef, pork, and chicken is eaten, and these are almost always cooked or served with a variety of vegetables. In this same vein, the seasoning agents used in the Balkans tend toward garden vegetables and herbs. Only on rare occurrences do the exotic spices of the East make an appearance. One of these is in the Greek classic, *Kotopoulo Stefado,* or "thieves' stew." It's not really a stew at all, and originally it was made with beef, gamebird, or hare rather than chicken. But today it is simply chicken and onions in a spicy sauce that includes cinnamon, cloves, raisins, red wine, and vinegar. Interestingly, Spain also has a well-known (and real) chicken stew called *Estafado,* which she has made popular in virtually every Spanish-speaking country in the world. The Italians have one too, called *Stufado*. The Greek version is rather spicy and the Spanish contains more vegetables, but they are all culinary cousins, joined together somewhere in the past by the unending cultural flow that has existed among Mediterranean nations since antiquity.

GREECE

KOTOPITTA—Chicken Pie

Kotopitta is very similar to the *bstilla* of the Maghreb, which the Moors brought back from Spain. Bstilla has more sweetening and nuts, but essentially it's the same dish.

Phyllo pastry or strudel leaves are readily available in specialty shops, but use ordinary pie crust if you wish, only roll it very thin.

1 3-pound chicken, cut up	½ cup Parmesan or Romano
1 onion, sliced	cheese
1 carrot, coarsely chopped	3 eggs, beaten
1 stalk celery, coarsely chopped	2 large onions, chopped finely
Salt and pepper	1 clove garlic, minced
Water	½ cup dry white wine
6 tablespoons butter	½ teaspoon nutmeg
4 tablespoons flour	2 tablespoons parsley flakes
2 cups stock	8 sheets phyllo pastry

In a large saucepan, place the chicken pieces, onion, carrot, celery, and a little salt and pepper. Cover with water and cook for 2 hours or until the chicken meat is falling off the bones. Remove the chicken pieces and strain the stock and reserve. Skin and bone the chicken and cut the meat into very small pieces.

Melt 3 tablespoons butter in a saucepan and stir in the flour. Remove the pot from the heat, add the chicken stock, and stir until a smooth paste forms. Now add a little more salt and pepper and bring to the boil, stirring constantly. Cook over moderate heat for 5 minutes, then stir in the cheese and remove from the heat. Let the sauce cool for a few minutes, then add the eggs and beat until thoroughly mixed.

In a skillet, sauté the chopped onions and garlic in the remaining butter. When golden add the chicken and a little salt and pepper and cook over moderate heat for about 15 minutes. Raise the heat, add the white wine, and cook for 3-4 minutes. This will drive off the alcohol but retain the wine flavor. Now remove from the heat, add the remaining ingredients, and mix thoroughly with the sauce. Adjust the seasoning if necessary.

Use a 9-inch pie plate. Place 4 layers of phyllo pastry on the bottom, one at a time, brushing melted butter onto each layer. Turn the chicken mixture into the plate and cover with 4 more layers of phyllo pastry, again brushing melted butter onto each layer. Seal the edges carefully and bake the pie in a preheated oven (400° F) for 15 minutes. Reduce the heat to 350° F and cook an additional 15 minutes. Serve right from the pie plate. Serves 4-6.

GREECE

KOTA YAHNI—Chicken Stew
This is almost identical to the *Tavuk Yahni* of Turkey, although the Turkish version does not include as many vegetables.

1 3-pound chicken, cut up	Salt and pepper
3 tablespoons butter	2 cups water
6 small onions	6 medium potatoes, peeled and quartered
4 tomatoes, peeled	1 pound peas
2 tablespoons tomato paste	4 tablespoons red wine (optional)

In a casserole or small Dutch oven, brown the chicken pieces in butter until golden. Add the remaining ingredients, cover, and cook over medium heat until the chicken is tender, about 30 minutes. Remove the cover and add the wine, if desired, and cook for 3 more minutes. Serves 4.

GREECE

KOTA MAITANO—Chicken with Parsley Sauce

1 3-pound chicken, cut up	Salt and freshly ground black pepper
4 tablespoons olive oil	2 cups chicken stock
2 cloves garlic, sliced	2 tablespoons butter
	Parsley sprigs for garnish

Parsley Sauce

2 tablespoons butter	6 tablespoons fresh parsley, chopped
2 tablespoons flour	Yolks of 2 eggs
1 cup cream	Juice of ½ lemon

Sauté the garlic in oil until golden, then brown the chicken pieces on all sides. Sprinkle the chicken with salt and a few grindings of fresh black pepper, add 1 cup of stock, and cook, covered, over medium heat for 30 minutes.

While the chicken cooks, prepare the parsley sauce: Melt the butter and stir in the flour, then add the cream and the remaining stock a little at a time, stirring constantly. When the sauce becomes smooth and somewhat thickened, add parsley and a little salt. Bring the mixture to the boil, then reduce the heat to low. Now beat the egg yolks and lemon juice together and stir into the sauce. Cook over low heat for about 5 minutes. Do not let the sauce become too thick.

Arrange the chicken on a warm platter and spoon some of the sauce over each piece, then garnish the platter with parsley sprigs. Serve the remaining sauce in a sauceboat. Serves 4.

GREECE

KOTOPOULO ATZEN PILAFI—Chicken Pilaf

1 onion, chopped finely	¼ teaspoon thyme
1 tablespoon butter	1 cup white rice
1 cup cooked white meat of chicken, cubed	4 cups chicken stock
	2 tomatoes, peeled and chopped
Salt and freshly ground pepper	¼ cup walnuts, chopped

Heat the butter in a large saucepan, then sauté the onions and meat slowly, about 10 minutes, until golden. Add the salt, pepper, and thyme and stir well for a minute or so, then add the rice and continue stirring until the rice is completely coated, about 5 minutes. Add the stock, tomatoes, and walnuts. Cover and simmer over low heat for about 20 minutes. Remove from the heat and leave covered in a warm place for 20 minutes before serving. Serves 4.

GREECE

AVGOLEMONO

Avgolemono is Greece's best-known contribution to international gastronomy. It is basically a sauce made of lemon juice and eggs, which is poured over chicken and other light meats, and it is also one of the world's great soups.

Avgolemono Sauce

3 eggs	Juice of 2 lemons
Salt	1 cup hot chicken stock

Separate the eggs, and beat the whites until thick. Add a little salt, then add the yolks one at a time and beat well. Now beat in the lemon juice and stock a little at a time. Don't rush this or the eggs will curdle. Now the sauce is ready to be stirred into a cream gravy or poured over the chicken (hot or cold) or mixed into stock for an unforgettable soup.

Chicken Soup with Avgolemono Sauce

1 4-5-pound stewing chicken	Salt and pepper
1 carrot, peeled and sliced length- wise	4 tablespoons cooked rice
1 stalk of celery, sliced	Chopped parsley or chives for garnish
2 shallots, sliced crosswise	Avgolemono sauce

Put the chicken, carrot, celery, shallots, and salt and pepper into a deep saucepan. Cover with water and bring to the boil over high heat. Then reduce the heat to low, cover, and simmer for 2 hours.

When done, remove the carcass and meat and strain the stock through cheesecloth. Save the meat for other chicken dishes. Now add 4 tablespoons of cooked rice and the Avgolemono sauce and a little salt and pepper to taste. Heat again before serving, garnishing with chopped parsley or chives.

GREECE

KOTOPOULO STEFADO—Chicken and Onion Stew

A stefado is a stew, and it's usually made with onions, but at first it was not made with chicken, rather beef or gamebird or hare in a highly spiced sauce. This was a "thieves' stew" originally, a pot into which went anything the band could steal. Although chicken was not one of the original ingredients, it has become more and more popular in recent years.

1 3-pound chicken, cut up
4 tablespoons butter
Salt and pepper
12-16 small white onions
1 teaspoon cinnamon
4 whole cloves

¼ cup raisins
½ cup red wine
1 tablespoon wine vinegar
½ teaspoon cumin
1 clove garlic, chopped
1 2-ounce can tomato paste

In a Dutch oven, melt the butter and brown the chicken until golden brown. Remove, add the onions to the pot, and sauté slowly. Now replace the chicken and add the remaining ingredients. Bake covered for 1 hour in a 350° F oven. Serves 4.

GREECE

KOTA ME ANITHO—Chicken and Dill
with Avgolemono Sauce

1 3-pound chicken, cut up
3 tablespoons butter
1 cup chicken stock
Salt and pepper

1 tablespoon dill, chopped
3 bunches of scallions cut into
    small pieces
Avgolemono sauce (page 215)

Melt the butter in a Dutch oven and brown the chicken pieces on all sides. Add the stock, a little salt and pepper, the dill, and the scallions, then cover and cook over medium heat for 30 minutes.

When the chicken is nearly done, make one recipe of Avgolemono sauce, using some of the stock from the chicken. Stir the sauce into the pan, making sure to lower the heat beforehand so as not to boil (this could cause the mixture to curdle). Serves 4.

GREECE

KOTOPOLO RIGANATI—Chicken Oregano

Oregano is basic to Greek cookery, and it does wonders for chicken. Chicken oregano from Greece is world-famous, and can be roasted, broiled, or braised.

Roasted
1 4-pound roasting chicken
Juice of 1 lemon

1 tablespoon salt
½ cup olive oil
2 tablespoons oregano

Combine the juice of 1 lemon and 1 tablespoon salt in ½ cup of olive oil. Rub some of this mixture all over the chicken, inside and out. Now sprinkle the bird with 2 tablespoons of oregano and roast in a moderate oven, covered, for 1 hour, basting frequently with the remaining lemon mixture. Uncover during the last 15 minutes to brown. Serves 4-6.

Note: A variation is to combine the remaining lemon mixture with 1 cup of tomato paste, 2 tablespoons oregano, and several grindings of fresh black pepper, and cook this very slowly for about 10 minutes. Then, 15 minutes before the bird is done, pour this sauce over the bird and finish roasting as above, basting frequently.

Grilled or Broiled
2 3-pound chickens, cut up   Juice of 1 lemon
2 cloves garlic, minced   1 tablespoon salt
½ cup olive oil plus 1 tablespoon   2 tablespoons oregano

First sauté the garlic in 1 tablespoon oil and brush on the chicken pieces. Now make a marinade of the same lemon mixture as above, then pour over the chicken in a large bowl, turning each piece to be sure it is covered with the marinade. Cover the bowl and refrigerate for several hours. Cook the chicken pieces in a broiler or as you normally would over charcoal, using the remaining marinade to baste. Serves 6-8.

Braised
Follow the above directions for broiling, but without the garlic. After marinating the chicken for several hours, brown the pieces in olive oil in a large skillet, then add ½ cup of water, cover, and simmer 1 hour or until tender. You may also add 2-3 tablespoons of tomato paste to the chicken with the water.

Greece

KOTA KAPAMA—
Chicken with Cinnamon and Tomato Sauce

1 3-pound chicken, cut up	2 tablespoons tomato paste
Salt and freshly ground pepper	¾ cup chicken stock
3 onions, chopped	3 small cinnamon sticks, ground
2 cloves garlic, minced	in a mortar
6 tomatoes, peeled, seeded, and	Grated Parmesan cheese
chopped	

Sprinkle the chicken with salt and several grindings of pepper. In a medium-sized Dutch oven, melt 3 tablespoons butter and brown the chicken thoroughly on all sides. Remove chicken pieces and set aside. Brown the onions and garlic in the same pot until golden, then add in the tomatoes, tomato paste, the chicken stock, cinnamon, and a little more salt and pepper. Bring the sauce to the boil, then return the chicken pieces to the pot, cover, and cook for 30 minutes. Serves 4.

Note: The best, and traditional, way to serve this dish is with some form of pasta. Macaroni is good, but thin spaghetti is better. Pour some of the sauce over the pasta on a serving dish and arrange the chicken pieces around it. Serve the remaining sauce in a sauceboat.

Romania

PIU CU GUTUI—Chicken with Quinces

Quinces are very popular in East Europe, much more so than in America. If you can't find quinces, use apples instead. It's a different taste, but good just the same.

1 3-pound chicken, cut up	Salt
1 medium onion, chopped	4 large quinces (or apples)
coarsely	1 cup chicken stock
4 tablespoons butter or olive oil	1 tablespoon flour

Sauté the onions in butter or oil, then add the chicken pieces and salt and simmer for 1 hour. Cut the quinces (or apples) into thin slices and add to the pan. Now add a little more salt and the stock and cook for 20-30 minutes (the quinces will take slightly longer). Remove the chicken and quinces to a platter and add 1 tablespoon flour to the gravy to thicken. Stir well, then serve in a separate gravyboat with potatoes or rice. Serves 4.

ROMANIA

CHICKEN VINAIGRETTE
This dish can be made just as well with duckling or goose.

1 3-pound chicken, cut up	3 cloves garlic, crushed
6 tablespoons butter	1 bay leaf
½ tablespoon flour	Salt and freshly ground pepper
2 medium onions, sliced	1 cup chicken stock
2 tablespoons tomato purée	4 tablespoons wine vinegar
	Parsley sprigs for garnish

In a large skillet, brown the chicken pieces in butter on all sides over moderate heat for about 10 minutes. Remove the chicken and sauté the onions until golden brown. Add the flour and stir into the onions thoroughly. Now add the tomato purée, crushed garlic, bay leaf (broken into pieces), a little salt, and about 6 or 8 good grindings of pepper and the stock. Stir well for one minute, then return the chicken pieces to the pan, spooning the sauce over each piece until thoroughly coated. Cover, reduce heat to low, and simmer for 20 minutes. If necessary, add a little more stock to keep the sauce moist, and stir every 5 minutes or so.

When the chicken is 10 minutes from done, add the vinegar and stir in well. Garnish with parsley sprigs. Serves 4.

ROMANIA

REIKACHEN MIT HUHN—Wedding Chicken Soup
This is traditionally served at weddings in Romania.

2 carrots, chopped	Salt and pepper
2 stalks celery, sliced	1 3-pound chicken, cut up
3 sprigs parsley, chopped	¾ cup rice
3 leeks, chopped	1 egg
4 onions, quartered	½ cup sour cream
6 cups water	½ cup white raisins

Put all the vegetables in a pot, add the water and salt and pepper, and bring to the boil. Add the chicken pieces, cover, and cook over moderate heat until done, about 1 hour. Now remove the chicken and keep warm. Strain the liquid and discard the vegetables. Add the rice to the liquid and cook gently for 20 minutes.

Whip the egg and mix with the sour cream. Pour the soup over the chicken pieces in a tureen or large bowl, and spoon in the egg and sour cream mixture, stirring well. Add the raisins, stir again, and serve. Serves 4-6.

BULGARIA

KOKOSKA KAPAMA—Chicken in Tomato Broth

1 3-pound chicken, cut up	1 bay leaf
4 tablespoons butter	1 teaspoon paprika
2 cloves garlic, sliced	12 peppercorns
3 onions, chopped	2 tablespoons parsley flakes
4 tomatoes, chopped	1 cup chicken stock

You'll need a skillet or Dutch oven with a tight-fitting lid. Brown the chicken pieces in butter for about 10 minutes, then add the remaining ingredients. Cover tightly, reduce heat to low, and simmer for about 30 minutes. Serve with rice. Serves 4.

BULGARIA

KOKOSKA LJUTIKA—Chicken with Green Peppers
This dish can be made equally well with duckling or goose.

1 3-pound chicken, cut up	4 medium green peppers, seeded
4 tablespoons butter	and sliced
2 onions, chopped finely	3 tomatoes, chopped
1 teaspoon paprika	Salt and freshly ground pepper
1½ cups chicken stock	Parsley sprigs for garnish

In a large skillet sauté the onions and chicken pieces for about 10 minutes, turning frequently to cook on all sides. Sprinkle over the paprika, add water, and simmer over low heat for 45 minutes. Now add the sliced peppers and chopped tomatoes. Cook for 10 minutes more. Add a little salt and a few grindings of pepper, and serve garnished with parsley. Serves 4.

BULGARIA

PILETA NA SKARA—Barbecued Chicken

In the Caucasian Mountains of Russia, there is a chicken dish called *Tabaka* in which the backbone is removed and the remaining carcass is flattened by pounding, and then cooked under a heavy weight. The idea is that the birds will brown and cook more quickly.

In Bulgaria there is a similar dish in which the chicken is cut in half with the backbone removed and then each half is pounded and a heavy weight (25 pounds) is put on each half for an hour. They flatten out like chops.

Using 1 chicken for each 2 people, prepare as above, and when ready to cook, rub salt and pepper over each flattened piece. The chicken halves can be fried in butter or grilled over an open flame with a butter basting or a barbecue sauce.

BULGARIA

CHICKEN WITH SAUERKRAUT AND SAUSAGE

This is a holiday dish that originates in the mountains of southern Bulgaria. It is much better if you use fresh, tangy homemade sauerkraut, but the store variety is an adequate substitute (but drain it well). Also use Italian blood sausage if you can. This you can get at most specialty meat stores or delicatessens; an Italian sweet sausage is excellent also.

3 pork chops	1 3-pound chicken
6 tablespoons butter or oil	1 pound ham (sliced) or bacon
2 onions, chopped finely	(cut in large pieces
½ cup rice	2 pounds sauerkraut
Salt and freshly ground pepper	1 pound blood (or Italian sweet)
½ cup chicken stock	sausage

Preheat oven to 350° F. First prepare a stuffing of pork and rice for the chicken: Cut the meat from the pork chops and mince it, saving the bones. Sauté the pork meat and onions gently in 2 tablespoons of butter for 5 minutes, then add the rice, a little salt, and ½ teaspoon of freshly ground pepper. Stir well for a minute, then add the stock. Simmer over low heat for 20 minutes, then stuff the chicken.

Place the ham or bacon pieces in the bottom of a large casserole or Dutch oven. Lay in 1 pound of sauerkraut, the stuffed chicken, and the pork bones. Place all but a little of the remaining sauerkraut over the chicken and grind on fresh pepper generously. Place the sausage on top of this, cover with the remaining sauerkraut, then cover the casserole tightly. Cook over moderate heat for 5 minutes, then place in the oven for 3 hours.

Serve the chicken and sausage on a large platter surrounded by the sauerkraut and ham (or bacon). Serves 6-8.

BULGARIA

KOKOSKA KESTENI—Chicken with Chestnuts

The Turkish influence in this dish is evident in the name, it being a direct descendant of the *Kestaneli Hindi* (turkey with chestnuts) from that country. The difference is in the sugar that the Bulgarians add, which gives the dish a somewhat sweeter taste.

1 3-pound chicken, cut up
2 tablespoons butter
1 onion, chopped
1 tablespoon flour
1 teaspoon paprika

In a deep skillet, heat the butter and sauté the onion until golden. Sprinkle in the flour, add paprika and stock, and cook for 10 minutes. Place the chicken pieces in the skillet and simmer over low heat for 30 minutes.

Meanwhile, slash the chestnuts (don't cut the meat) and boil for 20 minutes in salted water. Peel off both outer shell and inner skin.

When the chicken is half done, add the chestnuts. Now brown the sugar to a caramel and add with tomato paste and cinnamon to the chicken. Simmer for 15 minutes. Serves 4.

BULGARIA

JAREBIZI SAS SOS OT MORKOVI—
Partridge (or Chicken) in Carrot Sauce

Gamebirds are frequently found on the Bulgarian table, far more so than in America. If you are lucky enough to find, or shoot, several partridge, you will enjoy this method of cooking them, but if not, spring chicken or Rock Cornish game hen are also superb with this carrot sauce. (See note.)

3 partridge, split in half	2 large tomatoes, peeled and chopped
1½ cups water	1 bay leaf
Salt and freshly ground pepper	2 tablespoons flour
4 carrots, sliced	Toast points
3 tablespoons butter or oil	Fresh parsley sprigs for garnish

Put the partridge halves in a large pot, add the sliced carrots, and salt lightly. Now add the water and cook over medium heat for 15 minutes. Remove the partridge and strain the liquid through a sieve, then force the carrots through the sieve into the strained liquid.

Melt the butter in a large skillet and cook the partridge halves on all sides until done (about 15 or 20 minutes). While the birds are cooking combine the chopped tomatoes, the bay leaf (crumbled), and several grindings of fresh black pepper with the carrot broth. Cook in a saucepan over low heat for 20 minutes.

When the birds are done, remove and keep warm. Stir 2 table-spoons flour into the butter used to fry the partridge. Stir over low heat for 2 minutes, then pour in the carrot broth and cook over moderately high heat for 10 minutes. The liquid should be brought to the boil and kept bubbling until the sauce becomes somewhat thickened.

Now place each partridge half on toast points, spoon a little sauce over each, and garnish with a parsley sprig. Serve additional sauce in a sauceboat. Serves 6.

Note: If you use Rock Cornish game hens, use the same recipe, only cut the game hens into halves. Use only 2 game hens for 4 people. If you use chickens, cut a 3-pound chicken into quarters. This recipe will serve 4.

Yugoslavia

PILECI PAPRIKAS SA NOKLICAMA—
Chicken Paprika Stew with Dumplings

Chicken Paprikash is a world-famous dish, the Hungarian version of which may be the best known. But there are also delightful variations in both Yugoslavia and Austria. This, from the Voivodina region, combines the chicken and paprika in a stew with semolina dumplings.

1 onion, chopped	Salt
4 tablespoons butter	½ teaspoon paprika
1 3-pound chicken, cut up	2 teaspoons flour
1 cup water	½ cup sour cream

Heat the butter in a large skillet and sauté the onion until golden. Add the chicken pieces to the pan with 1 cup of water, cover, and simmer over low heat for 1 hour. Remove the chicken and sprinkle with salt and paprika. Now stir the flour into the sour cream and pour into the skillet. Replace the chicken to heat for a few moments, and then serve.

Dumplings

3 cups milk	1¼ cups semolina
½ teaspoon salt	1 egg

As soon as the chicken starts cooking, begin making the dumplings. Bring the milk to the boil and add salt. Stirring constantly, add the semolina to the pot, reduce the heat to low, and cook for 10 minutes. Let the mixture cool for 30 minutes, then beat the egg and stir it into the pot. Wet your hands in cold water and form as many dumplings as you wish to the size desired. Now drop them into boiling water (salted) and cook for 10-12 minutes. Serve hot with the chicken with sour cream sauce. Serves 4.

YUGOSLAVIA

CHICKEN IN SOUR CREAM

1 3-pound chicken, cut up	3 eggs
Salt and pepper	2 cups sour cream
½ cup mushrooms, sliced	1 tablespoon olive oil
2-3 tablespoons melted butter	1½ cups chicken stock
2 tablespoons flour	1 clove garlic, crushed
	Paprika

Rub the chicken pieces with salt and pepper, then broil in the oven or over charcoal until done, basting each side with melted butter. Cook the mushrooms in water over moderate heat for 5 minutes, then remove and drain.

Mix the flour and eggs together, then add the sour cream and stir over low heat for 2 or 3 minutes until very smooth. Add 1 tablespoon of olive oil and 1 cup of chicken stock and cook over low heat, stirring constantly until the sauce thickens (about 8-10 minutes). Add the remaining stock, mushrooms, and the crushed garlic, and continue stirring until the sauce achieves the consistency of heavy cream.

Place the chicken on a warm platter and pour over the sauce. Sprinkle with paprika. Serves 4.

YUGOSLAVIA

PILECI RISOTTO—Chicken and Oysters with Rice

This is a Dalmatian dish from the region along the Adriatic Coast, which had been occupied by the Venetians in the Middle Ages. This relatively simple risotto sets off oysters in their shells against a basic chicken background in a typical Italian manner.

1 3-pound chicken cut up	1 cup chicken stock
2 tablespoons olive oil	4 medium tomatoes, peeled and
1 onion, chopped	chopped
Salt and pepper	¾ cup rice
½ teaspoon paprika	1 cup water
	1 dozen oysters (in shells)

Clean the oysters with water and a stiff brush to remove sand and grit.

Heat the olive oil in a large skillet and sauté the onions until golden. Add the chicken pieces and salt, pepper, and paprika and brown for 10 minutes over low heat. Now pour in ½ stock and simmer for about 15 minutes, then add chopped tomatoes.

While the chicken simmers, boil the rice in 1 cup of salted water for 10 minutes, then drain and add to the chicken. Pour in the rest of the chicken stock, place the oysters on top, and cook over medium heat until the rice is done (10-15 minutes). The oysters should be opened and well cooked. Serves 4.

YUGOSLAVIA

PECENA CURICA S TESTOM MLINCIMA—
Roast Turkey (or Chicken) with Mlinci Paste

Mlinci paste is very much like the noodles of Italian origin, and it may be that an ancient Italian pasta is the forerunner of this one. The turkey of course did not show up in Europe until the explorers brought it back from America several hundred years ago. So while neither the bird nor the paste is native to the Croatian region, which is where this dish comes from, it is nonetheless very popular.

1 10-12-pound turkey	4 strips bacon
Salt	3 cups water
6 tablespoons butter	1 recipe for mlinci paste (below)

Preheat the oven to 325° F. Rub the turkey all over with salt, then cover with butter. Fry the bacon until brown. Place the turkey in a roasting pan, crumble the bacon over it, and pour in 1 cup of water. Cover and slow-roast the bird for 4 hours, then add the remaining water. Re-cover and continue roasting for 1 more hour. About 30 minutes before done, add the mlinci paste and remove the cover. Carve the turkey and place the meat on a mound of the hot paste. Serves 6-8.

Note: If you cook a 4-5-pound chicken, reduce the amount of butter to 2 tablespoons and the water to 2 cups. Cook covered for 30 minutes to the pound, adding the mlinci paste 30 minutes before the bird is done.

Mlinci Paste

4 cups flour	3 tablespoons water
1 egg	1¼ teaspoons salt
	1½ cups milk

Combine the flour, egg, water, and ¼ teaspoon salt and work into a dough. Keep kneading until smooth, then let it stand for 10-15 minutes. Now roll the dough out as thinly as possible. Cut the dough to fit a (greased) 12-inch by 15-inch sheet and bake each portion in a 350° F oven for 5 minutes. Remove and repeat this step until all the mlinci is baked, then break the baked dough into small pieces. About 40 minutes before the turkey is done, heat the milk and add the remaining salt. Pour this over the mlinci pieces and let stand for 10 minutes. Now drain and add the paste to the roasting pan, and finish the recipe above.

YUGOSLAVIA

KISELA CORBA—Sour Soup

This soup dish originates in Serbia, an eastern region that borders both Bulgaria and Romania.

1 3-pound chicken, cut up	2 bay leaves
2 quarts water	1 tablespoon olive oil
Salt	1 teaspoon flour
12 peppercorns	⅛ teaspoon paprika
1 carrot, cut in half	Juice of 1 lemon
1 onion, quartered	1 egg yolk
1 celery stalk, sliced	¼ cup cream
1 green pepper, seeded and sliced	1 tablespoon chopped fresh
2 tomatoes, quartered	parsley

Put the chicken pieces in a pan, add water and a little salt, and bring to the boil. After 15 minutes, skim off the scum that rises, and add 12 peppercorns. Now cover, reduce heat to low, and simmer for 1 hour. Add the carrot, onion, celery, pepper slices, tomato quarters, and bay leaves and continue cooking for 15 minutes. Remove the chicken pieces and save for another recipe. Strain the stock.

In a pan, heat the olive oil, then stir in the flour and paprika. Add

2-3 tablespoons of the strained stock and stir well, then return the mixture to the rest of the stock. Add the lemon juice and heat for 3 minutes, then remove and set aside. Beat the egg yolk with the cream and add to the soup.

Serve at once sprinkled with chopped parsley. Serves 4-6.

Albania

PULE ME DROP—Chicken with Sweet Stuffing

Albania has closed its frontiers to the Western world in recent years, but it is unique among Balkan nations for the fact that it became a completely Moslem culture after the downfall of the Ottoman Empire, whereas the others did not. It is a rugged mountainous land, agricultural essentially, with a great taste for chicken and lamb.

2 4-pound roasting chickens
2 cups soft breadcrumbs
8 tablespoons butter
¼ cup currants

¼ cup raisins
½ cup chopped almonds or
   walnuts
¼ cup sugar
1 tablespoon chicken stock

Brown the breadcrumbs in 4 tablespoons butter. Mix together with the other ingredients, then stuff the cavity of the chicken. Sew or skewer the opening and smear with the remaining butter. Then roast the bird, covered, in 350° F oven for 1½ hours. Uncover 15 minutes before done, to allow the breast and legs to brown. Serves 4-6.

❧ Chapter 8 ❧

Western Europe

During the Dark Ages, innovations in chicken cookery, along with all other Western European cooking, came to a standstill. The monasteries were the only ones that practiced animal husbandry, kept vegetable gardens, and tended vineyards. They invented the *vol-au-vent* (puff pastry filled with chicken and other meats), and they experimented with sauces, but that's about all.

In the fourteenth century, the Renaissance dawned over Italy. There was a steady trade between Venice and Genoa and Middle Eastern ports, and the basic commodities were spices, which brought exorbitant prices but no end of buyers. At the time, chicken was a familiar dish in northern Italy and was becoming popular in Spain and France. Cooks for royalty and the aristocracy used spices copiously in preparing their birds, as they did with just about all their other foods. Already established in Spain was *Arroz con Pollo,* a rice and chicken dish into which, centuries before, the Moors had introduced saffron for taste and coloring. Until the end of the fifteenth century, however, there was little to distinguish the Western European cuisine, chicken or otherwise.

In 1543, the Turks conquered Constantinople and blocked the overland spice routes to India, thereby denying Europe the condiments they coveted so much. In one respect it was the best thing that could have happened. Instead of dipping into the spice pot, chefs and cooks hoarded their spices, and went back to the seasonings that grew in their own gardens—basil, garlic, thyme, and others. They stepped up their use of wine in cooking and found that extracts developed from chicken, beef, and veal produced an entirely new kind of taste.

By the end of the fifteenth century, chicken was a well-known meat in Western Europe and was rapidly becoming the aristocrat's tour de force in haute cuisine. But it was cooked with truffles, wine, garlic, basil, and oregano and not with the spices of the East, except on occasion. In short, the cuisines of Europe were developed with the foods and seasonings they had always had, not with those they coveted.

Apparently the Europeans didn't realize they stood on the brink of culinary perfection, for their quest to break the spice blockade was undiminished; in fact it seems it was ingrained in them. In antiquity, Roman soldiers were paid in pepper; medieval dowries frequently included spices along with gold and silver; and during the early Renaissance the most successful banquets were those that offered the greatest variety of ornate and highly seasoned food. It was only from the East that cinnamon, nutmeg, mace, saffron, cumin, coriander, turmeric, clove, and, most particularly, pepper were obtained. But during the fifteenth century none of those were available to the Western European chef, except at a dear price.

At the end of the fifteenth century, two relatively minor countries, Spain and Portugal, provided the initiative that was to lead to a greater political, social, economic, cultural, and gastronomic upheaval than all that had gone before in history. Diaz and da Gama had found the sea route to India, and Columbus discovered the new world.

The exploits of these three men were to have a most profound effect on Europe's future. In scarcely more then a decade not only were two new continents discovered, but the blockade of the spice route was overcome. Within 50 years, the Aztec and Incan empires had been found, looted, and destroyed, the world had been circumnavigated, and European flags were flying over countless new possessions previously unheard of.

During the next centuries, chicken cooking, and the European cuisines in general, profited greatly. Europe saw foods from the Americas for the first time: corn, tomatoes, beans, chili peppers, chocolate, white potatoes, chicle, vanilla, and the turkey. Most found immediate acceptance in Europe and some in other cuisines. Tomatoes became an institution in France and Italy. Corn became the main ingredient in the *mamaliga* of Romania and the *polenta* of Italy and still is the staple for the chicken-breeding industry of Europe. The white haricot bean is basic to the great cassoulets of Southern France, and chili peppers went on to Africa and Asia, where they are used in just about everything.

The important thing is that finding the sea route to India turned out to be only the stimulus but not the fulfillment. Once Europe's cooks found out how well they were using the materials at hand, spices never again became as important as they once were thought to be.

PART I:

Italy-Sicily

Italian cooking has been called the "Mother Cuisine" of Europe, for Rome's was the only cuisine of any sophistication that existed in antiquity.

The most significant early contributor to the development of Rome's kitchen was the army. The legions returning from the provinces brought back asparagus, mushrooms, carrots, lettuce, and a variety of nuts, spices, and herbs, and introduced pomegranates, apricots, peaches, figs, lemons, grapes, and the forerunner of today's cantaloupe. From Africa came truffles and the Nubian or Carthaginian chicken, which was in reality the guinea fowl. In Greece and Egypt they found the real chicken and in time developed an enormous and very successful chicken-breeding industry. The Romans had discovered the improved quality that sterilization had brought to their beef and, by applying this technology to the chicken, developed the science of caponizing, which yielded larger, better quality, and more tender fowl. A Tuscan brought the first grapes to Marseilles. *Foie gras* was the invention of a Roman named Scipio Matellus, who discovered that force-feeding a goose resulted in the enlargement of the bird's liver.

Apicius, a Roman of the first century, is credited with writing the Western world's first cookbook, and in it he gives numerous recipes for sausages, meat dishes, vegetables, sauces, and, very possibly, the world's first recorded chicken recipe.

It was in the Renaissance kitchens of Florence, Bologna, and Venice that Italy earned her gastronomic credits. The wealth derived from the spice trade re-established Italy as the center of culture in

233

Europe in the fourteenth and fifteenth centuries, and gave rise to powerful merchant, banking, and political families such as the Sforzas, de Medicis, and Borgias, who lavished their immense fortunes on such artistic giants as Michelangelo, Da Vinci, and Ralphael, and who brought Italian cooking to unequaled rank among Europe's cuisines.

In terms of cooking and eating styles, the Italian peninsula can be cut roughly in half, with Rome in the middle. In the north, the food is richer, lighter, and more varied, and butter is the cooking oil. In the south, the land and people are poorer, and the food is spicier. Olive oil is the cooking medium. The popular Italian cooking we know in this country (pizza, spaghetti, and tomato sauce) originated in the south. Being strategically situated between the north and south, Rome borrows from both, changes the name, and offers the most representative "Italian" cuisine in the country.

The cuisine of Florence is still the most delicate and dignified in Italy, and perhaps the most famous Florentine chicken dish is *Pollo alla Fiorentina.* This is a simple, delicious chicken and white wine dish, which for some reason in France and America particularly, is presented as chicken on a bed of spinach. Not so in Florence.

Bologna is the other distinguished kitchen in Northern Italy, and its style is hearty, heavy, and rich. Some of its greatest chicken dishes illustrate the spirit of gustatory adventure that characterizes the Bolognese cuisine. *Pollo alla Bolognese* combines slices of Parma ham and cheese tucked between the fillets of a chicken breast and simmered in white wine. (This recipe, incidentally, is prominent in Swiss and French kitchens, where it is also known as *Poulet à la Suisse* and *Poulet Cordon Bleu.*) Another is *tortellini,* small ring-shaped pasta filled with chopped chicken or other meats. The Roman chefs borrowed this, made it into a pinched triangular shape, called it *cappelletti* (little hats), and served it in chicken broth. In still another the Bolognese simmer chicken and sausages in a white wine sauce with mushrooms to achieve a totally unexpected and robust medley of tastes.

On a lesser level, Venice has developed a cuisine that's different from those of her northern neighbors. Venetians are basically fish, rice, and pasta eaters, and though chicken is held in rather low regard, Venice can claim one outstanding dish—chicken risotto, a combination of chicken and rice usually served with a variety of vegetables.

Most of southern Italy is so poor that the natives subsist almost exclusively on what they can take from the sea, and poultry is rather scarce. Nevertheless, Naples and the Campagna region offer cuisines of some distinction in southern Italy. Here the food is highly seasoned with garlic, dill, and oregano and frequently cooked with tomatoes. Tomatoes came from Central America about four hundred years ago, and the Neapolitans bred them into the beautiful plum-shaped *pomo d'oro*. They combined it with chicken into Italy's best-known chicken dish—*pollo alla cacciatore* (Hunter's Chicken).

Off the southern coast of Italy lies Sicily. Chicken cookery stands a poor third behind fish and mutton there, but Sicily has two chicken dishes that have become well known. The first is *Pollo al Marsala,* a chicken simmered in the excellent dry marsala wine for which Sicily is famous. The second is *Pollo fra Diavolo* (deviled chicken), a spicy chicken, tomato, and wine concoction that is served up with a legend. *Fra Diavolo* means literally "Brother Devil." Allegedly the original Fra Diavolo was a sort of Sicilian Robin Hood who gave to the poor some (not all) of the plunder he took from the rich, all the while disguised as a monk.

RECOMMENDED READING: Naomi Barry and Beppi Bellini, *Food Alla Florentine* (Garden City, N.Y.: Doubleday, 1972); Robin Howe, *Regional Italian Cookery* (New York: Drake Publishers, 1972); Joe Famularo and Louise Imperiale, *The Festive Famularo Kitchen* (New York: Atheneum, 1977)

Italy (Milan)

POLLO ALLA MILANESE—Chicken in the Milanese Style

1 chicken, cut up and skin removed	1 egg, whipped
1 lemon, cut in half	1 cup fine breadcrumbs
Salt and freshly ground pepper	6 tablespoons butter
¼ cup flour	Parsley and another lemon for garnish

Rub each piece of chicken thoroughly with half of the lemon, then sprinkle with salt and pepper and dredge lightly with flour. Dip the pieces in the whipped egg and then into the dry breadcrumbs, covering thoroughly. Now heat the butter in a very large skillet and cook the chicken a few pieces at a time until done (about 30 minutes). When done, sprinkle the juice of the remaining lemon half over the pieces and slice the other lemon thinly for garnish. Add the parsley sprigs and serve on a warm platter. Serves 4.

Italy (Rome)

STRACCIATELLA—Chicken Egg Drop Soup

1 pound chicken giblets (hearts, necks, gizzards, and livers)	1 onion, sliced
1 quart cold water	Salt and pepper
1 stalk celery, sliced across	2 eggs
1 carrot, sliced across	3 tablespoons semolina
	¼ cup grated Parmesan cheese
	1 tablespoon parsley, chopped

Put the chicken giblets in a large kettle with the water and bring to the boil. Keep skimming the scum as it rises, then add the celery, carrot, onion, and a little salt and pepper. Cover, reduce the heat, and cook slowly for 2 hours, then strain the broth into a large saucepan and discard the rest.

Beat the eggs in a bowl and stir in 3 tablespoons semolina. Now add the cheese and parsley and stir well for 3 minutes with a fork. Bring the remaining broth to a boil and pour the egg mixture in very slowly, stirring constantly. Add a little salt and pepper to taste, once all the egg mixture has been added, then reduce the heat to low and simmer for 5 minutes more, stirring all the while. Serve in a tureen or in individual bowls with a little parsley added. Serves 4.

ITALY

CHICKEN TETRAZZINI

1 3-pound chicken, cut up	4 tablespoons flour
3 quarts water	Pinch cayenne
1 medium onion, sliced	1 egg yolk
2 carrots, sliced across	¾ cup light cream
2 stalks celery	¼ cup dry sherry or Marsala wine
1 bay leaf	½ pound mushrooms, sliced
Salt and 12 peppercorns	½ pound very thin spaghetti
6 tablespoons butter	Butter
	1 cup Parmesan cheese, grated

Place the chicken in a large kettle with 1 quart of water, and bring to the boil. Reduce the heat to low, and skim the scum off the water as it appears. Now add the onion, carrots, celery, bay leaf, a little salt, and the peppercorns and cook, covered, for about 45 minutes. Remove the chicken, strain the stock, and allow to cool. Discard the vegetables.

Remove the skin from the chicken pieces and then bone each piece. You should have between 3 and 4 cups of meat. When the stock is cool, skim off the surface fat with a spoon and measure out 1¾ cups and reserve.

Melt 4 tablespoons butter in a medium-sized (3-quart) saucepan, then remove from the heat and add the flour, a little salt, and the cayenne pepper. Stir for several minutes until smooth, then gradually mix in the reserved chicken stock. Now bring the pot to the boil, stirring constantly, then reduce heat and simmer for 2 or 3 minutes until the mixture thickens somewhat. Remove and set aside.

Bring 2 quarts of water to the boil for spaghetti. Add 1 teaspoon salt. While waiting beat the egg yolk and cream with a fork, then add a spoonful or two of the hot sauce and stir together well. (This will heat up the egg and cream and prevent curdling.) Now add the egg and cream mixture to the sauce and cook for several minutes over low heat, stirring all the while. Do not allow the mixture to boil. Add the wine, mushrooms, and chicken and heat very gently for 12-15 minutes.

At this point turn the oven on to broil. Now, add the spaghetti to the boiling water and cook for 10-12 minutes, then drain. Turn the spaghetti into a baking dish and spoon the chicken mixture over the top. Dot with butter and sprinkle with Parmesan cheese. Place the dish under the broiler for 3 minutes or so, until the top is golden brown, then serve piping hot directly from the dish. Serves 4-6.

SOUTHERN ITALY

POLLO CON SALSA VERDE—Chicken with Green Sauce

2 tablespoons olive oil	Salt and freshly ground pepper
1 medium onion, chopped coarsely	¾ cup dry white wine
	1 large tomato, peeled and chopped
1 3-pound chicken, cut up	1 cup chicken stock

Salsa Verde

¼ cup vinegar	2 small gherkins, chopped finely
1 clove garlic, chopped finely	½ teaspoon capers
4 anchovy fillets, chopped finely	3 tablespoons fresh parsley, chopped

Heat the oil in a large skillet and sauté the onion until golden. Salt and pepper the chicken and add to the pan and brown on all sides, about 15 minutes. Add the wine and cook over low-moderate heat for about 15 minutes (the wine should be about evaporated), then add the chopped tomato and the cup of stock. Cover and cook for 30 minutes. When the chicken is done, remove it to a platter and keep warm.

Now make the salsa verde: Add the vinegar to the pan liquid and cook slowly for 5-6 minutes, until it reduces somewhat. Stir the garlic, anchovies, gherkins, capers, and parsley into the sauce and stir well. Simmer very gently for 5 minutes, then pour over the chicken and serve warm. Serves 4.

ITALY (ROME)

POLLO ALLA CREMA—Chicken with Cream Sauce

Rome stands between the northern and southern provinces and thus has absorbed the food of both into her cuisine. Actually Roman cooking is characterized more by the international concept of Italian cooking than by the provincial. This recipe is one adapted by Roman chefs from northern Italy.

1 3-pound chicken, cut up
2-4 tablespoons butter
1 onion, chopped
½ pint cream

6-8 mushrooms, sliced thinly
Salt and freshly ground pepper
½ cup flour
Parsley sprigs for garnish

Heat the butter in a large skillet and sauté the onion lightly. Meanwhile put the flour, salt, and pepper in a bag, shake to mix, then put in each piece of chicken and shake until completely covered. Now add the chicken to the pan a few pieces at a time and brown thoroughly on all sides. Add more butter as needed. When the chicken is thoroughly browned, add the cream and mushrooms. Cover, reduce the heat, and cook for 20 minutes over low heat. When done serve on a warm platter with parsley. Serves 4.

ITALY (BOLOGNA)

POLLO AL PARMIGIANO—Chicken with Parmesan Cheese

2 whole chicken breasts, split,
  skin removed, and boned
1 cup Parmesan cheese
6 tablespoons butter
2 cloves garlic, sliced

2 tablespoons flour
1 cup chicken stock
½ cup Marsala wine
10 medium mushrooms, sliced
Salt and freshly ground pepper
Parsley sprigs for garnish

Roll the chicken breasts in the cheese until well coated. Melt the butter in a skillet and then gently sauté the garlic. Now brown the chicken pieces on all sides for about 15 minutes. Remove the chicken to a baking dish and keep warm.

Preheat the oven to 350°F. Pour off most of the melted butter, retaining 2-3 tablespoons. Now add the flour and stir into a smooth mixture, then add in the cup of stock, stirring all the while. Now add the wine, mushrooms, salt, and a few grindings of pepper. Cook gently for 10-12 minutes, then pour over the chicken in the baking dish. Place the chicken in the oven for 30 minutes, then serve in the dish, garnished with parsley sprigs. Serves 4.

ITALY (NAPLES)

POLLO CON PEPPERONI—Chicken with Peppers

4 tablespoons olive oil
2 onions, chopped
2 cloves garlic, sliced
1 3-pound chicken, cut up
Salt and freshly ground pepper
Pinch each thyme and marjoram

1 large green pepper, sliced and seeded
4 pimentos, seeded and cut into strips
3 tomatoes, peeled and chopped
Pinch basil
1 cup dry white wine
Parsley sprigs for garnish

Preheat the oven to 350° F. In a casserole, heat the oil and gently sauté the onion and garlic. Sprinkle the chicken pieces with salt and a few grindings of pepper and a little thyme and marjoram and brown on all sides, a few pieces at a time, for 10 minutes. Remove the chicken pieces to a plate and keep warm.

Now sauté the pepper and pimentos over low heat until they become soft, then remove them to a plate and keep warm. Add the chopped tomatoes, the wine, and a pinch of basil to the pan and cook for 5-6 minutes, or until the wine reduces in volume to about half. Now return the chicken and peppers to the casserole, cover, and bake for 40 minutes. Garnish with parsley and serve from the dish. Serves 4.

SICILY

POLLO AL MARSALA—Chicken with Marsala Wine

Marsala wine is the best-known of Sicily's several good wines. It was developed by an Englishman named John Woodhouse toward the end of the seventeenth century. Lord Nelson was one of the first to enjoy the wine in Sicily, and shortly thereafter it became a favorite among the wealthy in England. There are four varieties of Marsala, mostly used as dessert wines, but the dry varieties are excellent for cooking.

1 3-pound chicken, cut up
Salt and freshly ground pepper
4 tablespoons olive oil

2 cups tomatoes, peeled, cored, and seeded
1 teaspoon thyme

1 medium onion, chopped
  coarsely
½ cup Marsala wine
1 cup chicken stock

1 teaspoon rosemary
8 large mushrooms, sliced
¼ cup parsley, preferably the
  Italian flat leaf variety
2 tablespoons butter

Season the chicken pieces in salt and pepper and brown in hot oil in a skillet on all sides for about 15 minutes. Remove to a medium Dutch oven or deep saucepan and keep warm. Now sauté the onion in the skillet gently until golden, then add the wine, scraping the bottom of the pan, and cook slowly until the liquid reduces by half. Add the chicken stock and bring up to the boil, then reduce heat to low. Chop the tomatoes and add to the skillet with the thyme and rosemary. Stir well and cook for 5 minutes. Now pour the sauce over the chicken, cover the pot, and simmer for 45 minutes or until done.

After 30 minutes, sauté the sliced mushrooms and parsley in butter for a few minutes and add to the chicken. Serve the chicken on a warm platter with the sauce spooned over. Serves 4.

ITALY (ROME)

CAPPELLETTI IN BROTH

Cappelletti, or "little hats," is a Roman variation of the Bolognese *tortellini,* or "little twisted ones." Both are made of pasta, stuffed with meat, cheese, or vegetables, in this case chicken, and served in a broth.

Pasta

1½ cups flour   2 eggs

Broth

Backs, neck, wings, and giblets of
  2-3 chickens
2 quarts water
1 carrot, sliced

1 stalk of celery
Salt and pepper
1 bay leaf
¼ pound (1 cup) boiled chicken,
  chopped finely

Filling

3 slices prosciutto ham, chopped
  finely
Meat from 1 pork chop, chopped
  finely

1 egg
Salt and pepper
Pinch nutmeg
2 tablespoons Parmesan cheese,
  grated

Put the ingredients for the broth into the water in a large kettle and boil for 2 hours. Strain the broth and keep hot. Pick the bones for chicken meat and return it to the broth, then discard the skin, bones, and vegetables.

On a pastry board, make a well in the flour and break the eggs into it. Now mix the flour and eggs together with your fingers, then knead the dough slowly for about 20 minutes until a smooth, pliant ball of dough is formed. Sprinkle some flour over the board and roll the dough out as thinly as possible, then cut circles about 2½-3 inches in diameter.

Mix together all the filling ingredients and place a little in the center of each pasta circle. Fold over the dough and roll it to give the shape of a dunce cap, then gently press the edges to seal.

Bring the broth to the boiling point, add the cappelletti, and simmer over reduced heat for 30 minutes. Serve in individual soup plates. Serves 6.

ITALY (LOMBARDY)

POLLO ALLA LOMBARDA—Chicken Lombardy Style

4 tablespoons butter
1 onion, chopped finely
1 clove garlic, minced
3 sprigs fresh parsley, chopped finely
1 tablespoon fennel, chopped finely
1 3-pound chicken, cut up
¾ cup chicken stock
¼ cup dry white wine
1 pound fresh shelled peas
Livers of the chicken, sliced rather coarsely
Salt and freshly ground pepper
2 egg yolks
2 tablespoons lemon juice

In a large skillet with a cover, heat 2 tablespoons butter and sauté the onion, garlic, and parsley very slowly and gently for about 10 minutes. Add the fennel, chicken pieces, stock, and wine, cover, and cook over low heat for 30 minutes. Cook the peas in a separate pot for 10 minutes in salted water. Then drain and add them and the sliced chicken livers to the main pot. Add a little salt and a few grindings of pepper and cook for another 10 minutes.

Remove the chicken pieces from the pot and keep warm. Mix together the egg yolks and lemon juice and beat them thoroughly, then stir the mixture into the sauce. Serve the chicken on a heated platter and spoon the peas and sauce over. Serves 4.

ITALY (PIEDMONT)

BOLLITO MISTO

This means mixed boiled meats. It's a favorite dish in the Piedmont, whose people are second only to the Bolognese in the Italian "trencherman" tradition of eating.

1 3-pound beef tongue, fresh or smoked
1 2-pound boneless chuck, or rump roast
1 2-pound piece of veal rump or shoulder, tied in a roll

1 pound Italian sausages, hot or sweet
1 4-5-pound stewing chicken
2 onions, coarsely chopped
2 carrots, scraped and sliced
2 celery stalks with leaves
6 parsley sprigs
Salt and pepper
1 recipe salsa verde (page 238)

You will need a large stewpot. Wash the tongue, then cover it with cold water and bring it to the boil; then reduce the heat and simmer for 1 hour, covered. Now add the beef and veal and simmer for 1 hour more, covered, skimming off the scum as it comes to the top. Prick the sausage with a fork in several places so it won't explode in cooking, and add it plus the chicken, onions, carrots, celery, parsley, and a little salt and pepper to the pot and simmer, covered, for another hour. Keep the water level up by adding more, if necessary, as the cooking progresses. Also continue skimming the surface of scum, and adding salt and pepper, a little at a time according to your taste.

When the meats are done, remove them to a warm platter. Peel the tongue, discarding any gristle or fat. Slice all the meat into edible pieces, and carve the chicken into 6 or 8 pieces. Spoon some of the broth over the meat and serve with fresh cooked vegetables and salsa verde. Serves 8-10.

ITALY (BOLOGNA)

CHICKEN AND SAUSAGE IN WHITE WINE

3 tablespoons olive oil
1 garlic clove, sliced
1 3-pound chicken, cut up
1 pound hot Italian sausage, cut into 1-inch pieces

1 cup dry white wine
10-12 mushrooms, sliced
½ teaspoon salt
2 tablespoons cornstarch
¼ cup water

Heat the oil in a large skillet with a cover and sauté the garlic until golden, then remove the garlic with a spoon and discard. Add the chicken and sausage pieces, three or four at a time, and brown on all sides. Remove and keep warm, then finish the remaining chicken and sausage pieces. Pour off all but 2-3 tablespoons of the pan drippings, then return the browned meat to the pan and add the wine, mushrooms, and ½ teaspoon salt. Bring the pan to the boil, then reduce the heat to low and simmer, covered, for 30 minutes. Spoon a little pan liquid over the chicken pieces every 10 minutes or so.

When done, remove the chicken from the skillet to a serving platter and keep warm. Blend the cornstarch with the water and gradually stir the mixture into the pan liquid until it is smooth. Increase the heat to medium and cook the sauce until it thickens slightly, stirring constantly. Spoon some of the sauce over the chicken and sausage and serve the remainder in a boat. Serves 4-6.

ITALY (BOLOGNA)

POLLO ALLA BOLOGNESE—
Chicken in the Style of Bologna

Though Italian in origin, this classic has come to be known (at least in this country) by French and Swiss names as well—*poulet cordon bleu* and *poulet à la suisse*. It all depends on the kind of ham and cheese you use.

½ cup flour
Pinch salt and a few grindings of
  fresh pepper
2 whole chicken breasts, skinned,
  boned, and split in half

2-4 tablespoons butter
½ pound prosciutto or Parma
  ham
Mozzarella cheese

Tomato Sauce
1 tablespoon olive oil
2 small onions, sliced
½ cup tomato paste

2 cups water
1 tablespoon oregano
1 bay leaf
Salt and freshly ground pepper

Preheat the oven to 350° F. Season the flour with a little salt and pepper, then put it into a bag. Add each half chicken breast individually and shake lightly until covered. Melt the butter in a skillet and brown the chicken pieces, a few at a time, over low to moderate heat. When all the chicken is browned, arrange the pieces in a baking dish with a little melted butter and place one slice of ham on each breast. The ham should be approximately the size of the chicken. Now cut the cheese into the same sizes as the chicken and lay that over the ham. Cover and bake for 15 minutes.

While the chicken bakes prepare the tomato sauce: Bring the oil to moderate heat in a skillet and sauté the sliced onions until golden. Add the tomato paste, water, oregano, and bay leaf and a little salt and pepper and cook until the sauce reduces by half. When the sauce reaches the desired consistency, cover the pan and turn the heat down to very low, just enough to keep it warm.

After 15 minutes, spoon 4 or 6 tablespoons of tomato sauce over the chicken and allow it to cook, covered, for 15 minutes more. Serve the chicken on a warm platter and the tomato sauce separately. Serves 4.

ITALY (NAPLES)

POLLO ALLA CACCIATORE—Chicken Hunter Style

From southern Italy, this is one of Europe's most famous chicken dishes. It is best known as a chicken simmered in a tomato and wine sauce, and its fame is well deserved. But another version of *Cacciatore* replaces the tomatoes with green or black olives and anchovy fillets, and this style is equally good. Sicily also has her version with tomatoes and Marsala wine.

With Tomato Sauce

1 3-pound chicken, cut up	2 cloves garlic, chopped finely
Salt and freshly ground black pepper	2 tablespoons chopped parsley
	1 bay leaf
½ cup flour	Pinch thyme
3 tablespoons olive oil	2 cups (1 pound) tomatoes,
2 medium onions, finely chopped	peeled, seeded, and chopped
	½ cup dry white wine

Sprinkle the chicken pieces with a little salt and cover thoroughly with flour. Brown the pieces in oil in a large skillet on all sides for 10-15 minutes, then remove and keep warm.

Now sauté the onions and garlic for about 5 minutes over low heat in the same pan and add in the parsley, the bay leaf, thyme, and tomatoes. Add a little more oil if necessary. Simmer for 10 minutes over low heat, then add the wine and return the chicken pieces. Spoon the tomato sauce over the chicken, then add a little salt and pepper. Simmer the chicken for 30 minutes, then serve hot with rice or pasta. Serves 4.

Note: You may also sauté ½ pound of sliced mushrooms for 5 minutes and add to the pan with the tomatoes, stirring in well.

With Olives and Anchovies

3 tablespoons olive oil
3 cloves garlic, chopped
1 3-pound chicken, cut up
Salt and freshly ground pepper
⅛ teaspoon basil
⅛ teaspoon thyme

½ cup dry white wine
2 tablespoons white wine vinegar
10 black olives, pitted and sliced
10 green olives, pitted and sliced
3 flat anchovy fillets, chopped
½ cup stock

Sauté the garlic slowly in the oil in a large skillet. Season the chicken pieces with salt and fresh pepper and brown on all sides, about 15 minutes. Add the basil, thyme, wine, vinegar, sliced olives, and anchovies and ½ cup stock. Now simmer, uncovered, over low heat for 40 minutes or until the chicken is done. Arrange the chicken on a platter and pour over the sauce. Serves 4.

ITALY

POLLO IN UMIDO CON POLENTA—
Chicken Stew with Polenta

In Italy, polenta is nearly as popular as pasta. The original polenta, in ancient times, was made from wheat and other grains, and was called *puls* or *pulmento*. When corn was introduced to Europe four centuries ago, the Italians substituted it for wheat to make their present product, and it continues as one of their national dishes.

1 3-pound chicken, cut up
2 tablespoons butter
2 tablespoons olive oil

2 tablespoons salt
10 peppercorns
1 teaspoon rosemary

1 cup onion, chopped coarsely
2 cloves garlic, sliced

2 cups Italian plum tomatoes,
  with juice
1 cup chicken stock

Heat the butter and oil in a large Dutch oven and brown the chicken pieces on all sides, about 15 minutes. When done, remove the pieces to a plate and sauté the onion and garlic in the same oil until golden. Return the chicken to the pot and add the salt and peppercorns, rosemary, tomatoes, and the stock. Stir all together, then cover and simmer for 1 hour. Stir the pot occasionally.

Polenta
1 tablespoon salt

2 cups yellow cormeal
1 quart boiling water

About 30 minutes before the chicken is done, bring 1 quart of water to the boil in a saucepan and add 1 tablespoon salt. Now gradually pour the 2 cups of cornmeal into the water, stirring all the while. Don't rush this or the polenta will become lumpy. Stir until the mixture becomes smooth, then reduce heat to low and cook uncovered for about 30 minutes. When done, turn the polenta out onto a warm plate and spoon the stew over it. Serve immediately. Serves 4.

ITALY

FRITO MISTO—Mixed Fry

Frito misto means mixed fried meats, but it usually includes vegetables and sometimes fruit. This is most easily compared to the mixed grill in this country, which combines several types of meat. Frito misto is popular all over Italy and varies in composition according to what meat, poultry, vegetable, or fish is available. One of the most popular dishes is made with calf's sweetbreads, but the dish can be prepared with virtually anything desired or to any taste. Usually the frito misto combines up to six different foods, which are dipped in a batter or beaten egg and rolled in breadcrumbs.

1 small cauliflower
1 pound zucchini
½ pound artichoke hearts
2 apples, peeled, cored, and cut into 1-inch cubes
1 whole chicken breast, skinned, boned, and cut into 1-inch cubes

½ pound veal cutlets, cut into 1-inch cubes
½ pound fillets of white fish, cut into 1-inch pieces
Vegetable oil or shortening for deep-frying
Parsley sprigs and lemon slices for garnish

Batter

1 cup sifted, all-purpose flour
¾ cup warm water

3 tablespoons vegetable oil
Salt
White of 1 egg

Bring 2 quarts of salted water to the boil. Break the cauliflower into small bite-sized flowerets and parboil for about 5 minutes. Then drain the boiling water and hold under cold water for a few moments to stop the cooking. Drain again and set aside. Peel the zucchini and cut it into 1-inch cubes. Cut the artichoke hearts into bite-sized cubes also.

Preheat the oven to 250° F, and place it in 2 baking dishes lined with paper towels. Now heat about 4 inches of vegetable oil or shortening in a deep-fryer to 375° F.

While the oven and oil are heating up, make the batter: Combine the flour, water, oil, and salt in a large mixing bowl and stir slowly until the batter is smooth, and all lumps are gone. Now beat the egg white until stiff and fold it into the batter. Stir gently until completely mixed.

Cook the meat, vegetables, apple, and fish (last) separately. Starting with the meat, dip several pieces of chicken or veal into the batter, then with tongs drop 4 or 5 pieces into the fryer. Deep-fry for 5 or 6 minutes, until the batter becomes a golden brown, then remove each piece with a slotted spoon, drain a moment, and place in the baking dish in the oven to keep warm.

Continue until all the ingredients are cooked, then arrange them on a platter and serve immediately. Garnish with lemon slices and parsley. Serves 4-6.

SICILY

POLLO FRA DIAVOLO—Deviled Chicken

1 3-pound chicken, cut up	1 cup dry white wine
4 tablespoons olive oil	4 tablespoons chopped parsley
2 cloves garlic, sliced	1 teaspoon salt
2 medium onions, chopped	Freshly ground pepper
2 cups whole Italian tomatoes with juice	¼ teaspoon dried red pepper

Preheat the oven to 350° F. Heat the oil in a large skillet and brown the chicken pieces on all sides for about 15 minutes. Remove the chicken to a large casserole.

In the same oil sauté the garlic and onions until golden, then stir in the tomatoes, white wine, chopped parsley, salt, and a little black and red pepper. Simmer over low heat for about 10 minutes, then pour over the chicken in the casserole. Now cover and place the casserole in the oven for 1 hour.

While the chicken cooks, prepare whatever pasta you desire and serve with the chicken pieces and sauce poured over. Serves 4.

ITALY (VENICE)

CHICKEN RISOTTO

Risotto is made of rice, especially Italian rice, which though short-grained, is larger than American or Oriental types. A risotto is cooked slowly over moderately low heat with water or stock added from time to time as the grains absorb it and swell. It is properly served somewhat more moist than American rice and is usually cooked with chicken, fish, or vegetables and seasonings in any number of variations.

1 3-4-pound chicken	4 tablespoons butter
6 cups water	1 clove garlic, crushed
1 teaspoon salt	6-8 medium mushrooms, sliced
12 peppercorns	2 tomatoes, peeled and coarsely chopped
2 onions	
2 cloves	¾ cup Italian rice or short grain white rice
2 carrots	
2 stalks celery	1 cup dry white wine
1 bunch of parsley, chopped	1 cup Parmesan cheese

Place the chicken in a large kettle and cover with the water. Bring the water to the boil, then reduce the heat to low (just enough to keep the water bubbling). Skim off the scum which will rise in the first 5-10 minutes, then add the salt, peppercorns, 1 quartered onion, cloves, 1 sliced carrot, 1 sliced celery stalk, and ½ the chopped parsley. Cover and simmer for 1½ hours. When done, remove the chicken and strain the stock and reserve. Discard the vegetables. Cut the chicken into pieces, remove the skin and bones from the breast, and cut the white meat into ½-inch cubes. Save the remaining chicken pieces for another recipe.

Chop the remaining onion, celery, and carrot. Melt the butter in a skillet and sauté the chopped vegetables and garlic very lightly for about 5 minutes. Now add the sliced mushrooms and chopped tomatoes and cook slowly for 2 minutes, then add the chopped chicken and wine. Keeping the heat low, cook this mixture for several minutes, then add a little salt and pepper.

Mix the rice with the chicken mixture thoroughly, then add 1 cup of the reserved stock. Continue stirring and add more stock as it is absorbed. When the rice is done, there should be just a little of the liquid remaining in the skillet, yet the rice will be cooked through. Turn the risotto onto a serving platter, drop a generous lump of butter on top and sprinkle Parmesan cheese over all. Serves 4.

Note: Another popular risotto is made with chicken livers—*risotto di fagitine*. Omit the chicken and replace it with ¾ pound of chicken livers from which all veins, fat, and gristle are removed. Brown the livers in butter for a few minutes, until they lose their color, then remove from the heat and chop them rather finely. Now proceed with the recipe above.

ITALY (TUSCANY)

POLLO ALLA FIORENTINA—
Chicken in the Florentine Style
Most authorities agree that the Florentines do not include spinach in this dish, but Larousse says they do, and that might be the source of

the conflict. Regardless, the chicken can be served either alone or on a bed of spinach with the sauce spooned over, with equally good results.

1 4-5-pound roasting or stewing chicken	1½ cups fresh chicken stock
	Salt and pepper
4 tablespoons butter	Yolk of 1 egg, beaten
1 tablespoon flour	1 pound fresh spinach (optional)

You may roast the chicken or boil it as you desire. When done, the breast meat should be sliced rather thinly and the skin removed, then served with the sauce spooned over.

Sauce: Melt the butter in a skillet over low heat and gradually stir in the flour. When the paste is smooth, add the stock and then cook for 6-8 minutes, stirring continually until the sauce starts to thicken. Remove from the heat, season with a little salt and pepper, and stir in the beaten egg yolk.

If you wish to serve with spinach, time it so both the spinach and sauce are done at the same time. Drain the spinach thoroughly, then place a portion on a warm plate, lay on 2 or 3 thin slices of chicken, and spoon over the sauce. Serve with rice. Serves 2-4.

ITALY (ABRUZZI)

CROSTINI DI FAGITINI—Chicken Liver Toasts

½ pound chicken livers, chopped finely	Salt and pepper
	¼ cup dry white wine
2 teaspoons parsley, chopped	2 tablespoons stock or water
2 tablespoons butter	2 teaspoons lemon juice
3 anchovies and 1 tablespoon capers, chopped together	Fresh Italian bread, cut into ½-inch slices

Over low heat, fry the livers and parsley in butter for 3 minutes. Add the chopped anchovies and capers, salt and pepper, wine, and stock. Bring to the boil, stirring continually, then remove from the fire.

Spread a little butter on the bread slices and toast under the grill until they just turn brown. Spread the liver mixture on each slice, sprinkle with a drop or two of lemon juice, and serve hot. Serves 6-8.

ITALY

SALSA DI FAGITINI—Chicken Liver Sauce

1 tablespoon olive oil
1 onion, chopped finely
1 clove garlic, minced
¾ pound chicken livers

1 pound fresh tomatoes, peeled and chopped
½ tablespoon basil
Salt and pepper

Remove the veins, fat, and gristle from the livers and chop finely.

Over low heat sauté the onion and garlic in olive oil for several minutes, until soft, and then add the chicken livers. Cook them, stirring constantly, until they lose all their color. Sieve the tomatoes to remove the seeds, and add the pulp and liquid to the pot along with the basil and a little salt and pepper. Now cover and cook slowly for 20 minutes. Check the pot from time to time and add a little water if it gets too dry.

This sauce goes well with most pasta but is particularly good with plain spaghetti, topped with grated Parmesan cheese. Makes enough for 1 pound of spaghetti.

SOUTHERN ITALY

POLLO ALLA SCARPARIELLO—
Sautéed Chicken, Shoemaker Style

1 3-pound chicken, cut up
1 cup flour
Salt and freshly ground pepper
¼ cup olive oil

2 cloves garlic, minced
½ cup dry white wine
Juice of 1 lemon
Parsley sprigs for garnish

Wash the chicken pieces and pat dry. Combine the flour with a little salt and pepper and dredge the pieces thoroughly.

Heat the oil in a large skillet and brown 1 clove of minced garlic, then remove with a slotted spoon and discard. Place the chicken in the pan and cook over low to moderate heat, uncovered, for 10-12 minutes on a side. When done remove and keep warm.

Now sauté the second clove of minced garlic in the same pan, then remove with a slotted spoon and discard. Deglaze the pan with the wine, add the lemon juice, and return the chicken, coating each piece. Cover and cook for 2 or 3 minutes to reheat. Serve on a warm platter garnished with parsley sprigs. Serves 4.

France

For some reason the French nation that emerged from the Renaissance was blessed with an almost divine appreciation of good food. This attitude, growing over time, was responsible for the astonishing innovations that have issued from French kitchens during the past five centuries.

Today, without question, French cooking is unequaled in the Western world, and for most people it shares a unique position with the Chinese at the pinnacle of the world's cooking.

By the seventeenth century, the French kitchen had become recognized as the finest in Europe, and her greatest chefs performed their magic for most of Europe's nobility: the Hapsburgs, the British, the Spanish, the Danes, the Swedes, the Germans, and the Russians were all bitten by the French bug. Despite this, however, very little of the French technique permeated the national cuisines of her neighbors. Perhaps it was too expensive or too difficult; more likely the average person never experienced or knew much about it, for it was the cuisine of the royalty, the nobility, and the aristocracy.

There are two basic levels of French cooking: *cuisine régionale* and *haute,* or *la grande, cuisine.* Others have come into vogue since the French Revolution—*cuisine bourgeois* (middle-class cooking) in the nineteenth century and *cuisine minceure* (low-calorie cooking) in the twentieth—but they are really nothing more than adaptations of the first two. *Cuisine régionale* is the simple cooking of the peasants, and a number of regional specialties have become world-famous. Normandy, in the north, is dairy and apple country, and the Norman cooks have combined chicken with butter, cream, cider, or apple brandy (*calvados*) with spectacular results. One of their better known is *Poulet à la Normande*—chicken simmered in cider or calvados and heavy cream.

Brittany made the French *crêpe* famous and Alsace and Lorraine, the *charcuterie*. The world's finest *foie gras* comes from Alsace, where they still force-feed the goose as the Romans did to enlarge its liver. In Burgundy, where one will find perhaps the best overall cuisine in France, the Bresse chicken helps make such an international classic as *Coq au Vin,* just one of an incredible assortment of dishes that make use of the region's great wines.

The second and higher level of French cooking might be considered the poetry of the French kitchen, but few Frenchmen over the centuries have ever tasted it. *La grande cuisine* is eggs, cream, and butter-based cooking that was created in the chateaus and palaces of the nobility, who prided themselves on the lavishness of their banquet tables.

Today, despite the seeming complexity of haute cuisine, the basic dishes are usually simplicity themselves, for the goal of the great chef is no different from that of the peasant who cooks her regional specialty; and that is to extract the ultimate flavor from the particular food at hand. This involves countless hours of cooking down meat, vegetables, fish, or poultry to produce a perfect base or essence, which is then used for the final preparation of the dish.

In French chicken cookery there are no better examples of the lengths the haute cuisine chef will go to, to produce an image or create an effect, than *Poulet Chaud Froid* or *Poularde Demi-deuil.* Poulet Chaud Froid is a cold roast chicken covered with aspic, dotted with truffles, pimentos, and egg slices, and garnished with tarragon leaves, parsley, or watercress. At first glance it seems a splendid bit of rococo art, more to be admired than eaten. Poularde Demi-deuil, which means chicken in half-mourning, has thin slices of black truffles inserted under the skin, and this gives it the deathly pallor suggested by its name.

Sauces and wine are the two things most people associate with French cooking, and every French chef since the Renaissance spent his apprenticeship learning the subtleties of making or using them before he became great or even good. A sauce is there to mask an unwanted taste or to enhance one that is desirable, or it is used to bind two or more elements of the dish together; but the ultimate function of a sauce is to raise the flavor of the food above the ordinary. The French have perfected hundreds of sauces, many of which have become world-famous (*niçoise, béarnaise, hollandaise, bourguignonne*), and virtually all are built on the basic brown (*espagnol*) or white (*béchamel*) sauce.

Wine can be added to a great many recipes with excellent results, provided it is the right one, and in some dishes more than one wine is used. in *Paté Foies de Volailles* (chicken liver paté), for example, both cognac and port wine help produce one of the world's great hors d'oeuvre. But just as with a sauce, wine is there merely to enhance a flavor, not to create one. When added, it must be cooked long enough to boil off the alcohol, otherwise not only the taste but the aroma will be spoiled. Different wines will give different accents to the same dish. For example, the classic *Coq au Vin Rouge* is chicken cooked in a good burgundy, but the same bird cooked in a dry white wine becomes *Coq au Vin Blanc*; very different, but equally good.

Since the French Revolution, another level of French cooking has emerged. It is an adaptation of cuisine régionale with occasional touches of la grande cuisine, and it's called *cuisine bourgeoise*. More accurately, it is good middle-class fare in the "French style" served in homes and restaurants around the world. Interestingly, it is a class of cooking Napoleon himself helped create.

After the French Revolution, Napoleon caused the heads of the nobility to roll and thereby put many master chefs out of work. With no one to provide a kitchen or retainer, these enterprising gentlemen opened restaurants of their own. Some of the greatest chefs of the last two centuries, most notably Brillat-Savarin, Carême, and Escoffier, made public their recipes, philosophies, and techniques in cookbook form. With such gospel and tradition to go by, restaurants and inns all over France upgraded their cuisines, and it wasn't long before not only the French middle class but the world became aware of just how great the country's cooking really was.

RECOMMENDED READING: Julia Child, *From Julia Child's Kitchen* (New York: Knopf, 1975); Prosper Montagne, *Larousse Gastronomique* (New York: Crown Publishers, 1961); Craig Claiborne, *The New York Times International Cookbook* (New York: Harper & Row, 1971); *Splendid Fare, The Albert Stockli Cookbook* (New York: Knopf, 1970)

FRANCE

POULET SAUTÉ À LA NORMANDE—
Chicken Sauté Normandy Style

1 3-pound chicken, cut up	1 small onion, chopped
Salt and freshly ground pepper	1 cup cider, or 2 tablespoons cal-
6 tablespoons butter	vados or applejack
8-10 large mushrooms, sliced	¾ cup heavy cream
	3 tablespoons chicken stock

Rub the chicken pieces with salt and fresh pepper, then sauté them in a large skillet, a few pieces at a time, in 4 tablespoons of butter. When brown on all sides, remove from the heat and set aside.

In a separate skillet melt 2 tablespoons of butter and sauté the mushrooms and onions over low heat for 10 minutes, turning occasionally with a wooden spoon. When done, return the chicken skillet to the fire and add the mushrooms and onions. Increase the heat slightly and cook for an additional 15-20 minutes. The chicken should be very nearly done by now. Add the cider or brandy and cook until it has almost disappeared, then add ¾ cup heavy cream and 3 tablespoons chicken stock. Season with a little salt and pepper and cook for 5 minutes.

Serve on a warm platter with a little of the mushroom sauce poured over and the rest in a sauceboat. Serves 4.

FRANCE

PETITE MARMITE—Chicken and Vegetable Soup

This is perhaps the best-known soup of France. It is cooked in a *marmite*, which is an earthen soup pot, just as is *pot-au-feu*. Actually the two are almost the same, only the petite marmite is served in individual casseroles. It is important to cook this soup slowly so as not to make the bouillon cloudy.

1 2-pound chicken	1 small parsnip, quartered
1 2-pound rump of beef	1 onion, stuck with 2 cloves
1 pound oxtail	1 clove garlic
1 quart chicken stock	1 bay leaf
1 quart water	¼ teaspoon thyme
2 carrots, sliced	Salt and freshly ground pepper
2 stalks celery, sliced	French bread
	Grated Swiss cheese

Place the chicken, beef, and oxtail in a large stewpot and cover with equal parts of stock and water (about 1 quart each). Put over low heat and skim the scum as it rises for the first 30 minutes or so, until the pot begins to simmer. Now add the vegetables, the garlic, bay leaf, thyme, salt, and a few grindings of fresh pepper. Cover the pot and simmer for 3 hours. The chicken should be done in an hour or so. Remove, and return it to the pot for the last 30 minutes to reheat it.

When done, skim the fat from the bouillon, remove the chicken from its bones, then slice the meats into serving portions. Place a slice or 2 of each meat in a small casserole or soup bowl and ladle in the bouillon. Now place a slice of French bread on top, sprinkle liberally with grated cheese, and place under the broiler for a minute or so to brown. Serves 6-8.

Note: Today, petite marmite is often served almost as a clear consommé or bouillon with only a small amount of meat and vegetables, cut into small cubes, included with the liquid.

FRANCE

COQ AU VIN ROUGE—Chicken in Red Wine

Most well-known recipes for this dish call for a good red burgundy wine as the cooking liquid, but another excellent dish is *coq au vin blanc,* the same chicken cooked in dry white wine. You may vary the amount of wine used, up to a full bottle, the main thing being just to cover the chicken in the pan.

1 3-pound chicken, cut up	*Bouquet garni* *
Flour	3 cups burgundy wine
6 tablespoons butter	3 medium onions, sliced
Salt and pepper	1 clove garlic, minced
2 ounces cognac	12 mushrooms, sliced
	Parsley sprigs for garnish

*(Mince one teaspoon of celery and one sprig of parsley. Add a good pinch of thyme and one bay leaf. Tie up in cheesecloth and add to the pan.)

Roll the chicken pieces in flour until they are thoroughly coated. Heat 5 tablespoons butter in a skillet with a cover and brown the chicken pieces on all sides for about 15 minutes. As the pieces are done, remove them to a platter and keep warm. When all are browned, return them to the skillet and sprinkle with salt and pepper. Warm the cognac in a cup, then pour over the chicken pieces and light. When the flame dies, add a bouquet garni and pour over the wine. Cover and simmer for about 45 minutes.

About 15 minutes before the chicken is done, sauté the onions and garlic over low heat for about 5 minutes in the remaining butter, then add the sliced mushrooms and continue to cook slowly for another 10 minutes or so, or until tender.

Place the chicken pieces on a serving platter and spoon the mushrooms and onion over. Remove the bouquet garni, strain the pan liquid, and then pour it over the chicken. Garnish with parsley sprigs. Serves 4.

Note: More recently, coq au vin has been cooked with a combination of chicken stock and wine. If you wish, substitute stock for up to half the wine, but still be sure the chicken is covered.

FRANCE

POULET A LA NIÇOISE—Chicken and Vegetables

According to Larousse, a dish cooked "à la niçoise" always features tomatoes as an ingredient, but more recently this definition has expanded to include all the popular ingredients of southern France and northern Italy—onions, garlic, basil, and olives as well as tomatoes. The French cook many large and small cuts of meat and poultry this way and frequently combine other vegetables on the serving platter with the sauce poured over the whole thing.

4 tablespoons butter	3 large tomatoes, quartered
1 3-pound chicken, cut up	8-10 small potatoes, peeled
Salt and pepper	Pinch each thyme, tarragon, sage
3 medium onions, chopped	1 cup white wine
2 cloves garlic, sliced in half	Green or black olives (or both)

Over low heat, melt the butter in a large Dutch oven, then sprinkle the chicken pieces with salt and pepper and brown gently on all sides, a few at a time. As they are cooked, remove and set aside. Add the onions and brown, then return the chicken to the pan and add the garlic, tomatoes, and potatoes, and sprinkle over the seasoning. Add the wine, cover, and cook over moderate heat for 30 minutes.

When done, arrange the pieces on a warm platter, and place the potatoes and tomatoes around the sides. Pour the pan juices over all and scatter on 12-15 green or black olives. Serves 4.

FRANCE

PATE DE FOIES DE VOLAILLES—Chicken Liver Paté

½ pound butter	½ teaspoon salt
1 pound chicken livers, cut into small pieces, veins and gristle removed	⅛ teaspoon each of: powdered clove
	pepper
2 shallots, chopped finely	thyme
1 clove garlic, minced	marjoram
2 hard cooked eggs, chopped	basil
1½ tablespoons cognac	ginger
1½ tablespoons Madeira wine	cinnamon
	Bay leaf

Over low heat, melt 8 tablespoons (¼ pound) of butter and sauté the chicken livers, chopped shallots, and garlic very gently, being careful not to brown. Remove from the heat and set aside. Now cream another 8 tablespoons of butter in a bowl and add in the livers and shallots and the butter they were cooked in. Mix in the chopped eggs, cognac, Madeira, the spices, and the seasonings and blend well in an electric blender, using the purée setting.

This should make about 1 pint. Spoon the paté into an earthenware terrine or crock and place a bay leaf on top. Cover the dish tightly and place in the refrigerator to chill. It is best if you let it sit for several days (up to a week) to mellow.

Note: There is a second method of preparing paté, which is just as good and just as popular—*paté maison*. A much larger paté, it is cooked in a loaf and served in slices as an hors d'oeuvre.

1 pound chicken livers	1½ tablespoons Madeira
1 pound fresh pork, no fat	⅛ tablespoon each of:
1 shallot, chopped	ginger
1 tablespoon fresh parsley, chopped finely	cinnamon
	clove
2 teaspoons freshly ground pepper	basil
	marjoram
2 teaspoons salt	thyme
1½ tablespoons brandy	Bacon strips

Preheat the oven to 350° F. Clean all the fat, veins, and gristle from the chicken livers, and all the fat from the pork. Put both through the finest blade of a meat grinder three or four times. Now put the ground meat in a bowl and add the remaining ingredients except the bacon. Mix very thoroughly, then line a loaf dish or pan with the bacon and spoon in the mixture, packing it down firmly as you go. Cook in the oven for 1½ hours, then remove to cool. The paté should be allowed to cool under pressure for an hour or more to pack the meat down firmly. Use a dish or other object about the size of the paté and put a heavy weight on it, then place in the refrigerator to chill.

Before serving, turn the paté out onto a plate and cut into ¼-inch slices. Serve with French bread and butter.

FRANCE

POULET EN COCOTTE—Chicken in Casserole

1 3-pound chicken, cut up
Salt and freshly ground pepper
½ tablespoon paprika
4 tablespoons olive oil
2 tablespoons butter
2 carrots, peeled and sliced
4 small onions, quartered

1 clove garlic, minced
½ cup ham, finely shredded
1 bouquet garni (page 257)
1 cup dry white wine
2 tablespoons cognac (optional)
1 pound potatoes, peeled and
   diced
Parsley flakes for garnish

Rub the chicken pieces with salt and freshly ground pepper and sprinkle each with a little paprika.

Brown the chicken pieces in a casserole in hot oil until golden on all sides, about 10 minutes. Remove the chicken pieces and set aside, and discard the oil. In the same pan, melt the butter, keeping the heat low, and sauté the carrots and onions, minced garlic, and shredded ham for about 6 minutes. Now return the chicken pieces to the casserole, add the bouquet garni, and spoon the vegetables and pan liquid over all. Add the wine, cover, and cook for 30 minutes.

While the chicken cooks, melt 3 tablespoons of butter in a skillet and add the diced potatoes. Toss them gently over low heat with a wooden spoon, then cover, and cook for 30 minutes. Stir gently every 5 minutes or so or they'll burn. Remove to a serving dish and sprinkle with parsley. When the chicken is done, place the pot on the table and, if you wish, spoon 2 tablespoons warm cognac over the meat and light it. Serve when the flame dies, with the potatoes. Serves 4.

FRANCE

POULET SAUTE A LA PAYSANNE PROVENÇALE—
Sautéed Chicken from Provence, Peasant Style

4 tablespoons olive oil	½ cup dry white wine
1 3-pound chicken, cut up	4 medium tomatoes, peeled,
Salt and freshly ground pepper	seeded, and chopped
Flour	1 clove garlic, sliced
1 small onion, chopped finely	4 sprigs parsley, chopped
	12 pitted, halved black olives

Heat the oil in a large skillet. Sprinkle the chicken pieces with salt and pepper, then coat lightly with flour and brown on all sides. Remove and keep warm. Now add the chopped onions to the skillet and cook gently for 5 minutes, then add the wine and cook for 5 more minutes to reduce the liquid somewhat.

Return the chicken to the pan and add the tomatoes, garlic, and chopped parsley. Cover and cook for 30 minutes over low heat. Add the pitted, halved black olives about 5 minutes before the chicken is to be served. Serves 4.

FRANCE

POULET SAUTE BOURGUIGNONNE—
Chicken in Burgundy Wine Sauce

4 tablespoons butter	15-18 small mushrooms, washed
1 3-pound chicken, cut up	and patted dry
Salt and pepper	2 medium onions, chopped finely

Sauce Bourguignonne

1 bouquet garni (page 257)	½ cup fresh chicken stock
1 clove garlic, minced	1 cup dry red burgundy

Heat the butter in a large skillet or Dutch oven. Season the chicken lightly with salt and pepper, then brown the pieces on both sides a few at a time for about 10 minutes. When done remove chicken and set aside.

Add the mushrooms to the pan and cook over moderate heat for 5 minutes, then add the onions and cook for 3 minutes, stirring all the while. Remove the pan from the fire.

Add in the bouquet garni, garlic, stock, and wine. Stir the pot a few times to blend, and then return the chicken. Spoon the liquid over each piece, then return the pan to the fire. Bring the liquid to the boil, then reduce to low, cover, and simmer the chicken for 30 minutes.

When the chicken is done, remove the pieces to a platter. Discard the bouquet garni and pour the sauce over the chicken. Garnish the platter with parsley sprigs and serve. Serves 4.

France

POULE AU RIZ PROVENÇALE—
Chicken with Saffron Rice

Poule au riz is a favorite throughout France, but in Provence they add saffron to the rice and more vegetables to the pot. Saffron was introduced to Spain and southern France almost a thousand years ago by the Arabs.

2 3-pound chickens, trussed	1 large clove garlic
6 tablespoons butter	1 cup white wine
4 onions (2 stuck with 2 cloves each)	2 cups water
	2 cups chicken stock
1 carrot, sliced crosswise	Salt and pepper
1 stalk celery, sliced crosswise	1 cup white rice
Bouquet garni (page 257)	½ teaspoon saffron
	Parsley sprigs for garnish

In a large kettle or Dutch oven (large enough to hold 2 chickens), melt 5 tablespoons butter and brown both chickens over moderate heat on all sides, then remove and set aside. Chop one onion and brown it in the pan, then return the chickens. Add the carrot, celery, 2 onions stuck with cloves, bouquet garni, garlic, wine, water, and chicken stock. Sprinkle with salt and pepper and then bring the pot to the boil. Reduce the heat to low, cover, and cook for 1 hour.

When the birds are done, remove them from the pot and keep warm. Strain the pot liquid and set aside.

In a skillet, melt 1 tablespoon of butter. Mince an onion and sauté slowly for 3-4 minutes, until golden, then add 1 cup white rice. Stir with a wooden spoon until all the rice kernels are coated, then add 1 cup of the strained cooking liquid and ½ teaspoon saffron. Cover and cook over low heat for 20 minutes. Check the pot after 5 or 6 minutes and, if the liquid is absorbed, add 1 cup of the reserved pot liquid. Re-cover and continue cooking. Check the pot again in 10 minutes and add more (½ cup or less) of the liquid if the rice is too dry.

To serve, mound the rice in the center of a platter. Carve the chicken and arrange the pieces around the rice. Drizzle any remaining pot liquid over the meat, then garnish with parsley and serve. Serves 6-8.

FRANCE

POULET MARENGO—Chicken Marengo

Legend has it that Napoleon came in from the field one night after defeating Austria at the battle of Marengo, in the Piedmont region of Italy, and found virtually nothing to eat. His chef scavenged the neighborhood and came up with a chicken, a tomato or two, some onions, and a few crayfish. He prepared this improbable combination with faint heart, but received great commendation from the Emperor.

2 3-pound chickens, cut up
4-6 tablespoons butter
2 medium onions, chopped
   coarsely
1 cup chicken stock
1 cup dry white wine
4 large tomatoes, peeled, seeded,
   and chopped

3 cloves garlic, sliced
1 teaspoon thyme
1 bay leaf
Salt and freshly ground pepper
15-18 crayfish, 1-inch cubes of
   lobster, or medium-size shrimp
12-16 medium-size mushrooms,
   sliced
Parsley sprigs for garnish

Brown the chicken pieces in butter gently on all sides for about 15 minutes, then remove and set aside. Pour off all but 2 tablespoons of oil and, in the same pan, sauté the onions until golden, then add in the chicken pieces, stock, wine, tomatoes, garlic, and seasonings. Bring quickly to the boil, then reduce the heat to low, cover, and simmer slowly for 40 minutes. If the shellfish have not been cooked, add them to the chicken pot about 7 or 8 minutes before the bird is done. If they are cooked, add them to the finished sauce for a minute or so to heat just before serving.

When the meat is done, remove and keep warm, then cook the sliced mushrooms in the pan juices for 15 minutes over low heat. Arrange the chicken and shellfish on a warm platter, pour over the pan sauce and mushrooms, and garnish with parsley sprigs. Serve at once. Serves 8.

FRANCE

FOIES DE VOLAILLES—
Chicken Livers with Cognac and Sherry

¼ pound bacon slices	1½ tablespoons flour
2 tablespoons butter	½ teaspoon thyme
1 cup finely diced leek	½ teaspoon marjoram
1 pound chicken livers	¼ teaspoon summer savory
2 tablespoons warm cognac	1 cup chicken stock
¼ pound mushrooms, sliced	Salt and freshly ground pepper
	⅓ cup dry sherry

Fry the bacon in a skillet until crisp, then remove to drain.

Discard the bacon fat and melt the butter in the skillet, then sauté the leek until tender but not browned. Add the livers and brown them quickly on all sides. Add the cognac and ignite and when the flame dies down, add the mushrooms and cook for 3 minutes. Sprinkle with flour and cook for 1 minute, while stirring.

Add the thyme, marjoram, savory, and stock and bring to the boil, stirring. Reduce the heat to low and simmer for 3 minutes, or until the livers are cooked but still pink in the middle. Season with salt and pepper and stir in the sherry.

Serve the livers on a bed of rice or chopped vermicelli. Crumble the reserved bacon over the top. Serves 4.

FRANCE

FRICASSEE DE POULET—Chicken Fricassee

The word *fricassee* comes from the French word *fricasser,* which means to fry or stew a meat and serve it in a sauce of its own making. Whether it's French or Italian (or both) in origin is hard to tell, but it really doesn't matter as both countries have made this dish into one of their classics.

1 3-pound chicken, cut up	Salt
1½ quarts water	10 mushrooms, sliced
1 carrot, sliced	⅓ cup flour
1 stalk celery, sliced	Freshly ground pepper
1 onion, sliced	3 cups reserved chicken stock
1 bay leaf	½ cup light cream
12 peppercorns	¼ cup dry white wine
	Chopped parsley

Place the chicken pieces in a Dutch oven and cover with water. Bring to the boil and cook for 10 minutes, skimming scum off as it rises. Now reduce the heat to low, add the carrot, celery, onion, bay leaf, 1 teaspoon of salt, and the peppercorns. Replace the cover and simmer for 1 hour. When done remove the chicken to a plate to cool. Strain the stock, reserving 3 cups for the sauce (save the remaining stock for another recipe). Sauté the sliced mushrooms in 1 table-spoon of butter over low heat for 5 minutes.

When the chicken has cooled, remove the skin and bones and discard. Cut the meat into bite-sized chunks and put aside.

Make the sauce by melting the butter in a saucepan. Remove the pan from the heat and add flour, salt, and a few grindings of fresh pepper and stir until you have a smooth paste. Now gradually stir in the chicken stock and the cream. Bring the sauce to the boil, then reduce the heat to low, stirring all the while. Add the wine and continue stirring over low heat.

When the sauce is thoroughly blended (about 2 minutes), add the chicken chunks and sautéed mushrooms, cover, and simmer for 10 minutes. Serve over rice or thin spaghetti garnished with chopped parsley. Serves 4.

Note: In Rome and northern Italy, the popular fricassee includes 4 or 5 peeled and seeded tomatoes with a cup of dry red wine instead of white.

FRANCE

POULET AU CELERIS—Chicken with Celery

One of the interesting aspects of cuisine régionale is the way the French will cook a duck or chicken with a single vegetable—*Poulet Sauté à la Vichy* (carrots), . . . *aux Fonds d'Artichauts* (artichokes), . . . *au Navets* (turnips)—among others. One of the most delightful is this one, cooked with celery. Though it's not well known in America, it has a most unique taste and a light, fresh, almost outdoors quality.

1 large bunch celery	1 3-pound chicken, trussed for
Salt and pepper	roasting
4 tablespoons butter	1 onion, chopped

Sauce Soubise

4 tablespoons butter	½ cup cream
1 tablespoon flour	2 onions, quartered
Salt and pepper	Water

Preheat the oven to 350° F. Separate the celery stalks, and cut away the leaves. Blanch in slowly boiling salted water for 10 minutes, then drain and set aside. Melt the butter in a Dutch oven or casserole and brown the chicken for 4-5 minutes on each side, then remove from the pot and sauté the onions for 5 minutes, until golden.

Return the chicken to the pot and sprinkle with salt and pepper. Place the celery pieces over and around the chicken, then cover the pot and roast in the oven for 1 hour.

Thirty minutes before the bird is done, make the sauce: Boil the quartered onions in a saucepan of water for 10 minutes. While the onions cook, melt the butter over low heat and add the flour, stirring until it just begins to turn brown. Remove the pan from the fire and add the cream a little at a time, stirring all the while until a smooth sauce is formed.

When the onions are soft, drain and purée them in a blender or chop them very fine. Add to the cream sauce, with a little salt and pepper to taste. You may adjust the consistency of the sauce by cooking a little longer over low heat.

The chicken may be carved at the table or cut into serving pieces beforehand. Either way, serve the chicken on a warm platter surrounded by the celery, with a little of the sauce spooned over and the rest passed in a sauceboat. Boiled new potatoes go well with this dish. Serves 4.

FRANCE

POULET GRILLE, SAUCE DIABLE—
Grilled Deviled Chicken

This is a grilled chicken served in a hot and slightly tart sauce. Another version uses a hot mustard, the best type of which is produced around Dijon, France. The seasoned chicken is coated on both sides with the mustard, then covered with breadcrumbs and broiled. In this country it has been popularized as chicken Dijon.

1 3-pound chicken, quartered	Butter
Salt and pepper	Parsley sprigs for garnish

Sauce Diable

¼ cup dry white wine	1 tablespoon butter
¼ cup wine vinegar	1 tablespoon flour
1 tablespoon chopped shallots	¾ cup stock
(white part only)	Dash red pepper

First make the sauce: Combine the wine, vinegar, and chopped shallot in a saucepan and cook over moderate heat for 10 minutes or so until the liquid reduces to about ¼ of its original volume.

Melt 1 tablespoon of butter in a skillet and stir in the flour. Cook over low heat for 2-3 minutes, but don't let the flour burn. Remove from the fire. Combine the wine and vinegar mixture with the stock and then stir into the skillet. When well blended, bring to the boil, stirring constantly, then reduce the heat to low and simmer for 5 minutes. Before serving, sprinkle with just a little red pepper and stir the pot once or twice.

Arrange the chicken pieces on a broiler pan and lightly salt and pepper each piece. Brush some of the sauce on the chicken and place a dot of butter on each piece. Grill the chicken for 10 minutes on a side.

To serve, arrange the chicken on a warm platter and spoon a little sauce over each piece. Garnish the meat with parsley sprigs and pass the sauce in a sauceboat. Serves 4.

FRANCE

POULET A L'ESTRAGON—Chicken Tarragon

This dish can be either boiled in water or stock, whole or disjointed, braised in stock and wine, or marinated in wine and tarragon and sautéed. In all cases, however, the bird is served with a white sauce mixed with the pan liquid. If possible use fresh tarragon—it does make a difference. Also, use a pan that just fits the chicken; otherwise more stock and water are necessary.

1 3-pound chicken	4 tablespoons butter
2 sprigs fresh tarragon, or 1½ teaspoons dried	2 cups chicken stock ¾ cup dry white wine Parsley sprigs for garnish

Sauce Blanche

2 tablespoons butter	Dash salt
1 tablespoon flour	1 egg yolk, beaten well
1 cup water	1 cup heavy cream
	2 tablespoons lemon juice

Preheat the oven to 325° F. Melt 2 tablespoons butter in a casserole or Dutch oven and place 1 tablespoon butter in the cavity of the chicken along with 1 tablespoon tarragon, then truss or skewer the openings. Now brown the chicken slowly on all sides, about 5 minutes to the side. Add the stock and the wine (it should cover only about half the chicken), cover, and cook in the oven for 1 hour and 15 minutes. Remove the cover during the last 15 minutes.

When the chicken is done, remove the bird and keep warm. Strain the pan liquid into a small saucepan and reserve.

Now make the white sauce: Over low heat melt the butter and stir in the flour, then add the water, a little salt, and the egg yolk. Bring to high heat, stirring constantly with a spoon or whisk. When near the boil, remove the pan from the fire and gradually add in the cream and the lemon juice. Stir until well blended.

When the white sauce has reached the appropriate consistency, add 1 cup of the reserved pan liquid and pour into a sauceboat. Sprinkle the sauce with the remaining tarragon and garnish the chicken with parsley sprigs. Serves 4.

FRANCE

POULET SAUTE AU CITRON—
Sautéed Chicken with Lemon Sauce

1 3-pound chicken, cut up	Salt and freshly ground pepper
	4 tablespoons butter

Sauce Lemon

¼ cup Madeira wine	1 cup heavy cream
¼ cup dry white wine	Peeled lemon slices and parsley
Juice and grated rind of 1 lemon	for garnish

Sprinkle the chicken pieces with salt and pepper, then brown on all sides in butter. Cover the pan tightly, then sauté the chicken over low heat for 30 minutes. When done and tender, remove to a serving platter and keep warm.

Deglaze the pan with Madeira and white wine over moderately high heat. Stirring continuously, add the juice and grated rind of the lemon and season with a little salt and pepper. Now lower the heat and slowly stir the cream in a little at a time. Return the chicken pieces to the pan, coating them on all sides with the sauce, then cover and simmer for 5 minutes.

To serve, arrange the chicken pieces on a warm platter and spoon over the sauce. Garnish the meat with lemon slices and parsley sprigs. Serves 4.

FRANCE

OMELETTE AUX FOIES DE VOLAILLES—
Chicken Liver Omelet

Brown Sauce

1 tablespoon butter	¾ cup chicken stock
1 tablespoon flour	Salt and pepper
1 small carrot, chopped finely	2 tablespoons butter
½ small onion, chopped finely	¼ pound chicken livers, veined
Small pinch thyme	and chopped finely
½ cup dry white wine	½ cup chicken stock
¼ bay leaf	4 eggs
½ tablespoon tomato paste	2 tablespoons light cream

Start the brown sauce first: Melt the butter in a small saucepan or skillet and stir in the flour. When the flour just starts to turn color, add the carrot, onion, thyme, wine, and bay leaf. Cook over low heat for 5 minutes, then add the tomato paste, stock, and a little salt and pepper. Cover tightly and simmer for 20 minutes.

While the sauce cooks, sauté the chicken livers in butter over moderate heat for about 5 minutes, until they have lost their pink color and are browned evenly. Now add the chicken stock and let the chicken livers cook for several minutes over low heat. Remove and keep warm.

Combine the eggs, cream, and a little salt and pepper and beat until thoroughly mixed. Melt the butter in a skillet over low heat, and stir in the egg mixture with a fork until it begins to thicken. Let the omelet cook for a minute or so without stirring. When ready to fold, spoon the chicken liver mixture into the center and spread evenly. Fold the omelet over the mixture and cook for just a few moments.

Serve either whole with the brown sauce spooned over or in individual portions with the sauce served on the side. Serves 2.

FRANCE

SUPRÊMES DE VOLAILLES—Breasts of Chicken

Suprêmes are chicken breasts that have been split and skinned and boned. The large and small fillets of each half breast are separated and then placed between layers of waxed paper and gently pounded flat with a mallet or other blunt instrument. After seasoning with a little salt and pepper, they are ready for cooking either as is (*côtelettes*) or stuffed (*farcis*).

The two fillets from each half breast should be ample for one person, so adjust the recipe according to the number of people you intend to serve.

Suprêmes de Volailles, Sauce Suprême

2-3 whole chicken breasts, split, skinned, boned, and flattened	4 tablespoons butter
	3 tablespoons chicken stock
Salt and black pepper	Parsley sprigs for garnish

Sauce Suprême

2 tablespoons butter	Pinch nutmeg (optional)
2 tablespoons flour	Pinch salt

2 cups clear chicken stock
½ bay leaf (optional)
Pinch thyme (optional)

Pinch white pepper
2-3 tablespoons heavy cream
2 egg yolks

Season the suprêmes lightly with salt and pepper. Melt the butter in a skillet over low fire and put in the suprêmes. Turn them to coat with the butter, add the stock, then cover the pan and poach the chicken very gently for 10 or 12 minutes, turning once. When done remove to a warm serving dish, garnish with parsley, and keep warm.

Now make the sauce: Stir the flour into 2 tablespoons of butter in the skillet, keeping the heat low. Add the stock and stir until smooth, then add the bay leaf, thyme, nutmeg, and salt and pepper. Stir well to blend, then cover and cook for 30 minutes.

Beat the cream and yolks together and add slowly to the pan, stirring constantly. Do not allow to boil. Cook for 3 minutes to thicken slightly, then remove from the heat. Pour the sauce over the suprêmes and serve at once. Serves 4-6.

Suprêmes de Volailles aux Champignons (with Mushrooms)

The suprêmes are cooked and the sauce is prepared as above. While the suprêmes are poaching, simmer 8-12 large mushroom caps in ½ cup of chicken stock with 2 tablespoons lemon juice for 5 minutes. Drain and set aside.

When the sauce is finished, place 2 mushroom caps on each suprême and spoon the sauce over all. Serve at once. Serves 4-6.

Suprêmes de Volailles, Sauce Chasseur (Hunter Style)

Season the suprêmes and cook as above.

Sauce Chasseur

3 tablespoons butter
½ pound mushrooms, chopped
　finely
1 tablespoon shallots, chopped
　finely

2 tablespoons brandy
½ cup white wine
¼ cup tomato paste
1 cup chicken stock
1 teaspoon minced parsley

Melt the butter in a skillet and sauté the mushrooms slowly for about 5 minutes, then add the shallots, brandy, and wine. Continue cooking until the liquid reduces by half, then turn up the heat to high and add the tomato paste, stock, and minced parsley. Cook for 2 minutes, stirring constantly, then remove from the fire. Spoon some of the sauce over the suprêmes and pass the rest in a sauceboat.

Suprêmes de Volailles, Sauce Madère (Madeira Sauce)
Season the suprêmes and cook as above.

Sauce Madère
¼ cup Madeira wine

1 cup stock
3 tablespoons butter

Deglaze the pan with 2 tablespoons of Madeira wine, scraping the sides and bottom of the pan to dislodge all the particles that remain from cooking the chicken. Add the stock and bring the pan to the boil, then stir in the butter a little at a time. Reduce the heat to low and add the remaining Madeira wine. Stir for 2 minutes, then strain the juices and pass in a sauceboat.

Suprêmes de Volailles Farcis, Duxelles (Mushroom Stuffing)
In French, *champignons* are mushrooms, but when they are ground or chopped finely, they become *duxelles* and are frequently used as a stuffing (*farcis*). This technique, or something like it, was likely the forerunner of the great Chicken Kiev of Russia, which was brought there by the French during Catherine's reign.

1 small onion, minced
4 tablespoons butter
¼ pound fresh mushrooms, minced
Salt and freshly ground pepper
¼ cup heavy cream

2 tablespoons flour
Large pinch each of thyme and sage
1 tablespoon smoked ham or bacon, minced
¼ cup Madeira wine
Lemon slices for garnish

Sauté the onions in 2 tablespoons of butter until golden. Add 2 tablespoons of butter and cook the mushrooms until they have lost all color. Add a little salt and pepper, then add the cream, flour, thyme, and sage and stir over low heat for 2 minutes longer. Now add the ham and wine and cook an additional 2 minutes. When done, remove from the heat and set aside.

Prepare the suprêmes as in the above. Spread the meat out and fill with the mushroom stuffing, then roll them up and skewer them securely. Melt 3 or 4 tablespoons of butter in a large skillet and cook the suprêmes for a few minutes on a side, turning frequently to avoid burning. Garnish with lemon slices and serve. Any of the above sauces will be excellent with this dish.

Note: The suprêmes may also be breaded in eggs and breadcrumbs after they have been stuffed, and then deep-fried in hot oil for 5 or 6 minutes.

FRANCE

CHARTREUSE DE PERDRIX—
Baked Partirdge (or Cornish game hen) with Vegetables

3 strips lean bacon
1 large green cabbage, cored and shredded
2 cups beef stock
6 tablespoons butter
1 large onion, chopped finely

8 large carrots, sliced thinly crosswise
8 white turnips, peeled and sliced thinly crosswise
1 cup peas
4 roasted partridge or Cornish game hens
Salt and freshly ground pepper

First cook the bacon partially in a skillet for about 30 seconds on a side. Do not brown. Now cut up the bacon in fine dice and set aside. Discard the fat.

Simmer the cabbage in the beef stock for 20 minutes, then drain and set aside. Reserve the broth. Sauté the chopped onion in 1 tablespoon of butter until golden, then add it and the diced bacon to the cabbage and mix well.

Preheat the oven to 350° F. Melt 3 tablespoons of butter in a large casserole or Dutch oven and remove from the fire. Arrange ½ the cabbage-bacon-onion mixture in the bottom of the pan and cover with half of the carrots, turnips, and peas. Now place the partridges or game hens on top of the vegetables, season with a little salt and pepper then spread over the remaining carrots, turnips, and peas. Cover all with the remaining cabbage mixture. Melt the remaining 2 tablespoons of butter and drizzle over the cabbage, then pour in 1 cup of the reserved broth.

Cover the pot and bake in the oven for 1 hour, then remove and serve directly from the pot. Serves 4.

FRANCE

POULE AU VINAIGRE—Chicken in Vinegar Sauce

2 3-pound chickens, cut up
Salt and freshly ground pepper
6 tablespoons butter

1 tablespoon dried tarragon (or 3 tablespoons of fresh)
½ cup tarragon wine vinegar
½ cup chicken stock

Sauce Vinaigre

2 cloves garlic, minced
2 tablespoons tomato sauce

¼ cup dry white wine
Parsley sprigs for garnish

Preheat the oven to 350° F. Sprinkle the chicken pieces with salt and pepper, then brown them in 2 large skillets in the butter for about 8 minutes on each side. When done remove the pieces to a large Dutch oven, sprinkling each with a little tarragon as you put them in. Combine ¼ cup of tarragon vinegar with ¼ cup of stock and pour over the chicken. Cover and bake in the oven for 30 minutes.

Pour the fat from 1 skillet into the second and sauté the garlic gently for 1 minute. Increase the heat and pour in the remaining vinegar, scraping the bottom and sides of the pan to loosen all the particles that remain from the chicken. Cook the vinegar down to half, then add the tomato sauce, the remaining stock, and the wine. Stir well, reduce the heat, and simmer for 15 minutes. The liquid should reduce somewhat.

When the chicken is done, remove from the oven and pour the sauce in, making sure to coat each piece. Garnish the meat with parsley sprigs and serve right from the pot. Serves 6-8.

PART III:

The Benelux Nations

One must put the cooking of France at one end of the world's gastronomic spectrum and that of the Netherlands near the other. This is not to demean the cuisine that the Dutch have developed, for the food is wholesome, solid, and rather basic—a direct reflection of the national character and priorities of the nation.

Home cooking in the Netherlands features fish (mostly herring), potatoes, *genever* (gin), beer, and plenty of bread and butter. When the Dutchman goes out to eat, however, it's just as likely he'll visit an Indonesian-style restaurant as one that specializes in Dutch food, for the Dutch acquired an irresistible passion for the *Nasi Gorengs* and *Rijsttafels* of their former Indonesian colonies and made them an integral part of their own cuisine. Chicken is very popular in the Netherlands, but as part of an industry, not the cuisine.

Chicken, eggs, and dairy products in general constitute a major Dutch export, and a roast chicken, *Gebraden Kip,* or turkey is frequently reserved for holidays and other special occasions. Goose is the traditional meal at Christmas.

Situated directly between France and the Netherlands, the Belgians have blended the two cultures into a unique combination. If one were to draw a line across Belgium through Brussels, it would roughly separate the Flemish north of the country from the Walloon south. The Flemings' dialect, clothes, and architecture show a strong Dutch influence, and so does their cuisine, although it is much more venturesome. Flemish cooking (*à la Flamande*) is well seasoned with chervil, shallots, and nutmeg and richly sauced with eggs and cream. The Walloons, on the other hand, speak a dialect very similar to French,

275

and their life style and cuisine are also very much in the tradition of neighboring French provinces.

The scope and character of the Belgian cuisine could not be better characterized than by these two international classics:

Waterzooi, a Flemish dish, originated as a fish stew, but is now more popular made with chicken. It may also be one of the most elaborate Flemish dishes there is, for it is rich with heavy cream, eggs, and fresh lemon juice.

Equally delicious, from the Walloon kitchen, is *Poulet à la Wallone.* It is chicken and sweetbreads cooked in a veal stock and served with a rich egg, cream, and wine sauce.

BELGIUM

POULET A LA WALLONE—Chicken in the Walloon Style

1-pound knuckle of veal	Bouquet garni (page 257)
Cold water	1 calf's sweetbreads
4 small carrots, chopped coarsely	1 3-pound chicken
4 stalks of celery, cut into 1-inch pieces	4 tablespoons butter
	4 tablespoons flour
Salt and pepper	4 egg yolks
1 onion	4 tablespoons heavy cream
	¼ cup dry white wine

Make a veal stock by covering the veal knuckle with cold water in a kettle. Bring the water to the boil and skim the scum as it rises. Now add the chopped carrots and celery, and the salt and pepper and the onion and bouquet garni. Cover and cook over low heat for 1 hour. Remove the knuckle and strain the stock.

Bring water to the boil in a separate kettle and cook the sweetbreads for 5 minutes. Now add the sweetbreads and the chicken to the veal stock and cook covered for 45 minutes, or until the chicken is tender. When done, remove the chicken and sweetbreads and keep warm. Retain the stock.

Melt the butter in a small skillet and add the flour, stirring constantly, for 2-3 minutes. Slowly stir in 2 cups of the retained stock. Remove from the fire. Mix together the egg yolks, heavy cream, and wine in a bowl, then add 2-3 tablespoons of sauce and stir well. Now add this to the sauce and beat well. Return the sauce to the fire and bring to the boil, then remove and set aside.

Cut the sweetbreads into cubes and the chicken into quarters, placing both in a deep serving dish. Pour over the sauce and serve at once. Serves 4.

BELGIUM

WATERZOOI A LA GANTOISE—
Chicken Soup/Stew From Ghent

This Flemish dish (from Ghent) is one of the most famous in Belgian cookery. *Waterzooi* means "boiling water" and is neither a soup or a stew, but falls somewhere in between. Originally a coastal dish, it was made just with fish, though inland the chicken version has become the classic.

1 4-5-pound chicken, cut up
Heart, gizzard, and liver of the
   bird
2 quarts water
2 large leeks, washed, green parts
   cut off, and chopped
2 carrots, scraped and chopped

2 celery stalks, chopped
2 large onions, chopped
Salt and pepper
Bouquet garni (page 257)
3 egg yolks
½ cup heavy cream
Juice of 1 lemon

Place the chicken pieces and giblets in a large Dutch oven or kettle and pour in the water. Bring to the boil over high heat and skim off the scum as it rises. After 10-15 minutes, reduce the heat to low. Add the chopped leeks, carrots, celery, onions, salt and pepper, and the bouquet garni, then cover and simmer for 1 hour.

When done, skin and bone the chicken pieces, keeping the meat in as large pieces as possible. Remove the bouquet garni and the giblets and discard. Now strain the stock into a bowl. Let the stock sit for 5 minutes, then skim and blot off as much fat as possible.

Return the stock to high heat and cook down to about 10 cups. Beat together the egg yolks, the cream, and a little of the lemon juice, and pour into a soup tureen. Slowly add the stock, stirring constantly, then add the chicken pieces. Taste for seasoning and tartness, adding more of the lemon juice if desired. Serves 6-8.

Note: Although the original recipe does not call for it, adding back the vegetables to the soup makes it a more interesting "stew." Also, some versions call for thickening the soup with a small amount of breadcrumbs (2 tablespoons or so).

BELGIUM

CREME DE VOLAILLE—Cream of Chicken Soup

2 quarts fresh chicken stock,
   skimmed and blotted of all
   grease
1 pint of milk
1 cup flour

Salt and pepper
2 egg yolks
½ cup heavy cream
Pinch nutmeg
1 cup diced cooked white meat of
   chicken

Bring the chicken stock to the boil, then reduce the heat to low. Mix the milk and flour together thoroughly, then gradually add it to the stock. Simmer for 1 hour, covered. Season to taste with salt and pepper.

Mix together the cream, egg yolks, and nutmeg. Pour this mixture into a tureen, add the diced chicken, and then pour the broth in very slowly, stirring constantly. Serve immediately. Serves 4-6.

THE NETHERLANDS

GEBRADEN KIP—Roast Chicken

Because many lack ovens in Holland, chicken is often "roasted" on top of the stove, which is similar to the braising method used in France. This may be the simplest recipe in the book, and there's nothing classic about it, but it is the perfect example of the uncomplicated style of the Dutch. It is also a favorite with the Flemish in Belgium.

1 3-pound chicken	⅛ teaspoon mace
Boiling water	¼ cup chicken stock
Salt and pepper	1 tablespoon cornstarch
4 tablespoons butter	2 tablespoons water
Heart, liver, and gizzard of the bird, chopped	Parsley sprigs for garnish

Pour boiling water over and inside the bird and pat dry. Sprinkle salt and pepper inside and out and rub in thoroughly.

In a large Dutch oven, melt the butter and brown the chicken all over gently (about 5 minutes on a side). Now add the chopped giblets, the mace, and ¼ cup of stock and cook, covered, over low heat for 1½ hours. Baste every 10 minutes or so. When the bird is done, carve and place the pieces on a warm platter and set aside.

Mix the cornstarch and water and stir into the liquid in the roasting pan. Dissolve all the particles and continue stirring over moderate heat until the sauce reaches the desired consistency. Spoon some of the sauce over the chicken pieces and serve the rest in a sauceboat. Garnish with parsley sprigs. Serves 4-6.

The Netherlands

NASI GORENG—Indonesian Fried Rice

The Dutch were involved in Indonesia for years, and during that period a great many Dutchmen served with the army or the government in one military or administrative capacity or another in the Islands. Still others were occupied with the enormously lucrative spice, rubber, and mineral trade that Indonesia had to offer. This meant that over the years a great many Dutch were exposed to Indonesian living for long periods of time and naturally acquired a taste for the food of the country. Today, the Indonesian restaurants in Holland are as popular as the Dutch. Here's a Europeanized version of one of the world's great rice dishes, *Nasi Goreng,* which features chicken, although chopped pork, shrimp, and ham are just as popular.

In Indonesia, leftover rice was used to make *Nasi Goreng.* In Holland they have adopted the custom of making the rice the day before, and serving it cold. The Dutch version of this dish adds several vegetables, whereas the Indonesian recipe calls for more spices and garnishes. Both, however, call for the omelet.

1 pound white rice	½ cup cooked peas
2 cups water	½ cup cooked, chopped carrots
4 tablespoons butter	Salt and pepper
2 medium onions, chopped finely	4 eggs
1 clove garlic, minced	3 tablespoons milk
1 cup cooked, diced white meat of chicken	Crushed peanuts
	Sliced cucumbers
	Chopped pickles
	Sliced bananas

Cook the rice in 2 cups of water the day before and drain well.

Heat 2 tablespoons of butter in a large skillet and sauté the onions and garlic gently. Now add the rice and cook slowly until golden, stirring frequently. Add the chicken and a little salt and pepper and continue cooking for 5 more minutes. Now add the peas and carrots and cook 5 minutes more.

Make an omelet by beating together 4 eggs with 3 tablespoons of milk and cooking gently in the remaining butter. Cut the omelet into strips and serve on top of the *Nasi Goreng.* Serve the remaining garnishes in side dishes. Serves 4-6.

PART IV:

Spain and Portugal

Considering that the Arabs occupied the Iberian Peninsula for seven hundred years, the roles Spain and Portugal played in opening the spice trade, and the vast array of new foods they brought back from the New World, one would expect the cuisines of these countries to be among the most innovative and wide-ranging in Europe. But they aren't; in fact the cooking of neither country, by European standards, is particularly distinguished.

The Arabs controlled most of Spain and Portugal from the eighth to the fourteenth century, but there is little in their cuisines to remind one of the Arab presence beyond rice, olive and citrus trees, and a few spices. The Moors brought the tart Seville orange to Spain, but it was the French who used it to create a masterpiece, *Caneton à l'Orange.*

Portugal discovered the sea route to India and for a while dominated the spice trade, yet saffron, pepper, cumin, and coriander are the only spices that are found in her cuisine with any regularity. Spain and Portugal introduced Europe to an incredible bounty of foods from Central and South America, but few found the favor at home that they did in other countries. Italy and Romania replaced wheat with corn in their national dishes, *Polenta* and *Mamaliga*; the Turks and British welcomed the turkey with open arms; the white *haricot* bean became the staple for *Cassoulet* in France. The Portuguese brought the capsicum pepper to an indifferent Europe, but when they further transported it to Southeast Asia, the chili became an ingredient in virtually every dish.

Spain has given international cookery two outstanding classics, and both include chicken. One is *Arroz con Pollo,* which is one of the

281

best-known chicken and rice casseroles in the world. The rice has a yellow color due to the addition of saffron, which makes it an extremely attractive dish as well as delicious.

The other is *Paella Valenciana,* which is a chicken, rice, sausage, and shellfish combination. The original paella was created on the banks of the rivers near Valencia, and included olive oil, rice, beans, and whatever fish the river yielded that day. It was the daily meal of the Valencians, but over time its fame spread to other Spanish cities and to Portugal and now there are any number of different versions.

Paella traveled with the Spanish explorers to Latin America and the Philippines and even found its way to early America. In the Spanish-speaking countries, it retained its original name—*paella*— but in Louisiana, the Creoles added chili peppers and called it *jambalaya.*

SPAIN

POLLO EN SALSA DE VINO—Chicken in Wine Sauce

1 3-pound chicken, quartered
Flour
3 tablespoons olive oil
1 clove garlic, minced
1 medium onion, chopped
  coarsely

Salt and pepper
⅔ cup dry white wine
Bouquet garni (page 257)
⅛ teaspoon ground saffron
⅛ teaspoon ground nutmeg

Dredge the chicken pieces in flour. Bring the oil to moderate heat in a skillet and sauté the garlic and onion until golden, then add the chicken pieces and brown all over.

Season the chicken with salt and pepper, then pour in the wine, add the bouquet garni, and dust the pieces with saffron. Cover, reduce the heat to low, and cook for 45 minutes.

When done, place the chicken on a warm platter and pour over any remaining pan liquid. Sprinkle the chicken lightly with nutmeg and serve. Serves 4.

SPAIN

POLLO VASCONGADO—Basque Chicken

1 3-pound chicken, cut up
Salt and pepper
Flour
2-3 tablespoons olive oil
1 green pepper, seeded and
  chopped coarsely
1 medium onion, chopped
  coarsely

2 cloves garlic, minced
1 cup serrano or presunto ham
2 tablespoons fresh parsley,
  chopped
1 cup dry white wine
¼ teaspoon paprika
½ pound shrimp, shelled and
  deveined
Parsley sprigs for garnish

Rub the chicken with salt and pepper, then dredge lightly in flour. Bring 2 tablespoons oil to moderate heat and brown the chicken on all sides for 10-12 minutes, then remove to a plate and set aside.

Add the remaining oil to the skillet and the pepper, onion, garlic, and ham and cook over low heat for about 5 minutes. Now add the parsley, wine, and paprika and cook for another minute, stirring all the while.

Return the chicken pieces to the pan and spoon the mixture over each piece. Now cover and simmer for 30 minutes, then add the shrimp and cook another 10 minutes.

Place the chicken on a warm platter and pour any pan liquid over each piece. Garnish with parsley sprigs and serve with white rice. Serves 4.

SPAIN

POLLO A LA CHILENDRON—
Chicken with Peppers and Tomatoes

Use fresh peppers, red or green, or both at once, as you wish. This dish is a favorite in the northern provinces of Spain.

1 3-pound chicken, cut up	2 large red or green peppers, sliced in rings and seeded
Salt and freshly ground pepper	1/3 cup pimentos, cut into strips
4 tablespoons olive oil	1 cup lean, smoked ham, cut into short strips
2 medium onions, chopped coarsely	3 tomatoes, peeled, seeded, and chopped
2 large cloves garlic, minced	

Rub the chicken pieces generously with salt and fresh pepper. Heat the oil in a large skillet and brown the chicken pieces gently on all sides for about 15 minutes, then remove them to a platter and set aside to keep warm.

Now add the onions, garlic, pimentos, and peppers to the skillet and cook gently for 10-12 minutes. Add the ham strips and chopped tomatoes and cook for another 10 minutes over moderate heat, then return the chicken pieces to the pan and mix thoroughly with the sauce. Cover the skillet and reduce the heat to low and cook for 30 minutes. Serve the chicken on a warm serving platter with the sauce spooned over. Serves 4-6.

SPAIN

POLLO EN PEPITORIA—
Chicken Casserole with Pumpkin Seeds or Nuts
Although originally made with pumpkin seeds, this dish is now quite popular with almonds or pistachios.

1 3-pound chicken, cut up	1 cup dry white wine
Flour	2 cups chicken stock
¼ cup olive oil	¼ cup dried pumpkin seeds, or
2 medium onions, chopped	blanched almonds or pis-
1 clove garlic, sliced	tachios, pulverized
1 tablespoon parsley, chopped	⅛ teaspoon saffron threads,
finely	ground to powder
Pinch thyme	2 raw egg yolks
1 bay leaf	Salt and freshly ground pepper

Dredge the chicken in flour. Heat the oil in a skillet and brown the onion and garlic very gently for 5 minutes or so. Now add the chicken, a few pieces at a time, and brown slowly on all sides for about 15 minutes. As the chicken pieces are done, remove and keep them warm in a large Dutch oven or casserole.

When all the chicken pieces are browned and placed in the Dutch oven, pour the pan drippings, onions, and garlic on top. Add the parsley, thyme, and bay leaf and the wine and stock (the liquid should just cover the chicken, but add more if necessary). Bring to the boil, then reduce the heat to low, cover lightly, and simmer for 20-30 minutes.

Just before serving, mix the pumpkin seeds or crushed nuts, saffron, egg yolks, and salt and pepper together thoroughly. Remove the chicken pieces from the pot to a warm serving platter, then slowly add the egg and seed (nut) mixture to the pan liquid. Stir constantly until thoroughly mixed. Cook the liquid down to the desired consistency (you may have to increase the heat slightly). When done, pour the sauce over the chicken and serve. This goes well with rice. Serves 4.

Spain

EMPANADA GALLEGA—Stuffed Pastries

Empanadas are pies (or *empanadillas*—little pastries) filled with any number of different meats, vegetables, fish, or various combinations. They resemble the Turkish *koftet ferak*, and the smaller empanadillas are very similar to the Greek (Turkish) *meze*, the Middle Eastern hors d'oeuvre. Empanadas come in all sizes and shapes and are popular not only in Spain, but in Spanish-speaking countries around the world.

Pastry Dough

1 cake dry yeast	1 tablespoon salt
Lukewarm water	1 tablespoon olive oil
3 cups flour	1 egg yolk beaten with 1 teaspoon
½ cup milk	water

Break up and dissolve the yeast in a little lukewarm water and let the mixture rest for a few minutes in a warm place. The yeast will begin growing in volume. Sift 2 cups of flour into a bowl and make a well. Warm the milk slightly, then add to the flour. Pour in the yeast mixture, ¼ cup warm water, the oil, and the salt, and stir together well with a wooden spoon. Gradually sift the remaining flour into the bowl and continue mixing it until the ingredients are thoroughly blended.

Now sprinkle some flour on a breadboard or counter top and place the dough ball on it. Knead the dough with the heel of your hand, folding it back into a ball as the dough flattens out. Continue this for 15 or 20 minutes, sprinkling flour on the board and the dough if it begins to stick. When the dough is firm and smooth, but still pliable, return it to the bowl. Cover it with a towel and place the bowl in a warm, draft-free place where it can rise. After the dough has doubled in size—about 1 hour—punch it with your fist, then re-cover and let it rise again another hour. Meanwhile make the filling:

Filling for Empanadas

1 3-pound chicken, cut up	1 red pepper, cleaned, seeded, and
1 bay leaf	diced
Water	½ pound cured ham, chopped
4 tablespoons olive oil	finely
2 medium onions, sliced	Pinch saffron
	Salt and pepper

Place the chicken in a saucepan with the bay leaf and cover with water. Bring to the boil, skim the scum as it rises, then reduce the heat to low and simmer, covered, for 1 hour. Remove the chicken (reserve the stock for another recipe) and let cool a bit, then strip the meat, discarding skin and bones, and cut it into small pieces.

Now heat the oil in a skillet and sauté the onion and red pepper gently for about 10 minutes. Add the ham and continue cooking slowly, stirring all the while, for about 18 minutes. Remove from the heat and mix into a bowl with the chicken pieces, adding a pinch of saffron and a little salt and fresh pepper.

When the dough is ready, divide it in two, place on a lightly floured surface, and roll each half into a circle, as thin as possible. Place one circle across a pie plate and spoon in the filling, spreading it evenly. Spread the second circle over the pie and press down firmly to seal all around the edges. Cut off the excess dough as you would for a pie and crimp the edge with a fork. Set the pie aside to rise for about 15 minutes. While waiting, preheat the oven to 400° F.

Brush the pie with the egg yolk, beaten with a little water, and place it in the oven for 30-40 minutes, or until the top is a rich brown. Serve immediately from the pie plate. Serves 6.

Filling for Empanadillas

6 tablespoons butter
1 medium onion, chopped finely
Meat from the breast, leg, and thigh of a chicken, skinned, boned, and cut into small cubes
1 tomato, peeled, seeded, and chopped finely

6-8 black olives, pitted and sliced
1 tablespoon raisins
1 tablespoon chopped green pepper
1 teaspoon sugar
Salt and freshly ground pepper
Olive oil for frying

Melt the butter in a large skillet and sauté the onions for about 5 minutes over low heat. Add the chicken meat, chopped tomato, sliced olives, raisins, green peppers, and sugar, then sprinkle with salt and several grindings of fresh black pepper. Stir all together until well blended and simmer for 5 minutes, stirring occasionally, to heat through.

Split the dough in half and roll each half out into very thin rectangles. Now cut as many 2-inch by 2-inch squares out of each piece as you can. Put one level teaspoon of filling onto a square, then cover it with another square of dough and press down around the sides to seal. Continue this until all the filling and dough are used up.

You may stop at this point and let the empanadillas cool until you are ready to cook them. They may also be covered and refrigerated for several days.

To cook the empanadillas, pour olive oil into a saucepan or deep-fat fryer to a depth of several inches. Heat the oil until it is hot but not boiling, and drop in several empanadillas at a time with a slotted spoon. They will sink to the bottom for a time but will rise in several minutes. Turn once or twice to assure even browning. Cook for 5 minutes or so, until golden, then drain on a paper towel and place on a serving plate in the oven to keep warm. Serve warm. Makes 12-16.

SPAIN/PORTUGAL

COCIDO MADRILENO—Boiled Meat and Vegetable Soup

Cocido (in Spanish it means "boiled") is a rich soup of mixed vegetables and meats. It can be served as one dish, but usually a little rice is cooked in the broth and served first, with the meat and vegetables following as a second course. The dish is very similar to the French *Pot au Feu* and is probably in some way related.

Beans and some sort of pork are the basis for the dish. A similar dish in Galicia is called *Caldo Gallego* and features white beans. Throughout Spain, however, *Cocido Madrileno* is made with chickpeas.

1 4½-5-pound stewing chicken, cut up	2 onions, quartered
1 cup dried chickpeas	1 bay leaf, crumbled
Water	Salt and freshly ground pepper
½ pound beef brisket	¼ pound chorizo or Italian sausage
¼ pound bacon, unsliced	1 small head white cabbage, cut into eighths and white core removed
½ pound smoked ham	
3 carrots, quartered lengthwise	
3 medium potatoes, peeled and quartered	½ cup white rice
	Parsley sprigs for garnish

A day before you intend to serve the cocido, wash the chickpeas and place in a bowl. Cover with water and soak for 12-24 hours at room temperature.

The next day, drain the soaking water and pour the beans into a large casserole or Dutch oven. Add in the chicken and beef and 3 quarts of water and bring to the boil. Skim off the scum as it forms, then cover and cook over low heat for 1 hour. Now add the bacon and smoked ham and cook an hour longer. Add the carrots, the potatoes, onions, bay leaf, and a little salt and fresh pepper. Cover and cook for another hour.

About 30 minutes before serving, prick the sausage in several places with a knife or fork, place in a saucepan, and cover with water. Bring the pot to the boil, then reduce the heat to low and simmer for 5 minutes. Now transfer the sausage to the Dutch oven and add the cabbage as well. Cover and continue cooking over low heat for 15 minutes.

Strain 6 cups of broth from the Dutch oven and pour it into a small saucepan. Add the rice and cook gently until tender.

Serve the broth and rice in cups first. Then arrange the beans in the center of a platter and place the chicken pieces around it. Slice the meat and intersperse it and the vegetables among the chicken pieces. Garnish with parsley sprigs. Serve the cabbage in a separate bowl with the sausages crumbled over. Serves 6-8.

PORTUGAL

CANJA—Lemon Chicken Soup

This soup is popular in the Alentezan province, and has a flavor reminiscent of the Middle Eastern dishes that combine mint and lemon juice. Canja was transported to Brazil when it was a Portuguese colony, where, entirely different in taste, it's a national dish.

1 3-pound chicken	1 onion, quartered
Heart, liver, and gizzard of the bird, chopped finely	1 carrot, sliced
2 quarts water	½ cup rice, preferably the short grain type
Salt and pepper	¼ cup fresh mint, chopped
	Juice of 1 lemon

Place the chicken and giblets in a large saucepan and cover with water. Bring to the boil, then reduce the heat to low and cook for 10-12 minutes, skimming off the scum as it rises. Now add the salt and pepper, onion, and carrot. Cover and cook slowly for 2 hours, then add the rice and simmer for another 30 minutes.

When the chicken is done, remove it from the pot and strip the meat, discarding the skin and bones. Cut the meat into fairly large serving pieces. Serve by placing one or two pieces of chicken meat in a soup plate and spooning in the soup. Serves 6-8.

SPAIN

ARROZ CON POLLO—Chicken with Rice

1 3-pound chicken, cut up	1 cup rice
Salt and freshly ground pepper	2½ cups chicken stock
6-8 tablespoons olive oil	⅛ teaspoon powdered saffron
2 onions, chopped finely	2 tomatoes, peeled and chopped
1 green pepper, seeded and	1 tablespoon paprika
chopped	Chopped parsley

Preheat the oven to 350° F. Rub the chicken pieces all over with salt and freshly ground pepper. Heat 3-4 tablespoons of olive oil in a casserole and brown the chicken pieces on all sides, a few at a time. When done, set aside and keep warm.

Add 3-4 tablespoons more olive oil to the pan and, over moderate heat, sauté the onion and green pepper together with the rice for 3 or 4 minutes. Stir constantly so as not to let the rice burn. Now add the chicken stock and saffron and bring to the boil. Add the chopped tomatoes and paprika, stir well for a moment, then place the chicken pieces on top. Cover and cook in the oven for 1 hour. Garnish with parsley and serve the Arroz con Pollo right from the casserole. Serves 4.

SPAIN

PAELLA VALENCIANA—
A Rice, Shellfish, and Chicken Dish from Valencia

Paella (pi-EE-ya) is unquestionably Spain's most distinguished contribution to the world's gastronomy. It is actually a rice dish but has become known as a classic in chicken and shellfish cooking also.

There are two interesting things to know when starting out on paella. First, the dish is named after the pan in which it is cooked. A *paella* is a fairly large pan (they come in different sizes), which is round, but with a flat bottom (like a flat-bottomed wok). Second, in Spain rice is cooked differently than in America. Spanish rice is short grained and is added to the pot and fried momentarily to coat it with oil and to get it warm, then water or stock is poured over it and it is permitted to absorb the moisture, first over high heat, then over low.

¾ cup olive oil

½ pound boneless pork, cut into ½-inch pieces

3 chorizos, or hot Italian sausages, cut into ½-inch pieces

1 3-pound chicken, cut up

Salt and freshly ground pepper

2 medium sweet red or green peppers, seeded and sliced into strips

2 tablespoons pimentos, chopped

2 cups white rice

1 large tomato, peeled, seeded, and chopped finely

¼ teaspoon saffron powder or 1 teaspoon saffron threads, pulverized

4 cups fresh chicken stock

1 pound medium-sized raw shrimp, shelled and deveined

3 6-ounce rock lobster tails, cut into 1-inch sections (optional)

½ pound peas

½ pound artichoke hearts

12 mussels or 12 clams (or both), washed well

2 lemons, cut into wedges

Preheat the oven to 350° F. Heat the oil in a large skillet. Brown the pork pieces and sausages on all sides for 6-8 minutes, then remove to a large casserole. Brown the chicken pieces evenly and remove them to the casserole when done. Add salt and freshly ground pepper to the meat in the casserole. Set aside.

Now add the chopped garlic, onions, and sliced peppers to the pan and sauté gently for 5 or 6 minutes. Next add the chopped pimentos, the rice, the chopped tomato, and the saffron, and cook, stirring frequently, for 5 minutes. Keep the heat low. Now spoon the rice and tomato mixture over the chicken.

Pour in the chicken stock and add a little more salt and pepper; place in the oven and cook for 15 minutes, uncovered, then push the shrimp down into the rice mixture and do the same with the rock lobster pieces. Return the casserole to the oven and continue cooking for another 15 minutes.

Add the peas and artichokes to the pot, stirring several times to distribute them evenly. Now push the mussels or clams into the top of the rice, and return the casserole to the oven and continue cooking.

Add a little broth (¼-½ cup) if necessary (if the paella seems to be getting dry).

The clams or mussels should open up in 5-7 minutes, indicating that they are done. Serve in the casserole or in a large serving dish, garnished with lemon wedges. Serves 6-8.

Spain

POLLO ESTOFADO—Chicken Stew

Estofado is a familiar dish throughout all of Spain's provinces. Frequently it calls for partridges (*perdice*) or other small birds which, if you have them, can be readily substituted for the chicken in this recipe.

2 spring chickens, or other small birds, oven ready	⅔ cup water
Salt and freshly ground pepper	1 large clove garlic, chopped
Flour	1 bay leaf
1 thin slice ham or 2 slices bacon	3 medium onions, peeled and quartered
3 tablespoons olive oil	3 large potatoes, peeled and diced
⅔ cup dry white wine	6 carrots, scraped and quartered lengthwise
	Parsley sprigs for garnish

Sprinkle the birds with salt and pepper inside and out. Rub the salt and pepper into the cavities with your fingers to be sure it is evenly distributed. Now dust the birds all over with flour, shaking off any excess, and truss the legs and wings with twine or skewers. Heat the oil in a large Dutch oven or casserole and cook the ham or bacon for about five minutes or so, then remove to drain.

Increase the heat and get the remaining oil very hot. Cook the birds in the hot oil, turning every 5 minutes or so, until they are evenly browned all over. Watch the heat so they don't burn. Remove the birds to a plate, then pour off any excess fat. Over high heat, bring the wine and water to the boil, deglazing the pan.

Return the birds to the pan and reduce the heat to low. Crumble the bacon or ham over the birds, then add the chopped garlic. Crumble the bay leaf and distribute it evenly all around, making sure it drops into the liquid. Cover and simmer for 30 minutes, then add the onions, potatoes, and carrots. Re-cover, and continue simmering for an additional 30 minutes.

Place the birds in the center of a large platter, arrange the vegetables around them, and garnish with parsley sprigs. If the pan liquid is too thin, add a small amount of cornstarch and cook it down over high heat for a few minutes, then pass in a sauceboat. Serves 4-6.

SPAIN

POLLO EN ESCABECHE—Chicken in Marinade

This has been transported to the Caribbean, South America, and the Philippines where, cooked with local ingredients, it enjoys the same popularity as it does in Spain.

1 3-pound chicken	½ onion, sliced
4 tablespoons olive oil	Lemon slices and parsley for garnish

Marinade

2 cups dry white wine	1 garlic clove, chopped
1 bay leaf	Juice of 1 lemon
Salt and freshly ground pepper	Juice of 1 orange
	½ cup white vinegar

Mix together the marinade ingredients and marinate the chicken for 2 hours, turning frequently. Heat the oil in a Dutch oven and sauté the onion, then slowly brown the chicken over low heat on all sides for about 15 minutes. Pour in the marinade, cover, and simmer for 1 hour.

When done the chicken should be cooled completely, and refrigerated in the same pot. It may be served chilled or it may be reheated and served. In either case serve with lemon wedges and parsley garnish. Serves 4.

PORTUGAL

FRANGO COM ERVILHAS—Chicken with Peas

4 tablespoons olive oil	¼ cup Madeira wine
2 onions, chopped finely	Salt and pepper
1 3-pound chicken, cut up	1 bay leaf
½ cup chicken stock	1 pound shelled peas
	Parsley sprigs for garnish

Heat the oil in a casserole and sauté the onions gently until golden. Remove to a plate and keep warm. Now brown the chicken in the remaining oil a few pieces at a time and remove when done to the plate.

Return the chicken pieces and the onion to the casserole and add the stock, wine, salt and pepper, and bay leaf. Cover and simmer over low heat for 45 minutes. Now add the peas, replace the cover, and cook for another 15 minutes. When done remove the bay leaf. Serve on a platter around a mound of cooked white rice garnished with parsley. Serves 4.

PORTUGAL

FRANGO A BIERA ALTA—Baked Chicken and Ham

This dish is supposed to be prepared with a small bird, on the order of a squab or spring chicken. If these are not available, use Rock Cornish game hens.

2 spring chickens or Rock Cornish game hens	1 teaspoon fresh parsley, chopped
	Salt and freshly ground pepper
2 thin slices presunto, serrano, parma, or prosciutto ham	3 tablespoons butter
	8 new potatoes, peeled
1 cup cottage or ricotta cheese	Parsley for garnish

Preheat the oven to 350° F. Rub the cavities of each bird with a little salt and pepper. Gently loosen the skin of each bird over the breast and insert a slice of ham. Mix the ricotta, parsley, and 2 tablespoons butter together thoroughly, and stuff the bird. Now truss or skewer both openings. Spread the remaining butter over the birds and place in a baking dish, breast up. Place the potatoes around the birds and bake for 1 hour, basting occasionally. Garnish with parsley. Serves 2-4.

PART V:

The British Isles

In ancient England, the banquet was the nobility's style of eating, and it remained in vogue for centuries. It happened every night in the great hall, where throngs of guests, served by platoons of servants, gorged themselves on fish, venison, boar, gamebird, mead, and black bread. What the guests didn't eat, the servants did.

Accounts of these binges reveal a surprisingly long and varied cuisine, which, though probably not cooked very well, must have been rather colorful. The British Isles were a haven for gamebirds, and those that were snared were hung along with the meat in the rafters to be cured by the smoke from the fireplace. The Britons of the time were equally happy with a meal of lark, sparrow, tern, swan, peacock, heron, crane, blackbird, starling, or gull.

One of Britain's greatest traditions was the pie. Early recipe books are filled with various concoctions cooked under some sort of cover: meat pies, vegetables pies, gamebird pies, fish and shellfish pies, fowl pies, and "shepherd's" or "cottage" pie, to name just a few. The popular nursery rhyme that sings of "four and twenty blackbirds baked in a pie" was not a fiction. At one time, this was fairly common; in fact, there's a record of one recipe that includes live frogs in one part of the pie and live birds in another. It's a tradition that continues and today includes several delightful chicken pies.

England's adventures in the Far East and the New World during the colonial period brought a number of pleasant additions to the British cuisine. Besides the traditional curries and tea, the British brought back mulligatawny, the spicy chicken soup-stew that over the years has become substantially milder in English cookery.

The cooking of the British Isles has come a long way from its rather mundane past, but it is still rather straightforward fare, and cooked with little embellishment. A fowl dinner is generally roasted with a stuffing and frequently is served with a simple onion, bread, orange, or apple sauce. With the exception of the curries, most of the seasoning is done with garden herbs and vegetables. One of the more widely used is the leek, an onion family member that is to the culinary repertoire of the British Isles what the endive is to Belgium or the tomato to the Italian. The Scotch have made Cock-a-Leekie (chicken and leek) Soup world-famous, and an Irish favorite is baked chicken with leeks, and of course the most famous of all may be the English Chicken and Leek Pie.

RECOMMENDED READING: Maxime McKendry, *The Seven Centuries Cookbook* (New York: McGraw-Hill, 1973); Robin Howe, *Cooking for the Commonwealth* (London: André Deutsch, 1958)

ENGLAND

SHEPHERD'S PIE

In Britain, meat pies are usually made with beef or lamb, but are becoming increasingly popular with chicken or turkey. When the meat is cut into small chunks and cooked between layers of mashed potatoes it's a "shepherd's pie"; when it's minced, it's called a "cottage pie."

1 pound white potatoes	1 cup leftover chicken cut into
2 medium onions	small chunks
Bacon drippings (or butter)	Salt and pepper
	½ cup gravy
	1 egg, beaten

Peel the potatoes and boil them in salted water. When done, mash them and set aside to keep warm. Parboil the onions for 10 minutes in water, then remove to drain and chop.

Preheat the oven to 350° F. Put some bacon drippings into a small casserole or pie dish and spread over the bottom, then cover with a layer of mashed potatoes. Now lay in the meat, add the chopped onions, and pour over the gravy. Sprinkle on some salt and a few grindings of fresh pepper and finish the pie by covering with the remaining mashed potatoes.

Now brush the pie with the beaten egg and place it in the oven and bake for 15-20 minutes or until the crust is well browned. Remove and serve at once right from the pie dish. Serves 4.

SCOTLAND

COCK-A-LEEKIE SOUP

12 prunes	Salt and pepper
6 leeks	⅛ teaspoon thyme
1 small boiling chicken	3 parsley sprigs
2 quarts water or stock	2 tablespoons rice

Soak the prunes overnight, but do not stone them. Wash the leeks and put them with the fowl in 2 quarts of stock or water in a large saucepan with a tight-fitting lid. Bring the stock to the boil, then reduce to moderate heat, skimming the scum as it rises.

Now add the salt and pepper, thyme, and parsley sprigs, cover, and reduce the heat to low. Simmer gently for 3 hours. An hour before the soup is done, add the rice. Thirty minutes before it is done, add the prunes. When the soup is done, remove the chicken and bone it, discarding the skin. Put the pieces of chicken meat in a tureen and pour in the soup and prunes. Serve at once. Serves 6-8.

IRELAND

BAKED CHICKEN WITH LEEKS

1 3-pound chicken, cut up	10-12 mushrooms, sliced
3 tablespoons butter or oil	1 leek, sliced thinly (white part only)
2 cups chicken stock	2 tablespoons lemon juice

Preheat the oven to 375° F. Heat the butter or oil in a skillet and brown the chicken pieces for 12-15 minutes. When done, arrange the pieces in a baking dish and pour the cooking oil that's left in also.

Combine the stock, sliced mushrooms, leek, and lemon juice in a bowl and mix together thoroughly. Now spoon the mixture over the chicken and bake for 30 minutes. Serve right from the baking dish, spooning the sauce over the chicken. Serves 4.

ENGLAND

ROAST CORNISH GAME HENS
(or Spring Chickens) with White Wine

2 Cornish game hens	1 cup white wine
1 tablespoon butter	2 shallots, chopped
1 medium onion, chopped	2 tablespoons fresh parsley, chopped
½ cup rice	Salt and pepper
2 cups chicken stock	

In a skillet, sauté the onions in butter very gently for 5 minutes, then pour the contents into the top of a double boiler. Add the rice and 1 cup of chicken stock and a little salt and pepper to the pot and stir well. Bring the water in the lower pot to a rapid boil, place the upper pot on top, cover, and cook for 20 minutes.

While the rice cooks, rub salt and pepper inside the birds and out. When the rice is done, spoon it into the birds and skewer or sew the cavities closed. Place the hens in a Dutch oven with the second cup of stock and the wine. Sprinkle over some more salt and pepper, cover, and simmer for 1 hour. Now add the chopped shallots and parsley, cover again, and cook slowly for another 20-30 minutes, or until tender. Serves 2-4.

IRELAND

ROAST CHICKEN WITH ORANGE SAUCE

The authentic way to make this is with duckling. It is outstanding, though, with chicken using the same recipe.

1 4-pound roasting chicken	1 stalk celery, chopped
Liver of the chicken, diced	Salt and pepper
4 tablespoons butter	1 cooking apple, peeled, cored,
1 cup white fresh breadcrumbs	and chopped
⅛ teaspoon fennel	Juice of 2 oranges
1 tablespoon fresh parsley,	Grated rind of 1 orange (optional)
chopped	1 tablespoon cornstarch
	1 tablespoon water

Preheat the oven to 350° F. Heat 1 tablespoon butter in a small skillet and sauté the diced liver very gently until the color is changed. Put the breadcrumbs in a bowl and add the sautéed liver, fennel, chopped parsley, and celery and a little salt and pepper. Melt 2 tablespoons butter in the skillet and cook the apple gently for 1 minute, turning several times, then add the apple and the melted butter to the breadcrumbs. Mix all the ingredients thoroughly, then stuff the bird and skewer or sew the cavities closed. Melt the remaining butter and brush the breast and legs of the chicken, then place it in a roaster, breast side up, and roast covered for 1 hour, basting frequently. About 15 minutes before the chicken is finished pour in the orange juice and grated rind and continue cooking until done, basting once or twice.

When the bird is done, remove it to a platter. On top of the stove, dissolve 1 tablespoon cornstarch in 1 tablespoon water, stir into the pan drippings, and cook over moderate heat, stirring all the while, until the sauce thickens. Spoon a little sauce over the chicken and serve the rest in a sauceboat. Serves 4-6.

ENGLAND

ROAST CHICKEN WITH SAGE AND ONION STUFFING

One of the most famous meals in history was the Christmas goose the Cratchits enjoyed in Dickens' *A Christmas Carol,* stuffed with sage and onion and "eked out by apple sauce and mashed potatoes." This stuffing is excellent with roast chicken as well.

Sage and Onion Stuffing

2 cups water	Pinch each thyme and rosemary
2 large onions, peeled	4 tablespoons butter, melted
3 cups breadcrumbs	1 4-5-pound roasting chicken
1 tablespoon dried sage leaves, crumbled	1 cup chicken stock
	Salt and pepper

Bring 2 cups of lightly salted water to the boil and cook the onions for 12-15 minutes, then drain and chop them rather coarsely. Combine the onions, breadcrumbs, sage, thyme, rosemary, and melted butter in a bowl and toss until thoroughly mixed. Preheat the oven to 325° F. Now stuff the chicken cavity tightly and sew or skewer it closed. Sprinkle the chicken with salt and pepper, then place it breast side up on a rack in a roasting pan. Pour over the stock and roast, uncovered, for 1 hour, basting the bird every 20 minutes or so.

When done, place the chicken on a heated platter and let stand for 10 minutes or so, then serve with mashed potatoes and apple sauce. Serves 4.

ENGLAND

ROAST STUFFED TURKEY (OR CHICKEN) WITH BREAD SAUCE

This is one of the traditional fowl dishes of England, and it is usually served on a platter surrounded by chipolata sausages, vegetables, and a bread sauce. Two of the most popular stuffings are sausage and veal, and chestnut.

To cook it, preheat the oven to 375° F. Cover the turkey with several strips of bacon (fasten them with toothpicks) and put a good-sized lump of butter in the pan. Now stuff the bird with one of the two stuffings below and roast for 15 minutes per pound for a 12-15-pound bird or 20 minutes per pound for a turkey of up to 20 pounds. When done remove to a serving platter and let stand for 20 minutes.

Note: If you use chicken, reduce to ¼ the ingredients in the stuffings. Roast the chicken for 20 minutes per pound, covered, in a 350°F oven.

Chestnut Dressing (for a 12-pound bird)

1 pound chestnuts
1 cup chicken stock
¾ cup breadcrumbs
3 parsley sprigs, chopped

2 strips lean bacon, fried and crumbled
2 tablespoons butter, melted
1 egg, beaten
1 tablespoon lemon juice
Salt and pepper

With a sharp knife, cut a slit in the skin of each chestnut. Bring a saucepan of water to boil and drop in the nuts for 12-15 minutes. Remove the nuts from the heat, drain, and let cool a bit, then remove the skins. Now place them back in the saucepan, add one cup of chicken stock, and simmer for another 10 minutes or so, until they are tender. Remove the nuts from the pan and mash them and then add to the breadcrumbs, parsley, crumbled bacon, butter, egg, lemon juice, and a little salt and pepper in a bowl. Mix well, then stuff the turkey about ¾ full (the stuffing will swell). Cook as described above.

Sausage and Veal Stuffing (for a 12-pound bird)

½ pound shoulder or breast meat of veal
½ pound bulk sausage
1 cup chopped onions
1 cup chopped celery

1 green pepper, seeded and chopped
8 cups white bread, shredded
Salt and pepper
1 teaspoon tarragon
1 egg, beaten

Grind the veal rather finely, then mix with the sausage. Cook over low heat for about 10 minutes or until the meat has browned slightly. Remove the meat to a bowl, then sauté the onion, celery, and pepper for 5-6 minutes in the pan drippings. Now mix the vegetables with the meat and shredded bread in the bowl. Season with salt and pepper to taste and add the tarragon and beaten egg. Mix all together thoroughly and stuff the bird. Cook as described above.

Bread Sauce

2 cloves	Salt and pepper
1 small onion, peeled	1 cup white breadcrumbs
1¼ cups milk	2 tablespoons butter
Pinch nutmeg	2 tablespoons cream

Stick the cloves in the onion. In a double boiler, heat the milk without letting it come to the boil. Add the onion and nutmeg and cook for 30 minutes. Add a little salt and pepper, butter and the breadcrumbs and stir together. Add the cream, and stir again. Now cook very gently for 20 minutes. Serve hot in a sauceboat with the turkey.

England

CHICKEN AND LEEK PIE

1 3-pound chicken, cut up	1 bay leaf
2 cups water	1 teaspoon dry thyme leaves
1 medium onion, chopped	Salt and freshly ground pepper
1 stalk celery, sliced	6 medium leeks
2 sprigs parsley, chopped	Boiling salted water
	1 cup reserved stock

Pastry

1 cup flour	¾ cup shortening
Pinch of salt	2-3 tablespoons cold water
	½ teaspoon lemon juice

Place the chicken pieces in a large kettle with the water, onion, celery, parsley, bay leaf, thyme, and salt and pepper and bring to the boil. Reduce the heat to low, cover, and simmer for 1 hour.

While the chicken cooks, trim the leeks of roots and green leaves and cut each into about 1½-inch lengths and cook for 5 minutes in boiling salted water. Remove from the heat, drain, and set aside.

Now prepare the pie pastry by adding the salt to the flour and sifting into a bowl. Add a little of the shortening to the flour and work it in with your fingers. Keep adding shortening until it has all been worked into the flour, then add the lemon juice and continue working the dough. Now add a little water and knead until the dough becomes firm but pliable. (Be sparing with the water, but the dough will be ready when it can be rolled out into a thin sheet.)

When the chicken is done, remove it from the pan. Strain the pan liquid and reserve 1 cup. Cut the chicken into pieces and strip the meat, discarding the skin and bones. In a 6 x 9-inch baking dish place the chicken pieces and leeks and pour over the reserved stock. Season with a little salt and pepper to taste. Roll the pastry out as thinly as you can, then place a sheet over the baking dish. Trim and seal the sides, then brush with butter and cook in a moderate oven (350° F) for 15-20 minutes, until the top starts to brown. Serve right from the dish. Serves 4.

ENGLAND

CHICKEN AND OYSTER PIE

Because England is an island, fish and shellfish have been a cornerstone of their cuisine for centuries. It's not uncommon to find both poultry and shellfish served at the same meal, and in this classic, chicken and oysters are cooked in a succulent combination under a flaky pie crust.

3 tablespoons butter	Breadcrumbs
1 small onion, chopped finely	2 hard cooked eggs, quartered
1 clove garlic, minced	Juice of ½ lemon
1 3-pound chicken, cut up	4 tablespoons chicken stock
Salt and pepper	1 tablespoon flour
1 tablespoon chopped parsley	Lemon slices and parsley sprigs
12 oysters, poached (5 minutes)	for garnish

Heat the butter in a large skillet and sauté the onions and garlic gently until golden, then remove from the pan and discard. Rub the chicken pieces with salt and pepper and brown slowly on all sides, a few pieces at a time. Remove the chicken pieces and strip the meat, discarding skin and bones.

Preheat the oven to 350° F. Place the chicken pieces in a fairly deep baking dish and sprinkle with parsley and a little more salt and pepper. Roll the poached oysters in breadcrumbs and place them in the dish among the chicken pieces. Now put in the hard cooked egg quarters and sprinkle over the lemon juice. Deglaze the skillet with 4-5 tablespoons chicken stock or broth and 1 tablespoon flour, stirring together well, then pour this sauce over the chicken pieces, oysters, and eggs.

Now make a pastry (see Chicken and Leek Pie, page 302), and roll it out as thinly as possible. Cover the dish with the layer of pastry, trim and seal the edges, and brush with a little melted butter or oil. Place the pie in the oven and bake for 30-40 minutes; the crust should be golden brown. Serve from the dish, garnished with lemon slices and parsley sprigs. Serves 4-6.

PART VI:

Scandinavia

The gastronomy of the early Scandinavians was the rough and ready campfire fare of the Germanic tribes of East Europe and the Anglo-Saxons of Britain: fish, wild game, and mead or beer. It remained that way well into the Renaissance, until the cultural revolution that swept the continent found its way into the northernmost countries. Danish and Swedish royalty were bitten by the French bug and for a time employed chefs who had been trained in the French technique in their kitchens. This is one reason their cuisines show a far greater scope than those of Norway, Finland, and Iceland; but Denmark and Sweden are richer in natural resources, have more moderate climates and longer growing seasons, and this too has contributed.

The many fine hotels and restaurants throughout Scandinavia offer elaborate menus with an international selection of dishes, but at home the cooking is uncomplicated, rather bland, and, though nourishing and plentiful, is cooked with few frills and flourishes. Fish is the basic meat in the cuisines of all five countries, with beef, pork, and domestic poultry following well behind.

The cuisines the world knows or describes as "Scandinavian" are those of southern Sweden and Denmark. There is no more famous seafood meal in the world than the Swedish *smorgasbord,* nor can any country match the reputation that Denmark has earned for its open-faced sandwiches, its pastries, and its fabulous hams; and though poultry is subordinate to other meats, both countries have developed several dishes that are rather unusual. One is roast chicken stuffed with a handful of fresh parsley, which imparts a fresh, earthy taste to the bird.

Sauces seem to accompany most chicken dishes in the four mainland countries, the most prominent of which is a very sweet cream sauce that is particularly popular in Denmark and Sweden. One might think this reflects the recent French presence, and perhaps it does, but the Norwegians and Finns also use cream sauces and flavor theirs with lemon, dill, or tomatoes.

The most important feast of the year in Scandinavia is Christmas Eve. Scandinavians believe that the Christmas Spirit is always present in the home, and for one to feel it, he must offer food to anyone who knocks on his door. Perhaps this means these people practice and enjoy the spirit of Christmas throughout the year, for in every Scandinavian country, a little something is always cooked or baked for visiting friends and guests.

NORWAY

ROCK CORNISH GAME HENS IN CREAM SAUCE

Norwegian forests abound in gamebirds, and the common method of cooking them is to lard them with bacon or other fat and then cook them in a sweet or sour cream sauce. A more recent touch has been to add cognac, a reminder of the French influence that pervaded the Scandinavian countries two centuries ago and which still persists.

Note: This recipe originally called for ptarmigan or grouse. Use them if you have them, but this is also excellent with Rock Cornish game hen or spring chicken.

2 Rock Cornish game hens, cut up	4 strips fat bacon
Salt and pepper	3 apples
4 tablespoons butter	2 tablespoons sugar
2 onions, chopped	1 1-inch stick vanilla
½ cup dry white wine	1 cup water
1 cup chicken stock	1 cup heavy cream
⅛ teaspoon sage	2 tablespoons cognac
	Parsley for garnish

Preheat the oven to 375° F. Rub the pieces with salt and pepper and set aside. In a large Dutch oven or casserole, sauté the onions in 1 tablespoon of butter and remove to a plate when golden. Add the remaining butter and brown the meat pieces, a few at a time, then remove and keep warm. When all the pieces are brown, return them to the casserole. Scatter the onions over the meat, then pour in the wine and chicken stock and add the sage. (Lay 2 strips of bacon across the meat, then place the casserole in the oven and cook covered for 40 minutes.)

While the game hens cook, peel and core the apples and cut them into rings. Boil the sugar and vanilla in water for 5 or 6 minutes, then add the apple pieces and cook for 10 minutes.

When the birds are done, place them on a serving platter and keep warm. Spoon off as much fat from the pan as possible, then cook the liquid down for 10 minutes or so, until it begins to thicken. Reduce the heat to low, then add the cream and cognac. Stir continuously for 3 minutes, then strain the sauce into a sauceboat. Garnish the meat with parsley and serve with the sauce on the side. Serves 4.

Sweden

ROAST CHICKEN WITH PARSLEY STUFFING

1 3-pound chicken	1 cup hot chicken stock
Salt and pepper	3 tablespoons flour
½ cup butter	⅔ cup heavy cream
1½ cups fresh parsley, chopped	Tomato slices and parsley sprigs for garnish

Wash the chicken and pat dry, then rub inside and out with salt and pepper. Mix 3 tablespoons of butter with the parsley and stuff the cavity, then close the opening with skewers and tie the legs. Heat the remaining butter in a Dutch oven and brown the chicken gently on all sides until golden in color. Now pour in the chicken stock and simmer over low heat for 1 hour. Baste occasionally, adding a little stock or water if necessary to keep the bird moist. When done, remove the chicken to a warm platter and let sit for 10 minutes.

Pour off the pan juices, reserving 1 cup, and heat this over moderate fire. Add the flour and stir continuously until the sauce begins to thicken. Now reduce the heat to low and cook for a minute or so, then add the cream. Stir a few times, then correct the taste with salt and pepper if necessary. Cover and simmer for about 5 minutes over very low heat. Garnish the bird with tomato slices and parsley sprigs and strain the sauce and serve hot. Serves 4.

Finland

KANAVATKULI—
Braised Chicken with Tomato Cream Sauce

1 3-pound chicken, cut up	3 tablespoons flour
Salt and freshly ground pepper	1 cup cream
¼ cup butter	½ cup tomato sauce
	Parsley for garnish

Preheat the oven to 350° F. Rub the chicken pieces well with salt and pepper. Heat the butter in a large skillet and then brown the chicken on all sides for about 15 minutes over low heat. Remove the chicken to a large casserole, pour over the pan drippings, then cover and cook for 45 minutes.

When the chicken is done, return the pan drippings to the skillet. Stir the flour in and add a little more salt and pepper. Over low heat, add the cream and the tomato sauce and, stirring continuously, blend thoroughly.

Place rice or potatoes in the center of a warm platter and surround with the chicken pieces. Spoon a little of the sauce over all and pass the rest in a sauceboat. Garnish with parsley sprigs. Serves 4.

FINLAND

PAISTETTU METSELINTU—Braised Gamebirds

This recipe calls for small birds such as dove, quail, ptarmigan, snow bird, or partridge. If you can get them, use them; if not, use Cornish game hens.

2 tablespoons butter	Flour
4 small gamebirds, or 2 Rock	2 cups water
Cornish game hens	4 tablespoons cooked currants, or
Salt and pepper	currant jelly

Melt the butter in a large Dutch oven. Rub the birds with salt and pepper, dredge in flour, then brown them on all sides lightly over low heat for 10 minutes or so.

Arrange the birds breast side up in the Dutch oven and pour in ½ cup water. Cover the pot and braise the birds for 45-50 minutes or until tender. When done, remove to a platter and keep warm. Add the currants or jelly to the drippings and stir over moderate heat until the sauce is thoroughly blended and reduced to the desired consistency, then pour into a sauceboat. Garnish the birds with parsley sprigs and serve. Serves 2-4.

Note: Any of the sauces on the following pages are excellent with this dish.

Poultry and Wild Gamebird Sauces

In Finland and in the northern parts of Sweden and Norway, gamebirds are eaten more often than domestic poultry simply because of the harsh climate. Dove, ptarmigan, snow bird, and grouse are the most popular, and they are usually braised or roasted and served with a sauce. Here are five (three of which are based on a simple white sauce) that are just as good with Rock Cornish game hen and chicken as with wild birds.

White Sauce

2 tablespoons butter	1 cup light cream or chicken stock
2 tablespoons flour	Salt and pepper

Melt the butter in a saucepan and stir in the flour until smooth. Slowly add in the cream or stock and cook, stirring constantly, until smooth and thick. Add salt and pepper to taste. Makes 1 cup.

Dill Sauce

Make a recipe for white sauce and blend in 3 tablespoons fresh dill, chopped finely.

Lemon Sauce

To one recipe for white sauce, add the juice and grated rind of 1 lemon, and stir well over low heat for a minute or so.

Tomato Sauce

This is called *tomatti kastike* in Finland, and is excellent with broiled chicken.

2 large tomatoes, peeled and chopped	2 tablespoons flour
	¼ cup fresh parsley, chopped
1 onion, chopped finely	½ teaspoon sweet basil
2 tablespoons butter	Salt

Pass the tomatoes through a sieve to remove the seeds, then set aside. Melt the butter and sauté the chopped onions over low heat for 3 minutes, then stir in the flour. Add the strained tomatoes, parsley, and basil and simmer slowly for 15 minutes, stirring occasionally. If necessary, add a little salt at the end.

Horseradish Sauce

In Denmark, horseradish sauce (*flodepeberrod*) is a particular favorite, and the Danes eat it with fish, meat, chicken, and gamebird with equal relish. If fresh horseradish is not available, use the bottled variety, but let it drain for an hour or so and omit the lemon juice in the following recipe.

2 cups heavy cream	¼ cup freshly grated horseradish root
1-2 teaspoons sugar	
1 teaspoon lemon juice	Salt and pepper

Whip the cream until it begins to stiffen, then add the sugar, a little at a time. Now add the lemon juice, horseradish, and the salt and pepper. Continue whipping until stiff, then chill.

Spoon the cold sauce over hot, boiled chicken and serve with boiled potatoes and vegetables.

✤ Chapter 9 ✤

Latin America

During the early sixteenth century, exploration and colonization were taking place in the New World at a pace equal to or exceeding that in the Orient, and the same nations were involved. The Spanish made Cuba their main base in the Caribbean, and from there Cortes in 1519 and Pizarro in 1531 departed on their plunderous adventures against the Aztecs and Incas. Other captains took exploring parties into Venezuela, Colombia, and down the eastern coast of South America to Brazil. Spain had an exclusive franchise on the gold, silver, and precious stones of Latin America at first, but the Dutch, British, Portuguese, and French soon came seeking their share.

Having led the way, the Spanish became the dominant force throughout Central America, much of South America, and along the northern Gulf Coast. But all nations occupied one or more of the West Indian Islands and waged such continual war with each other that few answered to one flag for any length of time.

Caribbean cooking, when the Europeans came, was essentially the primitive offerings of the aboriginal Arawaks and Caribes, tribes that preceded the Spanish by thousands of years. Their gastronomy was fish, root, and berry oriented and of such little sophistication that it died out just as the natives did under the harsh subjugation of the Europeans. Despite the immediate change the Europeans brought, however, the lack of political stability in the Islands prohibited any one culinary style from becoming dominant, so a curious mixture of Spanish, Dutch, British, Danish, and French styles developed through which ran the thread of *Criolla* (Creole) cooking, created by the descendants of African slaves.

When the Spanish arrived in the New World, they found a plethora of foods they'd never seen before, the most important of which was corn. They also discovered the white potato in the cool high Andes valleys; a wide variety of beans, one of which was the white haricot, which the French ultimately popularized in cassoulet. The Spanish found squash and pumpkin in the Incan cuisine, sweet potatoes, vanilla and cacao (from which chocolate is made), avocadoes, pimentos, chicle, the turkey, and strange plants with red and green pods, which when used in cooking gave the food a fiery, hot taste. The Spanish called them chili peppers and took them back to Europe as one of the few "spices" the New World had to offer.

Once the Europeans arrived, it was only a matter of years before Latin American cooking became that of the Old World, flavored with local ingredients. Even the names of the dishes remained the same. Because they occupied so much territory during the early colonial period, the Spaniards' style of cooking became more dominant than any other and has remained so. *Arroz con Pollos* abound throughout the Islands, Mexico, Panama, Colombia, Peru, and Chile, and every Spanish-speaking country has its *Escabeche, Empanadas,* and *Cocido.* In Martinique and Trinidad one finds the *Poulet Rôti* and *Poulet à l'Orange* of the French kitchen, while a standard British cuisine greets one in Jamaica and Barbados.

Since the coming of the Spanish to Latin America, two very superior cuisines developed. One is in Mexico, and today it exists on two levels. First there is the corn and beans tradition of the Indians, which has its roots in antiquity and which features tortillas, tacos, tamales, and frijoles. Superimposed on this are the higher-styled Spanish imports *Adobo, Pollo en Jugo,* and *Paella,* with a touch or two of the French kitchen which Maximilian brought with him in the nineteenth century. Even the Seville orange is found in Mexican cooking, the Moorish fruit the French distinguished in their *Caneton à l'Orange.* But in Mexico it's a Spanish dish, and it's made with chicken rather than duck.

Less well known is Bahian or Afro-Brazilian cooking, which combines Brazilian, Portuguese, and African influences into one cuisine. It is easily the most outstanding in South America. Considering that the Portuguese first landed in Brazil just over four hundred years ago, it's surprising that this cuisine has such scope and sophistication today, starting as it did literally from scratch.

Finding the natives unwilling and unable to stand up to the rigorous conditions demanded in the sugar cane fields, the Portuguese imported thousands of slaves from Africa. The climate was almost identical to that of their native land, and as the slaves thrived so did the Portuguese. The landowners gave over the cooking chores to the slaves, which turned out to be a very fortuitous move for, with the transfer, the rather mundane fare of the landowners was raised several levels at least.

Bahian cooking is characterized by extensive use of coconut meat and milk, the fiery hot malagueta pepper of Brazil (a close cousin to the Mexican chili pepper), and dried shrimp. Its most characteristic feature however, is *dende,* the oil of the West African palm, which gives the food its distinctive flavor and yellow color.

Couscous, the classic multi-ingredient grain dish of North Africa, was introduced by slaves to Brazil where it became *cuscuz.* It is made of semolina in Africa and corn meal in South America, but it's just as traditional in either place, and it is prepared in the same way: steamed in a *cuscuzeiro* (or *couscousìere* in Africa) and then served with any combination of meat, chicken, fish, or vegetable.

African slaves played a part in the development of another Latin American cuisine of some distinction—the *Criolla* (Creole) cooking of the Caribbean. This too blends native Indian, European, and African cooking in the same pot, but without the shrimp or the dende oil. The Islanders use more okra, chili pepper, pimento, pineapples, and other native ingredients such as achiote, cassava, and corn.

RECOMMENDED READING: Margarite De Andrade, *Brazilian Cookery, Traditional and Modern* (Rutland: Chas. Tuttle Co., 1965); Jan Aaron and Georgine Sachs Salom, *The Art of Mexican Cooking* (Garden City, N.Y.: Doubleday, 1965); Diana Kennedy, Cuisines of Mexico (New York: Harper & Row, 1972); Robin Howe, *Cooking for the Commonwealth,* (London: André Deutsch, 1958); Elisabeth L. Ortiz, *The Complete Book of Caribbean Cooking* (New York: M. Evans, 1973)

TRINIDAD

PEPPERPOT—Chicken and Pork Stew

Today, pepperpot is a favorite in many of the Lesser Antilles islands, but it originated with the ancient Indian tribes of Guyana. The best-known pepperpots are found in Trinidad and Jamaica, and they are significantly different, most particularly because Jamaica's usually contains beef and Trinidad's, chicken.

The Trinidad version also contains *cassareep* (pronounced cassarip), an ingredient used only in some South American and Caribbean kitchens. Made by squeezing the fluid out of a grated raw cassava root, cassareep is used as a flavoring and coloring agent, and as a tenderizer. (Bottled cassareep can be bought in Latin American markets.)

1 4-5-pound stewing chicken, cut up	½ cup cassareep, using the following:
2 quarts water	1 cassava root
1 tablespoon salt	1-2 tablespoons brown sugar
Meat of 4 lean pork chops, cubed	3 cloves
1 pound chuck beef, cubed	1 stick cinnamon
1 tablespoon oil or butter	1-2 hot red chilies (to taste)
	1-2 tablespoons wine vinegar (optional)

Bring the water to the boil, then put in the chicken and 1 tablespoon of salt and boil for about 10 minutes over moderate heat. Skim off the scum, then reduce the heat to low and simmer for about 45 minutes. While the chicken cooks, brown the pork and beef cubes quickly in the butter (about 5 minutes), then set aside.

Now make the cassareep: Grate the cassava into fine shavings. Wrap these in cheesecloth and squeeze hard, in a downward direction, until all the juice is extracted. Grind the cinnamon stick and cloves into fine powder, then mix with the brown sugar until thoroughly blended.

Now place the cassava juice in a saucepan and bring to moderate heat. Stirring constantly, allow the liquid to cook until it reduces somewhat and becomes smooth. As it just starts to turn color, remove the pan from the fire and stir in the spice and sugar mixture, blending thoroughly. This sauce is cassareep.

When the chicken has cooked 45 minutes, add the browned meat, the cassareep, and the chili peppers. Cook this for about 30 more minutes, then remove from the fire. Remove the chilies and serve at once with boiled white rice. You may stir in 1 or 2 tablespoons of vinegar, if you wish, but taste as you go. Serves 6.

HAITI

SPICY CHICKEN

Spicy Marinade

Juice and grated rind of ½ lemon
½ cup white wine vinegar
2 cloves garlic, minced
Salt and pepper

1 fresh red pepper, seeded and chopped
1 tablespoon chopped parsley
6 tablespoons butter or peanut oil
1 3-pound chicken, cut up
½ cup dry white wine
½ cup chicken stock

Make a marinade of the lemon juice and rind, vinegar, garlic, a little salt and pepper, red pepper, and parsley. Place the chicken pieces in a bowl and pour the marinade over, coating each piece thoroughly. Let sit for 1 hour or more.

Heat the oil in a large skillet and slowly fry the chicken pieces until golden, for 10-12 minutes. Remove to a Dutch oven and pour the marinade into the skillet. Over low heat, scrape the bottom of the skillet to loosen and dissolve all particles. Now add the wine and broth and a pinch of salt.

Pour this mixture over the chicken and cover the pot. Cook over low heat for about 45 minutes and serve directly from the pot with hot white rice. (This is also good cold.) Serves 4.

TRINIDAD

CHICKEN PILAF—Chicken and Rice

A sizable Moslem community exists today in several of the Caribbean Islands, and most particularly Trinidad, so it's not surprising to find pilafs and other familiar Middle Eastern dishes. This pilaf, however, with the inclusion of peanuts and other local ingredients, hardly resembles its Asian cousins.

1 3-pound chicken, cut up
4 tablespoons butter
Salt and freshly ground pepper
1 hot red pepper, seeded and
    chopped finely
½ teaspoon thyme
1 clove garlic, chopped
1 large onion, chopped finely

2 medium tomatoes, peeled,
    seeded, and chopped coarsely
2-3 cups water
1 cup long-grained white rice
¼ cup crushed peanuts (or al-
    monds, blanched, skinned, and
    chopped)
½ cup green olives with pimentos
Parsley sprigs for garnish

Season the chicken with salt and pepper, then brown the pieces in 3 tablespoons of butter in a large skillet over low heat for about 8 minutes on a side.

While the chicken cooks, combine the chopped pepper, thyme, garlic, onion, and tomatoes in a bowl and mix well. Spoon this mixture over the chicken, then pour in 2 cups of water, cover, and simmer for 30 minutes.

When the chicken is done, remove it to a warm platter, strain the pan liquid, and add enough water to bring it back to 2 cups. Return the liquid to the pan and stir in the rice. Add 1 tablespoon of butter, then, keeping the heat fairly low, cover the pot and cook the rice for about 20 minutes or until all the liquid is absorbed. During the last 10 minutes return the chicken pieces to reheat and replace the cover.

To serve, mound the rice in the center of a warm platter and arrange the chicken pieces around. Sprinkle the rice and chicken with the chopped nuts and garnish with olives and parsley. Serves 4.

PUERTO RICO

ASOPAO DE POLLO—Chicken and Rice Stew

Asopao means "soupy" and that's just what this national dish of Puerto Rico is.

2 cloves garlic, minced
¼ teaspoon oregano
1 teaspoon salt
3 tablespoons butter or oil
1 3-pound chicken, cut up
1 green pepper, chopped
2 onions, chopped
½ cup lean ham, diced

4 tomatoes, peeled, seeded, and
    chopped
2 cups rice
6 cups chicken stock
1 cup fresh or frozen peas
6-8 small green pimento-stuffed
    olives
1 tablespoon grated cheese

Grind the garlic, oregano, and salt into a paste and rub it on the chicken pieces. Heat the butter or oil in a Dutch oven or large casserole and brown the chicken pieces on all sides for 10-12 minutes over moderate heat. Remove the meat and keep warm.

Now add the chopped pepper and onion to the pot and cook slowly for 3 minutes. Add the ham and cook for a minute, then the tomatoes and cook 2 minutes more. Pour the tomato mixture into a bowl and then return the chicken pieces to the pot. Now spoon the tomato mixture over the chicken, coating each piece completely. Cover the pot and cook over low heat for 40 minutes. When done, remove the chicken to a plate to cool.

While the chicken is cooking, pour 2 cups of rice into a pot with the stock. Add a little salt and pepper and stir to mix the rice and tomato mixture. Replace the cover and cook over low heat for 20 minutes.

When the chicken is cool, strip off the meat, discarding skin and bones, and cut the meat into bite-sized chunks. When the rice is done, add the chicken chunks to the pot along with the peas and simmer, covered, for 10 minutes. Now add the olives and sprinkle on the grated cheese. Simmer 2-3 minutes more, then serve directly from the pot. Serves 4-6.

CUBA

POLLO FRITO A LA CRIOLLA—
Fried Chicken, Creole Style

1 3-pound chicken, cut up	2 cloves garlic, minced
Salt and freshly ground pepper	½ cup Seville orange juice, or
5 tablespoons butter or oil	substitute (page 336)
	Flour

Rub the chicken pieces with salt and pepper. Melt 2 tablespoons of butter in a skillet and sauté the minced garlic for about 1 minute, then remove with a slotted spoon and discard. Place the chicken pieces in a large bowl or baking dish and spoon some of the garlic butter over each piece. Now pour the orange juice (or substitute) over the chicken, cover, and refrigerate for 4-6 hours. You should turn the pieces 4 or 5 times while they marinate.

When ready to cook, remove the chicken pieces from the marinade, pat dry with a paper towel, and dredge in flour. Heat the remaining butter in a large skillet and brown the chicken over moderate heat for about 10-12 minutes, then lower the heat and pour the marinade over the pieces. Cover the pan and cook the chicken for 30 minutes. Serves 4.

ARUBA

SAUCOCHI DI GALLINJA—Chicken Soup with Vegetables

Although this is a standard dish in Dutch-speaking Aruba, other versions show up all through the Spanish-speaking islands as *Sancocho de Pollo*. The latter, however, are spicier and contain exotic West Indian vegetables.

1 3-pound chicken, cut up
3 quarts fresh chicken or beef stock
Salt and pepper
3 large tomatoes, peeled, seeded, and chopped
2-3 ears of corn, cut into 2-inch pieces
2 large onions, chopped
½ cup fresh peas

2 yams or sweet potatoes, peeled and sliced
3 small potatoes, peeled and sliced
1 cup West Indian pumpkin or Hubbard squash, peeled and diced
1-2 (to taste) hot red chili peppers, seeded and sliced
Chopped chives or parsley for garnish

Place the chicken pieces in a large kettle and pour over the stock. Bring to the boil and skim off the scum as it rises. Now add salt and pepper, reduce the heat to low, and simmer, covered, for 40 minutes. While the chicken cooks, prepare all the vegetables.

When the chicken is done, add the tomatoes, corn, onions, peas, yams, potatoes, pumpkin (or squash), and chili peppers. Cover the pot, and continue simmering for 15-20 minutes. Serve in a tureen garnished with chives or parsley. Serves 4.

DOMINICAN REPUBLIC

POLLO CON PIÑA A LA ANTIGUA—
Chicken with Pineapple, Old Style

1 3-pound chicken, cut up	3-4 (1 cup) fresh tomatoes, peeled
Juice and grated rind of 1 lime	and chopped
Salt and pepper	1 hot chili pepper, seeded and
4-5 tablespoons butter or oil	chopped
2 cloves garlic, chopped	2 cups pineapple (with juice),
2 onions, chopped	chopped coarsely
4 tablespoons seedless raisins	¼ cup dark Jamaican rum
1/3 teaspoon oregano	

Season the chicken with salt and pepper, then rub it with the juice and grated rind of the lime. Set the meat aside for 1 hour.

Heat the butter or oil in a large skillet and lightly brown the chicken pieces on all sides, then transfer them to a large casserole or Dutch oven. Now sauté the garlic and onion for 4 minutes in the skillet. When done, add the raisins, oregano, tomatoes, and the chopped chili pepper and cook slowly for 6 minutes, stirring constantly.

Pour the sauce over the chicken in the Dutch oven and add the stock. Cover and cook slowly for 35-40 minutes. When the chicken is done, cook the pineapple chunks and juice in a small pan for 2 minutes, then add the rum. Heat for another minute, then pour over the chicken and cook over low heat for another 3 minutes. Serve directly from the pot. Serves 4.

Note: In Cuba, a very similar and popular dish is *Pato con Piña*. This is a duck dish, which is cooked the same way, only it is cooked whole with a bread and ham stuffing into which the onions and garlic and other ingredients are added. The pineapple chunks and juice are mixed with a dry white wine and served as a sauce.

DOMINICAN REPUBLIC

CHICARRONES DE POLLO—
Marinated Chicken Cracklings

This dish reflects the influence of the Oriental races that flourish in the West Indies. *Chicarrones* actually refers to bits of fried pork skin, but there is no similar word to describe fried chicken pieces; thus "chicarrones de pollo."

1 3-pound chicken, cut up	5 tablespoons dark rum
5 tablespoons soy sauce	Salt and pepper
Juice and grated rind of 1 lime	6-8 tablespoons flour
	Lemon slices for garnish

Chop the wings, thighs, and breasts of the chicken in half. Chop the bone ends off the drumsticks. (This should give you 14 pieces.) Place the pieces in a deep bowl.

Mix the soy sauce, grated rind and juice of 1 lime, and rum in a bowl and pour over the chicken pieces, coating them well, then set aside for 2 hours or more.

Blend the salt and pepper with the flour and roll the chicken pieces in it. Now heat the oil to fairly high temperature and fry the chicken pieces, turning to brown all sides for 8 minutes. When completely done, garnish with lemon slices and serve with hot white rice. Serves 4.

CUBA

PASTEL DE MAIZ—Chicken and Corn Pie

4 cups fresh corn kernels	2 tablespoons peanut oil
8 tablespoons butter	2 onions, minced
1 tablespoon sugar	10 fresh tomatoes, peeled, seeded,
4 egg yolks	and chopped
1 3-pound chicken, cut up	1 tablespoon seedless raisins
2-3 cups water (to cover)	1 tablespoon pimento
2 teaspoons salt	4-6 stuffed green olives, chopped
12 prunes, pitted	1 tablespoon capers
	2 hard cooked eggs, sliced thinly

Purée the corn in a blender for about 30 seconds. Over moderate heat melt the butter in a skillet and stir in the puréed corn and sugar. Mix thoroughly, then reduce the heat to low and cook slowly for 20-25 minutes. Stir occasionally. When done set aside in a bowl to cool, then whip the egg yolks and stir into the corn.

Place the chicken pieces in a kettle and add water to cover. Add salt and bring to the boil. Skim off the scum as it rises, then reduce the heat and cook, covered, for 45 minutes over low heat. When done remove the chicken pieces and strip the meat, discarding skin and bones. Cut the meat into bite-sized pieces and set aside. Retain the chicken stock.

Place the pitted prunes in a saucepan and cover with some of the hot chicken stock. Let the prunes soak for 10-12 minutes off the heat, then drain and set aside.

Preheat the oven to 350° F. Pour about half (or more) of the corn mixture into a shallow baking dish and spread into a thin, even layer across the bottom and up the sides. Heat the oil in a large skillet and slowly cook the onions until golden, then add the chopped tomatoes. Cook over low heat for 10 minutes, until the liquid cooks down somewhat and the mixture begins to thicken. Add this to the chicken meat in the bowl along with the prunes, raisins, chopped olives, pimentos, and capers. Mix thoroughly and pour into the corn-lined baking dish, spreading evenly. Top with the sliced hard cooked eggs and spread the remaining corn mixture over the top.

Bake in the oven for about 4-5 minutes, until the top is a rich and golden brown. Serve directly from the baking dish. Serves 4-6.

GUADELOUPE/MARTINIQUE

COLUMBO DE POULET—Chicken Curry

Over a hundred years ago, there was a rather large influx of Hindu and Moslem workers into the Lesser Antilles islands. Their descendants are still there and still practice the cooking of their forebears; however, they have added local ingredients to arrive at some very unusual tastes. *Le Columbo* is a classic example of the culinary wedding of the Indian style and that of the West Indies. (The mango, tamarind pulp, taro, and chayote may be found in Latin American and specialty stores.)

1 3-pound chicken, cut up	1 teaspoon turmeric
5 tablespoons butter or oil	1 cup dry white wine
2 onions, peeled and chopped	1 cup fresh chicken stock
3 cloves garlic, minced	1 tablespoon tamarind pulp
½-1 hot red pepper (to taste), seeded and chopped	1 mango, peeled and chopped
	1 pound taro, peeled and sliced
1 teaspoon ground coriander	½ pound West Indian pumpkin
½ teaspoon ground cumin	(or Hubbard squash)

1 teaspoon mustard powder
1 chayote (squash), peeled and
  sliced
Salt and pepper

½ pound eggplant, peeled and
  sliced
2 tablespoons dark Jamaican rum
1 teaspoon lime juice

Heat the butter or oil in a large skillet and brown the chicken pieces over moderate heat for about 8 minutes on a side. Remove to a large casserole or Dutch oven. In the same pan sauté the onions over low heat for 3 minutes, then add to the chicken with all the remaining ingredients except the rum and lime juice. Cover and cook over low heat for 1 hour. Before serving, add the rum and lime juice and stir several times. Serve right from the pot over white rice. Serves 6-8.

HAITI

POULET ROTI A LA CREOLE—
Roast Chicken, Creole Style

4 tablespoons butter
1 clove garlic, minced
1 tablespoon chopped onion
3 tablespoons dark Jamaican rum
Juice and grated rind of 1 lime
1 teaspoon brown sugar
Large pinch nutmeg

1 hot red pepper (or less), minced
Salt and freshly ground pepper
2 cups shredded white bread,
  crusts removed
1 cup fresh chicken stock
Parsley sprigs or watercress for
  garnish

Preheat the oven to 350°F. Sauté the garlic for ½ minute in 2 tablespoons of butter, then remove with a slotted spoon and discard. Add the chopped onion and sauté for 2 minutes, until golden, then remove the pan from the heat.

Add 2 tablespoons of rum, ½ the lime juice, the lime rind, brown sugar, nutmeg, red pepper, and a little salt and black pepper, then add the breadcrumbs and stir the pan until all ingredients are mixed well. Now stuff the bird and skewer or truss the cavities.

Place the chicken on a rack in a roasting pan and pour over it the remaining rum and lime juice and dot the breast and thighs with 2 tablespoons of butter. Cover and roast for 1½ hours, basting every 10-12 minutes with the pan juices. Remove the cover to let the breast brown during the last 15 minutes.

When the chicken is done, remove it to a warm platter and set aside.

Deglaze the pan with 1 cup of chicken stock, scraping the brown particles from the bottom of the pan. Check the seasoning, then pour into a sauceboat. Garnish the bird with parsley or watercress and serve. Serves 4-6.

MEXICO

POLLO EN NOGADO—Chicken in Nut Sauce

1 3-pound chicken, cut up	1 slice white bread, cut into
1 quart water	½-inch cubes
1 stalk celery, sliced	½ cup walnuts, shelled
3 onions	2 tablespoons oil or butter
1 bay leaf	1 clove garlic, minced
Salt and pepper	⅛ teaspoon ground cinnamon
4 green ancho chilies, sliced, seeded, and deveined	⅛ teaspoon ground cloves
	½ teaspoon oregano
1 cup boiling chicken stock	1 large tomato, peeled, seeded, and chopped

Place the chicken pieces in a large kettle and cover with the water. Bring to the boil and skim off the scum as it rises, then add the celery, 1 quartered onion, bay leaf, and a little salt. Reduce the heat to low and cook the chicken for 45-50 minutes. Do not cover.

Nut Sauce

While the chicken cooks, prepare the sauce: Cover the sliced chilies with 1 cup of boiling stock and let sit for 30 minutes. Fry the cubes white bread and walnuts in oil for several minutes, until they are toasted. Remove to drain, then put into a blender. Add the garlic, 2 chopped onions, cinnamon, cloves, oregano, tomato, and a little salt and pepper. Blend at high speed to form a purée. Add the chilies and the soaking liquid and blend again for 30 seconds. Now pour the purée into a large skillet and cook over moderate heat for 10-12 minutes, stirring occasionally.

When the chicken is done, pour off the pan liquid and strain, reserving 2½ cups. Stir the reserved stock into the sauce and blend thoroughly. Then add the chicken pieces. Be sure each piece is thoroughly coated. Reduce the heat to low and simmer for 15 minutes or so until the sauce thickens somewhat. You should turn the pieces several times during this last stage. Serve the chicken on a warm platter with the sauce poured over. Serves 4.

CENTRAL AMERICA

POLLO EN SALSADE ACEITANAS—
Chicken in Olive Sauce

1 3-pound chicken, cut up	16 large stuffed olives, sliced
2 cloves garlic, minced	3 pimentos, sliced
4 tablespoons oil	Salt and pepper
2 large tomatoes, peeled, seeded, and chopped	½ cup fresh chicken stock

In a large skillet with a cover, bring the oil to moderate heat and brown the garlic for 2-3 minutes. Remove with a slotted spoon and discard. Add the chicken pieces and brown on all sides slowly for 10-12 minutes.

Olive Sauce

Put the tomatoes, olive slices, pimentos, salt, pepper, and chicken stock in a bowl and mix well. Pour the mixture over the chicken pieces and cover. Reduce the heat to low and cook for 1 hour. Serves 4.

MEXICO

POLLO PIBIL—Pit-Roasted Chicken

A *pib* is an underground oven much the same as the Polynesian *imu* or *hima'a*. Stones are placed in the bottom of a large pit or trench and brought to high heat by means of a roaring wood fire. When ready, the meat (pork, chicken, turkey, or fish) is wrapped in banana leaves; then, these packages are put in a pan or fireproof bowl and placed on the stones. The pit is then covered with wet sacking and then with dirt to seal in the heat. The meat is left to steam for several hours, whereupon the cover is removed and the meat is served.

Pibs are very common in Yucatán, where they've been used since the days of the Mayans. It isn't recommended that the average person attempt to cook this dish as the Mayans did, because preparing a pib requires special knowledge and skill. The recipe that follows suggests the use of foil, but the dish can also be simulated quite well by simply steaming the chicken or turkey in a tightly covered skillet.

Pollo pibil requires in its seasoning achiote seeds. These can be found in Mexican-American markets and frequently in specialty stores in metropolitan areas. If you don't find them, omit them.

1 tablespoon achiote seeds
½ cup water
½ teaspoon cumin seeds
2 cloves garlic, minced
1 teaspoon oregano
¼ teaspoon ground allspice
Salt and freshly ground pepper
½ cup Seville orange juice (or substitute, page 336)

1 3-pound chicken, skinned, boned, and cut into large bite-sized pieces
4-6 pieces of foil, 5″ x 8″
2 tablespoons oil or butter
1 onion, chopped finely
1 tomato, peeled, seeded, and chopped
8-12 tortillas

The day before, put the achiote seeds in a saucepan with ½ cup of water and bring to the boil. Reduce the heat to moderate and cook for 5 minutes, then remove and set aside for an hour or more to cool completely. Now drain and crush the seeds in a mortar. Put the crushed achiote, cumin, garlic, oregano, allspice, salt and pepper, and orange juice (or substitute) in a blender and grind to a smooth paste.

Now place the chicken pieces in a bowl and mix in the seasoning paste. Turn well to coat each piece. Place one piece of chicken and 3 or 4 tablespoons of the paste in the center of a piece of foil and fold into a package. Continue this until the chicken and paste are used up. Place the packages in the refrigerator and let marinate for at least 12 hours.

Preheat the oven to 375° F. Heat the oil over a moderate to low fire and gently fry the onion for 2-3 minutes. Add the tomato and cook for another 3 minutes. Now unwrap the packages and spoon the tomato and onion mixture evenly into each. Rewrap and place them in the oven on a large cookie sheet. Cook for 1 hour. About 15 minutes before the pollo pibil is done, wrap the tortillas in a damp towel and then, tightly, in foil. Place in the oven and let them warm.

Serve immediately. The packages should be passed directly to your guests for them to unwrap. The meat is eaten with the tortillas, which should be covered and kept warm in a bread basket. Serves 4-6.

MEXICO

MOLE POBLANO DE GUAJOLOTE—
Turkey (or Chicken) in Chili and Chocolate Sauce

Chili peppers and chocolate in a sauce make as unusual a combination as there is anywhere, but the result is outstanding. This is Mexico's traditional Christmas dinner.

1 12-pound turkey, cut up
1 quart water
2 cloves garlic
2 onions, sliced
1 carrot, scraped and cut into 1-inch pieces
1 stalk celery, cut into 1-inch pieces
1 bay leaf
Salt and pepper
⅔ cup oil
2 tortillas
½ cup peanuts or almonds

1 tablespoon hot red chili pepper, chopped
3 tablespoons sesame seeds
1 teaspoon aniseed
½ cup raisins
2 green peppers, seeded and chopped
1 1-inch stick cinnamon, crushed
1 teaspoon ground coriander
¼ teaspoon ground clove
6 tomatoes, peeled, seeded, and chopped
3 ounces unsweetened chocolate, grated
Parsley sprigs for garnish

Place the turkey pieces in a large kettle and cover with the water. Bring to the boil and skim off the scum as it rises, then reduce the heat to low. Add 1 clove of garlic, 1 sliced onion, the carrot, celery, bay leaf, and a good sprinkling of salt and pepper. Cover and simmer for about 2 hours. Remove from the heat and place the turkey pieces in a large skillet with ½ cup oil. Strain the stock and reserve 4 cups.

Over moderate heat, brown the turkey on all sides for 8-10 minutes, then set aside. Fry the tortillas in the skillet for 2 minutes on each side, then set aside to drain. Pour off the oil and cook the peanuts (or almonds) for 2-3 minutes, then remove with a slotted spoon and set aside.

Crumble the tortillas into an electric blender, then add the nuts, chili pepper, sesame seeds, aniseed, and raisins and blend until all ingredients are well mixed.

Pour the remaining oil into the skillet and genly sauté the second sliced onion, the second garlic clove, and the chopped green peppers, for 4 or 5 minutes.

When done, combine the onion, garlic, and green peppers in a bowl with the blender ingredients. Add the cinnamon, coriander, and clove and mix well. Now pour in 4 cups of retained stock and continue stirring. Add the tomatoes and the grated chocolate. When blended thoroughly, pour into the original kettle, bring to the boil, then reduce heat, cover, and cook slowly for 12-15 minutes. Stir the pot every minute or so.

Now, add the turkey pieces and coat with the sauce. Simmer for 15 minutes, turning the pieces several times, until hot. Arrange the pieces on a platter, sprinkle with the remaining sesame seeds, and garnish with parsley. Serve with rice. Serves 6-8.

CENTRAL AMERICA

CHICKEN AND CHILI SOUP

2 tablespoons butter or olive oil
2 medium green chili peppers, peeled, seeded, and cut into thin strips
1 onion, chopped coarsely

8 cups chicken broth
Salt and pepper
1 cup cooked chicken, cut into thin 1-inch strips
4 tortillas, cut into thin 1-inch strips

Heat 1 tablespoon butter or oil in a skillet and cook the onion and chili for about 3 minutes over low heat. Pour the chicken broth into a kettle and bring to the boil. Reduce the heat to low, then add the cooked onions and chilies and the strips of chicken meat. Sprinkle with a little salt and pepper.

Heat the remaining butter or oil and fry the tortilla strips until brown. Set aside to drain. When the soup is hot, serve it in individual soup plates with a few of the tortilla chips floating on top. Serves 4-6.

MEXICO

ENCHILADAS DE POLLO CON SALSA ROJAS—
Chicken Enchiladas with Red Sauce

An enchilada is much like a taco. A tortilla is wrapped around a filling, but then it is topped with a sauce and shredded cheese and baked, whereas a taco is fried.

Salsa Rojas

4 tablespoons olive oil	3 large tomatoes, peeled and chopped
1 clove garlic, minced	
1 onion, minced	4 tablespoons tomato sauce
2 tablespoons hot green chilies, diced	Salt

Filling

1 onion, minced	½ cup water
1 clove garlic, minced	1 tablespoon red wine vinegar
3 large tomatoes, peeled and chopped	12 tortillas
2 cups cooked chicken, diced	½ cup jack or cheddar cheese, shredded

First make the sauce: Heat the oil in a skillet and gently cook 1 clove of garlic (remove and discard when done) and then 1 onion for 3-4 minutes. Add the chilies, 3 chopped tomatoes, tomato sauce, and sprinkle with salt. Simmer over low heat for 10 minutes. Remove from the fire when done and keep warm.

While the sauce cooks, prepare the filling. Combine the onion, garlic, and tomatoes in a saucepan, then add the chicken and water and sprinkle with a little more salt. Cook over a low flame for 10 minutes, then stir in the vinegar and simmer for 10 more minutes.

Preheat the oven to 350°F. Prepare the enchiladas by dipping a tortilla into the sauce and then spooning 2 tablespoons of the chicken mixture across the center. Roll the tortilla tightly and place in a shallow, greased baking dish, seam side down. Do each tortilla this way and arrange in the dish, then pour the remaining sauce over all, spreading it evenly. Sprinkle the shredded cheese across the top of the enchiladas and place in the oven for 10 minutes, or until the cheese melts. Makes 12 enchiladas.

Note: The variations on this dish are numerous. A Green Enchilada, for example, is made by adding avocado and chopped green peppers. Also try it with a little sour cream, or raisins, or nuts.

MEXICO

POLLO EN ADOBO—Chicken in Spicy Sauce

An *Adobo* is a spicy, sourish sauce that can be used with chicken, turkey, pork, veal, and even beef. This is a cousin of the Philippine classic, but because of the chili peppers, the taste is much different. This recipe calls for ancho chilies, the dried poblana chili. These are relatively mild and are available in most netropolitan specialty stores, or in areas where there is a sizable Mexican population. If you don't find them, use canned green chilies.

6 green ancho chilies, sliced, seeded, and deveined
1 cup fresh chicken stock
4 whole cloves, or ¼ teaspoon ground cloves
¼ teaspoon ground cinnamon
6 peppercorns
1 teaspoon salt

¼ teaspoon cumin seeds, or pinch ground cumin
3 cloves garlic, minced
2 tablespoons white vinegar
4 medium tomatoes, peeled, seeded, and chopped
3 onions, chopped
¼ cup olive oil (or less)
1 3-pound chicken, cut up

Bring the stock to the boil in a saucepan, then pour over the cleaned chilies in a bowl. Let sit for 30 minutes, then pour the chilies and stock into a blender and purée for 20-30 seconds. Add the cloves, cinnamon, peppercorns, salt, cumin, garlic, vinegar, tomatoes, and 2 chopped onions and purée for 30 seconds, until a smooth paste is formed.

Now heat 1 tablespoon of olive oil in a medium skillet and pour in the sauce. Cook over moderate heat for 10-12 minutes, stirring several times. When the sauce is fairly thick it is done. Remove and keep warm.

Bring the remaining oil to moderate heat in a large skillet and brown the chicken pieces, a few at a time, for 10-12 minutes. While the chicken cooks preheat the oven to 375° F.

Place the browned chicken pieces in a casserole and pour the warm sauce over. Cover and bake in the oven for 30-40 minutes. When done, remove the cover and sprinkle the last chopped onion over the chicken. Serve directly from the casserole with boiled white rice. Serves 4.

MEXICO

TOSTADOS DE POLLO—Chicken Tostados

A tostado is nothing more than a tortilla that has been fried until it becomes crisp. This usually takes only a couple of minutes and can be done well beforehand to save time. As with tacos, enchiladas, and other Mexican dishes, a great variety of tostado dishes find their way to the Mexican table. This one is made with chicken, tomatoes, and chilies, but other meats can be substituted, and almost any vegetable can be used also.

Tostados
12 tortillas	Oil or butter for frying

Tomato and Chili Sauce
1 cup tomato sauce	1 tablespoon red wine vinegar
1 tablespoon green chilies, seeded and chopped	¼ teaspoon oregano
	¼ teaspoon ground coriander
	1 tablespoon onion, minced

Filling
1 tablespoon olive oil	Shredded lettuce
1 small onion, minced	4 pimentos, chopped
1 cup tomatoes, peeled, seeded, and chopped	1 cup avocado, cut into ½-inch cubes
2 cups cooked chicken, diced	Green stuffed olives
Salt	3-4 radishes, sliced thinly

First, fry the tortillas in hot oil for about 2 minutes on a side. Remove to drain, keeping them flat.

Next make the sauce: Combine all the ingredients in a bowl and blend thoroughly.

Start the filling by heating 1 tablespoon of olive oil in a skillet and cooking the onion slowly for 3-4 minutes. Now add the tomatoes and chicken and cook for 5 minutes, stirring well. Sprinkle with a little salt.

Stir the sauce into the skillet, blend well, and cook for 5 more minutes. Pour into a sauceboat. Place a little shredded lettuce on top of a fried tortilla and spoon some of the chicken mixture on top of that. Sprinkle on a little pimento, a few avocado cubes, several olives, and some radish slices and serve. Spoon on the sauce at the table. Serves 12.

CENTRAL AMERICA

TAMALE DE POLLO—Chicken Tamales

Tamales are meat and/or cornmeal mixtures wrapped in corn-husks and then steamed. Their origins go back to the beginnings of Central American civilization and, though most popularly associated with Mexico's cuisine, they are eaten all through Central America.

2 cups cooked chicken, minced	2½ cups fresh chicken stock
1 tablespoon salt	4 cups cornmeal
1 onion, minced	1 cup olive oil
2 cloves garlic, minced	12-16 cornhusks, trimmed
3 green chilies, sliced, seeded, and deveined	Boiling water

Mix the chicken, salt, onion, garlic, and chilies in a saucepan with ½ cup of chicken stock. Cover and simmer for 15 minutes. Meanwhile, pour the cornmeal into a large bowl and stir in 1 cup of stock and the olive oil. Beat well for 5 minutes, then add the remaining stock. Beat again for 5-10 minutes.

Now dip the cornhusks into boiling water for a few seconds, then remove and dry. Spread the cornmeal on one husk to a thickness of about ¼ inch, then spoon 1-2 tablespoons of the meat mixture on top. Fold the sides of the corn husk in, then fold the ends together, making an envelope. Tie with a string.

When all the tamales are prepared, bring the water back to the boil in a steamer and place the tamales on a rack above the water. Cover and steam for 1 hour. Serve them on a platter to be unwrapped and eaten by the guests. (The Indians ate tamales with beans and corn, but rice is excellent also.) Serves 4-6.

MEXICO

TACOS DE POLLO—Chicken Tacos

A *taco* is a sandwich and is standard fare for everyone in Mexico, rich or poor. Starting with the most basic of all Mexican foods, the tortilla, a taco combines meat, sauce, cheese, vegetables, nuts, and virtually anything else in an endless variety. Tacos have become extremely popular in the United States, spreading from the West and

Southwest, where the association with Mexico has always been strongest.

½ cup olive oil
1 clove garlic, minced
1 onion, chopped
1 cup tomatoes, peeled and
  chopped
2 cups chicken (preferably white
  meat), shredded or diced
Salt and pepper

2-4 red or green chili peppers,
  seeded and chopped
¼ cup grated jack or cheddar
  cheese
Shredded lettuce
12 tortillas
Avocado cubes
Green olives

Heat 2-3 tablespoons of oil in a skillet and slowly cook the garlic for 1 minute, then remove with a slotted spoon and discard. Next cook the onion for 2 or 3 minutes, then add the tomatoes, chicken, salt and pepper, and the chili peppers. Cook for 2-3 minutes until heated through.

Spread 2 tablespoons of filling and 1 teaspoon of grated cheese on each tortilla. Roll up and place on a platter seam side down. Prepare all the tortillas in this manner.

Now bring the remaining oil to medium heat in a large skillet and carefully place in 2 or 3 tacos seam side down. Fry for a minute or so until crisp, turning once, then repeat with the remaining tacos until complete. Serve with shredded lettuce, avocado cubes, and olives. Serves 4-6.

Note: In America, a more popular way of making a Taco is by frying the tortilla for 30 seconds on each side in hot oil. Before the tortilla gets crisp it is folded in half. The chicken is spooned in first, then some shredded lettuce, 1 or 2 tablespoons of salsa rojas (page 331) and 1 tablespoon of shredded cheese. This taco is then eaten just like a sandwich.

MEXICO

TORTA COMPUESTA—Mexican Sandwich
This is another and perhaps more modern sandwich from Central and Southern Mexico. An American or European influence is obvious in that a hard roll is used rather than a tortilla. One of the ingredients is *queso fresco*—fresh cheese—a creamy moist cheese that

is not found outside of Mexico. A more than adequate substitute, however, is California's Monterey Jack.

Sliced chicken breast
Sliced avocado
Green chili pepper, chopped
Sliced cheese

Frijoles Refritos (Refried Beans)

1 cup pinto beans	½ (or less) red hot chili pepper,
1 small onion, diced	seeded and diced
Boiling water	Salt and pepper
	2 slices bacon, diced
	1 small clove garlic, minced

Wash the beans, then soak in cold water overnight.

When the beans are ready to be cooked, drain them and place in a kettle. Add the diced onion to the pot, then cover the beans with boiling water and cook for 20 minutes over moderate heat, or until done.

Now drain the beans and mash them with a fork. Add the chili pepper (to taste) and a little salt and pepper and stir until well blended, then set aside.

In a large skillet, brown the bacon bits, and then the garlic, then add in the beans and cook, stirring often, until they turn brown.

This will make enough for 4-6 tortas.

To make each torta, split a hard roll in half and lay on one-half a spoonful of frijoles refritos, then a slice or two of chicken breast meat, several thin slices of avocado, 1 teaspoon chopped green chili pepper, and a good slice of cheese. Butter the other half or sprinkle it with a few drops of olive oil. Close the sandwich and eat it with your fingers. Serves 4-6.

MEXICO

POLLO EN JUGO DE NARANJA—Chicken in Orange Juice

From Yucatán comes this blending of the Old World and the New. The original recipe calls for Seville oranges, which are thick-skinned and rough and have a rather bitter flavor. Finding them in this country is a difficult task at best, as they are grown and used almost exclusively for marmalade. One reasonable substitute is equal parts of orange, lemon, and grapefruit juice with a little grated grapefruit rind, to make about 1 cup.

1 3-pound chicken, cut up	½ cup pineapple, chopped
4 tablespoons oil	1-2 tablespoons sugar
Salt and pepper	1 cup dry white wine
1 cup Seville orange juice (or	⅛ teaspoon ground cloves
substitute)	⅛ teaspoon ground cinnamon
½ cup raisins	⅓ cup blanched almonds,
	skinned and chopped finely

Preheat the oven to 350° F. Bring the oil to moderate heat in a skillet. Rub each piece of chicken with salt and pepper, then brown slowly on all sides for 10-12 minutes.

Combine the orange juice (or substitute), raisins, pineapple, sugar, wine, ground clove, and cinnamon and blend together thoroughly. Place the chicken in an ovenproof baking dish, then pour the sauce over and around the pieces. Bake for 40 minutes. Turn the chicken onto a warm serving platter and pour on the sauce. Sprinkle with almonds. This dish is excellent with rice. Serves 4.

CENTRAL AMERICA

CASEROLA DE POLLO Y ELOTE—
Chicken and Corn Casserole
This basic Central American casserole is made equally well with turkey or duck.

4 tablespoons oil	1½ cups chicken stock
1 3-pound chicken, cut up	1½ cups fresh corn kernels
Salt and pepper	4-6 green ancho chilies, sliced,
4 tablespoons flour	seeded, and deveined
	8 green stuffed olives, sliced

Preheat the oven to 350° F. Bring the oil to moderate heat. Rub the chicken pieces with salt and pepper and brown slowly for 10-12 minutes on all sides. Set aside and keep warm.

Mix the flour, stock, corn, and chilies in a saucepan, season with a little salt and pepper, then cook over moderate heat for 10 minutes.

Place the chicken pieces in a casserole and pour in the corn and chili sauce. Cover and bake in the oven for 40 minutes. When done, garnish with sliced olives and serve right from the pot. Serves 4.

Brazil

XIN-XIN—Bahian Chicken and Shrimp Stew

This is Bahian cooking at its best. Dried shrimp and dende, the oil from the West African palm, give this dish its characteristic flavor and color, and both can be found in specialty food stores.

1 cup dried, peeled shrimp	1 small onion, chopped finely
1 3-pound chicken, cut up	1 teaspoon ground coriander
Salt and pepper	seeds
1 clove garlic, minced	1-2 red or Tabasco peppers,
6-8 sprigs fresh parsley, chopped	minced
finely	⅔ cup dende oil
	2 cups water

Soak the shrimp in water for 2-3 hours, then drain and grind them to a paste in a blender. Place the chicken in a large kettle and sprinkle with salt and pepper. Add the shrimp paste, minced garlic, parsley, onion, coriander, peppers, dende oil, and water.

Bring the pot to the boil, then reduce the heat to low, cover, and cook for 1 hour. When done, serve on a platter with rice. Serves 4.

Chile

ESCABECHE DE GALLINA—Pickled Chicken

Breast meat of 3 whole chickens, skinned and boned (retain the bones)	Salt and freshly ground pepper
	¾ cup white wine
	½ cup fresh chicken stock
¾ cup olive or peanut oil	5 tablespoons white vinegar
2 onions, sliced thinly	Pinch cayenne pepper
¼ cup pimento, chopped finely	3 sprigs parsley, chopped
4 medium carrots, scraped and chopped	Lemon slices for garnish

Coat the bottom of a casserole or Dutch oven with 5 tablespoons oil and place in 1/3 of the chicken meat. Spread a layer of onions, 1 tablespoon pimento, and about ⅓ of the chopped carrots over the meat, then sprinkle with a little salt and pepper. Place on top of this another layer of meat and then the vegetables, and season, and then another layer of each. Arrange the chicken bones across the top layer, then pour over the wine. Cover tightly and cook over low heat for 3 hours.

While the chicken cooks, combine the remaining oil, wine, stock, vinegar, salt, and cayenne pepper in a bowl and stir well. Cover and place the bowl in the refrigerator.

When the chicken is done, remove the bones and allow the pot to cool uncovered. When cool, replace the cover and refrigerate overnight.

Unmold the chicken just before you intend to serve it. Garnish with chopped parsley and lemon slices, and serve the sauce separately. Serves 4.

BOLIVIA/PERU

AJI DE GALLINA—Spicy Chicken

Aji is the fiery red chili pepper cultivated originally by the Incas, and which today finds almost everyday use in the cooking of Bolivia, Chile, Peru, and Ecuador.

Aji de Gallina is cooked with *annato* oil, one of the foundations of South American (and Caribbean) cooking. Called *aceite de achiote,* the oil is made by heating achiote seeds in a little oil, and then putting it away for a day or so in the refrigerator. When strained it is ready for use as a coloring (red) and flavoring (hot) agent for any meat, fish, or chicken sauce. Just combine 2 parts vegetable or peanut oil to 1 part achiote seeds (which you will find in specialty stores), heat for a minute or so, then cool, bottle, and chill. Strain before using.

6-8 slices fresh white bread, trimmed of crusts and shredded finely
1 cup light cream
⅔ cup olive or peanut oil
1 3-pound chicken, cut up
1-2 dried red chili peppers
2 large onions, minced
1 clove garlic, minced
2 cups fresh chicken stock

2 large tomatoes, peeled and chopped
2 tablespoons annato oil
1 teaspoon salt
¼ teaspoon freshly ground pepper
6-8 tablespoons grated cheese
12 ripe olives
6 hard cooked eggs, halved
Parsley sprigs

Soak the bread in cream, then mash it into a paste. Heat the oil in a large, deep skillet or Dutch oven and brown the chicken pieces evenly over low heat.

Soak the chili peppers, while the chicken cooks, for 15 minutes, then seed and grind them to a paste in a mortar or blender.

When the chicken is done, remove the pieces and keep warm (strip the meat if you wish) and lightly brown the onions and garlic for 4-5 minutes, until golden. Now add the chili paste, tomatoes, annato oil, and the bread paste. Cook for 4-5 minutes, stirring constantly. Now add the stock and season with salt and pepper.

Bring the pan to the boil and return the chicken. Stir the pot several times to blend all ingredients, then cover, reduce the heat to low, and simmer for 1 hour. Sprinkle liberally with cheese and cook, covered, for another few minutes, until the cheese melts, then serve on a warm platter garnished with olives, egg halves, and parsley sprigs. Serves 4.

BRAZIL

VATAPA DE GALINHA—Chicken Vatapa

Another from the Afro-Brazilian kitchen, *Vatapa* is a favorite throughout South America and the Caribbean as a fish, shellfish, chicken, or combination dish. It features the ever-present dende oil and freshly made, thick coconut milk. This recipe also calls for *malagueta* peppers, a small fiery-hot pepper from Brazil. They will be difficult to find, but red chili peppers may be substituted.

2 medium onions, chopped finely
2 tablespoons butter or oil
3 medium tomatoes, peeled, seeded, and chopped
1-2 malagueta peppers, or hot red peppers

1 3-pound chicken, cut up
5 cups water
1 cup thick coconut milk (page 82)
½ pound ground roasted peanuts
1 cup dried ground shrimp
½ cup dende oil

Sauté the onions in butter or oil in a large kettle for 3-4 minutes over low heat, then add the chopped tomatoes and continue cooking for another 1 minute or so. Now add the peppers, chicken pieces, and the water and cook, uncovered, for 1 hour. Remove the chicken to cool, then strip the meat, discarding the skin and bones.

Add the coconut milk to the pot, the ground peanuts, and then the dried shrimp. Season with a little salt and pepper, then cook slowly until the liquid begins to thicken. (If the liquid is too thin, thicken it with a little flour or cornstarch mixed in water.)

Return the chicken pieces to the pot and simmer for 3 minutes, then add the dende oil. Stir for a moment then serve. Serves 4.

BRAZIL

FRANGO AO MOLHO PARDO—Chicken in Brown Gravy
The base for the brown gravy is the chicken's blood, which means the chicken must be fresh killed and some of the blood saved. A kosher butcher can provide this, or, if possible, arrange to get the chicken freshly killed at a poultry farm. Be sure to stir the fresh blood into ½ cup or so of vinegar or it will coagulate, and store it in the refrigerator until ready to use. (If using chicken blood doesn't suit your taste, purée the chicken livers in a blender and use them instead.)

1 3-4-pound chicken, cut up	1 cup water
3 tablespoons butter or oil	1 large tomato, peeled and diced
Salt and pepper	1 teaspoon sugar
2 onions	1 tablespoon flour or cornstarch
1 bay leaf	for thickening, if necessary
1 tablespoon vinegar	Blood of 1 freshly killed chicken
½ cup chicken stock	or the bird's liver, puréed

Heat the butter or oil in a Dutch oven and brown the chicken pieces on all sides. Sprinkle with salt and pepper and add 1 onion, coarsely chopped, the bay leaf, vinegar, chicken stock, and water. Cover and cook over low heat. After 30 minutes, add the tomato and cook, covered, for another 30 minutes. Now slice the second onion very thinly and add to the pot. Re-cover and cook another 15-20 minutes.

When done, add the sugar, the blood (or puréed livers) and a little thickening if you wish. Simmer a moment, then serve. This goes well with rice. Serves 4.

COLOMBIA

ARROZ CON POLLO—Chicken and Rice

This Spanish masterpiece is also popular throughout South and Central America, but with a difference—Latin Americans add chili peppers. This dish, from Cartagena, Colombia, also illustrates the Latin method of browning rice before cooking it in water or stock.

⅓ cup olive or peanut oil
1 chicken, cut up
2 onions, chopped coarsely
2 cloves garlic, minced
1 cup white rice
4 large tomatoes, peeled, seeded, and chopped

1-2 red chili peppers (to taste), chopped
1 tablespoon salt
⅛ teaspoon freshly ground pepper
1½ cups fresh chicken stock
1 cup cooked ham, diced
3 pimentos, sliced

Preheat the oven to 325° F. Heat the oil in a Dutch oven and brown the chicken pieces on all sides for 10-12 minutes over moderate heat. Remove and set aside. Reduce the heat and lightly cook the onions and garlic for about 5 minutes. Remove with a slotted spoon and set aside. Now sprinkle in 1 cup of rice and brown lightly, stirring constantly with a spoon (about 5-6 minutes).

Return the chicken, onions, and garlic to the pot. Add the tomatoes, chili peppers, salt and pepper, and diced ham, then pour in the chicken stock. Cover and bake in the oven for 1½ hours.

Remove the cover and garnish with slices of pimento. Serve right from the Dutch oven. Serves 4.

BRAZIL

CUZCUZ DE GALINHA—Chicken Cuzcuz

This dish originated in the Middle East, and traveled with the sultan's armies to North Africa and Sicily over a thousand years ago. It came to Brazil in the sixteenth century with the slaves the Portuguese imported to work their plantations. Of course, the combination stewpot-steamer, the *couscousière (cuzcuzeiro* in Brazil) came with it.

Though cooked the same way, *couscous* and *cuzcuz* have become substantially different dishes. Instead of the semolina-like grain that the North Africans use, the Afro-Brazilians substitute cornmeal. Brazilians will usually add a chili pepper or two to their cuzcuz, which is absent from the Arab dish.

(See page 160 for instructions on how to cook with the cuzcuzeiro, or couscousière, or how to improvise a steam pot using a colander.)

1 3-pound chicken, cut up
Juice and grated rind of 1 lemon
6 tablespoons vinegar
5-6 tablespoons peanut oil
2 onions, chopped coarsely
1 clove garlic, minced
⅛ teaspoon ground coriander
   seeds

6 sprigs fresh parsley, chopped
   finely
1 teaspoon dried savory
Salt and freshly ground pepper
2 medium tomatoes, peeled,
   seeded, and chopped
1 cup fresh chicken stock

Place the chicken pieces in a large shallow pan or baking dish. In a saucepan, mix together the lemon juice and rind, vinegar, oil, onions, garlic, coriander, parsley, and savory, then add a little salt and fresh pepper. Bring this mixture to the boil, stir several times to blend thoroughly, then pour it over the chicken pieces. Turn each piece several times to coat, then cover and let sit for 6-8 hours or overnight. (Turn the pieces every hour or so to be sure each is marinated evenly.)

When the chicken is ready to cook, arrange the pieces in a Dutch oven or large casserole and pour in the marinade. Sprinkle with a little more salt and pepper, then bring the pot to the boil. Reduce the heat to low and add the tomatoes and stock, then cover and simmer for 1¼ hours. When done, remove the chicken, strain the cooking liquid, and return it to the pot. Strip the chicken meat and discard the skin and bones. Cut the meat into medium-sized chunks or shreds, place them in a bowl and cover, and keep warm.

Cuzcuz Preparation

½-¾ pound smoked, spicy pork
   sausage
2 tablespoons peanut oil
4 cups white cornmeal
1 cup boiling water
1 tablespoon salt
1 cup butter (2 sticks) or oil
6-8 sprigs fresh parsley, chopped

1-2 malagueta, Tabasco, or red
   chili peppers, seeded and
   minced
3-4 tomatoes, sliced
1 cup hearts of palm, sliced
12-15 green stuffed olives, sliced
3 hard cooked eggs, sliced
1 cup peas
Orange slices for garnish

Slice the sausage into ½-inch rounds and fry in a little oil for 4 or 5 minutes. Remove from the heat and set aside.

Preheat the oven to 350° F. Return the reserved chicken liquid to the fire and reheat, but don't boil. While it heats, spread the cornmeal on a cookie sheet and heat in the oven for about 5 minutes, stirring several times. When the meal just begins to brown, it has cooked enough. Remove from the oven and add to 1 cup of boiling salted water slowly, stirring constantly until the water is absorbed (about 2-3 minutes). Return to the oven and cook for 2 more minutes, then remove the pan and stir in 8 tablespoons (1 stick) of melted butter or oil.

When the chicken stock is hot, add the remaining butter, parsley, and peppers and stir to blend well. Now remove from the heat and sprinkle in the cornmeal mixture, stirring constantly. Stir, or knead (if cool enough), until you can form a small ball between your fingers. If it stays together, it's fine, but if it is too dry and falls apart, add just a little more stock until it is the right consistency.

Use a cuscuzeiro if you have one, or the substitute described on page 160. Fill the bottom pot partly with water, then fit on the top pot or colander, making sure it does not touch the water. Arrange slices of tomato, hearts of palm, and slices of egg and olive across the bottom of the colander, then spread a layer of the cuscuz mixture over that. Next arrange some of the shredded chicken and sausage rounds and ½ cup of peas on the cuscuz and follow with another layer of cuscuz. Now arrange another layer of tomatoes, hearts of palm, egg and olive slices, then spread another layer of cuscuz. On top of this spread the remaining peas, chicken, sausage, and any remaining vegetables, then cover with the last of the cuscuz. Cover the colander with a cloth and bring the water to a slow boil. Cook for 45 or 50 minutes, adding water to the bottom pot if it boils away.

When done, remove the cloth and unmold the cuscuz onto a serving plate. This is best done by inverting a plate and placing it over the colander, then inverting the colander. The cuscuz should unmold easily onto the plate, but if it doesn't, just tap the bottom of the colander gently once or twice.

Garnish with orange slices and serve along with the chicken, while hot. Serves 6-8.

ARGENTINA

CAZUELA CRIOLLA—Argentine Chicken Stew

Although the Argentines are overwhelmingly disposed toward beef, they have one dish that has become a national favorite. A *cazuela* is the pot the chicken cooks in, and what goes in it under the name *Cazuela Criolla* varies considerably according to the ingredients at hand and the cook.

1 3-pound chicken, cut up	1 cup pumpkin pieces
1 quart water	2 onions, sliced
1 tablespoon salt	2 cloves garlic
10 peppercorns	1 medium squash, sliced
6 medium potatoes, peeled and quartered	6 carrots, sliced in 1-inch pieces
	¼ cup parsley, chopped
½ cup raw rice	1 cup peas
1-2 red chili peppers, seeded and sliced	3 cobs fresh corn, cut in half
	3 tomatoes, peeled and quartered

Place the chicken in a large kettle and add the water. Bring to the boil, skimming off the scum as it rises, then add salt and peppercorns. Reduce the heat, cover, and cook for 30 minutes, then add the remaining ingredients. Return the cover and simmer for another 30-45 minutes. Serve when done right from the kettle. Serves 6.

BRAZIL

CANJA—Chicken and Rice Soup

Canja translates into something like "rice cream." In Portugal, where it originated, canja has distinct Arabic overtones. The Brazilian version is a far more substantial dish, and is an excellent example of the improvements the Afro-Brazilians made in Portuguese cookery.

1 4-5-pound chicken, cut up	2 large tomatoes, peeled and chopped
2 tablespoons butter or oil	
1 onion, coarsely chopped	¾ cup white rice
1 clove garlic, sliced	1 cup raw carrots, sliced thinly
2 quarts water	1 cup cooked ham, diced
Salt and pepper	4 sprigs fresh parsley, chopped

Heat the butter in a Dutch oven or large, deep skillet, and lightly brown the chicken pieces, onion, and garlic. Now add the water, half the parsley, the tomatoes, and a little salt and pepper. Bring the water to the boil, then reduce the heat to low, cover, and cook for 1 hour.

When done, remove the chicken pieces and strip away the meat, discarding the skin and bones. Cut the meat into strips and return to the pot. Stir in the rice and cook for 10 minutes, then add the carrots. Re-cover and cook an additional 10 minutes, then add the ham and cook 10 minutes longer.

Serve the canja in a tureen, sprinkled with chopped parsley. Serves 6.

❧ Chapter 10 ❧

The United States/Canada

With better organization and crucial assistance from friendly Indians, the New England Pilgrims fared far better than the Virginia settlers, so it was in New England that traditional American cooking began.

The core of the earliest American cuisine was corn and turkey, and without them the Pilgrims might not have survived their first winter. The Indians helped the Americans by showing them how to plant and cultivate maize (corn) and then to grind it into cornmeal or pound it into a sort of hominy called *nausamp* (or *samp*). From corn came the johnny-cake, corn bread, and an adaptation of the British hasty pudding, in which corn was used instead of oats. The Indians introduced the Pilgrims to the quahog, a clam not unlike the treasured oysters of British waters, and also showed them how to make a clambake by alternating layers of clams between layers of seaweed in a firepit.

But, once established, the early settlers turned to agriculture as their basic means of subsistence. And this rural mode of life set the tone for the emerging nation for the next two hundred years. Wheat came to America from Europe in the seventeenth century and so did the pig, and both, along with corn, provided the first commercial agricultural endeavor the early settlers enjoyed.

In the eighteenth century whaling and shipping became important industries along the eastern seacoast. The rum trade brought ships from Nova Scotia to Georgia into the West Indies, and this turned into the slave trade when rum was bartered in Africa for a cargo of human beings. American and Canadian captains profited heavily from this invidious traffic, but at the same time, they contributed to the early cuisines of both countries. At sea for months at a time, they fashioned their own recipes of chicken and fish, heavily laced with spices, which became known as "Country Captains," and every seaport from Halifax to Savannah claimed theirs to be the original. Though they used a wide variety of ingredients and a lot of imagination, Country Captains were all rather similar chicken or fish curries.

The slaves they brought to America were used as cheap labor for tobacco, sugar, and cotton plantations. The men worked the fields while the women tended the houses and children of their masters, and also did the cooking. Through the eighteenth and nineteenth centuries they developed Southern and Creole cooking, two of the more prominent of America's early regional cuisines.

Southern cooking started below the Mason-Dixon Line and traveled south and west to Texas as the country was settled. The dishes varied from one region to another, but basically it was hearty farm style cooking, featuring ham and pork dishes, fish and shellfish (near the seacoast), wild game, and, at first, a relatively sparse number of vegetables.

As the chicken became more plentiful in the South during the latter part of the eighteenth century and the early nineteenth, black Southern cooks discovered the versatility of its meat, and a whole tradition of chicken cookery began to emerge. Though this encompassed all the conventional methods of preparing the bird, it was the fried version that eventually became the South's tour de force. Southern Fried Chicken is undoubtedly the most famous chicken dish in America today and is served in homes and restaurants from coast to coast. As one would expect, it has its variations, several of which—Kentucky Fried, Maryland Fried, and Alabama Fried—are almost as well known as the original, and depending where you are in the South, that's where it's "best."

Early in America's history, a curious mixture of nationalities came to Louisiana to produce the Creole and "Cajun" cuisines. The Creoles of Louisiana were the French and Spanish elite who developed the sugar and cotton plantations and the storied affluence that grew up with them. The Cajuns came from Acadia, which is now the Canadian provinces of Nova Scotia and Prince Edward Island, and they brought a somewhat different French cooking with them, one that had its roots in Normandy, France. It was earthy, hearty food, heavily accented with shellfish and well seasoned, but less refined than Creole cooking at first. Now it's hard to tell them apart.

Two of Louisiana's most famous dishes are *Gumbo Filé* and *Jambalaya*; the first is Cajun and the second is Creole, and both feature chicken. Gumbo filé is an adaptation of the original chicken gumbo that was developed in other areas of the South. In Southern cooking it is made with okra (*n-ghumbo* in the Bantu tongue of Africa), which tends to thicken the dish more than add to the taste. In Louisiana, the

Cajuns borrowed the dried sassafras leaf from the Choctaw Indians, ground or pounded it to a powder, and then added it to the stew in place of okra just before it was served. Called *filé*, this powder gave the same slippery, smooth quality to the gumbo without thickening it quite so much.

Jambalaya is a true Creole dish; in fact there is no other which so typifies the Creole kitchen. It is an adaptation of the Spanish paella, but has overtones of France and Africa in it. The base of the word is *jambon,* which in French means ham, and the rest is *à la ya,* which comes from an African tongue and means rice. Nowhere, however, through the centuries did it lose the features of the original Spanish dish, which meant the presence of shellfish. Today, as in the past three centuries, jambalaya is rice-based, with sausage or ham, to which are added shrimp, mussels, crabs, lobster or crayfish, and, invariably chicken.

In the nineteenth century, America was growing rapidly, and regional cuisines were forming in virtually all parts of the country. In the South and Middle South, the farmers used every excuse to get together: political rallies, county fairs, horse races, fish fries, barn raisings, weddings, births, even funerals. The occasion always produced a mass cookout, and from these some of America's classic chicken dishes emerged. From Virginia came the Brunswick Stew. Originally made of rabbit, chickens became the favored meat as they became more abundant and rabbits fewer. Later, Kentucky Burgoo became famous as the dish for horse sales and political rallies. It's an enormous stew cooked outdoors in huge iron pots over wood fires from a recipe that starts with one ton of potatoes, peeled and diced, 200 pounds of chicken, and ends with "salt and pepper to taste."

Through the eighteenth and nineteenth centuries the settlers came to America in droves: Scandinavians to Minnesota, a fish country just like their own, and their cuisine still reflects it; the Germans to the Mid-Central states, again practicing what they did best in Europe— in this case it was dairy farming, fishing, and laying the table with huge satisfying meals; the Germans again to Pennsylvania and Ohio farms, but there with a more typically Eastern European cuisine; the Mexicans to the Southwest—but their influence had been there so long that even the Indians adopted their food, dress, and language; and the Chinese in the Far West—brought there originally to help build the nation's railroads, but who added that final international dimension to the country's cuisine.

With subtle exceptions only, the Canadian kitchen developed essentially in the same way. Born in the eastern Provinces of Canada with the coming of the explorers from France and England, the cuisine has a decided French flavor through Quebec, but otherwise it is very similar to that of New England and Great Britain, until one gets to the Great Lakes area, where Scandinavian and German influences become evident. Throughout most of Canada, cooking is little different from that of America.

Canada does have at least one element in her gastronomic armamentarium that she has stamped indelibly as her own—the Canada goose. Though these magnificent birds wing their way south across the United States in the autumn, their natural home is Canada. A freshly-killed Canada goose, served with an orange and wine gravy, is like no other in the world.

Country cooking, developed over several centuries, has turned out the regional cuisines that we consider traditional in America, but there is another style, just as American, that is probably better known on the international scene. This is the eating style of the city dwellers and suburbanites, reflecting at once the casual and yet frenetic lifestyle of its urban population. It is directly opposed to those of our ancestor nations, the French particularly, who make their midday meal a multi-coursed feast, complete with a bottle or two of wine. Not so the American city dweller (or for that matter his Canadian counterpart), for he has made the sandwich, the salad, the leftover, and the barbecue a cuisine in and of itself. Despite this almost calculated disrespect for the niceties of good eating, a number of unpretentious but excellent dishes have become part of the American/Canadian tradition. Chicken salad, for one, either hot or cold, is a widespread favorite as a sandwich spread, and is probably served at more ladies' luncheons than any other dish. Then there's the club sandwich, a three-decked affair, with turkey or chicken, bacon, and tomatoes, which is another favorite in homes and restaurants across the country. But the barbecue has become the symbol of American cooking for most of the world. It was conceived centuries ago on the steppes of ancient Tartary, but the grilling of meat over an open fire has been glorified by Americans and Canadians into an art form. Hamburgers and hot dogs undoubtedly share first place in popularity on the barbecue, but chicken, chops, and steak are not far behind.

The Jews have added an urban cooking tradition that is just as "old-world" in its origins as the others. Coming as it did from East Europe, the Jewish menu originally favored goose and duck, but through the years these birds have given way to chicken and turkey. Today, the heart and soul of the Jewish cuisine is chicken soup. Actually it starts out the same as any other, but the Jewish cook will add several chicken feet to the pot to build up the body and strengthen the character of the final product. Once done, the soup is a vehicle for a variety of accompaniments such as farfel, noodles, kreplach, mandelin, or knaidlach.

In North America, the popularity of chicken and other fowl extends beyond the table, to our everyday life and lexicon. During the dreary days of the Great Depression, for example, "chicken every Sunday" was a treat to look forward to; an American President in this century is said to have campaigned on the promise of "two chickens in every pot"; something that's easy to do is "duck soup"; and when one talks seriously, one "talks turkey"; good fortune comes to whomever breaks the chicken's wishbone correctly (is it the short or the long piece that wins?), and more often than not the weathervane on the barn is the silhouette of a cock. And finally, the chicken is involved in the ultimate philosophical puzzler—"which came first, the chicken or the egg?"

RECOMMENDED READING: Ruth Berolzheimer, Ed., *The United States Regional Cookbook* (Chicago: Culinary Arts Institute, 1947)

UNITED STATES

KENTUCKY BURGOO

This is one of the most startling dishes in the American repertoire. It originated in the Middle South and became extremely popular at political rallies, races, fairs, and farm gatherings. One man became so famous for his recipe that he was invited to various events, all over Kentucky, to supervise the preparation of incredible quantities of food, their seasonings, and finally the incantation over the food by a local preacher. The stew, which was cooked over open fires in enormous cauldrons, would feed hundreds. Such a stew is too big for most of us, so here's one of somewhat smaller dimensions:

2 3-pound chickens, cut up
2 pounds chuck beef
2 pounds lean pork
4 squirrels, cut up (optional)
1 pound veal
6 quarts water
Salt
4 carrots, cleaned and sliced
1 small head cabbage, cored and
  shredded
4 onions, peeled and quartered
4 green peppers, seeded and cut
  into strips
12 peppercorns
1 bouquet garni (page 257)
8 tomatoes, quartered
2 cups okra
2 cups corn kernels
2 cups fresh peas
4 potatoes, peeled and quartered

Place the chicken pieces, beef, pork, squirrels (if you use them), and veal in water in a large kettle. Sprinkle over 4 tablespoons salt and bring to the boil. Reduce heat to moderate and gently boil the pot for 2-2½ hours. When done remove the meat. Bone the chicken and squirrel pieces and cut all the meat into 1-inch cubes.

Return the cubed meat to the pot and add the carrots, cabbage, onions, pepper, 1 tablespoon salt, 12 peppercorns, and the bouquet garni. Reduce the heat to low and simmer for 45 minutes, then add the tomatoes, okra, corn, peas, and potatoes. Continue to simmer for another 30 minutes, turning the contents of the pot occasionally with a spoon. Serves 10-12.

United States

BRUNSWICK STEW

From the South comes this all-time classic. Originally, it was made in great quantities to feed large gatherings at political rallies, fairs, or other events where many people were on hand. The first Brunswick stew was made with rabbits, but this gave way to chicken as the basic meat, and so it remains today.

2 3-pound chickens, cut up	4 large tomatoes, skinned and
2 pounds beef (chuck) or veal	chopped
1 bone from baked Virginia ham	2 cups celery, chopped
Salt and freshly ground pepper	4 onions, peeled and quartered
3 quarts water	3 cups corn kernels
1 bay leaf	1 red pepper pod
1 teaspoon basil	4 large potatoes, peeled and
4 sprigs parsley	boiled
3 cups butter (or lima) beans	

Place the chicken pieces, the pieces of beef or veal, and the ham bone in a large (10-quart) kettle. Sprinkle with salt and several grindings of fresh pepper. Add the water, bay leaf, basil, and parsley and bring to the boil. Skim off any scum that rises, then reduce the heat to low and cook for 1½ hours. When the meat is done, remove it from the broth to a platter. Add the beans to the broth, along with the tomatoes, celery, and onions and cook for about 15 minutes, stirring every few minutes. While the vegetables cook, remove the skin and bones from the chicken and cut the meat into 1-inch cubes. Cut away any remaining ham from the bone and cut it into small pieces. Cut the beef or veal into cubes also. Now return all the meat to the kettle with the vegetables and add the corn. Continue simmering for 10-12 minutes, then add the red pepper pod and a little more salt and pepper. Mash the potatoes and stir into the stew, then cook, stirring constantly for 15 minutes. Serves 10-12.

United States/Canada

CHICKEN SANDWICHES

Across North America, the sandwich is probably the most commonly eaten everyday food, and its variety is endless. Two of the most popular include chicken.

Chicken (or Turkey) Club Sandwich

3 slices white bread	1 medium tomato, sliced
4 slices cold roast breast meat of chicken or turkey	Butter or mayonnaise
	Lettuce
4 strips lean bacon	Salt and pepper

Fry the bacon until crisp, then drain on a paper towel. Toast the bread, then spread butter or mayonnaise on each slice. Lay the chicken or turkey meat on one slice and sprinkle on just a little salt and pepper. Cover with the lettuce and the second piece of toast. On top of that lay the bacon and tomato slices (add a little more salt and pepper), more lettuce, then top with the third slice of toast. Cut diagonally into triangles and serve with dill pickle and cold potato or macaroni salad.

Chicken Salad Sandwich

4 tablespoons cold chicken salad (below)	Butter or mayonnaise (optional)
	Lettuce
	2 slices white bread

(You'll want to mash or dice the chicken cubes in the chicken salad recipe with the end of a fork so the mixture spreads evenly.)

Toast the bread and spread each slice with butter or mayonnaise. Now spread the cold chicken salad over one slice and top with lettuce and the second slice of toast. Serve with dill pickle and cold potato or macaroni salad. (An excellent addition is slices of hard cooked eggs over the chicken salad.)

UNITED STATES/CANADA

CHICKEN SALAD

This dish, hot or cold, is one of the most popular luncheon dishes in North America.

Hot Chicken Salad

2 cups cooked chicken meat, cubed	Salt and pepper
	1 cup mayonnaise
½ cup chopped, toasted nuts (almonds, cashews, or pistachios)	2 teaspoons onion, minced
	¼ cup pimento, chopped
1 cup thinly sliced celery	2 tablespoons lemon juice
½ cup green pepper, seeded and chopped	Paprika

Preheat the oven to 350° F. Mix all the ingredients (except paprika) thoroughly in a bowl, then turn into a baking dish. Cover and bake for 30 minutes. Remove the cover and sprinkle with paprika, then return to the oven and bake, uncovered, for 5 minutes. Serve right from the dish. Serves 6.

Alternative: Omit the paprika, but cover with grated cheese and bread cubes.

Cold Chicken Salad

2 cups cooked chicken meat, diced
1 cup diced celery
1 tablespoon lemon juice
⅓ cup mayonnaise

Salt and pepper
1 tablespoon onion, minced
Lettuce leaves
4-6 ripe tomatoes
Parsley sprigs for garnish

Combine the diced chicken and the celery in a bowl. Mix the lemon juice, mayonnaise, salt, pepper, and onion in a separate bowl, then stir into the chicken mixture. (Add a little more mayonnaise if you want it more moist.)

Arrange a large, fresh lettuce leaf on each plate and spoon some of the chicken salad into the center. Cut the tomatoes into wedges and curround each salad with 4 pieces, garnish with parsley sprigs, and serve. Serves 4-6.

Alternatives: Add chopped nuts, fruit (apples, pears, pineapple), coconut, curry powder, chutney, vegetables (peas, beans), or capers. Hard cook several eggs, then slice or halve them for another good accompaniment, or hollow out avocados or tomatoes and stuff with the salad.

United States

JELLIED CHICKEN RING (OR LOAF)

This is from the Pennsylvania Dutch country. The Mennonites cook the bird until done in water and then strip away the meat. They extract the essence from the skin and bones by returning them to the broth to simmer for an hour or so, thus giving it an extremely thick and rich texture, which jells naturally. Time-consuming—yes—but you'll end up with a much tastier ring or loaf than if you use gelatin.

1 5-6-pound stewing chicken	1 onion, peeled and quartered
1 quart water (or more)	1 carrot, cut into 1-inch pieces
Salt and pepper	1 stalk celery, cut into 1-inch
1 bay leaf	pieces (leaves and all)
	Parsley for garnish

Put the chicken into a kettle and add the water (it should just cover the bird). Bring to the boil and skim off the scum as it rises. Now add salt and pepper, bay leaf, onion, carrot, and celery, cover, and cook for 1½ hours. When done, remove the chicken to cool, then strip the meat.

Return bones to the broth and simmer covered for 1 hour. Now skim or blot all the fat from the broth (this is essential, or the jelly will have a cloudy, unappetizing appearance to it).

Shred the chicken into thin strips and pack it into a loaf pan or aspic ring. Pour in the broth, making sure it completely covers the meat. Now refrigerate until firmly jelled. (This can be done the day before.) Unmold on a serving plate and garnish with parsley. Serve with tomato wedges, sliced chilled cucumbers, cold sliced ham, and cold mayonnaise or other sauce. Serves 4-6.

UNITED STATES/CANADA

CHOP SUEY

One of the best-known dishes in Chinese-American restaurants, chop suey, isn't Chinese at all. It is cooked in the Chinese style, though, and according to legend credit for its invention goes to a Chinese cook in America who was asked at the last moment to prepare a meal for a number of guests. With little food in the pantry, he put together what he had, and to the delight of everyone, chop suey was born. In Canton the word *suey* means hash—and that's just what this is, chicken hash, Chinese style.

Breast meat of 1 chicken, skinned, boned, and shredded finely	½ teaspoon sugar
	Salt and pepper
⅓ cup peanut or sesame oil	1 cup celery, sliced very thinly
2 scallions, sliced thinly	½ cup bamboo shoots, sliced
2 cloves garlic, minced	thinly
1 slice fresh ginger, minced	½ cup bean sprouts
1 tablespoon sherry	1 tablespoon cornstarch dissolved
3 tablespoons soy sauce	in 2 tablespoons water

In a wok or large skillet, bring 3 tablespoons oil to moderately high heat and quickly fry the scallions, garlic, and ginger until lightly browned. Add the chicken shreds and continue frying for 3-4 minutes, stirring constantly. Remove the chicken and vegetables from the pan with a slotted spoon and set aside.

Make a sauce by combining the soy sauce, sherry, sugar, and a little salt and pepper.

Add the remaining oil and stir-fry the celery, bamboo shoots, and bean sprouts for 3 minutes, then return the chicken. Add the sauce and stir-fry for 1 more minute. Now add the cornstarch mixture and stir-fry for 1 more minute, then serve with rice and crisp fried noodles. Serves 4-6.

United States/Canada

CHICKEN A LA KING

2 tablespoons butter	1 cup light cream
4 large mushrooms, chopped finely	1 egg yolk
	Salt and pepper
½ green pepper, seeded and cut into coarse dice	Dash paprika
	1 cup cooked chicken (or turkey)
1 tablespoon flour	1 pimento, chopped
½ cup chicken stock	4 pieces toast, crusts removed

Melt the butter and sauté the mushrooms and pepper slowly for 4-5 minutes. Add the flour and stir until completely blended, then stir in the stock and the cream. Beat the egg yolk, salt, pepper, and paprika together in a bowl, then slowly stir it into the pan. Return the pan to the fire and add the chicken. Don't let the pan boil, but heat thoroughly for about 10 minutes. When done, spoon the chicken and sauce over the toast and sprinkle with a little chopped pimento. Serves 4.

UNITED STATES/CANADA

CHICKEN (OR TURKEY) CROQUETTES

This is one of the best ways known to use up leftover chicken or turkey. It may not be as fancy as some of the world's great dishes, but it is a standard, and classic, dish in America and Canada.

½ cup flour
Dash cayenne pepper
¼ cup melted butter
1 cup light cream
1 teaspoon lemon juice
2 cups cooked chicken or turkey, chopped finely

3 large mushrooms, chopped finely
2 hard cooked eggs, chopped finely
Salt and pepper
1 egg, beaten
1 cup breadcrumbs
Oil for frying

This entire dish should be prepared cold, and allowed to refrigerate for a while.

In a small saucepan, blend ¼ cup flour and cayenne pepper with the melted butter until smooth. Add the light cream and lemon juice and return the pan to moderate heat. Cook the sauce for several minutes, stirring constantly, but don't let it boil. Pour the sauce into a dish and set aside to cool completely.

When the sauce is cold, mix it with the chicken, mushrooms, and eggs. Add a little salt and pepper, and blend thoroughly. Now form the mixture into small croquettes about 2 inches high. Dust the croquettes in flour, lightly brush them with the beaten egg, then roll them in breadcrumbs. When all are ready, place them on a plate in the refrigerator for 1 hour, then fry them in deep hot oil until golden brown. Serve with a cream gravy (page 379). Serves 4.

UNITED STATES/CANADA

CHICKEN AU GRATIN

1 3-4-pound chicken
Water (about 6 cups)
1 bay leaf
1 stalk celery, cut up (leaves and all)
1 carrot, cleaned and cut up

Salt and pepper
4 tablespoons butter
3 tablespoons flour
2 egg yolks, beaten
4-6 tablespoons grated cheese
1 cup finely shredded white bread or soft breadcrumbs

Place the chicken in a large kettle and cover with water. Bring to the boil, removing the scum that rises, then add the bay leaf, celery, carrot, and a little salt and pepper. Reduce the heat to low and simmer for 1½ hours. When the chicken is done, remove it from the kettle, then strain the broth and set aside.

Remove the skin and bones from the chicken and shred the meat. Place these shreds in a large casserole.

Preheat the oven to 350° F. Melt the butter in a saucepan and blend in the flour and the retained broth. Mix a little of the hot broth mixture with the beaten egg yolks and then add back to the pan. Stir for a moment, then cook this mixture over low heat until it begins to thicken. Pour it over the chicken in the casserole, then cover and place the dish in the oven to cook for 15-20 minutes.

Now remove the cover, sprinkle the grated cheese and breadcrumbs over the chicken, and return the casserole to the oven. Do not cover. Cook for 8-10 minutes, or until the cheese melts and the breadcrumbs begin to brown. Serves 4-6.

Alternative: Cook 1 cup elbow macaroni in water until done. Add to the casserole just before covering with the cheese and breadcrumbs. (You should increase the broth in the previous step to 2 cups if you plan to add macaroni.)

United States/Canada

CHICKEN (OR TURKEY) HASH

As common as it may seem, hash has been a mainstay in America's culinary repertoire since early times. Thomas Jefferson was fond of a version of chicken hash, which he enjoyed at breakfast, and more than one great restaurant has featured it. Regardless, the economical American or Canadian housewife has made good use of chicken or turkey leftovers in making a quick, easy, and delicious hash dinner. This is also known as *scalloped* chicken.

3 cups cooked chicken, diced	1 medium onion, chopped
1 cup heavy cream	2 egg yolks, beaten
2 tablespoons butter	3 tablespoons grated cheese
2 tablespoons flour	4 tablespoons white wine
1 cup milk	4 slices white toast
Dash salt	Fresh, chopped parsley for garnish

Combine the chicken and heavy cream in a saucepan and cook over low heat until the cream has reduced somewhat. Remove from the fire and set aside.

While the chicken cooks, make a cream sauce: Melt the butter, then remove from the fire and stir in the flour, making a smooth paste. Add the milk, salt, onion, and egg yolks. Put the pan back on the fire and heat over low flame.

Blend the chicken in with the sauce and add the cheese and wine. Cook over low heat for 15 minutes, then serve, garnished with chopped parsley, on toast points. Serves 4.

Note: In the South, this dish is made with the addition of oysters. Cook the oysters in water for 3 minutes, then chop them and add to the chicken mixture. Serves 4.

In the West, this dish is served in avocado halves. Cut firm avocados in half, lengthwise, and remove the pits. Place the chicken or turkey mixture in the well, mounding it as high as you can, then sprinkle with a good layer of grated cheese. Bake in a 350° F oven for 15 minutes. Serves 4-6.

UNITED STATES/CANADA

CHOPPED CHICKEN LIVER

Along with chicken soup, chopped chicken liver is one of the mainstays of the Jewish culinary tradition. Made with chicken fat and *grebenes,* it is a delightful first course at dinner or canapé at cocktail time.

1½ cups fresh chicken fat, diced	Salt and freshly ground pepper
4 large onions, peeled and minced	3 hard cooked eggs, chopped
2 cups fresh chicken livers	finely
	Grebenes for garnish

Render the chicken fat in a skillet over low heat for 25-30 minutes. As it cooks, stir in one of the minced onins. When the fat has been reduced and the onions are brown, strain the liquid and save the browned particles (these are the *grebenes*).

Return the liquid fat to the skillet and stir in the remaining onion, livers, and a little salt and freshly ground pepper. Cook over low heat for 6-8 minutes, then remove and chop into fine dice. Return the diced livers to the pan, chop two of the hard cooked eggs into fine dice, and add. Cook slowly for 5 minutes, stirring frequently. Remove from the heat and pour the liver mixture into a crock or bowl large enough to hold it.

Cover tightly, or seal, and refrigerate for several hours. Serve cold on a large leaf of lettuce garnished with grebenes and thin slices of the third hard cooked egg. Serves 4-6.

UNITED STATES

NEW ENGLAND CHICKEN POT PIE

Chicken, meat, fish, and clam pies were favorites among New England's early settlers, and came here directly from England.

1 4-5-pound stewing chicken	1 onion, sliced thinly
1 quart water plus 1 cup	Salt and pepper
2 stalks celery, chopped (leaves and all)	4 tablespoons flour
	1 tablespoon butter
2 carrots, cut into 1-inch pieces	1 cup egg noodles
	1 hard cooked egg, sliced

Pastry Dough
2 cups flour	⅔ cup shortening
½ teaspoon salt	4-6 tablespoons cold water

Place the chicken in a large kettle and cover with water. Add the celery, carrots, onion, a little salt, and pepper, then bring the water to the boil, skimming off the scum as it rises. Now reduce the heat to low and simmer for 2 hours. Season with salt and pepper (to taste) again, and continue simmering for another 45 minutes, or until the chicken is tender. Remove the chicken from the pot and set aside to cool. Strain the stock.

Heat the butter in a pan and stir in the flour. When smooth, add the strained stock and stir over low to medium heat until the liquid begins to thicken. Remove and set aside.

When the bird has cooled, cut it into pieces and remove the skin. Now cook the noodles in boiling salted water for 8 minutes or so, until nearly done, then drain.

While the noodles cook, make the pastry dough: Sift 2 cups of flour and the salt into a bowl and cut in the shortening until it has a rather coarse consistency. Add the cold water a little at a time, and work the dough with a spoon or your fingers until it is smooth and firm, but pliant. Separate the dough into 2 equal balls and roll each out as thinly as possible. Place one dough sheet over the bottom of a deep 9-inch pie plate, being careful not to tear it. Lay the noodles over the bottom of the pie and the chicken pieces on top. Pour the liquid over the chicken and noodles and add the egg slices. Now cover the pie with the second sheet of dough and trim off the excess around the edges. Seal the edge by pressing with the end of a fork. Cut 3 vents in the top layer for the steam to escape. Bake in a hot (450° F) oven for 20 minutes, then serve immediately. Serves 6.

UNITED STATES/CANADA

FRIED CHICKEN

Fried chicken is a culinary institution in America, and there is no end to the variations that play on this theme. There are three basic styles, however, which are world-famous, and even these have as many versions as there are cooks who cook them. They are, of course, Maryland Fried, Kentucky Fried, and Southern Fried Chicken.

Maryland and Southern Fried Chicken are dredged in seasoned flour, then browned quickly in hot butter or oil, and covered while the cooking is completed. The difference is that water is added to the Maryland version, but not the Southern, so that one is finished by steaming, and the other by frying. Kentucky Fried Chicken is first rolled in beaten egg, then dredged in seasoned flour before browning.

Each style is delicious, coming to the table inside a brown crust that goes well with or without a gravy. Here are authentic recipes for each, with suggestions for gravy, garnishes, and sauces, which you may include according to your own taste.

Maryland Fried Chicken

1 3-pound chicken, cut up	Salt and freshly ground pepper
1 cup flour	$\frac{1}{3}$ cup oil
	$\frac{2}{3}$ cup water

Wash the chicken pieces and pat dry. Over moderate heat, heat the oil in a large skillet with a cover. Rub the chicken pieces with salt and freshly ground pepper, then dredge with flour. Brown the chicken pieces on all sides for about 15 minutes, then remove from the fire and pour off the oil. Pour the water into the skillet with the chicken, cover, and reduce the heat to low. Cook for 30 minutes, then remove the cover and fry slowly for 10 more minutes. Serve with succotash, iced cucumbers, and mashed potatoes. Serves 4.

Serve, if you wish, with cream gravy (page 379).

Southern Fried Chicken

Prepare the same way as above, only add no water. Cover the pan as soon as the chicken is added, and keep it covered until done. You should turn the chicken about midway through, and serve with cream gravy (page 379).

Kentucky Fried Chicken

1 cup (or more) flour	1 teaspoon baking powder
¼ teaspoon salt	½ cup milk
⅛ teaspoon pepper	1 egg
¼ teaspoon thyme	1 3-pound chicken, cut up
	4 tablespoons butter or oil

Sift the flour, salt, pepper, thyme, and baking powder together. Beat the milk and egg, then combine in a bowl with the flour mixture, and stir until completely blended. Dip each piece of chicken in the batter and drop into hot oil or butter in a large skillet. Cook, turning several times, for about 30 minutes. The chicken should have a golden brown crust. Serves 4.

Oven Fried Chicken

1 3-pound chicken, cut up	½ cup cracker meal
4-6 tablespoons butter	Salt and pepper
	1 teaspoon thyme (or rosemary)

Preheat the oven to 400°F. Melt the butter in a baking dish and turn the chicken pieces in it until completely coated.

On waxed paper, mix the cracker meal, thyme, and salt and pepper, then roll the chicken in the meal until each piece is covered on all sides. Place the chicken back in the baking dish and cook in the oven for 40 minutes. Serves 4.

UNITED STATES

CHICKEN IN BUTTERMILK

Cooking chicken using buttermilk is a widespread practice in the South. This may have come over with the slaves, for buttermilk has been used for centuries to tenderize the small, scraggly birds that grow in Africa.

Whatever the origin, buttermilk lends a flavor to chicken that is unique—so much so, in fact, that many Southern cooks use it as part of their Southern Fried Chicken recipes.

1 3-pound chicken, cut up	1 teaspoon sugar
3 tablespoons butter	1 cup buttermilk
2 onions, peeled and chopped	Salt and pepper
4 large tomatoes, peeled, seeded, and quartered	2 tablespoons fresh dill, chopped

Melt the butter in a large skillet with a cover, or a Dutch oven, and brown the onions slowly for about 5 minutes. Remove the onions and set aside, then brown the chicken pieces for 10-12 minutes. Now add back the onions, and the tomatoes, sugar, and buttermilk, and a little salt and pepper. Cover and cook slowly for 30 minutes. Remove the cover and sprinkle the dill over the chicken. Cook another 5 minutes. Serves 4.

UNITED STATES

SOUTHWESTERN CHICKEN CASSEROLE

1 3-pound chicken, cut up	Heart, liver, and gizzard of
¾ cup flour	chicken
3 tablespoons grated cheese	8 tablespoons butter or oil
1 teaspoon paprika	10 ripe olives, pitted and sliced
½ teaspoon black pepper	1 green pepper, seeded and sliced
2 cups water	2 tomatoes, peeled and quartered
	1 teaspoon oregano
	1 teaspoon salt

Combine the flour, 2 tablespoons of cheese, paprika, and pepper and dredge the chicken pieces. (This can be done easily by shaking the pieces with the flour mixture in a paper bag.) Bring the water to the boil and cook the giblets for 5-6 minutes. Remove the giblets and chop them finely. Reserve the broth.

Preheat the oven to 350°F. Heat the butter or oil in a large skillet and brown the chicken pieces, 4 at a time, for 10-12 minutes. Remove to a casserole and add the olives, green pepper, and tomatoes. To the skillet, add the oregano, salt, and the remaining seasoned flour. Add 1 cup of the giblet broth, stir, and cook over moderate heat until the liquid begins to thicken. Now add the chopped giblets and the remaining cheese. Pour this gravy over the chicken and vegetables in the casserole, cover, and bake for 35-40 minutes. Serve right from the casserole. Serves 4.

UNITED STATES/CANADA

BAKED CHICKEN

1 3-pound chicken, cut up
1 stalk celery, chopped
1 onion, chopped
½ cup dry white wine

¼ teaspoon oregano
Pinch each of rosemary, paprika, thyme, cayenne
½ cup olive oil
2 cloves garlic

Put all the ingredients (except the chicken) into a blender and blend into a paste. Pour this over the chicken and marinate for 12 hours.

Preheat the oven to 375°F and cook the chicken in a Dutch oven or covered casserole for about 2 hours. Remove the cover, raise the temperature to 400°F, and cook for 15 minutes more until the chicken is brown. Serves 4.

UNITED STATES/CANADA

CHICKEN AND RICE

4-6 tablespoons flour
Salt and pepper
1 3-pound chicken, cut up
3-4 tablespoons butter or oil
1 onion, chopped coarsely
4 scallions, chopped coarsely
1 green pepper, seeded and cut into thin strips

3 medium tomatoes, peeled, seeded, and chopped coarsely
3 cups chicken broth
2 sprigs parsley, chopped
1 bay leaf, crumbled
1 cup raw rice
½ cup chopped ham
6 tablespoons dry sherry

Mix together the flour, salt, and pepper, then dredge the chicken pieces. Melt 3 tablespoons of butter in a large deep skillet with a tight cover, or in a Dutch oven, and brown the meat for 12-15 minutes, then remove and keep warm.

Add the remaining butter and sauté the onion, scallions, and pepper slowly for about 5 minutes. Return the chicken to the pan and add the broth, chopped tomatoes, parsley, and crumbled bay leaf. Cover and cook over fairly low heat for 15 minutes. Add the rice, ham, and wine, then re-cover and cook for another 20 minutes.

Serve directly from the pot. Serves 4.

UNITED STATES

CHICKEN TAMALE PIE

Over a century ago, American settlers in the Southwest adapted traditional Mexican ingredients to their own cooking techniques and produced this regional classic.

Corn Meal Mush
½ cup cornmeal   1 teaspoon salt
3 cups boiling water

3 cups cooked chicken, shredded   ½ teaspoon chili powder
Salt and pepper   10-12 ripe olives, pitted and
½ green pepper, seeded and   sliced
   chopped   2 tablespoons olive oil
1 cup tomato sauce   1 tablespoon sugar
1 cup corn kernels   ¾-1 cup grated cheese

Preheat the oven to 350°F. Dissolve the salt in boiling water, then slowly add the cornmeal. Set aside for 5 minutes, until all the water is absorbed, then spread the mush over the bottom of a casserole.

Place the shredded chicken over the mush and sprinkle with a little salt and pepper. Combine the remaining ingredients, except the cheese, in a blender and mix at medium speed for 20 seconds. Pour this mixture over the chicken, then sprinkle with cheese until well covered.

Place the pot in the oven and bake for 45 minutes. When done, serve immediately right from the casserole. Serves 4-6.

United States/Canada

COUNTRY CAPTAIN—Captains' Curries

The early American and Canadian merchant ships usually spent weeks and months at sea, and as time went by the food that issued from the galley became monotonous, tasteless, and—frequently—spoiled. To overcome this, captains experimented with different spices and spice mixtures, and in due time every port from Nova Scotia to Savannah, Georgia, boasted a variety of spicy meat, fish, or vegetable dishes that became known as country captains or *Captains' Curries*.

4-5 tablespoons flour
Salt and pepper
1 3-pound chicken, cut up
8 tablespoons butter or oil
1 teaspoon coriander
½ teaspoon cumin
¼ teaspoon turmeric

½ teaspoon ginger
2 cloves garlic, minced
3 stalks celery, chopped
1 small green pepper, seeded and
  chopped
2 onions, chopped
4 large tomatoes, peeled, seeded,
  and chopped

Combine the flour, salt, and pepper and dredge the chicken, then brown the pieces slowly in butter or oil in a large skillet on all sides. Remove and keep warm.

Stir the spices into the oil in the skillet, then add the garlic, celery, pepper, and onions and cook over low heat for 10-12 minutes. Add the chopped tomatoes and return the chicken to the pan, mixing the pieces in with the vegetables. Cover and simmer for 40 minutes.

Serve with rice. Serves 4-6.

United States

JAMBALAYA—Chicken, Rice, and Shellfish Stew

One of Louisiana's great chicken dishes, jambalaya has its origins in the Spanish paella. However, its evolution in America was strongly influenced by the transplanted French and African kitchens as well as by ingredients native to the New World.

1 3-pound chicken, cut up
Salt and freshly ground pepper
3 tablespoons butter or oil

3 cups water
½ teaspoon hot red chili pepper,
  chopped finely

1 pound smoked link sausages
2 tablespoons flour
2 large onions, minced
6 tomatoes, peeled, seeded, and chopped
1 clove garlic, crushed
1 large green pepper, cored, seeded, and minced

½ teaspoon thyme
2 cups long grain white rice
2 cups shrimp, cleaned and deveined (or lobster chunks, or crayfish)
2 tablespoons fresh parsley, minced

Sprinkle the chicken pieces with salt and pepper. Heat the butter or oil in a large iron kettle and brown the chicken over fairly low heat for 10-12 minutes, then remove and set aside. Brown the sausages on all sides for about 5 minutes, then remove from the pot and set aside.

Stir the flour into the oil, scraping down the sides and bottom of the pot to loosen and dissolve the brown particles. When the roux is smooth and turns a light brown, return the chicken and sausages. Now add the onions, tomatoes, garlic, green pepper, water, chili pepper, thyme, and a good sprinkling of salt and pepper. Bring the pot to the boil and stir continuously to blend the ingredients thoroughly, then stir in the rice, cover tightly, and simmer for 1 hour.

About 20 minutes before the jambalaya is done, add the shrimp and parsley. Stir the pot well to mix, re-cover, and continue cooking. When done, serve right from the pot. Serves 6.

UNITED STATES

CREOLE CHICKEN

¼ cup oil
2 3-pound chickens, cut up
3 tablespoons butter
6 medium tomatoes, peeled, seeded, and chopped
Salt and pepper
Pinch thyme
Pinch basil

1 tablespoon parsley, chopped
2 bay leaves
1 teaspoon cayenne
2 cloves garlic, chopped finely
2 tablespoons flour
1 onion, chopped finely
1 green pepper, seeded and cut into ½-inch wide strips
1 cup dry white wine

Heat the oil in a Dutch oven and brown the chicken slowly on all sides, a few pieces at a time, then remove to a warm platter. Add half the butter and the chopped tomatoes and sprinkle with a little salt and pepper, then simmer for 15 minutes.

Now add the thyme, basil, parsley, bay leaf, cayenne, and chopped garlic. Increase the heat slightly and cook for another 15 minutes. The sauce should thicken somewhat.

In a separate saucepan, melt the remaining butter and stir in the flour. Cook for 1 minute and then add the chopped onion, pepper strips, and the wine. Stir over low heat for 5 minutes, then add to the other ingredients in the Dutch oven. Return the browned chicken, cover, and simmer for 1 hour. Serve with rice. Serves 6-8.

United States/Canada

ROAST STUFFED CHICKEN

"Chicken every Sunday" is a theme of bygone days when times were hard and delicacies came few and far between. For many people, the Sunday dinner was the high point of the week, and the table was set with the finest linen, china, and silver and heaped with the best food that could be afforded. Chances are, as the slogan suggests, the meat was chicken and the likelihood is that the chicken was roasted.

Oven roasting can be one of the easiest ways to cook a chicken, but it can also take the longest time. It's best to use a slow oven and cook longer, so the bird will retain more of its juice and flavor. The average cooking time for a 4-5 pound roasting chicken is 30 minutes a pound in a 325° F preheated oven, provided, of course, the bird is completely thawed. Let the chicken sit out with a cloth over it for several hours if it has been refrigerated, or overnight if it is frozen.

Before putting the chicken in the oven, wash it thoroughly inside and out, and pat dry with a towel. Rub the cavity with salt then stuff it if you wish, or add any vegetables, fruits, seasonings, or sauces you choose. Some recommend covering the breast and thighs of the bird during cooking to prevent it from drying or browning too much. This is not necessary if you baste it frequently (every 10-15 minutes). The chicken should be cooked covered until the last 15-20 minutes, when the cover is removed and the breast and thigh skin allowed to brown.

A roast chicken is good all by itself, but it takes on extra character if it is stuffed or served with a gravy. Here are some of the traditional accompaniments that are popular in both America and Canada:

Basic Bread Stuffing

½ cup butter
3 onions, chopped finely
10 slices shredded white bread, crusts removed

1 teaspoon salt
¼ teaspoon pepper
1 tablespoon paprika
1 egg
2½ cups fresh chicken stock

Sauté the chopped onion in butter until translucent. Add the shredded bread and cook until it starts to brown. Combine all the other ingredients and add to the bread and onion mixture. Blend well, then stuff the cavity and sew or skewer the openings. This should be adequate for 2 large chickens or one small (12-pound) turkey.

Mushroom Stuffing

To the basic bread stuffing, add 1 cup of sliced mushrooms and sauté them with the onions.

Apple-Prune Stuffing

Pit and chop 1 cup of prunes and peel, core, and chop 2 medium apples, then mix with the basic bread stuffing.

Celery and Onion Stuffing

Add to the basic bread stuffing 1 more chopped onion and ½ cup chopped celery.

Giblet Stuffing

Dice the gizzard, heart, and liver and sauté very quickly with the onion in the basic bread stuffing.

Matzo Stuffing (Jewish Cookery)

Use the basic bread stuffing, only substitute chicken fat for the butter and 10 crumbled matzos for the white bread.

Seasoned Bread Stuffing

In the basic bread stuffing, replace the paprika with ½ teaspoon of poultry seasoning.

Orange Stuffing for Chicken or Gamebirds
This is enough for a 2½-pound bird.

2 cups shredded white bread, crusts removed	2 tablespoons butter
	1 stalk celery, chopped coarsely
Juice and grated rind of one orange	¼ onion, chopped coarsely
	Salt and pepper
½ cup orange sections (½ orange)	¼ teaspoon thyme

Put the shredded bread in a bowl and sprinkle it with orange juice, tossing the bread as you do. Sprinkle in the grated orange rind, then add the orange sections. Continue to toss until the bread and orange ingredients are well mixed.

Melt the butter and sauté the celery and onion slowly for 3 minutes, then add to the bowl. Season with salt and pepper to taste; add the thyme. Toss again to blend thoroughly, then stuff the bird and close the cavities.

Chestnut Dressing
This is enough for a 12-pound Thanksgiving or Christmas turkey.

8 cups chestnuts	Salt and freshly ground pepper
1 cup oil	¼ teaspoon marjoram
6 cups water or stock	½ teaspoon thyme
2 tablespoons butter	2 teaspoons parsley, chopped
1 onion, chopped coarsely	½ cup milk
½ pound bulk sausage	¾ cup shredded white bread, crusts removed

Slash the flat sides of the chestnuts and cook them in the oil over moderate heat for 3 minutes, turning frequently. Remove to drain and let cool, then peel off the shells and the skins that cover the meat. Bring the water or stock to moderate heat and cook the chestnut meat for 12-15 minutes until tender, then mash half of the nutmeats, and chop the other half and set aside.

Melt the butter in a skillet and sauté the onion slowly for 3 minutes, then add the sausage, salt, pepper, marjoram, thyme, and parsley and cook for 5 minutes. As it cooks, chop the sausage and stir the pan so it becomes very crumbly and well mixed. Remove the sausage and onions with a slotted spoon and add to the chestnuts.

Now soak the bread in the milk and squeeze dry. Add to the sausage and chestnuts and toss to blend well. Stuff the bird and close the cavities and it's ready to roast.

White Rice Stuffing
2 medium onions, chopped
1 cup diced celery
4 tablespoons butter

3 cups cooked white rice
2 teaspoons salt
¼ teaspoon pepper
1 teaspoon sage

Sauté the celery and onions in the butter until golden and tender. Remove from the fire and mix in the remaining ingredients, stirring to blend thoroughly. This makes enough for one large roasting chicken, and should be doubled for a 10-12-pound turkey.

Fruit and Nut Dressing (especially good with a goose)
3 cups dry, shredded bread
Salt
2 apples, peeled and chopped

1 orange, peeled and cut into
  small pieces
½ cup chopped almonds
1 tablespoon sugar

Combine all ingredients in a bowl, mix well, then stuff and close the bird's cavities.

Forcemeat Dressing
This is enough for two 4-5 pound chickens or one small turkey.

½ cup ground veal
½ onion, chopped finely
1 teaspoon parsley flakes
Juice and grated rind of ¼ lemon

2 cups shredded white bread,
  crusts removed
½ teaspoon salt
½ teaspoon pepper
1 egg, whipped

Mix all the ingredients in a bowl, then stuff the bird(s), close the cavities, and roast.

Farfel Dressing (Jewish Cookery)
½ pound farfel
2 tablespoons chicken fat
½ cup chicken stock
1 onion, chopped finely
2 stalks celery, chopped

1 small carrot, grated
1 teaspoon parsley flakes
½ teaspoon salt
⅛ teaspoon pepper
⅛ teaspoon paprika
1 egg, whipped

Sauté the farfel in chicken fat for about 3 minutes, then add the stock and stir over low heat until all the liquid is absorbed. Add the remaining ingredients, stir for a few minutes, then let cool.

This should be enough for two chickens, 4-5 pounds each, or one small turkey.

Mashed Potato Stuffing

4 tablespoons butter or oil
2 onions, chopped

2 cups mashed potatoes
2 teaspoons salt
½ teaspoon pepper

Sauté the chopped onions gently in 2 tablespoons of butter or oil. Remove when golden to a bowl with a slotted spoon, then add the remaining ingredients and mix well. Stuff the bird and sew up the cavities.

This is enough for a 4-pound roasting chicken, but will have to be increased for a turkey.

Oyster Stuffing

This is enough for a 12-15-pound turkey. Use ¼ for a 4-5-pound chicken.

⅓ pound butter
2 cups oysters in their liquid
2 cloves garlic, minced
½ green pepper, seeded, deveined, and chopped
6 stalks celery, chopped (leaves and all)
2 large onions, chopped finely

8 cups white bread, shredded finely
1 cup parsley, chopped finely
Salt and freshly ground pepper
½ teaspoon nutmeg
¼ teaspoon whole cloves
½ teaspoon thyme
1 teaspoon sage, chopped finely

Drain the oysters, reserving ⅓ cup of the liquid. Over low heat melt 1 tablespoon butter and sauté the oysters for 1 minute (until the edges start to curl). Remove and set aside.

Keeping the fire low, melt the remaining butter in a large skillet and cook the garlic, pepper, celery, and onions for 2 or 3 minutes, stirring constantly. Now add the shredded white bread, the reserved oyster liquid, parsley, and seasonings. Return the oysters, and blend all the ingredients thoroughly, then stuff the bird.

UNITED STATES

SPIT-ROASTED CHICKEN

Spit-roasting a chicken over a barbecue or on a rotisserie is popular all over America, but one variation, which has become a favorite in the West and Southwest, inserts a grapefruit or several oranges in the cavity of the bird. The skewer is run through and the bird is placed on the barbecue to turn slowly over the coals until a golden brown. The heat will release some of the oils and juice of the citrus and give the meat a faint, but delicious, flavor. You may also brush the bird with an herb sauce if you wish. A duck or small turkey done this way is excellent, also.

Citrus fruits may be inserted in a goose also, but this should be cooked in an oven roaster. Place the goose on its side for the first half-hour, then turn it over on the other side for the second half-hour. Finish cooking by turning the goose on its back. That way the entire goose will take on the citrus flavor.

UNITED STATES/CANADA

HICKORY-SMOKED CHICKEN (or Turkey or Duck)

Meat was smoked originally to help preserve it, a technique that has been used in many countries for centuries. Certain woods impart unusual flavors to various meats and fowl, and early epicures around the world discovered that fact.

Today, with refrigerators in common use in America and Canada, smoking is done almost strictly for taste, though it is not commonly practiced on a large scale anymore. (The exception, of course, is smoked ham and bacon.) Though individual smokehouses still exist on many farms, the outdoor barbecue has taken over as the smoking device for most people.

If you don't have a hood over your barbecue, you can fashion one very easily by stripping the cloth off a medium-sized lampshade and covering it tightly with foil. Or straighten several wire clothes hangers and make a frame, then cover it in the same way. Or, simplest of all, just fold foil into the shape of a large bowl and cover the meat.

8-10 hickory chips	1 teaspoon salt
2 2-2½-pound broilers, split in half or quartered	¼ teaspoon paprika
	Freshly ground pepper
½ cup butter or oil	Parsley for garnish

First soak the hickory chips in water for about 30 minutes, then drain. Melt the butter in a saucepan, then stir in the salt, paprika, and pepper. Brush the skin side of each piece of chicken with this.

When the coals have reached the desired heat (covered with white ash), adjust the grill to about 3 inches above the fire, and place on it the chicken pieces, meaty side down. Grill for 15 minutes, basting once, then turn the pieces and brush again with the seasoned butter.

Place the soaked chips on the coals, then place the hood over the chicken. Do not raise the hood to baste again, or you'll lose the smoke. Grill for 20 minutes, then remove to a serving platter. Dribble any remaining butter mixture over the pieces and garnish with parsley. Serves 6-8.

United States/Canada

BROILED CHICKEN

Broiled chicken, turkey, or duck can be done easily in the oven or outdoors over a charcoal or wood fire, and with the variety of marinades, sauces, and glazes available to them, North American cooks turn out a surprising number of different dishes.

When broiling in the oven, allow up to 40 minutes for the chicken to cook. The time will vary with the size of the bird, but this should be adequate for one of about 3 pounds. Keep the meat about 4½-5 inches below the broiler. Place the meaty or skin side down first, then turn after 20 minutes or so. If you use a sauce, brush the bottoms of the chicken pieces once, then 2 or 3 times after it is turned.

In charcoal broiling, the fire tends to be hotter at first, so the meat pieces must be turned more often to avoid burning. Place the cooking rack 3-4 inches above the coals and place the chicken on. Brush with sauce or marinade and turn every 5-6 minutes at first, brushing each time. Chicken may cook faster on a charcoal fire, depending on how hot the coals are when you start. The heat of the charcoal diminishes rapidly after it reaches its peak, so it's important to put the chicken on just when a white ash forms on the coals. This will provide at least

45-50 minutes of good heat, which should be adequate. It's a good idea to remember also that adding tomatoes or tomato sauce to a marinade increases the chances of burning.

Barbecue Marinade and Sauce

½ cup wine vinegar	1 teaspoon Worcestershire sauce
1 small onion or scallion, sliced thinly	Salt and pepper
	Dash paprika
1 clove garlic, sliced thinly	2 tablespoons tomato paste
	½ cup oil

Mix all the ingredients together thoroughly in a bowl and put the chicken in, coating each piece on all sides. Let sit for an hour or more, turning 2 or 3 times. Grill the chicken either in the broiler or on a charcoal fire. Brush the pieces with the marinade several times during cooking. The remaining marinade may be refrigerated in a covered jar for a week or so, and can be used equally well with steaks or chops.

Lemon Glaze

⅓ cup corn syrup	Juice and grated rind of 1 lemon
	Pinch salt

Combine all the ingredients and brush the chicken pieces frequently as the meat broils.

Mustard Barbecue Sauce

1 cup salad oil	½ teaspoon freshly ground pepper
2 cloves garlic, quartered	
1 tablespoon dry mustard	1 teaspoon paprika
Juice of ½ lemon	1 small onion, chopped finely
2 teaspoons salt	1 teaspoon Worcestershire sauce
	¼ cup catsup

Combine all the ingredients in a large bowl and blend thoroughly. Put the chicken pieces in to marinate and turn to coat well, then set aside for 2 hours. Turn the chicken 2 or 3 times while it marinates. As the chicken broils, brush with the marinade sauce several times.

Ginger Barbecue Sauce

1 medium onion, minced
3 slices fresh ginger root, minced

½ cup soy sauce
4 tablespoons wine or cider
    vinegar

Combine all the ingredients and mix well. Coat the chicken and let it sit for 30 minutes, then grill, brushing each piece several times. This is also excellent with broiled shrimp.

Lemon/Wine Marinade

½ cup white wine
1 teaspoon Worcestershire sauce
5-6 tablespoons salad oil

6 tablespoons brown sugar
Juice and grated rind of 1 lemon
2 teaspoons rosemary
Salt and pepper

Mix all the ingredients together. Place the pieces of 1 3-pound chicken, cut up as you like it, in a large shallow baking dish and pour the marinade over the pieces, coating each completely. Let stand at room temperature for 1 hour or refrigerate for 3 hours, but either way turn the pieces several times. Barbecue or oven-broil the chicken using the marinade for basting.

Oyster Sauce

3 teaspoons parsley, chopped
1 teaspoon onion, chopped
1 cup light cream
2 tablespoons butter

2 tablespoons flour
Pinch salt
1 teaspoon Worcestershire sauce
1 cup fresh oysters (with juice),
    chopped finely

Combine 1 tablespoon parsley and the onion and cream in a saucepan and bring quickly to high heat, but don't let it boil. Remove from the heat and set aside.

Melt the butter, then add the flour and stir until a thin smooth paste forms. Pour in the cream and onion mixture and cook for several minutes over low heat. Add the salt, Worcestershire sauce, oysters, and the remaining parsley and increase the heat to bring the pot to the boil. Remove from the heat and pour into a sauceboat.

Cranberry Glaze

2 tablespoons butter

Juice of 1 small orange
1 can cranberry sauce

Melt the butter over low heat, then stir in the orange juice and cranberry sauce. Stir constantly until smooth and hot. Spread over the chicken (or turkey, duck, or wild bird) just before serving.

Brown Gravy

2 tablespoons flour
2 tablespoons cornstarch

¾ cup cold water
2½ cups boiling water
Salt and pepper

Mix the flour, cornstarch, and cold water until a smooth paste forms. Remove the chicken from the roasting pan when done and spoon off as much grease as possible. Now, over moderate heat, pour in the boiling water, and scrape off all the particles that cling to the sides and bottom of the pan. Slowly add in the flour-cornstarch mixture and let it cook, stirring constantly, until it begins to thicken. Remove and serve in a gravyboat. This is enough for 1 turkey or 2 chickens.

Alternate: Another way to make brown gravy is to use ¾ cup of chicken stock instead of water in mixing the flour and cornstarch. It makes a richer gravy.

Herb Sauce

¼ cup butter
½ teaspoon dried savory
½ teaspoon dried thyme
¼ teaspoon dried tarragon

1 onion, chopped finely
2 tablespoons flour
1 cup dry white wine
½ cup light cream
½ cup chicken stock

Heat the butter in a skillet, then add the savory, thyme, and tarragon and the chopped onion. Sauté slowly until the onion is golden, then remove from the heat and blend in the flour. Add the wine, stock, and cream and stir until completely mixed. Return the pan to the fire and bring to the boil, stirring constantly. Remove from the heat and serve in a sauceboat. This is excellent with roast, baked, or braised chicken.

Cream Gravy

This is the gravy that goes with Southern or Maryland Fried Chicken, or with Chicken Croquettes.

¼ cup pan drippings
¼ cup flour
Dash salt

Dash paprika
Dash pepper
1 cup light cream
1 cup chicken stock

Stir the flour, salt, paprika, and pepper into hot pan drippings, then add the cream and stock, stirring constantly until the sauce begins to thicken. Pour, serve over the chicken, or serve in a sauceboat. (This can also be made with four cream, but that is not traditional.)

Giblet Gravy

4 tablespoons butter
¼ cup flour
3 cups stock

Salt and pepper
Cooked giblets of chicken or
    turkey, chopped finely

Melt the butter over medium heat in a small skillet or saucepan and stir in the flour. Cook for about 2 minutes, then add the stock, salt, and pepper and cook for 5 more minutes, stirring constantly. Add the chopped giblets and cook 1 more minute. Serve in a sauceboat.

Hot Mustard Sauce

3 tablespoons dry mustard
1 teaspoon sugar
½ teaspoon salt

Dash Tabasco
½ cup milk or light cream
Juice and grated rind of 1 lemon

Combine all the ingredients except the lemon juice and rind and mix well. Over moderate heat, cook the sauce for 5 minutes, stirring several times, but do not boil. When ready to serve, add the lemon juice and rind and cook for 1 more minute. Serve in a sauceboat. This is enough for 1 chicken or duck; double the recipe for a 10-12-pound turkey.

Chestnut Sauce
Here's an early White House recipe for a Thanksgiving turkey sauce:

1 pound chestnuts
1 teaspoon coriander seeds
½ teaspoon salt
1 bay leaf

¼ cup (½ stick) butter
1 onion, chopped finely
1 cup chicken stock (or a little
    more)

Slash each chestnut, taking care not to cut the meat. Cook in boiling water for 10 minutes, then peel off the shells and skin. Return the chestnut meats to the water and bring back to the boil, then add the coriander seeds, salt, and bay leaf. Cook for 10 minutes, then drain.

Crush the chestnut mixture into a paste in a mortar or blender. Melt the butter and sauté the onion until golden over low heat. Add the chestnut paste and the stock and cook for 3-5 minutes, stirring constantly. Strain and pour into a sauceboat. Serve with a turkey stuffed with chestnut dressing (page 372).

Mayonnaise Sauce

2-3 tablespoons dry white wine
1 tablespoon parsley, minced
1 cup mayonnaise
3 tablespoons sour cream

Juice and grated rind of ½ lemon
1 teaspoon chives, finely chopped
½ teaspoon tarragon leaves,
    crumbled

Blend all the ingredients thoroughly, then cover and refrigerate for 30 minutes. Serve with cold, boned chicken or turkey.

Lemon Sauce

1 cup strained chicken stock

2 egg yolks, whipped
Juice and rind of ½ lemon

Combine the stock and eggs a little at a time, stirring constantly. Place over low heat and cook for 5-7 minutes. Don't allow it to boil or the sauce will curdle. When it starts to thicken, add the juice and rind of the lemon. Serve in a sauceboat over simmered or poached chicken.

New England Fruit Sauce

1 cup cranberry jelly
2 tablespoons honey
Juice and grated rind of ¼ orange

2 tablespoons butter
½ cup cider
2 tablespoons cornstarch
Dash salt

Combine all the ingredients in a saucepan. Cook over medium heat for 15 minutes or so, stirring frequently. Serve over roast chicken or turkey.

UNITED STATES/CANADA

CHICKEN SOUP

No matter what country you're in, good chicken soup demands fresh chicken stock, and that is just as true for any other recipe that calls for stock. Bouillon cubes, which Americans tend to use as a substitute in order to save time and effort, simply do not have the quality nor the character of the real thing.

If you boil a chicken with several vegetables and a few seasonings, you automatically end up with a quart of good stock, more or less, so it's always good to let it cool, scoop and blot off the fat, then strain it and put it away for another time. Refrigerated, stock will keep for several weeks and frozen for several months.

The best chicken stock, though, is made with only a minimum of seasonings, for too many strong tastes will alter a sauce or gravy you're making for a particular dish. One economical way to make stock is to save (freeze) the backs, giblets, and wing tips of chickens or turkeys (even a cooked carcass) and boil them in 3 or 4 quarts of water (depending on how many chicken parts you have) with 1 tablespoon salt, 2 bay leaves, 6-8 peppercorns, 1 sliced carrot, and 1 sliced stalk of celery. Bring to the boil and skim off the scum as it rises, then reduce the heat until the water is barely moving, cover, and simmer for 2-3 hours. When done, remove the chicken pieces and strain the stock. It's ready for chicken soup or for any other recipe in which you might need it.

American and Canadian Jews are probably better known for their chicken soup than for any other dish they cook. The Jewish cook will cut away as much fat as possible, then add the chicken to the pot along with the giblets, neck, and feet (in fact, if she has them, she'll put in extra feet, as this builds the body and strength of the stock). Finally, when the soup is just about done, she'll add some sort of accompaniment made of grain—farfel, knaidlach, noodles, or mandelin—to make the dish more interesting.

Farfel (Dough Pellets)
2 cups sifted flour   ½ teaspoon salt
2 eggs, beaten   Water

In a bowl, make a well in the center of the flour and drop in the eggs and salt and 2 tablespoons of water (or a bit more as needed). Mix well with your fingers, then knead the dough until it becomes very stiff. Roll it into a ball and let dry in an open place for an hour. Now chop or grate the dough into very small, coarse pieces (farfels) and let dry again.

To cook, drop the farfels into the boiling chicken soup or salted water and cook for 10 minutes. Add as much as you wish for a thick or a thin soup. (The farfels can be kept for months stored in a tightly covered container.)

UNITED STATES

CHICKEN AND CORN SOUP WITH RIVELS
This is traditional Pennsylvania Dutch cookery.

4 quarts water
Salt and pepper
1 4-5-pound stewing hen, cut up
¾ cup chopped celery (leaves and all)

8-10 ears fresh corn, cut from the cobs
1 onion, chopped coarsely
2 hard cooked eggs, chopped

Rivels
1 cup flour
1 egg, whipped

Pinch salt
Milk

Bring the water to the boil and add 1 teaspoon of salt. Put in the chicken pieces, and skim off the scum as it rises, then reduce the heat to low and simmer until tender (about 1½ hours). Remove the chicken and let cool, then cut away the meat, discarding skin and bones. Add the chopped celery, corn, onion, and a little salt and pepper and continue to simmer for 30 minutes.

While the soup simmers make the rivels: Combine the flour, whipped egg, salt, and a little milk. Working with your fingers, blend thoroughly (use the milk sparingly so the rivels are crumbly), then form small pellets. Drop the rivels and the chopped egg into the soup and cook for 15 minutes. Serve in individual soup plates or in a tureen. Serves 4-6.

The Pennsylvania Dutch frequently pass a pitcher of cream, which is added to the soup, 1 or 2 tablespoons at a time, at the table.

United States

CHICKEN GUMBO

Gumbo is a Bantu work meaning okra, and both the dish and the vegetable were brought here from Africa by the slaves. One of the staples of the South, its major alteration came when filé was added to the pot. This is the ground or powdered sassafras leaf, which the Choctaw Indians of Louisiana introduced to the early settlers. Today either the okra or filé powder (rarely both at once) is included in an authentic gumbo.

4 tablespoons butter or oil
1 3-pound chicken, cut up
½ pound smoked ham, diced
1 pound okra, sliced, or 3 teaspoons filé powder
4 medium onions, chopped
2 tablespoons flour
1 quart chicken stock

4 cups tomatoes, skinned and
   chopped
Salt and freshly ground pepper
1 teaspoon thyme
1 green pepper, seeded and
   chopped
1 tablespoon fresh parsley,
   minced

Heat 3 tablespoons of the butter or oil in a large kettle and slowly brown the chicken pieces. Remove and set aside. Now gently cook the ham pieces without browning (about 3 minutes), then remove from the kettle. Next brown the okra slices and onions in the same oil for about 5 minutes. Remove the vegetables and set aside.

Add the remaining butter or oil and stir in the flour until a roux or paste is formed. When the roux is smooth, add the chicken stock and bring to the boil. Stir the liquid several times, then replace the chicken pieces, ham, okra, and onion. Now add the chopped tomatoes, salt, a few grindings of fresh pepper, and thyme. Cover and simmer for 1½-2 hours.

When the gumbo is nearly done, add the green pepper and parsley and simmer another 4-5 minutes. If you use filé powder, omit the okra from the recipe. When the pot is finished cooking, remove it from the fire and stir in the filé powder. Do not let it cook. Let the pot sit for a minute or so and then serve in individual soup plates or in a tureen. Serves 4-6.

CHICKEN NOODLE SOUP

This is an all-time favorite in North America, although mostly today it comes out of a can. Chicken noodle soup can be made quickly if fresh chicken stock is already on hand.

1 pound egg noodles	1 stalk celery, chopped
Boiling salted water	½ cup cooked ham, diced
1 quart fresh chicken stock	2 scallions, chopped finely
Giblets of 1 chicken, chopped finely	Salt and freshly ground pepper

Cook the noodles in boiling salted water until about half done (6-8 minutes). Bring the stock to the boil, then reduce the heat to low. Add the chopped giblets, celery, ham, scallions, and salt and fresh pepper. Drain the half-cooked noodles and add them to the pot. Cover and simmer for 20 minutes. Serves 4-6.

CHICKEN AND RICE SOUP

Repeat the above, only omit the ham and substitute 1 cup of cooked rice for the noodles.

CANADA

PATE A LA RAPURE—Rappie Pie

This is an Acadian classic, which is popular on Sunday in Newfoundland. It's unusual because the potatoes are first grated, then squeezed dry of as much water and starch as possible to form the base of the pie.

1 3-pound chicken	1 large carrot, cut into 1-inch sections
1 quart water	3 onions, quartered
1 bay leaf	Salt and pepper
1 tablespoon rosemary	10-12 large white potatoes
1 teaspoon rhyme	4 tablespoons butter
1 stalk celery, cut into 1-inch sections	4-5 strips bacon

Place the chicken in a kettle with the water. Add the bay leaf, rosemary, and thyme. Add the celery (leaves and all), carrots, and 1 quartered onion, then sprinkle over salt and pepper to taste. Bring the pot to the boil and skim off the scum as it rises. Cover, reduce the heat to low, and simmer for 1 hour.

While the chicken cooks, peel the potatoes and pass them through the coarse side of a grater. Put the grated potatoes in a muslin bag or in the center of several folds of cheesecloth, then close and squeeze them until as much water and starch are removed as possible. (You should take care to measure how much liquid comes out, as it must be replaced with chicken stock.)

Now place the potato meal in a large pan and add enough stock to replace the water squeezed out. Stir over low heat for 6-8 minutes until smooth.

Preheat the oven to 400° F. When the chicken is done, let it cool, then remove and discard the skin and bones and cut the meat into shreds. Cover the bottom of a rather deep baking dish with half the potatoes, then add the chicken shreds. Spread the remaining onion quarters over the chicken, then arrange 4 or 5 thin pats of butter over the top. Now cover the dish with the remaining potatoes, and more butter. Finally, lay 4 or 5 strips of bacon on top. Place in the oven and cook for 2 hours. Serves 4-6.

CANADA

TOURTIERE DE LA GASPESIE—Three Meats Pie
This is a traditional Christmas Eve dish served in French-speaking sections of Eastern Canada.

1 3-pound chicken	2 cloves garlic, minced
2 onions	Meat from 1 pork chop, cut into small cubes
1 stalk celery (leaves and all), cut into 1-inch sections	½ pound beef, cut into small cubes
1 quart water	1 recipe pastry dough (page 362)
Salt and pepper	¼ cup flour

Place the chicken in a large kettle. Quarter 1 onion and add it and the celery pieces to the pot. Pour in the water, then add salt and pepper to taste. Bring the kettle to the boil and skim off the scum as it rises. Cover, reduce the heat to low, and simmer for 1 hour or until tender.

While the chicken cooks, chop the second onion coarsely. Heat the butter or oil in a skillet and sauté the onion and garlic slowly for about 3 minutes, until golden. Remove the onions from the pan and set aside. Now add the pork cubes to the skillet and brown for 7-8 minutes. Remove and set aside. Brown the beef cubes in the same pan for 5 minutes, then remove and set aside.

When the chicken is done, remove it from the pot and allow to cool. Strain and retain the broth. When the chicken can be handled, remove and discard the skin and bones and shred the meat. Now combine the chicken, pork, beef, and onion in a bowl and sprinkle over a little salt and pepper.

Make a pastry dough (page 362).

Preheat the oven to 425° F. Line the bottom of a 9-inch pie plate with 1 round of pastry and spread in the meat mixture. Add ¼ cup of the retained broth, then lay the second round of pastry over the top. Trim around the edge of the plate, then seal the edge with a fork. Cut 2 or 3 vent holes in the top. Put the pie in the oven and bake for 30-35 minutes, or until golden brown.

Add the flour to 4 cups of the retained broth and blend well. Allow this to simmer for 5 minutes or so just before the pie is done. Serve in a sauceboat. Serves 6-8.

Index

389